HOUSING

Carol B. Meeks

CORNELL UNIVERSITY

PRENTICE-HALL, INC. Englewood Cliffs, NJ 07632

Library of Congress Cataloging in Publication Data

MEEKS, CAROL B
  Housing.

  Includes bibliographies and index.
    1. Housing—United States.   2. Housing policy—
United States.   I. Title.
HD7293.M36   301.5'4'0973   79-22303
ISBN 0-13-394981-8

Printed in the United States of America

10 9 8 7 6 5 4 3 2 1

Editorial/production supervisor: Penelope Linskey
Interior design by Emily B. Dobson
Cover design by Miriam Recio
Manufacturing buyer: Anthony Caruso/Harry P. Baisley

PRENTICE-HALL INTERNATIONAL, INC., *London*
PRENTICE-HALL OF AUSTRALIA PTY. LIMITED, *Sydney*
PRENTICE-HALL OF CANADA, LTD., *Toronto*
PRENTICE-HALL OF INDIA PRIVATE LIMITED, *New Delhi*
PRENTICE-HALL OF JAPAN, INC., *Tokyo*
PRENTICE-HALL OF SOUTHEAST ASIA PTE. LTD., *Singapore*
WHITEHALL BOOKS LIMITED, WELLINGTON, *New Zealand*

Contents

Preface

Housing and its environment is a major dimension of the quality of life. Thus, it is a reflection of a nation's economic and social well-being.

This book explores the social, economic, and political components of housing in the United States. It uses a social-economic approach to analyze how consumers and producers behave with regard to housing and how government action affects housing consumption, production, and distribution.

The reader is provided with an overview of what the population of the United States looks like and how its demographic characteristics relate to the housing stock, demand for housing, and housing policy. Following a look at the population is a view of housing in the United States and the needs, values, and satisfaction it fulfills.

This background sets the stage for the introduction of an economic framework for analysis of the interaction of consumers, producers and government in the determination of housing supply and policy.

Part II then analyzes consumer and producer behavior in detail for a set of housing alternatives whereas Part III details the housing programs and policies of federal, state and local governments as well as the role of other major policies which impinge on housing.

Statements in this book are backed up by research where research exists. The serious student will want to follow-up the original research in the areas of his or her interest. It is important for all students to understand the role of research in defining and developing knowledge and the limitations of studies based on sample size, quality of data, level of analysis and interpretation.

In sum, this text provides an overview of housing in the United States. It emphasizes contemporary issues, a framework for analysis of those issues and how the sectors of American society behave in regard to housing.

Carol B. Meeks

Acknowledgments

Many thanks to:

Gwen Bymers and **E. Scott Maynes** for their encouragement;

Jennifer Gerner and **Jean Robinson** for reviewing and commenting on parts of manuscript;

the reviewers, **Professor Constance C. Whitaker** and **Dr. Jacquelyn W. McCray** for their helpful comments and ideas;

Eleanor Oudekerk for her numerous trips to the library, editing and checking; **Patricia Baker** and **Bonnie Huff** for their diligence in typing and retyping the manuscript;

my daughter **Catherine** for the welcome diversions she created;

HOUSING PERSPECTIVES

I

THE AMERICAN
POPULATION: A PROFILE

1. HOW DO CHANGES IN POPULATION GROWTH AFFECT HOUSING DEMAND?

2. WHY ARE HOUSEHOLD FORMATIONS INCREASING?

3. HOW DOES HOUSEHOLD SIZE INFLUENCE DWELLING CHARACTERISTICS?

4. WHAT IS THE ROLE OF MOBILITY IN HOUSING?

5. HOW DO EMPLOYMENT AND INCOME AFFECT HOUSING DEMAND?

The study of housing in the United States begins with a review of its occupants. Which population groups are growing, shrinking, or remaining stable? Where do they live? Such trends provide insight into housing needs. How are family size and life style changing? Such characteristics determine space needs and locational preferences. How are employment, income, and wealth distributed? Such information indicates the ability to buy goods and services, and reflects the country's economic conditions.

This chapter helps the reader understand what the U.S. population looks like. With this background, we can then examine how and whether the housing provided matches people's needs.

POPULATION GROWTH

Population growth is basic in determining total housing demand. From 1790, when the first official census was taken, until today, the U.S. population has grown from about 3.9 million people to 220 million in 1978[1] (Figure 1-1). This continued growth has been due to a gradual improvement in average life ex-

---

[1] U.S. Department of Commerce, Bureau of the Census, *Historical Statistics of the United States, Colonial Times to 1970*, (Washington D.C.: U.S. Government Printing Office, 1975); ——, "Estimates of Population of the U.S. and Component of Change: 1940–1978," *Current Population Reports*, Series P-25. No. 802 (May 1979), p. 1.

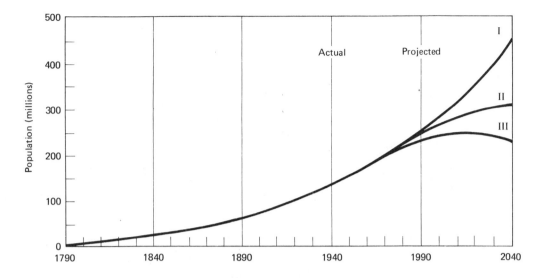

Figure 1-1. Population Growth: 1970—2040. Data from 1790 to 1970 are based on official census figures. Data from 1980 to 2040 are projections. "Series I assumes that the future fertility of young women now entering the childbearing years and of the women who follow will yield an average of 2.7 children per woman during the entire childbearing period. Series II assumes that the fertility of these women will result in an average of 2.1 children per woman, which is the number required under current mortality conditions for each generation to be replaced by one of equal size (ignoring immigration). Series III, finally, assumes that the fertility of these women will yield an average of 1.7 children per woman." Future death rates are assumed to gradually decline, in line with observed trends; net migration is assumed to be 400,000 persons per year. [*Source:* U.S. Department of Commerce, Bureau of the Census, *Social Indicators 1976* (Washington, D.C.: U.S. Government Printing Office 1977), p. 37.]

pectancy, continued immigration, and fluctuating fertility levels.

If our current fertility levels continue relatively unchanged, the population would continue to grow but at a slower rate.[2] In fact, this is now taking place. Viewed over the country's 200-year history, the current decline in the growth rate is normal.

Small changes in fertility levels can have a tremendous impact. A shift from 2.7 to 1.7 children per woman would decrease the total U.S. population to 211

million by the year 2040, other things equal. In 1974 50 percent of the women under twenty-five expected to have 2 children. In contrast, 25 percent of the women in their later thirties expected to have 2 children and 25 percent 3 children.[3]

The long-term effect of past fluctuations in birth rates is evident in the dramatic contrast in rates of population change among the different age groups (Figure 1-2). "In particular, the declining

---

[2] Current fertility is defined as on average of 2.1 children per woman.

[3] U.S. Department of Commerce, Bureau of the Census, "Population Characteristics" *Current Population Reports,* Series P-20. No. 336 (April 1979) p. 8.

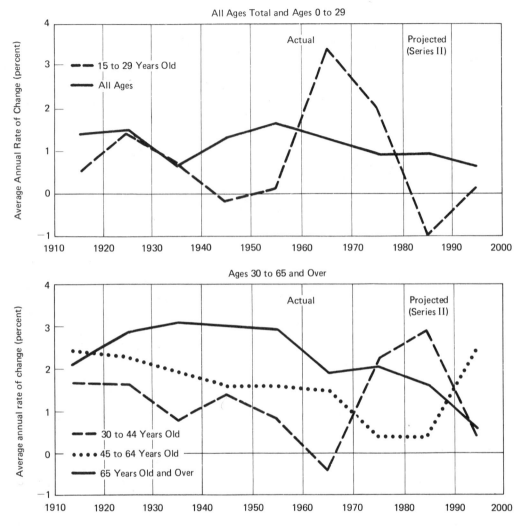

Figure 1-2. Rate of Population Change, by Age, 1910-2000. [*Source:* U.S. Department of Commerce, Bureau of the Census, *Social Indicators 1976.* (Washington, D.C.: U.S. Government Printing Office, 1977) p. 8.]

birth rates of the 1920–35 period, the 'baby boom' of the post World War II period (1947–61) and the second decline in birth rates since the early 1960's result in major fluctuations in the demand for goods and services associated with per-sons at different stages in the life cycle."[4] This recent decline in births is caused by

---

[4]U.S. Department of Commerce, Bureau of the Census, *Social Indicators 1976* (Washington, D.C.: U.S. Government Printing Office, 1977) p. 2.

4

changes in the roles and aspirations of women, increased concern over the quality of life, increased abortions, growing acceptance of more effective forms of contraception, and changes in religious views.

At current fertility levels, the U.S. population will gradually continue to age, with a growing proportion over age 45 and a smaller proportion under 15. In fact, the population has become older in the 150 years surveyed. In 1820 the median age was 16.7 years; by 1978, it had increased to 29.7.[5] Household formation and the demand for certain types of housing and second homes vary with age. For example, blacks have recently been increasing about half again as fast as whites. These rates are expected gradually to converge, with the black rate falling somewhat faster.

In addition to fertility levels, population change is related to death rates and net migration. The Bureau of the Census assumes that future death rates will gradually decline, in line with observed trends, and net migration will stay at 400,000 persons per year.

For a long time to come, the U.S. population will continue to increase. In the long run, housing growth depends on population growth. In the past eighty years, the only two periods when housing lagged far behind population growth were the Great Depression of the 1930s and World War II. However, the relationship between population growth and housing demand is complex. The demand for housing and household-related goods and services in the 1980s and 1990s is already determined by past birth rates. Housing demand, however, does not depend on population growth alone; other factors must be considered.

HOUSEHOLD FORMATION

Apart from population growth, the demand for housing is also affected by the rate of *household* formation. The higher the rate, the greater the need for new homes. Between 1890 and 1970, household formations in the United States generally rose (Figure 1-3).

The formation of a household is related to marriage and divorce rates, the ability to live as a separate unit, a preference for living alone, and society's attitudes about household and family composition. The ability to live as a separate unit, in turn, depends on income and the price of housing relative to other goods. Price may also be related to housing availability.

Households are often classified by composition. *Families* as part of total households have dropped steadily over the last twenty years. In 1940, the proportion was 90.1 percent; in 1978, only 74.9 percent. However, the husband-wife household continues to be the dominant living arrangement in the United States. The reduced proportion of all married-couple households has resulted from the increase in other household types. For example, the proportion of female-headed families has grown for both blacks and whites. In 1978, 39 percent of black families were headed by women,

---

[5]U.S. Department of Commerce, Bureau of the Census, *Historical Statistics of the United States, Colonial Times to 1970*, Bicentennial Ed., Part 2 (Washington, D.C., 1975), p. 19; "Population Characteristics," p. 15.

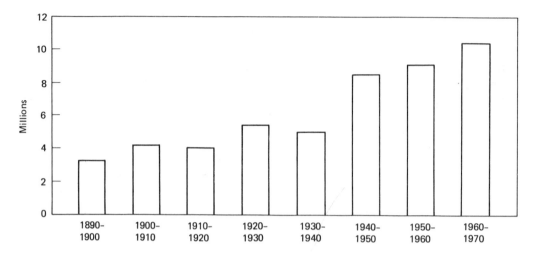

Figure 1-3. Household Formation, by Decade, 1890-1970. [*Source:* U.S. Department of Commerce, Bureau of the Census, *Historical Statistics of the United States, Colonial Times to 1970,* Bicentennial Ed., Part 2. (Washington, D.C.: U.S. Government Printing Office, 1975) p. 41.]

compared with 11.5 percent of white families.[6]

Many analysts have neglected the importance of these other household types. Household composition affects the kinds of housing needed. According to Glick and Norton, unmarried adult couples accounted for only 2 percent of all households.[7] The rise in households other than families has been caused by the women's rights movement, liberalized divorce laws, and the lowered legal age of adulthood.

FAMILY STABILITY   We can gain some idea of family stability by examining data on first marriages, divorces, and remarriages. Marriages have declined and divorces increased. Factors associated with divorce include young age at marriage, premarital pregnancy, and lower educational level.

The ratio of divorces to first marriages has risen sharply over the past decade, while the ratio of remarriages to divorces has begun to drop. If this trend continues, the number of formerly married persons who remain single will greatly increase. This may change the kind of housing needed. There will be not only more single households with a need for smaller housing units but also more children living with only one parent.[8]

[6]U.S. Department of Commerce, Bureau of the Census, *Statistical Abstract of the United States: 1978,* Table 56 (Washington, D.C.: U.S. Government Printing Office, 1978), p. 43 and ———, "Household and Family Characteristics," *Current Population Reports,* Series P-20. No. 340 (March 1978) pp. 1, 5.

[7]Paul C. Glick and Arthur J. Norton, "Marrying, Divorcing and Living Together in the U.S. Today," *Population Bulletin,* 32 (October, 1977), 33.

[8]Over 60 percent of all divorce decrees involve at least one child. *Social Indicators,* p. 54.

HOUSEHOLD SIZE

The number of persons in a household affects how much space and how many rooms are needed. The average American family size peaked at 3.70 persons in 1964, mainly as a result of the "baby boom" of the 1950s. Since then, it has steadily declined, reaching 3.33 by 1978 (Table 1-1). Most of this decline can be attributed to a decrease in the proportion of persons under age eighteen. Average household size has always been smaller than average family size since single individuals, by definition, are not a family.

In 1978, one- and two-person households made up more than half of all households in the United States. Only 6 percent of all households had six or more members. The trend toward smaller households results from lower fertility rates, later marriages, divorce rates, and the ability of young singles and the elderly to live alone.

Since 1970, the proportion of both young adults and older women living outside families has risen greatly. In contrast, the proportion of men over sixty-five living alone has remained fairly constant at about 11 percent. Most of the women—33 percent in 1978—lived alone. The number of women aged sixty-five and over who live alone is expected to rise from about 5 million in the

TABLE 1-1. Average Population Per Household and Family, 1940–1978

Year	AVERAGE POPULATION PER HOUSEHOLD All Ages	AVERAGE POPULATION PER FAMILY All Ages
1940	3.67	3.76
1950	3.37	3.54
1955	3.33	3.59
1960	3.33	3.67
1961	3.34	3.70
1962	3.31	3.67
1963	3.33	3.68
1964	3.33	3.70
1965	3.29	3.70
1966	3.27	3.69
1967	3.26	3.67
1968	3.20	3.63
1969	3.16	3.60
1970	3.14	3.58
1971	3.11	3.57
1972	3.06	3.53
1973	3.01	3.48
1974	2.97	3.44
1975	2.94	3.42
1976	2.89	3.39
1977	2.86	3.37
1978	2.81	3.33

Source: U.S. Department of Commerce, Bureau of the Census Current Population Reports, "Population Characteristics" Series P-20, No. 313 (September 1977), p. 4 and No. 327 (August 1978), p. 3.

mid-1970s to about 7.9 million by 1990.[9]

Household size varies with the type of housing occupied. In owned units, median household size decreased from 3.3 persons in 1940 to 2.8 in 1976. In rental units, the decrease in median household size was greater, from 3.2 persons in 1940 to 2.1 in 1976. In both cases, single-person households increased both in number and as a percent of all households. Larger households—7 or more—declined both as a percentage and numerically for rented units. For owned units, they increased in number but decreased as a percent. Given the shrinking family size, the large suburban home of the 1970s may go the way of the large home of the 1920s.

FAMILY LIFE CYCLE

Housing is closely related to family life cycle. This consists of the stages through which a family goes, from formation to final dissolution. Changes in family composition imply changes in space needs and desires.[10]

Thus, family life cycle relates to space, type of housing, *tenure* and services desired. A single person who marries usually requires a change in housing. With many young single people now living alone, one person may simply move in with the new spouse. If there are children, space, environment, and community service needs will change. Further, children of different ages affect the household and housing needs differently.

As the composition of household units changes, a model other than one with a family orientation may be needed. Thus, a person may participate in the life cycle and live as shown in table on facing page.

Not all persons will participate in every stage. However, these stages show the variety of households and housing situations needed. Other life-cycle conceptions have been and could be developed.

Family life cycle interacts with other factors, such as location, mobility, and tenure. In terms of location, young and old families in the mature childbearing stage are found disproportionately on the outskirts of the central business district, while single heads and primary individuals are found more often near the center.[11] However, the age of the neighborhood may directly affect family location.[12] In addition, age, site, and space variables interact in many ways. These variations determine where various types of families live.[13]

Family life cycle is also related to mobility. "Persons of the same age but at different life cycle stages are often quite different in their mobility behavior. Similarly, persons of the same life cycle stage but of different ages exhibit different mobility rates."[14] Mobility rates drop sharply with length of residence, except for the newly married and eighteen-to-twenty-nine year olds.[15] Again, life cycle

---

[9]"Household and Family Characteristics," pp. 2, 3.

[10]Kevin F. McCarthy, "The Household Life Cycle and Housing Choices," Santa Monica, Calif. Rand Crop., P-5565, 1976.

[11]Avery M. Guest, "Patterns of Family Location," *Demography,* 9 (February 1972), 162.

[12]Ibid. 169.

[13]Ibid. 170.

[14]Alden Speare, Jr., "Home Ownership, Life Cycle Stage, and Residential Mobility," *Demography,* 7 (November 1970), 457.

[15]Ibid. 454.

STAGE IN LIFE CYCLE	CHARACTERISTICS OF STAGE	RESIDENCE SELECTION
1. Single-person household	Active and mobile, economic independence	Rental of a small apartment
2. Young couple	Both persons employed, active and mobile, no children	Rental of a larger apartment as income increases; may choose luxury high rise, townhouse, apartment, or condominium; prefer central city location.
3. Young married household	Young couple with at least one child under six years, still active and mobile	Own townhouse or condominium
4. Expanding household	Couple has one or more children	Space needs predominate; single-family home on the edge of a city or in a suburb
5. Established household	Couple approaching peak, has discretionary income again	Prestige; single family home in a suburb
6. Contracting household	Couple with children gone; discretionary income	Less space needed, no maintenance desired; quality not quantity luxury apartment, condominium, or townhouse
7. Retired household	Fixed income	Reduced space needs, no maintenance
8. Widowed	Fixed income	Widow relinquishes own home and lives in the home of a grown child or in a smaller unit alone
9. Older single-headed household	Older single person with no children	Quality, not quantity, of housing
10. Single-headed household	Single head with children; income less than couple's	Space needs for children, little maintenance

interacts with factors other than mobility, and mobility influences the decision to rent or buy.

Mobility

POPULATION DISTRIBUTION

Before 1970, there were three major population shifts: (1) the continuing but slowing overall westward movement, (2) migration toward both oceans, the Gulf, and the Great Lakes regions, and (3) the ongoing redistribution of blacks northward and westward to the major cities. These shifts have changed dramatically since 1970.[16]

Every census since 1790 has shown a further westward population movement. However, since 1970, the South has grown as fast as the West, while the Northeast and North Central regions have lost population (Table 1-2). And, although blacks have traditionally moved

[16]For a review of research on migration, see Michael J. Greenwood, "Research on Internal Migration in the United States: A Survey," *Journal of Economic Literature*, 13 (June 1975), 397–433.

TABLE 1-2. Population Trends, By United States and Regions, 1900–1978

	UNITED STATES		NORTHEAST		NORTH CENTRAL		SOUTH		WEST	
	(mill)	% change	(mill)	% change	(mill)	% change	(mill)	% change	(mill)	% change
1900	76.1[a]		21.1		26.3		24.5		4.1	
1920	106.5[a]	40.0	29.7	40.8	34.1	29.7	33.1	35.1	8.9	117.1
1940	132.0[a]	23.9	36.0	21.1	40.1	17.6	41.7	26.0	13.9	56.2
1950	151.3[b]	14.7	39.5	9.8	44.5	11.0	47.2	13.2	20.2	45.3
1960	180.7[b]	36.9	44.8	24.5	51.7	29.9	55.2	32.4	28.3	103.6
1970	204.9[b]	13.4	49.2	9.8	56.7	9.6	63.0	14.2	24.9	23.3
1976	215.1[b]	5.0	49.5	0.6	57.7	1.8	68.9	9.4	38.6	10.6
1977	216.4[c]	0.6	49.3	−0.4	58.0	0.5	69.8	1.3	39.3	1.8
1978	218.1[c]	0.8	49.1	−0.4	58.3	0.5	70.6	1.1	40.1	2.0

[a]U.S. Department of Commerce, Bureau of the Census, *Historical Statistics of the United States, Colonial Times to 1970,* Part I, (Washington, D.C.: U.S. Government Printing Office, 1975) Table Series A172-194, p. 22.

[b]_____, *Statistical Abstract of the United States, 1978,* 99th ed. (Washington, D.C.: U.S. Government Printing Office, 1978), p. 14.

[c]_____, *Current Population Reports,* "Population Profile of the U.S.: 1978," Series P-20, No. 336 (April 1979), pp. 18, 22.

from the South northward, this movement appears to have stopped.

The coastal areas of the United States attracted people by their climate and job opportunities. Between 1940 and 1970 the population within fifty miles of the coastline (including the Great Lakes) increased from 46 to 54 percent of the total U.S. population. Today, however although some coastal areas—such as Florida and Oregon—have continued to grow since 1970, the movement to the coasts has ceased. Trends in regional growth aggravate environmental problems, especially air pollution.

Landform, too, affects where people live. Populations gather in valleys rather than on mountain peaks. They locate along rivers. They respond to transportation needs—waterways, rails, and highways.

The United States has changed from a relatively scattered colonial population to an urban nation. Between 1910 and 1970, the percentage living in *rural* areas declined from about 50 to about 25 percent (Figure 1-4). Between 1970 and 1978, the population in metropolitan areas increased by 4.4 percent, while in nonurban areas it rose by 12.2 percent. This reverses one of the long-standing patterns of U.S. population redistribution—urbanization. Many factors have contributed to this reversal: increased job opportunities in some nonurban areas; new retirement communities in nonurban areas that attract older city residents; and suburban development. However, this new movement does not indicate a return to farm living. The farm population stabilized in the 1970s at about 9.5 million.

The larger urban areas have shown the least growth since 1970. Of the eight such areas with more than 3 million people, only the Washington, D.C., *Standard Metropolitan Statistical Area* (SMSA) has grown significantly. However, many of

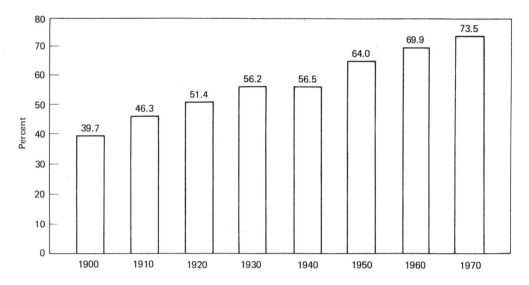

Figure 1-4. Percent Urban Residence, 1900-1970. (*Note:* Alaska and Hawaii were excluded before 1950. The definition of "urban" changed in 1950.) [*Sources:* U.S. Department of Commerce, Bureau of the Census, *Historical Statistics of the United States, 1789-1945* (Washington, D.C.: U.S. Government Printing Office, 1949.) Table Series B 13-23, p. 25; *Statistical Abstract of the United States, 1963* (Washington, D.C.: U.S. Government Printing Office.) Table No. 7, p. 10; *Statistical Abstract of the U.S., 1977* (Washington, D.C.: U.S. Government Printing Office, 1977.) Table 19, p. 18.]

the smaller urban areas are growing faster than adjacent nonurban areas. The principal population corridors are Boston–Washington, D.C.; Buffalo west to Cleveland-Detroit; Chicago-Milwaukee; north of Daytona Beach to Miami to the Florida Keys: Seattle-Portland; San Francisco, Oakland, and Monterey; Los Angeles-San Deigo.

The central cities have lost population since 1970, all of it due to "white flight." This shrinking of the central cities, racial concentration, and expansion in suburban and outlying areas are continuing policy issues for all levels of government.

The massive population movements of this century from farm to city to suburb are reflected in the proportions of the population who move each year—about 20 percent. This figure has been rela-

tively stable over the last thirty years.[17] Reasons for moving include divorce, job opportunities, forced moves, change in family size, increased income, and psychological satisfaction.

FACTORS AFFECTING MOBILITY

Since mobility affects not only the household that moves but also the community it leaves and the one it goes to, researchers have attempted to analyze the reasons and choices behind it. Characteristics of the household, its dwelling unit, and the community all influence mobility. Mobility is related to

---

[17]"Population Characteristics," No. 336; and "Population Profile of the U.S.: 1978" *Current Population Reports.* Series P-20, No. 340, p. 34.

age. It generally increases through the late teens, peaks in the early to mid twenties, and then gradually decreases (Figure 1-5).

Unemployment or job dissatisfaction push a family to move. Families whose heads are unemployed or who are employed but looking for a different job are more likely to move than those whose heads are not job hunting. Also, recent arrivals who cannot find acceptable work are especially prone to move again.

Local economic conditions affect outmigration, primarily for the unemployed. Unemployed persons and others looking for work are more responsive to such economic factors as family income, origin, wage rates, and expected earnings increases than persons apparently satisfied with their jobs.

Past mobility behavior of a family influences current behavior. Families are more likely to move if they have moved in the recent past,[18] primarily because people tend to return to places they have recently left. Families who have moved several times are more likely to move again then are families who made one or no recent moves if those multiple moves involved no return. Families whose multiple moves ended with a return to a previous place are, in some cases, no more likely to move again than families who have not moved at all.

Movers tend to be younger, have higher income, and be renters.[19] How-

[18]U.S. Department of Labor, *Why Families Move,* R&D Monograph 48 (Washington, D.C.: U.S. Government Printing Office, 1977), p. 98.

[19]U.S. Department of Commerce, Bureau of the Census, *Annual Housing Survey,* Part D, "Housing Characteristics of Recent Movers" (Washington, D.C.: U.S. Government Printing Office, January 1978).

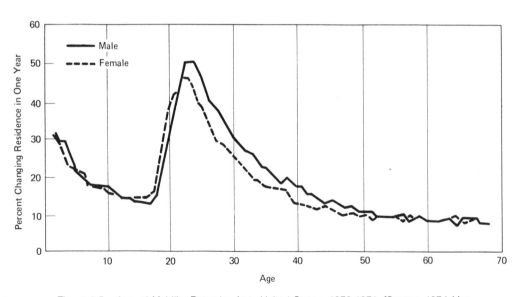

Figure 1-5. Annual Mobility Rates by Age, United States, 1970-1971. [*Source: 1974 Manpower Report of the President,* Chart 13. (Washington, D.C.: U.S. Government Printing Office, 1974) p. 83.]

ever, other things equal, age and education are not important.[20] Mobility is inversely related to the number of school-age children.[21] Crowding increases mobility, but lack of space to separate children by sex is more important than persons per room.[22] Families are less likely to move when family size decreases than when it increases.[23]

The birth of the first child is more likely to result in a move than the birth of other children.[24] The first child puts the greatest strain on available space because of the furniture and equipment not needed in the childless home. In addition, schools and the neighborhood are evaluated differently.

Although unmarried renters move less then married renters, renters are much more mobile than homeowners regardless of family characteristics.[25] Tenure may be the most powerful predictor of mobility. However, tenure choice is partially based on the expectation of future moves.

Mobility is hindered by neighborhood ties. The longer people have lived in one place, the less the likelihood of a move.[26]

Wives have a significant influence on whether and where the family moves.

Families with working wives are not necessarily less likely to move than families with nonworking wives, other things equal. Families in which the working wife earns only a small part of the family's income, or is fairly young and earns less than she could elsewhere, are more likely to move than families with nonworking wives. Also, families who move tend to choose areas where both the husband's and wife's earnings will be highest; maximizing the wife's contribution is an important consideration.[27]

Bach and Smith conclude that:

1. Community satisfaction is important in predicting who is likely to move.

2. An evaluation of the community occurs that negates the effect of background characteristics.

3. The main effect of satisfaction on mobility is substantial if expectation to move is included.

4. People who are quite dissatisfied plan to move and then do move.[28]

Homeownership, young children, age, and indirectly, income contribute to satisfied groups who probably will not move.[29] "Quality of attachments," rather than quantity, accounts for the low migration of people who are dissatisfied but do not expect to move.

Mobility obviously results in housing changes. According to Rossi, "Mobility is the mechanism by which a family's hous-

[20]U.S. Department of Labor, *Why Families Move,* p. 99.

[21]Alden Speare, Jr., Sidney Goldstein, and William H. Frey, *Residential Mobility, Migration and Metropolitan Change* (Cambridge, Mass.: Ballinger, 1975).

[22]David R. Fredland, *Residential Mobility and Home Purchase* (Lexington, Mass.: Lexington Books, 1973).

[23]Ibid., p. 69.

[24]Albert Chevon, "Family Growth, Household Density, and Moving," *Demography,* 8 (November 1971), 455.

[25]Fredland, *Residential Mobility,* pp. 86, 89.

[26]Speare and others, *Residential Mobility,* p. 132.

[27]U.S. Department of Labor, *Why Families Move,* p. 99.

[28]Robert L. Bach and Joel Smith, "Community Satisfaction, Expectations of Moving, and Migration," *Demography,* 14 (May 1977), 164–66.

[29]Ibid., 158–59.

ing is brought into adjustment to its housing needs."[30]

Moving is expensive. There are the actual costs of moving and transportation. There are information costs, psychic costs, and opportunity costs (time spent moving could be used in another way). In addition, one loses the benefit of knowing about one's community. Other living areas generally become less familiar with distance.

Employment and Income

Employment and income enable households to buy or rent housing. They also influence the kind of housing chosen.

EMPLOYMENT

The U.S. labor force has about 100.4 million workers, or 63 percent of the civilian noninstitutional population over age sixteen.[31] From 1970 to 1978 the labor force grew by about 17 million persons: 7.4 million men and 10.7 million women. Among male family heads in 1978, about 81.6 percent were in the civilian labor force; about 43 percent of all wives and 58.5 percent of all female family heads worked.[32]

There are now more two-income than one-income families, since more married women work. Since 1950, the proportion of women engaged in or seeking work climbed from about one-third to nearly one-half. Prior to World War II, most female workers were young. After the war, more women aged forty-five to fifty-nine began to work. Since the mid 1960s the greatest increase has been in women under forty-five years. Factors associated with the wife's decision to work include:

1. Economic pressure—the need to supplement the husband's earnings.
2. Wife's skills and earning potential.
3. Number and ages of children and the presence of other adults.

The percentage of working mothers, husband present, with children under six has increased from 18.6 percent in 1960 to 41.6 percent in 1978. The percentage of those with children under three has more than doubled since 1960 to 1975 from 15.3 to 32.7 percent.[33] As more women are employed outside the home, less time is available for home and family care.

Other aspects of employment also relate to housing choice, such as length of the workday. A shorter workday means more time at home or for recreation. Paid vacations have the same effect.

INCOME

The distribution of total income among fifths of families has been one of the most stable relationships since the Current

---

[30]Peter H. Rossi, *Why Families Move* (Glencoe, Ill.: The Free Press, 1955), p. 178.

[31]U.S. Department of Commerce, Bureau of the Census, *Current Population Reports*, "Population Profile of the United States: 1974," Series P-20, No. 336 (April 1979), p. 41.

[32]Ibid.

[33]U.S. Department of Commerce, Bureau of the Census, "A Statistical Portrait of Women in the U.S.," *Current Population Reports*, Special Studies, Series P-23, No. 58 (April 1976), pp. 22, 31; "Population Profile of the U.S.: 1978," p. 42.

Population Survey began in 1947.[34] Total income is distributed as follows:[35]

FAMILIES	PERCENT OF TOTAL INCOME RECEIVED, 1977
lowest fifth	5.2
2nd fifth	11.6
3rd fifth	17.5
4th fifth	24.2
highest fifth	41.5

The top 5 percent of families received 15.7 percent of the total income, while the lowest 40 percent of all families received 26.8 percent.

Median family income increased from $3,319 in 1950 to $16,009 in 1977 (Table 1-3). However, the most important figure here is median income in terms of con-

[34]U.S. Department of Commerce, Bureau of the Census, "Population Profile of the United States: 1974," *Current Population Reports*, Series P-20, No. 279 (March 1975), p. 26.

[35]U.S. Department of Commerce, *Statistical Abstract 1978*, Table 734, p. 455.

stant purchasing power. In constant dollars (1977), median family income increased from $8,356 in 1950 to $16,009 in 1977, but gains have been slow and sometimes negative in recent years. Median family income for blacks in 1950 was 56.3 percent of total median family income; by 1977, it had risen to 63.4 percent. Trends in median income should be kept in mind as housing prices are discussed in later chapters.

Median family income is closely related to the number of earners per family. Education also increases income. Family life cycle studies indicate that income typically increases with age up to about the mid-fifties and then gradually declines. Urban families usually have higher median incomes than nonurban families—who, in turn, have higher median incomes than farm families.

Earnings comprise the largest source of family income. However, only about 25 percent of families have income from earnings alone. Approximately 12 percent of all families have only nonearned

TABLE 1-3. Median Family Income, 1950–1977

Year	Median Income, All (Current $)	DEFLATED FOR INFLATION Constant Purchasing Power (1977 Constant $)	Median Income, Blacks (Current $)
1950	3319	8,356	1869
1955	4,421	9,999	2,549
1960	5,620	11,500	3,233
1965	6,957	13,362	3,904
1970	9,867	15,399	6,516
1974	12,902	15,855	8,265
1975	13,719	15,447	9,321
1976	14,958	15,923	9,821
1977	16,009	16,009	10,142

Source: U.S. Department of Commerce, Bureau of the Census *Statistical Abstract of the United States, 1978*, Table 734, p. 452, based on *Current Population Reports*, Series P-60, No. 114. (Washington, D.C.: U.S. Government Printing Office, 1978).

income. The remaining 63 percent have income from earnings and other sources, such as interest dividends, unemployment compensation, or pensions.

POVERTY

Poverty is highest among blacks, Spanish, the elderly, and female-headed households. In 1977 there were about 25 million persons below the poverty level, which was defined as $6,191 for a non-farm family of four persons.[36]

Between 1976 and 1977, persons below the poverty level declined from 25 million to 24.7 million. This was in contrast to 1974–1975, when the number rose by 2.5 million. This was the largest single annual increase since 1959, the first year for which poverty data are available.[37] The increase affected black, whites, and Spanish, and the young as well as the elderly (Table 1-4).

---

[36]U.S. Department of Commerce, "Population Profile of the U.S.: 1978," p. 54.

[37]Ibid.

The number and kinds of persons living in poverty influences the kind and cost of government housing programs. It affects the size, cost, and location of housing needed and chosen. For example, if a government housing program is designed to serve the single elderly when the greatest need is to house families with four children, funds are misused and the "housing problem" is no closer to being solved.

Social Class

The concept of social class represents a more complex view of housholds than either income level or occupation. Social class includes similarities in the life style and values of its members regardless of income or occupation. Different classes have different expectations about the kind of housing that is symbolically correct for each stage in the life cycle. ". . . Knowing a family's (or individual's) social-class identification is crucial for

---

TABLE 1-4. Poverty Status, 1959–1976

Year	Poverty Level for Nonfarm Family of Four	PERSONS BELOW POVERTY LEVEL		PERSONS IN HOUSEHOLDS WITH FEMALE HEADS	
		Number (1000's)	% of Total	Number (1000's)	% of Total
1959	$2,973	38,490	22.4	10,390	50.2
1960	3,022	39,851	22.4	10,663	49.5
1965	3,223	33,185	17.3	11,058	46.0
1970	3,968	25,420	12.6	11,154	38.2
1974	5,038	23,370	11.2	11,469	33.6
1975	5,500	25,877	12.3	12,268	34.6
1976	5,815	24,975	11.8	12,586	34.4
1977	6,191	24,700	11.6	12,600	32.8

Source: U.S. Department of Commerce, Bureau of the Census, Current Population Reports, "Consumer Income, Characteristics of Population Below Poverty Level, 1976," Series P-60, No. 115 (July 1978); Table 1, p. 15; Table A-1, p. 205 and _____, Statistical Abstract of the United States 1978 (Washington, D.C.: U.S. Government Printing Office, 1978) p. 465.

understanding its housing aspirations."[38]

Social class has been defined in a variety of ways, but the categories usually include an upper class, an upper middle class, a middle class, and working class, and a lower class. The upper and upper middle classes are college-educated, with above-average incomes. The middle class is typically white-collar, with a college education and an intermediate income. The working class is blue-collar, with a high school education and incomes at the intermediate or lower levels. The lower class often consists of school dropouts, with poverty-level incomes, unemployment, or employment in unskilled jobs.

Social class influences housing choice, neighborhood location, consumption level, and services needed. The mingling of different social classes in a neighborhood seems to negatively affect the residents' life style and makes the area less desirable. Gans notes that differences of more than 20 percent in house values leads to unsalable homes.[39] Gutman reports that working-class wives have trouble adjusting in a mixed-class suburb since they lack the social skills of the middle class.[40] Gans suggests that instead of making friends with their middle-class neighbors, working class residents isolate themselves.[41] Keller claims that both classes have a fuller social life when they are not mixed.[42]

Summary

Demographic, sociological, and economic factors all affect housing demand. The U.S. population will continue to grow, but at a decreasing rate. More housing is needed to accommodate single-person households. With fewer traditional couple households, a greater variety of housing is needed.

The population will still be mobile, with the South and West both continuing to grow. There will be new demand for housing in these areas, while no-growth areas will see housing abandoned.

The economic situation of consumers will influence their ability to pay for housing. Income in relation to housing costs is a critical issue. The social class of consumers influences housing choice, housing perceptions, and satisfaction, as well as behavior.

Terms

family household or family two or more persons in a household who are related by blood, marriage, or adoption.

head of household person designated as the head, except married women living with their husbands.

household all persons who occupy a house, apartment, or room that constitutes a housing unit. A household may contain a single indi-

[38]David Birch and others, *America's Housing Needs: 1970 to 1980* (Cambridge, Mass.: Joint Center for Urban Studies, 1973), pp. 5–6.

[39]Herbert Gans, *The Levittowners* (New York: Pantheon, 1967), p. 281.

[40]Robert Gutman, "Population Mobility in the American Middle Class," in *The Urban Condition,* ed. Leonard Duhl (New York: Basic Books, 1963), pp. 172–84.

[41]Gans, *The Levittowners,* p. 170.

[42]Suzanne Keller, "Social Class in Physical Planning," *International Social Science Journal,* 8 (1966), 504.

vidual, a group of unrelated individuals, a single family, or two or more families living together.

migrants movers whose change of residence involved crossing county boundaries.

movers persons who changed their residence during the specified year.

standard metropolitan statistical area (SMSA) except in the New England states, a county or group of contiguous counties that contains at least one city of 50,000 inhabitants or more, or "twin cities" with a combined population of at least 50,000. In addition to the county or counties containing such a city or cities, contiguous counties are included in an SMSA if, according to certain criteria, they are socially and economically integrated with the central city. In the New England states, SMSAs consist of towns and cities instead of counties. Each SMSA must include at least one central city, and the complete title of an SMSA identifies the central city or cities. With a few exceptions, central cities are detemined according to the following criteria: (1) the largest city in an SMSA is always a central city; (2) one or two cities may be secondary central cities if they have at least 250,000 inhabitants or if the additional city or cities each have a population one-third or more of that of the largest city and a minimum population of 25,000.

tenure ownership status of a housing unit. It is "owner occupied" if the owner(s) lives in the unit, even if it is mortgaged. All other units are "renter occupied" including those for which cash rents are paid as well as those rented for services.

urban residence residence in urbanized areas and in other places of 2,500 inhabitants or more. (Urbanized area: in 1970 consisted of at least one city of 50,000 inhabitants or more and the surrounding, closely settled area that meets certain criteria of population density or land use.) This includes all persons living in places of 2,500 inhabitants or more incorporated as cities, villages, boroughs, and certain towns, unincorporated places of 2,500 or more, and other territory included in urbanized areas.

rural residence all territory or area not classified as urban.

Suggested Readings

Advisory Commission on Intergovernmental Relations, *Urban and Rural America: Policies for Future Growth.* Report A-32, Washington, D.C.: U.S. Government Printing Office, 1968.

Commission on Population Growth and the American Future, *Population and the American Future.* Report of the Commission on Population Growth and the American Future. Washington, D.C.: U.S. Government Printing Office, 1972.

Fuguitt, Glenn V., and Calvin L. Beal, *Population Change in Nonmetropolitan Cities and Towns.* Economic Report No. 323, Washington, D.C.: U.S. Department of Agriculture, Feb. 1976.

National Goals Staff, *Toward Balanced Growth: Quantity with Quality.* Washington, D.C.: U.S. Government Printing Office, 1970.

President's National Advisory Commission on Rural Poverty, *The People Left Behind.* Washington, D.C.: U.S. Government Printing Office, 1969.

U.S. Department of Housing and Urban Development, *National Growth and Development.* Washington, D.C.: Committee on Community Development, Dec. 1974.

HOUSING IN AMERICA:
A MACRO VIEW

1. HOW DOES THE HOUSING STOCK CHANGE?

2. IS OWNED HOUSING AFFORDABLE? WILL IT CONTINUE TO BE SO?

3. IDENTIFY CHARACTERISTICS OF MOBILE HOME OCCUPANTS.

4. WHAT IS THE TREND IN STARTS FOR PUBLIC HOUSING UNITS?

5. WHAT ARE THE IMPLICATIONS OF FLUCTUATIONS IN HOUSING STARTS?

With a profile of the U.S. population in mind, let us now consider the types of housing in which people live. We will first review characteristics such as size, age, structure, and value of housing stock, and then analyze how residents use energy. Finally, housing and population are interrelated on a macro scale.

First, however, a *housing unit* must be defined. This is more difficult than it first appears; the Census Bureau has changed its definition between 1940 and 1970. In 1940 a dwelling unit was defined as living quarters occupied or intended for occupancy by one household. In 1950 it was defined as a group of rooms occupied or intended for occupancy as *separate living quarters* and having either separate cooking equipment or a separate entrance. The 1960 definition was similar to 1950

except that "dwelling unit" was changed to "housing unit." In 1970 and in the Annual Housing Survey, the definition remained relatively unchanged.

Most information on U.S. housing is obtained from the decennial censuses conducted by the Census Bureau. Annual information on housing stock became available in 1973 with the Annual Housing Surveys developed by the Census Bureau and the Department of Housing and Urban Development.

Housing Stock

Although a housing unit is built to last several decades, each year units are lost because of *demolition*, casualty (e.g., fire),

19

With urban growth come increasing high rise buildings.

conversion to other uses, and *mergers.* Such losses total less than 5 percent of the housing stock.[1] Also, each year units are added through construction, *conversion* of a housing unit into two or more, or conversion of another type of structure into a housing unit.

The U.S. housing stock has grown from 14.5 million units in 1900 to over 80 million units in 1976 (Figure 2-1). The

number of occupied units has grown with it. As the housing stock has increased, its composition has greatly changed. One-family detached homes have accounted for about two-thirds of all detached units since 1940.[2] The number of two- to

---

[1]Joint Center for Urban Studies of MIT and Harvard University, *America's Housing Needs: 1970 to 1980:* (Cambridge, Mass., December 1973).

[2]U.S. Department of Commerce, Bureau of the Census, *Census of Housing,* 1940, 1950, 1960, and U.S. Department of Housing and Urban Development. *Annual Housing Survey:1976,* Part A, (Washington, D.C.: U.S. Government Printing Office, 1978). Series H-150. "General Housing Characteristics for the United States and Regions."

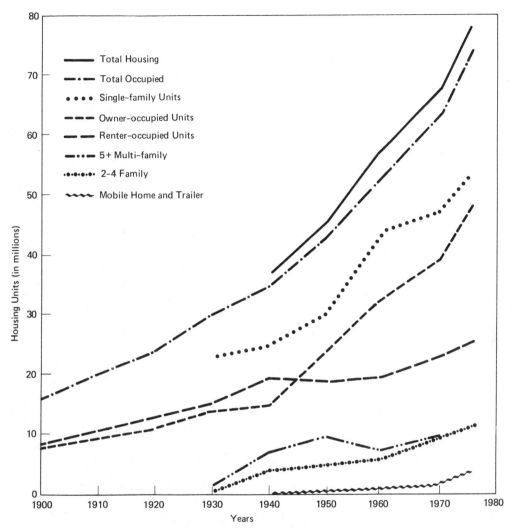

Figure 2-1. Housing Units, 1900–1976. (*Note:* Due to the way some of the data were assembled, and changes in definitions, data on housing units prior to 1940 may not be comparable. This chart indicates trend lines only. Data on breakdown of dwellings by one-, two-, or three- or more family units before 1930 are not available.) [*Sources:* U.S. Department of Commerce, Bureau of the Census, U.S. Census, 1900–1930; *U.S. Census of Housing*, 1940–1970; *Statistical Abstracts of the United States*, 1933, 1943, 1953, 1977; *Annual Housing Survey of 1976*.)

four-family units has declined somewhat, while the number of dwellings with five or more units has increased. Although in 1940 and 1950 mobile homes made up less than 1 percent of the housing stock, by 1976 they had risen to close to 5 per-

cent. In 1976, there were about 80.8 million housing units in the United States; 74 million were occupied, about two-thirds of these by homeowners (Figure 2-1). Of all housing units, 26.9 million were located outside SMSAs.

HOUSING VACANCIES

Vacancy rates are important in determining the type and amount of housing needed. According to the Census Bureau, a housing unit is *vacant* if no one is living in it at the time of the census, except when the residents are temporarily gone, on a vacation for example.

Units are vacant for many different reasons. The owner may be waiting for the market to improve before selling it; the unit is going to be demolished; it is a transition period between closing of a sale or rental. The unit may be vacant for an involuntary reason, such as a drop in local employment. National vacancy rates in 1978 were 5.0 percent in rental housing and 1.0 percent in homeowner housing.[3] *Homeowner vacancy rates* have re-

---

[3]U.S. Department of Commerce, Bureau of the Census, *Current Housing Reports*, "Housing Vacancies," Series H-111 (May 1979), p. 1.

mained stable in the last four years. During the 1970s *rental vacancy rates* peaked in 1974 at 6.2 percent (Figure 2-2).

In 1977, the vacancy rate in rental housing inside SMSAs (5.3 percent) differed only slightly from the rate outside (5.2 percent). The rental vacancy rate inside central cities was higher (5.7 percent) than the rate in the suburbs (4.6 percent).

In 1978, there was a higher vacancy rate for rental units built in 1970 or later. In addition, vacancy rates were higher in more expensive units and in small units. There were few vacant single-family homes. Some similarities existed among homeowner units. Vacancy rates were highest in units built after 1970 or before 1940 and in those with three rooms or less. Units in multiunit structures and without plumbing facilities—a small part of the total inventory—had relatively high vacancy rates.

Thus, vacancy rates reflect demand—the kind of housing people want. Eco-

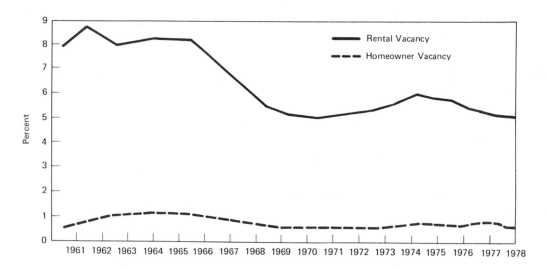

Figure 2-2. Vacancy Trends in Rental and Homeowner Housing: 1960–1977. [*Source:* U.S. Department of Commerce, Bureau of the Census, "Housing Vacancies," *Current Housing Reports,* Series H-111, May, 1979.]

nomic changes at the end of the 1970s should raise the demand for rental units, lower rental vacancy rates, and ultimately stimulate production. Some vacancies are needed at any time to insure mobility and consumer choice.

CONSTRUCTION ACTIVITY

Housing construction is based on household demand, the need to replace units lost through demolition and abandonment, and finally, the need for units to assure enough vacancies. Improvement of substandard housing conditions also increases the need for housing. Since World War II, total construction has more than kept pace with the increased population. For every two units built for a new household, another has been built for some other purpose. However, annual housing construction is small compared to the total housing stock.

Let us now begin to examine production trends and characteristics of new units. As we do so, we should keep in mind that housing production depends upon two things: (1) the amount of resources—labor, land, and capital—available for expansion and maintenance of housing and (2) management, marketing, financing, insurance, and related services.

Public housing construction depends

U.S. Department of HUD

Housing construction.

on the political situation. The post-World War II period, for example, saw considerable building to meet the housing shortage. This production was stopped by the Korean War and an unfriendly administration. In the late 1960s, a concern for poverty increased public housing until the Nixon moratorium. These fluctuations in housing production have important economic and social costs. Resources are unemployed or poorly used, income is poorly distributed, and a price structure with potential inflation is created. The effect on housing availability is less clear.

HOUSING STARTS

A housing start is a measure of new construction activity. It consists of the start of construction of a housing unit designed as a permanent residence. "Start of construction for private housing units is defined as the beginning of excavation for the foundation of a building; for public housing units it is defined as when the construction contract is awarded."[4]

The cyclical nature of new construction can be seen in Figure 2-3. The first decline occurred at the beginning of World War I, when resources were used elsewhere. The 1920s showed a rapid increase in housing starts, partly in response to the pent-up demand. The Great Depression of the 1930s resulted in a drastic decrease. Recovery from the Depression led to a slow construction upturn, which was again reduced by World War II. Housing starts dramatically increased after the war. New housing starts peaked in 1972 at about 2.4 million (Table 2-1). Public housing units started have declined steadily since 1968, the peak year, with 37,800 units. However, data on

[4]U.S. Department of Commerce, Bureau of the Census, "Housing Starts," *Construction Reports*, C-20-76-11, November 1976 (January 1977), 16.

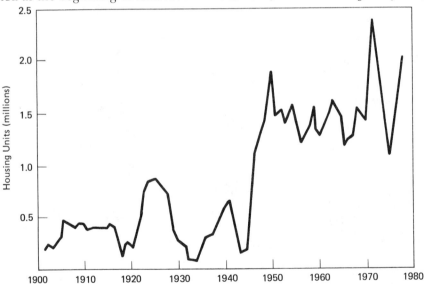

Figure 2-3. Housing Starts in the United States, 1900–1978. [*Source:* U.S. Department of Commerce, Bureau of the Census, "Housing Starts," *Construction Reports*, Series C-20.]

public housing starts give a misleading picture of government support for housing, since some programs are considered part of the private sector.

Privately owned housing starts decreased in 1973, 1974, and 1975. In 1976 this trend was reversed, primarily for single-family units. In the early 1970s, one-family homes accounted for about 55 percent of all private housing units started; by 1976 and 1977, the figure was about 75 percent (Table 2-1). The number of households that usually demand single-family homes has increased so that demographic data support this trend. A *Professional Builder* study reports an overwhelming (about 94 percent) preference for single-family detached homes in 1975, 1976, and 1977.[5]

In the early 1970s, the location of housing starts changed. Urban areas in the South and West grew. Whether this in-

crease will continue depends on economic improvements. Another factor is the interest rate on mortgages. Generally, as interest rates have increased, housing starts have declined (Figure 2-4). When interest rates are high, mortgage funds are usually scarce and harder to obtain. Credit requirements are also stricter. The increased cost of housing that results from high interest rates reduces the demand for housing; thus fewer units are started.

Skyrocketing construction and financing costs have today dampened the investment in multi-family buildings. "In the past several years, investors also saw diminished profit prospects as rental vacancy rates rose and the spectre of rent controls grew in many areas."[6] Large increases in energy costs, maintenance and repair, and property taxes have de-

[5]*Professional Builder,* 42 (January 1977), 143.

[6]Aaron Sabghir, "The New Construction Outlook for 1977," *Construction Review,* 22 (November 1976), 5.

TABLE 2-1. Housing Starts (in Thousands of Units)

	TOTAL HOUSING STARTS	PUBLICLY OWNED [a]	NEW, PRIVATELY OWNED HOUSING UNITS STARTED			ONE-FAMILY HOMES, AS % OF TOTAL HOUSING UNITS
			Total	1 Unit	5 Units	
1970	1,469.0	35.4	1,433.6	812.9	535.9	57
1971	2,084.5	32.3	2,052.2	1,151.0	780.9	56
1972	2,378.5	21.9	2,356.6	1,309.2	906.2	56
1973	2,057.5	12.2	2,045.3	1,132.0	795.0	55
1974	1,352.5	14.8	1,337.7	888.1	381.6	66
1975	1,171.4	10.9	1,160.4	892.2	204.3	77
1976	1,547.6	10.1	1,537.5	1,162.4	289.2	75
1977	1,989.8	2.7	1,987.1	1,450.9	414.4	73
1978	2,023.3	3.0	2,020.3	1,433.3	462.0	71

[a]Publicly owned housing includes housing units for which construction contracts were awarded by federal, state, or local governments. Units built by private developers for sale upon completion to local public housing authorities under the U.S. Department of Housing and Urban Development "Turnkey" program are classified as private housing.

Source: U.S. Department of Commerce, Bureau of the Census, "Housing Starts," *Construction Reports,* Series C-20-79-3 (May 1979), 3.

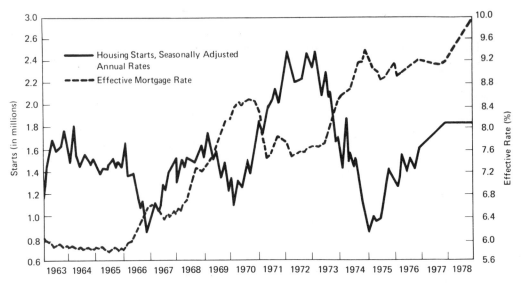

Figure 2-4. Relationship Between Housing Starts and Effective Mortgage Rates on New Homes Sold, 1963–1978. [*Source:* U.S. Department of Commerce, Bureau of the Census, *Construction Reports,* "Housing Starts 1959–1971," C-20 supplement; *Construction Reports,* "Housing Starts," Series C 20. (Office of Economic Research Federal Home Loan Bank Board, "Interest Rates on Conventional Home Mortgage Loans Closed," January 1978.)]

creased profit margins. "Surveys by the Institute of Real Estate Management show that average operating expenses of rental buildings increased 26 percent from 1972 to 1975, while the average rent increased only 13 percent."[7] As profit margins dropped, builders turned away from multi-family units, and lenders were reluctant to finance such construction.

In the early 1970s there was a glut of rental units, and the fact that newer units competed with older ones that were built at lower costs increased the difficulty. The Section 8 housing assistance program is designed to help multiunit construction (see Chapter 11, p. 256).

---

[7]David E. Bloom, "Housing Activity in the Recent Recovery," *Survey of Current Business,* 56 (September 1976), 15.

HOUSING COMPLETIONS

Housing completion data are released jointly by the Bureau of the Census, the U.S. Department of Commerce, and the U.S. Department of Housing and Urban Development.[8] Since housing completions have been recorded only since 1968, historical analysis is limited.

Housing completions peaked in 1973 and dropped substantially in 1974 and 1975 (Table 2-2). Whereas 1976 saw a slight increase over 1975, 1977 saw a strong increase as did 1978. The rise in units completed privately resulted from an increase in single-family units completed. The number of multi-family units completed declined every year since 1973

---

[8]Housing completions and "under construction" statistics do not include mobile home units.

TABLE 2-2. New Housing Units Completed by Ownership and Type of Structure (in Thousands)[a]

Year	Total All	Total Publicly	PRIVATELY OWNED Total	One Unit	2 Units or More
1970	1452	34	1418	802	617
1971	1740	34	1706	1014	692
1972	2032	28	2004	1160	844
1973	2120	19	2100	1197	903
1974	1744	16	1729	940	788
1975	1333	16	1317	875	442
1976	1387	10	1377	1034	343
1977	NA	NA	1657	1258	399
1978	NA	NA	1867	1369	498

[a]Mobile homes are not included.

Source: U.S. Department of Commerce, Bureau of the Census, "Housing Completions," *Construction Reports*, Series C-22-79-2 (April 1979), p. 3.

but rebounded slightly in 1977 and somewhat more in 1978.[9] This will result in a tight rental market. The number of publicly owned units completed has declined throughout the 1970s. Since 1968 about 33 percent of all units completed have been located outside SMSAs. About 40 percent are found in the South and about 25 percent in the West and North Central regions; the remainder are in the Northeast.

The lag between starts and completions affects the cash flows into the mortgage market. Permanent financing rather than construction financing is received upon completion.

Units under construction rose from 1970 to 1973 and then began to decline until late 1975. Privately owned single-family units under construction then started increasing and continued to increase strongly throughout 1978. At the end of that year, about 1.3 million housing units were under construction.[10] In the early 1970s, multi-family units under construction exceeded one-unit structures. But after reaching peak construction in 1972 and 1973, multi-family units dropped below single-family units and remained there until mid-1977. Even then, the rate was somewhat slower than that of single-family units.

CHARACTERISTICS OF ONE-FAMILY HOUSES COMPLETED[11] Since 1972 the average size of a new one-family house increased from 1,555 to 1,720 square feet; the median from 1,405 to 1,610. This is a 9 per-

[9]For an economic discussion of the allocation of construction resources between single-family and multi-family housing, see Alan R. Winger and John Madden, "The Application of the Theory of Joint Products: The Case of Residential Construction," *Quarterly Review of Economics and Business*, 10 (Summer 1970), 61–69.

[10]U.S. Department of Commerce, Bureau of the Census. "Housing Completions," *Construction Reports*, Series C-22-79-3 (May 1979), 7.

[11]The Census Bureau provides data on size, equipment, and design characteristics of housing units completed. See U.S. Department of Commerce, Bureau of the Census, and U.S. Department of Housing and Urban Development, "Characteristics of New Housing," *Construction Reports*, Series C25.

An A-frame is a typical vacation dwelling.

Manufactured Housing Institute

cent increase and a 13 percent increase, respectively. However, the percentage of homes with three bedrooms has remained constant at about 66 percent. The number of bathrooms increased, with 47 percent of 1977 homes having two baths and 23 percent two and a half.

The number and percentage of homes with central air conditioning have increased; by 1977, 54 percent had central air conditioning. In the Northeast, few homes have central air conditioning; in the South, 80 percent do. Due to shifts in energy availability and price, home heating fuels have completed changed. Gas decreased from 54 to 38 percent and electricity increased from 36 to 50 percent from 1972 to 1977. Use of oil decreased slightly. About 75 percent of all homes completed from 1972 to 1977 had a central warm air heating system. During this period, the percentage of homes with one or more fireplaces increased from 38 to 61 percent, up 23 percent.

One-story homes have been the main type of housing unit completed, although falling from 72 percent in 1972 to 63 percent in 1977. The exterior was usually of brick or wood/wood products. Over 60 percent of the homes had garages for two or more cars. The percentage of homes with full or partial basements increased from 37 percent in 1972 to 44 percent in 1977.

CHARACTERISTICS OF MULTI-FAMILY UNITS COMPLETED Since 1971 nearly all (99 percent) multi-family buildings completed had fewer than four floors. By 1977, 61 percent were two- to four-unit buildings, compared to 48 percent in 1973. Only 4 percent had twenty or more units, down 6 percent.

Since 1973 the size of the average multi-family unit has dropped from 1,031 to 938 square feet. The median was about 900 square feet for the same time period. Thus, multi-family units completed were smaller than single-family units. Since 1971 about 50 percent of all units have had two bedrooms, and 35 percent had one bedroom. One bathroom was most common (68 percent in 1977). About 80 percent of 1977 multi-family units had air conditioning, compared to 85 percent in 1975. From 1973 to 1977, electricity was the heating fuel used for over 60 percent of the units. Gas was used for 34 percent in 1973 but declined to 29 percent by 1977.

VACATION HOMES/SECOND HOMES

A small part of the housing stock is made up of second homes, vacation homes, seasonal homes, and homes held for occasional use.[12] Most new second homes are in the Northeast or the South (32 percent each) and fewest in the West (10 percent).[13] For the country as a whole, 75 percent of new second homes are in rural areas. However, both the South and the West have a large proportion of new second homes in urban areas (43.7 and 35.0 percent, respectively).

Summarily the housing industry is marked by cycles of high and low production, usually influenced by current economic conditions. These fluctuations are related to the business cycle (recession) and credit availability. Housing starts have generally led total economic activity, whether on the upswing or the downswing.

The number of single- and multi-family units started or completed are related to both supply and demand. In the 1960s and early 1970s the population bulge was in the fifteen to twenty-nine age group, which normally demands apartment housing. An increase in the number of single households further added to the demand. Rentals have not risen as fast as homeownership costs. An oversupply of rental units has helped keep rentals below the cost of a home. In the middle to late 1970s the population bulge shifted to the thirty to forty age group, which usually demands single-

---

[12]For a thorough review of vacation home studies before 1970, see Richard Lee Ragatz, "The Vacation Home Market: An Analysis of the Spatial Distribution of Population on a Seasonal Basis" (unpublished Ph.D. thesis, Cornell University, 1969).

[13]U.S. Department of Commerce, U.S. Bureau of the Census and U.S. Department of Housing and Urban Development, *Annual Housing Survey: 1976, Part A,* "General Housing Characteristics for the United States and Regions" (February 1978). (Washington, D.C.: U.S. Government Printing Office.)

family homes. Land and energy costs may dampen the demand somewhat.

Growth in second homes or vacation homes is related to periods of affluence, improved transportation, and paid vacations. Many such homes are within a short driving distance of the permanent residence, which is usually also owned. Rising housing and transportation costs could limit growth in vacation homes.

Housing Costs

Important to both production and consumption is the price of housing. Housing costs have been of continual concern in the last twenty-five years. They have been the focus of congressional action and the subject of presidential commissions. In the 1970s the cost of building, buying, and operating a home increased faster than family income. This section examines housing prices, indexes of housing cost, and housing cost components.

In 1978, consumers spent $207.3 billion dollars on housing.[14] This was 12 percent more than in 1977 and 120 percent more than in 1970, when consumers spent $94.0 billion dollars for housing. In addition, another $91.3 billion dollars were spent in household operation in 1978, of which $43.0 billion dollars were for electric and gas. Household operation expenditures increased 181 percent from 1970.

The *Consumer Price Index* (CPI) shows that housing costs rose faster than all items but slower than food and slightly slower than medical care (Table 2-3). Costs of apparel, transportation, personal care, and other goods and services, all rose at a slower rate than housing.

As housing prices increase, production has shifted somewhat from production of shelter to production of replacement housing for those who want to move up or change their life style. According to Gruen, "Estimating replacement demand requires a far higher level of sophistication than forecasting the shelter housing market."[15] Preferences play a greater role since households can wait for the market to provide what they want.

HOUSING PRICE

The price of housing increased dramatically in the 1970s (Figure 2-5). From 1970 to 1978, the median price of a new one-family home went from $23,400 to $55,700, a jump of 238 percent. Existing homes sold went from $23,000 in 1970 to $48,700 in 1978, an increase of 111 percent. In addition, the median value of all owner-occupied units went from $17,100 in 1970 to $32,300 in 1976, an increase of 88 percent.[16]

In a period of inflation, a house for sale is likely to be priced high, since presumably it will be worth more in the future. Thus, the sales price is high in relation to amount and quality of housing received in the short run.

[14]U.S. Department of Commerce, Office of Business Economics, *Survey of Current Business,* 59 (June 1979), 10. Figures represent current dollars.

[15]Nina J. Gruen, "Will Consumer Demands Continue to Influence Residential Development?" *Urban Land,* 35 (October 1976), 10.

[16]U.S. Department of Commerce, Bureau of the Census, "New One-Family Houses Sold and For Sale," *Construction Reports,* Series C25-79-2 (April, 1979), p. 7; U.S. Department of Commerce, Bureau of the Census, *Statistical Abstract of the U.S., 1977,* 98th annual ed. (Washington, D.C.: U.S. Government Printing Office, 1978), p. 798.

TABLE 2-3. Consumer Price Index of Housing Costs and Selected Other Items[a] (1967 = 100)

	1970	1972	1974	1976	1978
All Items	116.3	125.3	147.7	170.5	195.3
Food	114.9	123.2	158.7	180.8	211.4
Housing	118.9	128.1	148.8	177.2	202.6
Shelter	123.6	134.5	154.4	179.0	210.4
Rent	110.1	119.2	130.6	144.7	164.0
Home Ownership Costs	128.5	140.1	163.2	191.7	227.2
Mortgage Interest Rate	132.1	117.2	140.2	140.9	146.7
Property Taxes	121.0	147.7	151.2	167.6	192.1
Property Insurance Rates	113.4	123.2	124.2	144.3	104.4
Maintenance & Repairs	124.0	140.7	171.6	199.6	233.0
Household Furnishings and Operation	113.4	121.0	140.5	168.5	177.7
Fuel & Utilities	107.6	120.1	150.2	182.7	216.0
Apparel and Upkeep	116.1	122.3	136.2	147.5	159.6
Transportation	112.7	119.9	137.7	165.5	185.8
Health & Recreation[b]	119.8	126.1	140.3	163.3	
Medical Care					176.2
Entertainment					219.4

[a]The Consumer Price Index is an index compiled by the U.S. Government that is designed to measure changes in the purchasing power of the urban consumer's dollar. It is an attempt to assess the degree to which consumer purchasing power is eroded by price increases.

[b]Health and Recreation divided in 1978 to Medical Care and Entertainment.

Source: U.S. Department of Labor, Bureau of Labor Statistics, Monthly Labor Review, Consumer Price Index, (April 1979 and various years).

MONTHLY HOUSING COSTS

In 1977 mortgage payments accounted for 62 percent of monthly expenses for a median-priced new single-family home (Figure 2-6). Real estate taxes and utilities each account for another 15 percent, while maintenance and repairs take 6 percent and insurance 2.5 percent. From 1970 to 1976 these costs increased at varying rates. Maintenance and repair jumped the most, followed by property taxes, insurance, mortgage payments, heat, and utilities.

Changes in home ownership costs can be examined for both median-priced new homes and fixed-quality homes.[17] Be-

[17]A fixed-quality home is one for which characteristics are controlled so that a similar unit is being examined over time.

tween 1970 and 1975 the total monthly cost of median-priced new homes increased 82.4 percent, monthly mortgage payment 75.9 percent, sales price 67.9 percent, interest rate 6.6 percent, maintenance and repairs 117.7 percent, and heat and utilities 72.8 percent.

Increases for fixed-quality new homes were lower for all categories. The total monthly cost rose 59.8 percent, monthly mortgage payment 54.9 percent, sales price 48.4 percent, interest rate 6.6 percent, maintenance and repairs 97.9 percent, and heat and utilities 50.5 percent.

OWNERSHIP PRICE INDEX

The nature of housing changes over time. When the average selling price increases, "it is difficult to determine

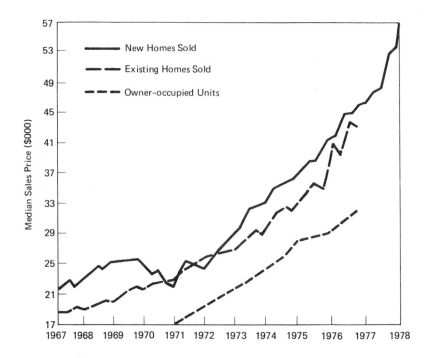

Figure 2-5. Median Sales Price, New and Existing Homes Sold, 1967–1978; Median Value—Owner Occupied Units. [*Source:* U.S. Department of Commerce, *Construction Reports,* "New One-Family Houses Sold and for Sale," C25-79-2 (April, 1979, p. 7,) and National Association of Realtors.]

whether the increase represents a true inflation in housing costs or whether the price increase indicates that the consumer is getting a larger and higher quality home for his money."[18] One approach to examining change in housing quality is to "compare the year-to-year change in the cost of a standard house (as measured by an appropriate cost index) with year-to-year changes in the price of housing that people actually buy. If the price of houses actually purchased rises more than the cost of a standard house, it is assumed that quality improved, since people are buying a house that is more

expensive than a standard quality house."[19]

The Census Bureau price index measures changes in the price of new houses sold for ten physical characteristics: floor area, number of stories, number of bathrooms, air conditioning, type of parking facility, type of foundation, geographic division within region, metropolitan area location, presence of fireplace, and size of lot. These characteristics account for about 70 percent of the variation in selling price. They do not take into account variations in workmanship, materials, and mechanical equipment. Because the price index is based on

[18]*Housing in the Seventies* (Washington, D.C.: U.S. Department of Housing and Urban Development, 1974), p. 205.

[19]Ibid., p. 218.

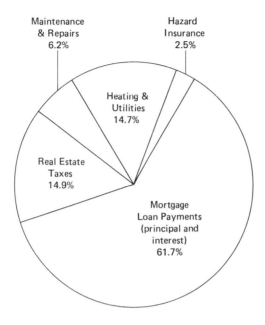

Figure 2-6. Typical Monthly Housing Costs to the Buyer of a Median Priced New Single Family House, 1977. (*Note:* Assumes sales price of $48,800, interest rate of 9.01 percent, downpayment of 25 percent, term of 25 years. Operating expenses based on actual experience under the FHA 203(b) program.) [*Source: HUD News,* HUD No. 78-175 (Washington, D.C.: U.S. Department of Housing and Urban Development, n.d.)].

fixed proportions of ten characteristics of the new houses sold in 1974, movements of the price index may differ from changes in the average sales prices of new houses actually sold during each period. The price index covers labor and material costs, land costs, direct and indirect selling expenses, and the seller's profits. Thus, it is influenced by supply factors such as wages, material costs, and productivity, as well as demand factors such as demography, income and cost, and mortgage funding.

The price index has risen steadily (Table 2-4)—104 percent between 1970 and 1978. Thus, the new house that sold in 1970 for an average price of $29,100 sold for $59,500 in 1976. The actual average price of new 1978 houses was $62,500.

The difference may be due to a shift in amenities, quality, and other factors. It should be noted that before 1973, lot size and fireplaces were not included. Thus, the index probably overstates the quality increase for two reasons: (1) lot size is not controlled in the early index and (2) more new homes are sold in the West, where prices are relatively high.[20]

RENTAL PRICE INDEX

The rent index measures quality improvements for renters, just as the housing ownership price index does for

---

[20] David E. Bloom, "Housing Activity in the Recent Recovery," *Survey of Current Business,* 56 (September 1976), 15.

TABLE 2-4. Price Index of New One-Family Homes Sold, 1970–1978

Year	Price Index[a]	AVERAGE SALES PRICE FOR KINDS OF HOUSES	
		Sold in 1974	Sold Each Year
1970	89.1	$29,100	$26,000
1971	93.9	30,700	28,300
1972	100.0	32,700	30,500
1973	108.9	35,600	35,500
1974	119.1	38,900	38,900
1975	131.0	42,800	42,600
1976	142.0	46,400	48,000
1977	159.6	52,100	54,200
1978	182.1	59,500	62,500

[a]Index based on kinds of houses sold in 1974.

Source: U.S. Department of Commerce, Bureau of the Census, "Price Index of New One-Family Houses Sold: Second Quarter, 1978" *Construction Reports,* Series C-27 (April, 1979). Pp. 2-3.

buyers. The rent index is calculated by comparing rent charges for the *same* apartment from month to month and year to year. Except for age, then most aspects of housing quality automatically remain constant over time. Thus, the rent index is more precise. It is not adjusted for depreciation; "depreciation appears in the index as a decline in price, rather than as a decline in quality."[21] For example, three prices could be compared: a 1976 new unit price, a 1977 new unit price, and a 1977 price for the 1976 unit. The index does not compare the 1976 and 1977 prices but rather the two 1977 prices. Thus, many statisticians regard the rental price index as biased downward.

Rent patterns were affected by rent control under Phase I and Phase II programs to fight inflation. In addition, rents reflect only the value of the services currently provided.

The rent component of the Consumer Price Index (CPI) is a reasonable guide to the cost of rental housing. This is especially true for changes in the index over relatively short periods, such as five years, "because depreciation and possible neighborhood changes are likely to have a smaller impact; their effects tend to be gradual and cumulative over fairly long periods for the Nation as a whole."[22]

AFFORDABILITY

Housing costs generally increased faster than prices (based on the CPI) during the 1960s and 1970s. For most households in the 1960s, this was not a serious problem; income kept pace with housing costs.[23] However, during the 1970s, family income lagged behind housing inflation as well as general prices. How can we estimate affordability of housing? Who is hurt by housing cost increases? The usual measurement systems are all somewhat arbitrary.

One method compares median family

[21]*Housing in the Seventies,* p. 232.

[22]Ibid., p. 233.

[23]U.S. Department of Housing and Urban Development (Washington, D.C.) *HUD News,* HUD No. 78-175, n.d.

income with median sales price and calculates a price-to-income ratio.[24] Since 1949, this ratio has been quite stable at 2.8 or 2.9 to 1 except during one period in the early 1970s when many subsidized homes were built.

Another method compares increases in median family income with increases in median-priced new houses and with median-priced existing houses.[25] The time period chosen is usually 1970 to the current year. Median family income rose much more slowly than housing prices during this time.

A third method examines the proportion of families able to purchase median-priced new or existing single-family houses.[26] Usually no more than 25 percent of gross income is expected to be spent on housing under this sytem. The percentage of families able to afford a median-priced new house went from 46.2 in 1970 to 27.0 in 1976, while for a median-priced existing house it went from 44.8 in 1970 to 36.0.[27] The critical assumption here is the proportion of income set aside for housing.

A related system asserts that a house cannot be purchased for more than 2.5 times a family's income. The median value of houses purchased is examined, and the proportion of the population with incomes less than 40 percent of median value is determined. If the proportion increases, it is assumed that housing has become less affordable. The problem with this system, of course, is the assumption of 2.5 times income.

These estimates of affordability raise certain questions:

1. What is the standard house that should be affordable?
2. Should all families be homeowners?
3. How do tax incentives lower the cost of home ownership? (See Chapter 13.)
4. How many people are really in the housing market?

2085692

Consumers, who were homeowners, at the start of the 1970s, face only increases in occupancy costs not increases in purchase price or financing. Previous owners who moved often benefitted by appreciation. Thus, although the ability of first-time home buyers to afford homes declined since 1970, that of repurchasers and nonmovers rose. The proportion of husband-wife families who are headed by a person under 35 years and who own their own home has been increasing. In 1950, it was less than 40 percent, while in 1974 it was 56 percent. In fact, the proportion of all husband-wife households as homeowners has increased.

Since the proportion of American homeowners did not decline during this period of rising costs, how did consumers adjust their behavior? Two-income families enabled many to buy housing. Others committed more income to housing than the standard rules suggest. Older housing needing renovation was another option, as were mobile homes.

---

[24]For example, see *9th Annual Housing Report of the President*, p. 17, U.S. Department of Housing and Urban Development, *1976 Statistical Yearbook* (Washington, D.C.: U.S. Government Printing Office), p. 237.

[25]*The Nation's Housing: 1975–1985* (Cambridge, Mass.: Joint Center for Urban Studies of MIT and Harvard University, April 1977), p. 103; also *HUD News*, HUD No. 78-175, n.d.

[26]*The Nation's Housing*, p. 103, and *Housing in the Seventies*, p. 242.

[27]*The Nation's Housing*, pp. 124, 126.

Some people rented out part of their house.

In general, the share of homeowners' income going for housing has declined. This does not mean that ownership costs relative to income or other prices have changed; what has changed is the homeowner's choice about how much housing to consume.

Renters' incomes in the 1970s kept pace with the rather modest rent increases during this period. Still, renters increasingly spend more than 25 percent of their income for housing. Little information is available on nonrent tenant costs, but utility costs have rapidly increased.

The proportion of income used for housing costs can be critical to the household's finances. Generally, it is hard to defer or reduce month-to-month housing costs without moving once a unit has been chosen. What form and quality of housing can be afforded remains an important issue.

Energy

FUELS

Energy use and cost are part of housing. Different energy fuels require different heating and cooling systems. In 1940, more than three out of four American homes were heated with coal or wood. Today the picture is very different. Utility gas has become the preferred fuel, used by 4 million households in 1940 and more than 40 million by 1975. The dramatic increase in use of electricity since 1960 should also be noted (Figure 2-7).

This change took place even though the United States now produces nearly one-fifth of the world's coal. The geographic distribution of home heating fuel has changed. For example, in 1950, coal or wood predominated in about two-thirds of all counties. East of the Mississippi, nearly all counties used these fuels except those in New England and Florida. By 1970 wood fuel had almost disappeared, and coal was favored only in coal-mining areas.

While most older buildings rely on utility gas or fuel oil, many newer ones are designed for electricity. In units built prior to 1940, about 87 percent were heated by gas or oil. In those built between 1970 and 1975, gas or oil use had declined to about 55 percent while electricity rose to about 36 percent. The largest buildings, with twenty or more units, are most likely to be heated by oil. In about three-fifths of the smaller buildings, with one to four units, gas is used.

Since 1950, individual room heaters have been increasingly replaced by central heating. To show the American family's desire for comfort and convenience, the number of occupied units with central heating systems more than quadrupled between 1940 and 1975.

Electricity has become the most important cooking fuel since data were first gathered in 1940. Although gas is still being used in about 45 percent of occupied units, it has declined gradually since 1950. In 1940, fuel oil was used in about one out of every ten households; in 1976 its use as a cooking fuel was practically zero.

Home air conditioning has increased

the demand for electricity. Between 1960 and 1975, the number of households with some form of air conditioning rose by about 30 million, an increase of nearly 6,000 per day!

CONSERVATION

With the emphasis on energy-saving measures, about 75 percent of single-family homes including mobile homes are protected by some attic or roof insulation, 56 percent have storm windows, and 60 percent have storm doors.[28] In the next few years, the availability and cost of insulation materials will be critical. The ret-

[28]U.S. Department of Commerce, Bureau of the Census and U.S. Department of Housing and Urban Development, *Annual Housing Survey: 1976* (Washington, D.C.: U.S. Government Printing Office, 1978), p. 90.

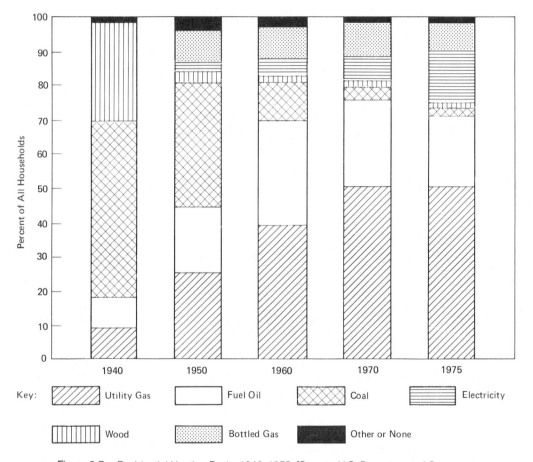

Key: Utility Gas   Fuel Oil   Coal   Electricity

Wood   Bottled Gas   Other or None

Figure 2-7. Residential Heating Fuels: 1940–1975. [*Source:* U.S. Department of Commerce, Bureau of the Census, "Residential Energy Uses," *Current Housing Reports,* H-123-77. Chart 2.]

rofitting of existing homes will compete with new housing and building construction for insulation products. Fuel cost economics, with emphasis on *life-cycle costing*, is now stimulating much retrofitting work. If tax incentives to home and building owners are provided, much more of this could be done. Higher insulation requirements for new homes by building codes, FHA minimum property standards, HUD Mobile Home Standards, and federal building specifications, will also boost the demand for insulation materials.

Can insulation producers meet this growing need? The answer is uncertain. However, major shortages are not considered likely. The 1973–1974 shortages were primarily for roofing insulation. Expanded insulation-producing facilities may now be sufficient to meet anticipated needs. Furthermore, the wide variety of insulation products on the market in loose fill, batt, board, film, and spray form—such as fiberglass, perlite, foamed plastics, cellulose, rock wool, vermiculite, aluminum foil, asbestos, and various chemical compositions—offer a wide choice to designers, contractors, and other users. However, given the dramatic increase in energy costs since 1973,[29] prices are expected to rise in the near future. Energy prices will influence housing quality and costs in several ways:

1. The cost of energy-intensive materials will rise and add to housing prices.

2. More insulation and other energy-conserving equipment and design will be used.

3. Housing location may reflect increased costs of transportation.

4. Space demands may change.

5. The density and kind of housing chosen may change.

Housing and Population

So far, population and housing characteristics have been considered in isolation. In reality, however, there is much interaction. This section examines owner, renter, and mobile home occupants in relation to their housing.

OWNER CHARACTERISTICS BY INCOME[30]

Among the 47,904,000 owner-occupied houses in 1976, demographic and housing characteristics varied greatly by income and value of the home. Let us compare upper-income ($20,000 or more) and lower-income (less than $5,000) households.

Upper-income households were mainly husband-wife families with children under eighteen, while lower-income households had almost as many one-person households as husband-wife households. In percentage terms, there

---

[29]Carol B. Meeks and Eleanor Oudekerk, "Housing and the High Cost of Energy: The Problem," *Focus on Energy and Housing* (Washington, D.C.: The American Home Economics Association, 1978), p. 27.

[30]U.S. Department of Commerce, U.S. Bureau of the Census, *Annual Housing Survey: 1976*, Part A, "General Housing Characteristics for the United States and Regions" (Washington, D.C.: U.S. Government Printing Office, 1978); *Annual Housing Survey: 1976*, Part C, "Financial Characteristics of the Housing Inventory for the United States and Regions" (Washington, D.C.: U.S. Government Printing Office, 1978).

were more female-headed and elderly households in the lower-income group.

The housing units of upper-income households were newer and larger. They usually had complete plumbing facilities and central or built-in heating equipment.

The median value of single-family, owner-occupied housing units in 1976 was $32,300. About one out of ten homes was worth less than $10,000, and two out of ten were worth less than $15,000. About 30 percent were worth $35,000 or more, and 20 percent $40,000 or more.

The median value varied greatly by the occupants' income: $19,750 for those with incomes below $5,000 to $44,233 for those with incomes above $20,000. Lower-income owners had homes worth almost four times their annual income, whereas the median ratio of value to income was 1.63 for upper-income households.

Homes valued at $40,000 or more contrasted greatly with those under $15,000. The more expensive homes were larger (Table 2-5), with three or more bedrooms and two or more complete bathrooms. Practically all had complete private plumbing facilities. They also tended to be newer and had proportionately more air conditioning, basements, and carports

TABLE 2-5. Characteristics of Owner-Occupied Units Valued Below $15,000 and $40,000 or Over

| | PERCENT | | |
Characteristics	Less than $15,000	$40,000 or over	All Owner Occupied Housing
Housing			
Median number of rooms a	5.0	6.4	5.9
3 or more bedrooms	45.7	87.9	73.1
2 or more baths	4.4	61.8	31.9
Air conditioning	42.8	63.4	57.7
Basement	36.4	55.6	51.5
Carport or garage	46.1	88.6	75.5
Warm air furnace	24.9	69.6	62.3
Steam or hot water heat	5.6	19.2	13.7
Mortgage debt	35.9	74.9	63.5
Age: Built 1960 or later	14.0	55.9	37.7
Built April 1970 or later	2.8	22.6	13.6
Household			
Median Size b	2.2	3.4	3.0
Male-head with wife present	45.3	86.1	76.9
Children under 18	31.3	55.1	47.0
Age of head:			
less than 25 years	2.1	0.6	1.8
25—34 years	8.8	17.4	15.9
35–44 years	8.4	23.3	17.0
45–64 years	22.6	36.8	31.6
65 or over	15.3	8.1	10.6

a Rooms, not percent.
b Number of persons.

Source: U.S. Department of Commerce U.S. Bureau of the Census and U.S. Department of Housing, *Annual Housing Survey: 1976,* Part A, Part C, Series H-150-76, Table A-2. (Washington, D.C.: U.S. Government Printing Office, 1978.)

or garages. Although the most common type of heating equipment was a warm air furnace, about 20 percent of the homes were heated by steam or hot water.

About 25 percent of the more expensive homes were not mortgaged. Almost none of the homes (.72 percent) had a failure in water supply. Of those units occupied the previous winter, 5.6 percent had heating equipment which was unusable for six hours or more.

Larger families were found in the most expensive homes. Usually the family was headed by a man whose wife was present; the largest proportion of men was in the forty-five to sixty-four age group. Over half of the families in the more expensive homes had children under eighteen; a relatively small proportion were occupied by one person.

The median income for those who owned homes worth $40,000 or more was $22,650. This was $7,150 higher than the median income of $15,500 for all owner-occupied households and $15,400 higher than the median income of $7,250 for households in the under-$15,000 home-value group.

RENTER CHARACTERISTICS BY INCOME[31]

Among the 26,101,000 renter-occupied units in 1976, housing characteristics varied greatly by income and rent. Among renters with low incomes— less than $5,000—the proportion of one-person households was much greater than that of husband-wife families (50.2 percent compared with 18.7 percent); among upper-income ($20,000 or more) renters, the reverse was true (16.0 percent one-person households compared

---

[31]Ibid.

with 72.6 percent husband-wife families). The percentage of lower-income renter households headed by women was much greater than among upper-income renters (25.1 percent compared with 5.4 percent), as was the predominance of households headed by an individual aged sixty-five or over (40 percent compared with 5.9 percent). About one-fourth (25.5 percent) of the lower-income families contained children under eighteen; for upper-income renters, the proportion was greater (37.6 percent). More of the lower-income households contained non-relatives (8.9 percent compared with 3.5 percent), but few of either type of household contained *subfamilies*.

Upper-income renter households were somewhat larger than those of lower-income renters, as were the units they occupied. A much higher proportion of upper-income renters occupied units built in 1960 or later. In addition, units with central or built-in heating equipment were much more common for the upper-income group. More lower-income units were crowded. Perhaps the most striking contrast was in the percentage of units lacking some or all plumbing facilities—.39 percent of the upper-income units but 9.6 percent of the lower-income units.

The 1976 median gross rent for all renter-occupied units was $167 monthly. About 1,802,000—7.1 percent—of all renters paid less than $70 a month, while 7,844,000 renters—30.9 percent—paid $200 or more. About 1,277,000 renter units were in the "no cash rent" category; for example, the unit was provided free of charge by relatives or in connection with employment.

Units renting for $200 or more contrasted strongly with the lower-rent units (Table 2-6). Like the homeowner units,

TABLE 2-6. Comparison of Renter-Occupied Units with Rents Below $70 and $200 or More

	PERCENT		
Characteristics	Rent Less than $70	Rent $200 or More	All Renter Occupied Housing
Housing			
Median number of rooms[a]	3.1	4.5	4.0
3 or more bedrooms	11.9	27.4	20.2
2 or more baths	1.2	16.6	6.9
Air conditioning	19.0	64.0	44.7
Single-family house	32.6	26.1	30.7
Five or more units	44.3	49.3	38.8
Age: Built 1960 or later	26.8	56.5	35.6
Built 1970 or later	11.6	26.5	14.6
Household			
Median size[b]	1.5	2.4	2.1
Male head with wife present	15.8	51.7	42.4
Head under 45 years	8.5	37.4	29.6
Children under 18	22.5	39.3	34.4
One-person household	60.6	21.3	33.3

[a]Rooms, not percent.
[b]Number of persons.

Source: U.S. Department of Commerce, U.S. Bureau of the Census and U.S. Department of Housing and Urban Development. *Annual Housing Survey: 1976,* Part A, Part C, Series H-150-76, Table A-3. (Washington, D.C.: U.S. Government Printing Office, 1978.)

the higher-rent units were larger, with more bedrooms and bathrooms. About .31 percent lacked some or all plumbing facilities. The higher-rent units tended to be newer. A smaller proportion were single-family houses and a greater proportion were in buildings with five or more units and air conditioned.

Households living in higher-rent units were larger. The typical household had a male head under forty-five years with a wife present. About one-third of these households had children under eighteen, and another one-third consisted of one person.

The median income for families paying higher rents was $13,250. This is 61.9 percent higher than the median income for all renter-occupied units and more than $8,500 higher than the median income of those who paid lower rents.

MOBILE HOME OCCUPANCY

Studies of mobile homeowners and their homes have yielded a general picture (Table 2-7). Most household heads were in their thirties, and about half had children. For 70 percent this was their first mobile home, and most of the homes were new. About 50 percent of the mobile homes were 12 feet wide. Width is probably most related to the time of the study.

Proportionately few black households own mobile homes. Black families constitute about 9.5 percent of the U.S. families but occupy only 2.4 percent of the mobile homes.[32] One possible reason is that

[32]Richard A. Smith, "An Analysis of Black Occupancy of Mobile Homes," *American Institute Planners Journal,* 42 (October 1976), 411.

TABLE 2-7. Summary of Mobile Home Studies

		STUDY CHARACTERISTICS			FAMILY CHARACTERISTICS		
Study	Year	Size of Sample	Location of Study	Family Income ($)	Mean Age of Head (Years)	Household Size (N)	Percent With Children
HUD	1967	2,900	40 states	6,620	35	2.5	53
Census Bureau	1970	2,073,994	U.S.	7,500	39.9	2.3	40
Owens-Corning	1974	1,400	U.S.	10,850	39.4	2.7	44a
Owens-Corning	1969	1,280	8 cities	7,500	34	2.2	52a
Greenough	1976	70	Saratoga Co., N.Y.	1,000	———	3.5	70
Moller	1970	105	Onondaga Co. N.Y.	——— ≤	35	———	44
Smith	1975	122	Delaware Co. N.Y.	———	———	2.3	50
FHLBB	1960s	—	—	———	———	———	———
Waind & Wright	1975	893	N.D.	———	———	———	———
Tri-State Region	1970	—	N.Y. Ct., N.J.	———	———	———	———
Macedon, N.Y.	1970	187	Wayne Co., N.Y.	300b	30b	2.5	40
Planning Dept.	1976	638	Riverside, Ca.	———	———	2.4	———
Spurlock	1972	522	Washington Co., Ark. (Fayetteville)	———	———	2.8	———

a Estimated.

b Male heads only.

c 7–8 percent expandables and doubles.

d Square feet.

	MOBILE HOME CHARACTERISTICS					
Study	Percent First Mobile Home	Percent in Park	Age of Unit (Years)	Size of Unit	Initial Price ($)	Lot Rental ($)
HUD	———	62	1	71%–2bd.	5,600	32
Census Bureau	———	———	5	4.0 rm	———	———
Owens-Corning	67	57	1	46%–12' 21%–14' 31%–24'	9,400	———
Owens-Corning	73	100 ≤	2	———	5,740	38
Greenough	75	100 ≤	5	67%–12' 30%–14'	8,000	———
Moller	———	100	2.6	46%–10' 54%–12'	———	40
Smith	72	34	———	684d	———	———
FHLBB	———	———	———	84%–12'c	5,700	40
Waind & Wright	———	93	———	———	———	45
Tri-State Region	———	———	———	20%–10' 72%–12c	———	———
Macedon, N.Y.	73	100	7	44%–10' 47%–12'	4,900	———
Planning Dept.	———	0	1	———	———	———
Spurlock	———	47 ≤	4	608d	5,500	———

Sources:

"A Study of the Mobile Home Industry" (Washington, D.C.: Federal Home Loan Bank Board, 1973).

Focus on the Mobile Home Market (Toledo, Ohio: Owens-Corning Fiberglas Corporation, 1970).

Greenough, Jeanne, "Mobile Home Consumer Study" (Ithaca, N.Y.: Cooperative Extension, Cornell University, 1976).

"Mobile Homes in Macedon, N.Y.," prepared at the request of the Macedon Town Planning Board (Macedon, N.Y., 1970).

Moller, William G., Jr., "Mobile Homes in Mobile Home Parks, New York State and Onondaga County" (Syracuse, N.Y.: Business Research Center, Syracuse University, 1970).

Riverside Co. Planning Department, "Mobile Home Owners Report: Own Your Own Lot Survey" (Riverside, Calif., 1976).

Smith, Frances, "1975 Survey of Mobile Home Owners and Renters" (Delaware Co., N.Y., 1975).

Spurlock, Hughes, H., "Mobile Home Situation in Washington County, Arkansas, 1972" (Fayetteville, Ark.: Agriculture Experiment Station, University of Arkansas Division of Agriculture, 1974).

The New Mobile Home Market (Toledo, Ohio: Owens-Corning Fiberglas Corporation, 1975).

"The Role of Mobile Homes in the Tri-State Region" Housing Series #8 (New York: Tri-State Transportation Commission, 1970). Internal report; not for public release.

U.S. Department of Commerce, Bureau of the Census, Mobile Homes: 1970 Census of Housing (Washington, D.C.: U.S. Government Printing Office, 1973).

U.S. Department of Housing and Urban Development, Housing Surveys, Part 2 (Washington, D.C.: U.S. Government Printing Office, 1968).

Waind, Dabid W., and Boyd L. Wright, "North Dakota Mobile Home Park Residents: An Attitudinal Survey" (Grand Forks, N.D.: Bureau of Governmental Affairs, University of North Dakota, 1975).

blacks prefer not to live in mobile homes. Or, they may be discriminated against in sales, financing, and location.

places, and garages. One-story houses are the most popular.

Summary

The U.S. housing stock continues to grow along with population. Over two-thirds of all units are owner-occupied. Single-family units dominate the current stock as well as construction of new units. Housing prices have increase dramatically in the 1970s and are a critical national issue. Affordability of housing, particularly ownership, is a primary concern as incomes lag behind housing prices and occupancy costs. Ownership costs have risen faster than rental costs.

Publicly owned unit starts almost disappeared in the late 1970s, a far cry from their 20 to 30 percent market share in the early 1970s. Housing production is related closely to financing and the economic situation.

Housing stock is gradually becoming newer and larger. New single-family housing also has more amenities: bathrooms, central air conditioning, fireplaces, and garages. One-story houses are the most popular.

Terms

consumer price index (CPI) a monthly statistical measure of the average change in prices for a fixed group of goods and services.

conversion additions in which one housing unit is converted into two or more units.

demolitions losses in which units are deliberately destroyed.

homeowner vacancy rate the percentage relationship between vacant homeowner units and all homeowner units. It is found by dividing the number of vacant units by the total owner-occupied units, vacant units sold and awaiting occupancy, and vacant units for sale. Vacant units that are seasonal or held off the market are excluded. In the reports published before 1972 (which includes the data from 1956 to 1959), vacant homeowner units that were rated as dilapidated were also excluded.

housing inventory a count of the number of housing units and an indication of their occupancy status.

housing unit house, apartment, single room, or group of rooms occupied or intended for occupancy as separate living quarters.

life cycle costing price of an item is related to its life and operation. Thus, although an item may have a higher initial purchase price, it may result in lower costs over time.

mergers losses in which two or more units are formed into a single unit.

persons per room computed for each occupied unit by dividing the number of occupants by the number of rooms.

rental vacancy rate the percentage relationship of vacant rental units to total rental units. It is found by dividing the number of vacant units by the total rental units, vacant units rented but not yet occupied at the time of enumeration, and vacant units for rent. Vacant units that are seasonal or held off the market are excluded. In the reports published before 1972 (which include the data from 1956 to 1959), vacant rental units rated as dilapidated were also excluded.

separate living quarters those in which the occupants do not live and eat with any other persons in the building and which have either (1) direct access from the outside of the building or through a common hall, or (2) complete kitchen facilities for the occupants' use alone. The occupants may be a single family, one person living alone, two or more families living together, or any other group of related or unrelated persons who share living arrangements.

subfamily a married couple with or without children; or one parent with one or more single children under eighteen years old, living in a household and related to, but not including, the head of the household or his wife—for example, a young married couple sharing the home of the husband's or wife's parents. Members of a subfamily are also included as members of a family. The number of subfamilies is not included in the number of families.

vacant absence of persons from a housing unit at the time of a census, unless the vacancy is only temporary. In addition, a vacant unit may be one that is entirely occupied by persons who usually live elsewhere. New units not yet occupied are classified as vacant if all exterior windows and doors are installed and final usable floors are in place. Vacant units are excluded if unfit for human habitation—for example, if the roof, walls, windows, or doors no longer protect the interior from the elements or if the unit is to be demolished or is condemned. Also excluded are units used entirely for nonresidential purposes, such as a store or an office, or quarters used to store business supplies or inventory, machinery, or agricultural products.

Suggested Readings

Bloom, David E., "Housing Activity in the Recent Recovery," *Survey of Current Business,* 56 (September 1976), 15.

Building the American City, Report of the National Commission on Urban Problems. House Document No. 91-34. 91st Congress, 1st Session (1968), Paul H. Douglas, Chairman.

Grebler, Leo and Frank G. Mittelback, *The Inflation of those Prices.* Lexington, Mass.: Lexington Books, 1979.

Joint Center for Urban Studies of MIT and Harvard University, *America's Housing Needs: 1970 to 1980.* Cambridge, Mass., December 1973.

———, *The Nation's Housing: 1975–1985.* Cambridge, Mass., April 1977.

Sabghir, Aaron, "The New Construction Outlook for 1977," *Construction Review,* 22 (November 1976), 4–8.

United States Department of Commerce, Bureau of the Census, *Census of Housing, 1940, 1950, 1960, 1970.* Washington, D.C.

———, "New One-Family Houses Sold and For Sale, *Construction Reports,* Series C25.

U.S. Department of Commerce, Bureau of the Census, and U.S. Department of Housing and Urban Development *Annual Housing Surveys.* Washington, D.C., U.S. Government Printing Office, yearly since 1973.

HOUSING IN AMERICA: A MICRO VIEW

Although we need to understand how population is related to housing, ultimately we want to know how human behavior is linked to the housing environment. Housing does affect social interaction, physical and mental health, and cultural patterns and the way they are expressed. Buildings are limited for technological, aesthetic, social, political, and economic reasons as well as by people's biological, psychological, and cultural needs. This chapter is concerned with the relationship between people and their living environment.

Rapoport has identified many important issues regarding people and their surroundings:

1. The nature and meaning of space and how people use it.

2. Crowding, density, and privacy.

3. Complexity.

4. Preferences and evaluation of environments.

5. Effect of the environment on people.[1]

How do people perceive their environment? To what extent are they satisfied or dissatisfied? How does the environment influence behavior? Finally, how is the environment evaluated? This chapter concentrates on the latter two questions, emphasizing the role of space and structure type.

---

[1]Amos Rapoport, "An Approach to the Construction of Man-Environment Theory," in *Environmental Design Research*, Vol. 2, ed. Wolfgang F.E. Preiser (Stroudsburg, Pa.: Dowden, Hutchinson and Ross, Inc., 1977), pp. 124–35.

In considering the effect of environment on behavior, the following concepts are useful to keep in mind:

1. Element types—qualitative description of different buildings.
2. Quantity—number or amount of space or area.
3. Density.
4. Grain—variety, size, and spacing of housing units.
5. Focal organization—crucial place.
6. General spatial distribution.[2]

Needs

The basic human need that housing provides is shelter or protection. This is the lowest level on Maslow's hierarchy of needs. On the higher levels, housing also provides safety or security, belongingness, self-esteem, and self-fulfillment.[3] "Lower" needs must be met before "higher" needs can be considered (Figure 3-1). Maslow's hierarchy concept suggests that certain problems may have to be solved before a given need is met. Table 3-1 analyzes user needs in relation to housing.

Housing fulfills needs in the following ways:

1. To give shelter, housing must provide warmth and coolness, light, air, and ventilation. Most Americans expect hot and cold water and plumbing fixtures. These needs are easily quantifiable and can be used to measure total housing quality.

2. Safety and security of the house and neighborhood is a growing concern. The greatest dangers related to housing are listed in Table 3-2. These dangers, with both human and nonhuman sources, represent a complex web of physical, social, and moral harm.

3. Safety features in all types of buildings are also receiving more attention. Regulations generally focus on the structure, materials used, or mechanical systems that protect occupants from danger. Hence the concern, for example, with using fireproof materials, and providing fire extinguishers and smoke detectors.

4. Buildings can be designed for protection by allowing residents to casually and continually survey public areas. Lighting also increases safety, as does the ability to control one's space. Thus, design does much to influence the perception of safety.

5. The interior environment influences health by controlling light, air, and noise.[5] Other factors include vibration, thermal conditions, space, and

---

[2]Keven Lynch and Lloyd Rodwin, "A Theory of Urban Form," *Journal of the American Institute of Planners,* 24, 4 (November 1958), 205–206.

[3]Abraham H. Maslow, *Motivation and Personality* (New York: Harper and Brothers, 1954).

[4]Oscar Newman, *Defensible Space,* (New York: Macmillan, 1972), and Franklin D. Becker, *Design for Living: The Resident's View of Multi-Family Housing* (Ithaca, N.Y.: Cornell University, 1974).

[5]Kiyoshi Isumi, "Psychological Phenomena and Building Design," *Building Research* (July/August 1965), 9–11. For a discussion of thermal, light, air, and acoustic needs, see M.S. Goromoson, *The Physiological Basis of Health Standards for Dwellings* (Geneva: World Health Organization, 1968).

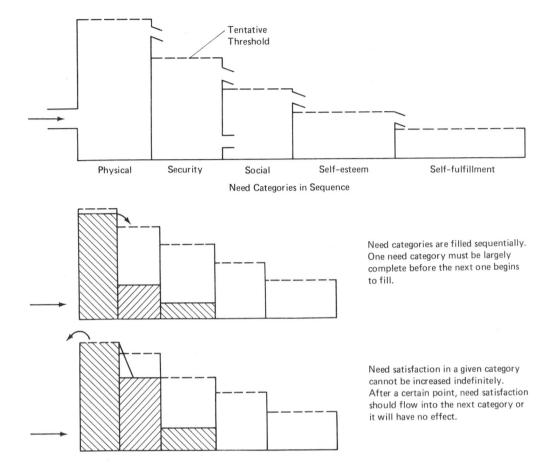

Physical   Security   Social   Self-esteem   Self-fulfillment

Need Categories in Sequence

Need categories are filled sequentially. One need category must be largely complete before the next one begins to fill.

Need satisfaction in a given category cannot be increased indefinitely. After a certain point, need satisfaction should flow into the next category or it will have no effect.

Figure 3-1. Conceptual Model of Maslow's Hierarchy-of-Needs Theory. [*Source:* U.S. Department of Housing and Urban Development, *Phase I—Volume I—User Needs, In-Cities Experimental Housing Research and Development Project.* PB 184 121 (Springfield, Virginia: Clearinghouse for Federal Scientific and Technical Information, March 1969, p. III-4.)]

dangerous design, which promote accidents or falls.[6]

6. The social or belongingness need depends largely on design and struc- ture type. Most people prefer a single-family detached home. Its location helps or hinders neighborliness and community feeling. The need for community must be bal-

[6]See also Wesley E. Gilbertson and Eric W. Mood, "Housing, the Residential Environment and Health—a Re-evaluation," *American Journal of Public Health and the Nation's Health,* LIV (December 1964), 2009–13; Robert G. Healy, "Effects of Improved Housing on Worker Performance," *Journal of* *Human Resources,* VI (Summer 1971), 297–308; U.S. Department of Health, Education and Welfare, *Proceedings of the First International Conference on Health Research on Housing and Its Environment* (Washington, D.C.), March 1970.

TABLE 3-1. The Relationship Between User Needs and Housing

Basic Human Need	Social Cost If Need Unmet	Relationship to Housing	Mechanism of Need	Relevant Housing Variable (psychological variable)	Measurement Techniques	Experiments in Assessment and Satisfaction
Survival	Death; retarded development; disease	Physical structure; utilities; location	Physiological	Shelter (territory)	Housing stock survey Structured interview	Industrial design
Safety and Security	Disability; retarded social development; conflict	Physical structure external environment: Physical Social Protective services	Perception of danger Perception of threat from others	Protection (trust)	Survey; participant observation; Story completion	Gaining community acceptance
Social Acceptance Belongingness	Envy; isolation; conflict	Image of housing; propinquity; organization of social relationships	Comparison with others	Possessions; privileges; services (status stigma)	Sociometrics; games; role play	Meeting rising expectations
Self-esteem	Self-degradation; Inefficiency Anti-social behavior	Housing as symbol of self-worth	Comparison with standards of achievement and justice	Power; competence; control (autonomy)	Projective techniques: Games Depth Interview Role play	Increasing self-determination and user participation

Source: U.S. Department of Housing and Urban Development, *Phase I—Composite Report—Volume I—User Needs, In-Cities Experimental Housing Research and Development Project* PB184 121 (Springfield, Va.: Clearinghouse for Federal Scientific and Technical Information), March 1969, p. III-5.

TABLE 3-2. Selected Dangers in the Lower-class Home and Environment, with Physical, Social, and Moral Consequences

SOURCE OF DANGER	
Nonhuman	*Human*
Rats and other vermin	Violence to self and possessions
Poisons	Assault
Fire and burning	Fighting and beating
Freezing and cold	Rape
Poor plumbing	Objects thrown or dropped
Dangerous electrical wiring	Stealing
Trash (broken glass, cans, etc.)	Verbal hostility, shaming, exploitation
Poorly protected heights	Own family
Other aspects of poorly designed	Neighbors
or rundown buildings (e.g.,	Caretakers
thin walls)	Outsiders
Cost of housing	Alternatives that draw oneself or valued
	others away from a stable life

Source: Lee Rainwater, "Fear and the House-as-Haven in the Lower Class," The Journal of the American Institute of Planners, 32 (January 1966), 23–31.

anced by the need for privacy. Housing entrances can provide privacy, opportunity for socializing, or loneliness. Finally, most people prefer to live near those of similar life cycle, life style, and social class.

7. The living room, more than any other room, reflects the individual's conscious and unconscious attempts to express a social identity.[7] Also, good friends and a respectable neighborhood are key concerns.

8. Self-esteem and self-fulfillment can be expressed in the type of housing or its location. If interior and exterior space can be individualized, these needs will be met. Moving to one's own home is strongly related to housing satisfaction. It also enhances one's social status.[8]

---

[7]Clare Cooper, "The House as Symbol of Self," *HUD Challenge*, 8 (February 1977), 4.

[8]Louis M. Rea, "Residential Satisfaction and Intraurban Mobility," *Housing and Society*, 5 (1978), 2.

NEEDS OF CHILDREN

Children's play and activities shape most of their housing needs. Obviously these activities change with age and possibly with sex. An ideal play area should provide for:

Physical development and bodily health
Emotional stability and mental health
Intellectual growth and learning
Friendliness and cooperation.[9]

It should include the tools to develop body awareness and integration, balance, spatial relationships, depth perceptions, and texture or touching awareness.

---

[9]Nancy Hargrave, "Designing Children's Playgrounds: Defining the Problem," *Environmental Analysis: Planning for Human Behavior*. A collection of students' research projects, ed. Edward R. Ostrander, Bettye Rose Connell, and Tony Sin, Department of Design and Environmental Analysis, N.Y.S. College of Human Ecology (Ithaca, N.Y.: Cornell University, 1975), p. 49.

Children like variety and mobility; thus, they will play anywhere, not just in designated play areas.[10] Preschool children need adult supervision, so play areas should be near their homes. Those over age five need more space, somewhat apart from younger children. Equipment needs to be durable. Space for games—baseball, basketball—is desirable. Teenagers need meeting places for socializing and watching, in addition to sports facilities and space for cars. All children need a place of their own at home and space for quiet as well as busy activities.

Values

Although housing provides many needs at varying levels, people can weigh each need and category differently. Let us examine the concept of values to see how consumers choose their home and decide how to furnish and maintain it.

Kluckhohn defines a value as "a conception, explicit, or implicit, distinctive of

an individual or characteristic of a group, of the desirable which influences the selection from available modes, means, and ends of action."[11] Values "provide the underlying meanings that give continuity to all decisions and actions."[12] Values related to housing show what is desirable and worthwhile to the occupant.

Values may be absolute or relative. Absolute values are independent of outside conditions, while relative values depend on the setting.[13] This distinction is important in terms of housing. In designing housing policy, it is important to know whether a value remains constant over time or changes with a household's situation or community. For example, does importance of housing for family interaction depend on one's peers or is it innate and constant over time? In measuring

[10]This paragraph adapted from Clare C. Cooper, *Easter Hill Village* (New York: Free Press, 1975), pp. 102–15.

[11]Clyde Kluckhohn and others, "Values and Value Orientation in the Theory of Action," in Toward a General Theory of Action, eds. Talcott Parson and Edward A. Shils (Cambridge, Mass.: Harvard University Press, 1962), p. 395.

[12]Ibid, p. 143.

[13]Ruth E. Deacon and Francille M. Firebaugh, *Home Management,* p. 140. Copyright © 1975 by Houghton Mifflin Company. Reprinted by permission.

Playgrounds provide opportunities for creative activity.

U.S. Department of HUD

Federal National Mortgage Association

Values and lifestyles can be expressed by furnishings.

values and interpreting the results, value type must be considered.

Values may also be intrinsic or extrinsic. An intrinsic value is "the desirable and self-sufficient quality of an experience," while an extrinsic value is "the meaning or worth desired from the relation of one thing to another."[14] Thus, intrinsic values are ends in themselves, while extrinsic values are designed for a purpose. This distinction may be applied to housing values. For example, owning a home may be valued in itself or as a means to obtain status or community services. Making this distinction would aid policy design.

Recognizing the need to study housing

values, Cutler[15] developed a test with ten values: beauty, comfort, convenience, cost, health, safety, privacy, friendship, personal interest, and location. Beyer and his colleagues did further research on human values linked to housing.[16] Nine values were studied: family centrism, equality, physical health, economy, freedom, aesthetics, prestige, mental health, and leisure. Downer, Smith, and Lynch

---

[14]Ibid., p. 140.

[15]Virginia F. Cutler, "Personal and Family Values in the Choice of a Home," Cornell University Agricultural Experiment Station Bulletin 840 (Ithaca, N.Y.: Cornell University, November 1947).

[16]Glenn H. Beyer, Thomas W. Markesey, and James E. Montgomery, *Houses Are for People* (Ithaca, N.Y.: Cornell University Housing Research Center, 1955), and Glenn H. Beyer, *Housing and Personal Values,* Cornell University Agricultural Experiment Station, Memoir 364 (Ithaca, N.Y.: Cornell University, July 1959).

reported that dominant housing values vary with life-style stages.[17] Meeks and Deacon found that a value ranked high in general may not be important in a specific housing situation.[18]

Rokeach and Parker found that although values differ between rich and poor, uneducated and educated, and blacks and whites, black-white differences disappear when socioeconomic status is controlled.[19] Cutler found that values *within* each class were roughly similar, while values *between* classes were quite different.[20] Children, however, had very similar values regardless of social status. Thus, somewhere between childhood and adulthood, the effects of age, training, and experience tend to show up.[21] Meeks and Sherman reported that for families who are similar socioeconomically and demographically, housing values remain relatively stable for short periods of time.[22]

Values influence how we perceive and use the physical environment, and how we feel about it in general.[23] In designing

housing, these underlying values should be kept in mind. However, Morris and Winter caution that "diverse and opposite kinds of housing behavior may be implied by a single value orientation."[24] For example, a high value on social interaction may result in the choice of a house with lots of space for entertaining or alternately a small house because all social relationships take place away from home. Montgomery sums up the relationship of values to the living environment as follows: "no sector of American life more faithfully portrays its values than its dwellings, neighborhoods, and communities."[25]

Quality

Housing quality indicates how well people are housed. Lansing and Marans define an environment of high quality as one that "conveys a sense of well-being and satisfaction to its population through characteristics that may be physical (housing style, condition, landscape, available facilities), social (friendliness of neighbors, ethnic, racial, or economic composition), or symbolic (sense of identity, prestige values)."[26] Fraser considers habitability the state or quality of a dwelling that varies according to purpose—

[17]Donna B. Downer, Ruth H. Smith, and Mildred T. Lynch, "Values and Housing: A New Dimension," *Journal of Home Economics,* 60 (March 1969), 173–76.

[18]Carol B. Meeks and Ruth E. Deacon, "Values and Planning," *Journal of Home Economics,* 64 (January 1972), 11–16.

[19]M. Rokeach and S. Parker, "Values as Social Indicators of Poverty and Race Relations in America," *The Annals of the American Academy of Political and Social Science,* 388 (March 1970), 97.

[20]Cutler, "Personal and Family Values," p. 104.

[21]Ibid.

[22]Carol B. Meeks and Barbara Sherman, "Housing Values of Families Living in an Economically Integrated Community," Department of Consumer Economics and Housing (Ithaca, N.Y.: Cornell University, 1977).

[23]Chester W. Hartman, "Social Values and Housing Orientations," *Journal of Social Issues,* 19, (April 1963), 113.

[24]Earl W. Morris and Mary Winter, *Housing, Family, and Society* (New York: John Wiley & Sons, Inc., 1978), p. 32.

[25]James E. Montgomery, "The Housing Environment: Crises and Challenges," Conference proceedings, second annual meeting, American Association of Housing Educators, Purdue University, October 11–14, 1976, p. 7.

[26]John B. Lansing and Robert W. Marans, "Evaluation of Neighborhood Quality," *American Institute of Planners Journal,* 35 (May 1969), 195–99.

camper, tent, and so on.[27] Van Fossen believes that a high-quality environment is one that shows a humanistic concern for the individual.[28] In summary, quality contributes to a person's sense of well-being and physical, social, and psychological satisfaction.

Every year houses and neighborhoods decline in quality. Some are lost from the housing stock as a result of casualties such as fire or floods. Others become physically unlivable or their physical characteristics are out of date with the present interests of consumers. Some housing units no longer attract investment or ownership. On the other hand, many houses are repaired and improved or revitalized each year.

Although Congress in 1949 established a national housing goal of "a decent home in a suitable living environment," this goal was not defined. Thus, it is difficult to measure progress toward it. In addition, housing quality is a normative concept.

Fraser stated that a person's response to the housing environment is a measure of its quality in meeting his or her physical, social or productive needs.[29] He noted that most measures of housing quality relate to the culture of the society, are interviewer opinions, or cannot be quantified.

Housing deprivation can be defined as a physically substandard unit; an occupancy problem of being overcrowded or poor; or an environmental problem. Until recently, the Census Bureau has measured housing quality in terms of missing plumbing, dilapidation, or need for major repairs and overcrowding (Table 3-3).[30] Using these measures, the condition of U.S. housing has improved dramatically (Table 3-4).

PHYSICAL STANDARDS

Physical standards are related to the condition and operation of the housing unit and neighborhood. However, even physical standards are greatly affected by values and culture choices.[31] For example, comfort zones vary by culture. Building and housing codes determine structural standards for housing and set minimum physical conditions. (See Chapter 12 for more detailed discussion.)

Housing in the United States is gradually becoming newer.[32] The proportion of housing stock aged thirty years or more dropped from 48 percent in 1940 to 40.6 percent in 1970. In 1976, 15.8 percent of the housing units were six years old or less, 22.3 percent were seven to sixteen years old, 17.4 percent were seventeen to twenty-six years old, 10.2 percent were twenty-seven to thirty-six years old, and 34.3 percent were older than thirty-six years.

[27]Thomas M. Fraser, "Relative Habitability of Dwellings—a Conceptual View," *Ekistics,* XXVII (January 1969), 15–18.

[28]Theodore van Fossen, "Informing What We Make," in *People and Information,* ed. Harold B. Pepinsky (New York: Pergamon Press, 1970), pp. 201–23.

[29]Fraser, "Relative Habitability of Dwellings," 15–18.

[30]James W. Hughes, *Methods of Housing Analysis* (New Brunswick, N.J.: Center for Urban Policy Research, 1977), pp. 450–59.

[31]Amos Rapoport and Newton Watson, "Cultural Variability in Physical Standards," in *People and Buildings,* ed. Robert Gutman (New York: Basic Books, 1972), pp. 33–53.

[32]U.S. Department of Commerce, Bureau of the Census, *U.S. Census of Housing,* 1940 through 1970, and *Annual Housing Survey: 1976,* Part A.

TABLE 3-3. Condition of Housing Units Defined, 1940–1970

CENSUS OR SURVEY	CONDITION	BASIC FACILITIES
1940 census	"Needing major repair"— a unit having serious defects requiring repair or replacement, or one whose continued neglect would jeopardize soundness of structure or safety of occupants	Lacking any of the following: Private bath Private flush toilet Running water
1950 Census	"Dilapidated"—providing inadequate shelter or unsafe conditions for the following reasons: One or more serious defects Enough intermediate defects to require much repair or rebuilding Poor original construction	Lacking any of the following: Private bath Private flush toilet Hot running water (at least part of the time; may be seasonal or part of the week)
1960 Census	"Dilapidated"—1950 definition used. In addition, an intermediate category, "deteriorating," was introduced with three conditions: dilapidated, deteriorating, sound.	1950 definition used
1970 Census	Structural quality not measured in 1970 census.	1950 definition used Lacking some or all plumbing facilities, mechanical serviceability, and occupant opinion
Annual Housing Survey 1973-76	Complete plumbing and persons per room.	

aSerious defects (e.g., holes, open cracks, or rotted, loose, or missing material over a large area).

bThe 1960 question on condition of housing unit (i.e., dilapidated, deteriorating, or sound) was eliminated because of serious problems with response reliability.

Source: U.S. Department of Commerce, Bureau of the Census, *Census of Housing* 1970, Vol. 1, "Housing Characteristics for States, Cities, and Counties, Part 1, U.S. Summary, Appendix B, "Definitions and Explanations of Subject Characteristics" p. App.-4. Also, U.S. Department of Commerce, Bureau of the Census and U.S. Department of Housing and Urban Development, *General Housing Characteristics for the United States and Regions,* H-150 (January 1978), Washington, D.C.: U.S. Government Printing Office.

TABLE 3-4. Measures of Housing Inadequacy

	1940	1950	1960	1970	1975	1976
Percent lacking some or all plumbing	45.2	35.4	16.8	6.5	3.5	3.3
Percent dilapidated or needing major repairs	17.8	9.8	6.9	4.6	NA	NA
Percent substandard: dilapidated or lacking plumbing	49.2	36.9	18.2	9.0	NA	NA
Percent with 1.51 or more persons per room	9.0	6.2	3.6	2.0	1.0	.9
Percent with 1.01–1.50 persons per room				6.0	4.0	3.7
Percent of "doubling up" (two families in one unit) or "subfamilies"	6.8	5.6	2.4	1.4	1.2	1.5

NA—Not applicable.

Sources: Decennial Census of Housing, U.S. Department of Commerce, Bureau of the Census, and the U.S. Department of Commerce, U.S. Bureau of the Census and U.S. Department of Housing and Urban Development. *Annual Housing Survey,:* 1976, Part A, "General Housing Characteristics for the United States and Regions." Series H-150 (Washington, D.C.: U.S. Government Printing Office).

Rural housing is generally newer than urban housing by an average of five years. This reflects the continued migration of people to the outer fringes of the suburbs and to rural areas. The median age of rural housing in 1975 was nineteen years, compared to twenty-four years for urban units. This was caused in part by a higher proportion of rural housing being built between 1970 and 1975—some 21 percent of all rural units, compared to 12 percent of urban housing built during the same period. More newer rural housing is being built in the outer fringes or rural portions of SMSAs than in the traditional countryside. In particular, the average rural home inside SMSAs is fourteen years old, or eight years less than rural homes outside such areas.

The median number of rooms increased from 4.7 in 1940 to 5.1 in 1976.[33] The proportion of dwelling units with three rooms or less has dropped since 1940; there have been about 11 million since 1950. In contrast, the number of units of all other sizes has increased. Since 1950, about 60 percent of all units have had four, five, or six rooms; the proportion with seven or more rooms has increased from 15 to 20 percent.

At the time (1934) of the National Housing Act, over one-third of all U.S. housing lacked complete plumbing facilities, particularly in rural areas and the South. Today, this condition is rare. However, a unit is more likely to lack plumbing if it is rented. In 1970, households with incomes of less than $6,000 made up 43.3 percent of the rural population and 34.7 percent of the urban population but occupied 76.3 percent and 76.5 percent of the housing without complete plumbing, respectively.[34]

Since housing quality is relative and most units today have plumbing, new measures have been developed to assess housing quality and problems. In the Annual Housing Surveys, seven major factors are examined: electrical, plumbing, heating, kitchen and bath, roof and basement, interior walls, ceiling and floor. Incomplete or poor equipment or materials in any of these areas is considered a defect. In addition, neighborhoods are examined and the presence of rats and vermin checked.

The biggest defect, reported by at least 20 percent of households, was water in the basement. Rural areas were most prone to this problem. Signs of rats or other vermin were reported by about 10 percent of the households. A fuse or switch blowout occurred in about 12 percent of those units occupied for three months or more. About 7 percent of the households who had lived in their home the previous winter had a heating breakdown, 6 percent had leaks through the roof, and 5 percent had cracks or holes in the interior walls and ceilings. Other defects were found in less than 5 percent of the units.

In addition, defects may overlap. A unit may have both water in the basement and a heating breakdown. In 1976, 68.9 percent of the units had no defect, and 25.2 percent had only one or two.[35] Since the majority of units had few defects and

---

[33]Ibid.

[34]Ronald E. Kampe, *Household Income–How It Relates to Substandard Housing in Rural and FmHA Areas* (Washington, D.C.: U.S. Department of Agriculture, Economic Research Service, June 1975).

[35]U.S. Department of Housing and Urban Development, *Tenth Annual Report on the National Housing Goal* (Washington, D.C., 1978), p. 62.

the defects varied, no single measure of housing quality is valid. Goedert and Goodman conclude that "No single housing feature is a reliable indicator of the presence, or absence, of a wider range of housing quality indicators."[36]

UPKEEP AND IMPROVEMENT   One reason the quality of existing housing has increased is the upkeep and improvements made by property owners. Demand for housing is related to improvement and maintenance. *Additions, alterations,* and *major replacements* increase the value of the original structure, while *maintenance* simply sustains the current value.

Housing upkeep and improvement totaled $37.5 billion in 1978, double the $18.5 billion spent in 1973 and 2.8 times the $13.5 billion spent in 1969.[37] Owners of one-family houses spent $26.3 billion in 1978.

Maintenance and repairs account for 25 percent of total spending on owner-occupied one-family homes and major replacements for another 21 percent; *construction improvements* account for the remainder. Painting and papering comprise 40 percent of all maintenance and repair costs. Siding accounts for 25 percent and roofing 32 percent of the money spent on major replacements. Both of these are more likely to be replaced than repaired, although roofs are repaired more often than siding.

Maintenance and repair work is more likely to be done on houses built before 1970. Major replacements are most likely for housing twenty to twenty-five years old or thirty-five or more years old. Given the lifetime of roofs and other major replacement items, this is to be expected. Construction improvements, in contrast, are made at any time.

About $16.5 billion of the $23.9 billion spent for jobs totaling $25 or more was paid to contractors or hired laborers. The rest was for materials bought directly by the owner. Over time, about two-thirds of all expenses for jobs of $25 or more were paid to contractors or hired workers. One-third of all painting and papering expenses are for materials used by the owner alone. Plumbing and remodeling are two other categories where the owner is likely to buy materials but is also likely to hire some help.

In 1978, the average outlay for property upkeep and repair by one-family homeowners was $562 up from $517 in 1977. Owners of higher-valued property spent almost twice as much as owners of lower-valued property. Age had some influence on spending. For properties worth less than $25,000, more money was spent on property twenty to twenty-five years old. For more valuable property, average spending was higher on both newer and older properties. Those about twenty to twenty-five years old had the lowest average expenditures.

For elderly homeowners, total income, wage income, market value, and homes with rental units increase the probability of upkeep investments, while the household head's age, business income, and rental income decrease the probability.[38]

[36]Jeanne E. Goedert and John L. Goodman, Jr., *Indicators of the Quality of U.S. Housing* (Washington, D.C.: The Urban Institute, September 1977), p. 29.

[37]U.S. Department of Commerce, Bureau of the Census, *Construction Reports,* "Residential Alterations and Repairs," C50-78A-5 (April, 1979).

[38]Carol B. Meeks and Michael Walden, "The Demand for Housing Upkeep by the Elderly" Department of Consumer Economics and Housing (Ithaca, N.Y.: Cornell University, 1976).

Wage income, business income, rental income, and households with some college education increase upkeep spending, while market value decreases it. Retirement income and reduced property taxes have no influence on either decision, while wage income increases both the probability and the amount of upkeep investment.

In another study of upkeep and improvement behavior, it was found that 124 family heads had performed a mean of 2.58 maintenance jobs in the past six months.[39] The number of jobs done varied inversely with the length of the work week. Job costs increased with skill. More skillful men may tackle more costly jobs, or may be willing to spend more for better-quality materials. A mean of 2.35 improvement jobs were completed by 90 of the husbands, at a mean cost of $91.56 ranging from zero to $6,000. The number of improvement jobs varied with skill, while none of the variables studied influenced job cost.

FUNCTIONAL STANDARDS

Functional standards refer to the social-psychological aspects of the environment that link the housing unit and occupant. An example is the ability of the unit to promote sociocultural aspects of family life or provide privacy. Housing should fulfill its occupants' needs. In addition, occupant perceptions give meaning to the environment.

SPACE Space plays an important role in human behavior. Rapoport has identified three components of space: physical, sociocultural, and perceptual.[40] Physical space is obviously the area defined by certain boundaries—walls, fences, highways. Sociocultural space is the setting for social interaction. Finally, perceptual space is the area defined by the individual. A space that may be large by most physical standards may seem small to some people.

Space not only indicates status but also reinforces it. Higher-status people usually have more space of higher quality and greater freedom to use it. Arrangement of the space depends on the tasks to be done, the personality of the doer, and the environment. The spatial environment is important in maintaining life style. Forced removal from a good environment can have severe social and psychological consequences.[41]

Closely related to the idea of space is that of *territoriality*. Lyman and Scott have identified four types of territories:

1. Public areas, such as parks, which people use because of some claim to the area. Behavior in such areas is determined by social norms and often by laws as well.

2. Spaces for social gatherings.

3. The home. Here the residents have relative freedom, a sense of intimacy, and control over the area.

4. The body as personal space.[42] There

---

[39]Carol B. Meeks and Francille M. Firebaugh. "Home Maintenance and Improvement Behavior of Owners," *Home Economics Research Journal,* 3 (December 1974), 114–29.

[40]Amos Rapoport, "Toward a Redefinition of Density," *Environment and Behavior,* 7 (June 1975), 133–58.

[41]Robert J. Diaiso, David M. Freedman, Lester C. Mitchell, and Eric A. Schweitzer, *Perception of the Housing Environment: A Comparison of Racial and Density Preferences* (Pittsburgh, Pa.: University of Pittsburgh, 1971), p. 67.

[42]Stanford M. Lyman and Marvin B. Scott, "Territoriality: A Neglected Sociological Dimension," *Social Problems,* XV (Fall 1967), 236–49.

is an area around a person's body into which intruders may not move. The size of this area is related to the culture.

"Defense of territories hinges on visible boundaries and markers. . . ."[43] One can invade a territory by using it improperly or without permission, by simply being there, or by contaminating it, such as by throwing trash in a space. Becker reported that visual privacy was closely related to territoriality and control.[44] Crowding results in the need for social rules to limit unwanted intimacy which is likely to arise when physical barriers are lacking.[45]

Defensible space is a concept popularized by Newman.[46] This space inhibits crime by creating a physical and social environment that defends itself. Basically, buildings and spatial arrangements create areas for which people feel responsible—perceived zones of territorial influence.[47] Physical design can allow people to survey each other and offer opportunities to meet casually. Design also influences our perception of the environment. It may emphasize uniqueness, isolation, or stigma, for example. The goal of defensible space is a safe, productive, and well-maintained living environment. Little is known of how density and crime add to environmental stress. It is important for us to learn more about the nature, meaning, and use of space.

DENSITY   Density has been a concern of urban sociology since 1938, when Wirth asserted that density, along with population size and heterogeneity, influence urban life styles.[48] Density has been studied by sociologists, geographers, and economists.[49] "A given level of population density in a community area can be achieved by different combinations of four components of density: (i) the number of persons per room; (ii) the number of rooms per housing unit; (iii) the number of housing units per structure; and (iv) the number of residential structures per acre."[50]

Density is related to culture. It may affect physiological reactions, psychological situations, and social interaction. A person may adapt to the setting, redefine or modify the setting, or move in response to density.[51]

Density is the number of persons or

---

[43]Robert Sommer, *Personal Space* (Englewood Cliffs, N.J.: Prentice-Hall, 1969), p. 45.

[44]Franklin D. Becker, *Design for Living: The Residents' View of Multifamily Housing* (Ithaca, N.Y.: Cornell University, 1974), p. 81.

[45]Ibid., p. 41.

[46]Oscar Newman, *Defensible Space* (New York: Macmillan, 1972).

[47]Ibid. p. 50.

[48]Louis Wirth, "Urbanism as a Way of Life," *American Journal of Sociology,* 44 (July 1938), 3–24.

[49]Amos Hawley, *Human Ecology* (New York: Ronald Press, 1950); R.D. McKenzie, *The Metropolitan Community* (New York: Russell, 1933); R.E. Park, Ernest W. Burgess, and Roderick D. McKenzie, *The City* (Chicago: University of Chicago Press, 1925); B.L. Berry, J.W. Simmons, and R.J. Tenant, "Urban Population Densities: Structure and Change," *Geographical Review,* 53 (July 1963), 389–405; E.M. Hoover and R. Vernon, *Anatomy of a Metropolis* (Cambridge, Mass.: Harvard University Press, 1959).

[50]O.R. Galle, "Population Density and Pathology: What Are the Realtions for Man?" *Science,* 176 (April 1972), 23–30.

[51]Ronald W. Manderscheid, "A Theory of Spatial Effects," in *Progress in Cybernetics and Systems Research,* Vol. 1, ed. R. Trappl and F.R. Public (Washington, D.C.: Hemisphere Publishing, 1975), pp. 75–83.

Partially covered slide
gives child a sense of space.

U.S. Department of HUD

units per space whereas overcrowding is concerned that there are too many persons or units per space. "Overcrowding is one of the oldest concerns of housing policy in the United States."[52] It has been viewed as a factor in physical and mental illness. However, the need for space is culturally determined. The housing unit provides, or should provide, access to privacy.

The Census Bureau measures overcrowding by counting the number of persons per room. This denotes the general amount of space and privacy available. This measure does not consider room size, age, sex, or the relationship of the occupants. A person is considered to be living in an overcrowded situation if there is more than one person, including children, per room. Another measure of housing space is the extent to which two households share the same housing unit, regardless of the number of rooms. Both overcrowding and doubling up have

steadily declined. ". . . Minority groups generally are much more likely to be living in overcrowded conditions than the majority population, regardless of geographic location or type of tenure."[53]

In contrast to the Census Bureau definition, Greenfield and Lewis have developed an overcrowding index based on these criteria:

1. A married couple may share a room.
2. No more than two children of the same sex may share a room past the age of 12.
3. No more than two children of the opposite sex may share a room past the age of three.
4. All other persons must have individual sleeping rooms.

In addition, a living room, kitchen, and

[52]William Grigsby and Louis Rosenburg, *Urban Housing Policy* (New York: APS Publishers, 1975), p. 42.

[53]U.S. Commission on Civil Rights, *Social Indicators of Equality for Minorities and Women* (Washington, D.C.: U.S. Government Printing Office, August 1978), p. 75.

bath are needed.[54] In a sample of 198 households, Greenfield and Lewis found that 11.6 percent were overcrowded according to the above definition.[55] In contrast, using the Census Bureau definition of 1.5 persons per room, only 1 percent of the owner-occupied and 2 percent of the renter-occupied units were overcrowded. Using number of persons per sleeping room, 58 percent of the households defined as overcrowded above were overcrowded.

Overcrowding may be related to mortality. (1) Increased contact with others increases the probability of catching infectious diseases; (2) people who are overcrowded tend to get rundown, thus increasing their susceptibility to disease; (3) rest and relaxation are prohibited by contact.[56]

Overcrowding may lead to tension and family situations that could cause a family breakdown. As a result of crowding, family members may leave home.[57] "Persons who feel crowded believe that their relationship with their spouse has deteriorated."[58] Privacy and interaction of family members are affected by available space and life-cycle living patterns.

Morris reported that crowding, as measured by a deficit of bedrooms, does not affect fertility but does influence mobility.[59] Chevan reported no difference in crowding at the end of the period studied between couples who did and did not have children.[60] Thus, additional space was had or obtained on the arrival of children.

Age is systematically related to crowding. Families in the middle of the life cycle are apt to have more children than those in the early stages.[61] Crowding does not influence how much parents play with their children. However, the more crowded they are, the more often they hit them.[62] Crowding also increases quarrels among children. Children may receive less effective care. If they find the home noisy and without privacy, they may seek relief by leaving.[63] Parents usually do not discourage them.[64]

Other research suggests that the more an individual is surrounded by a cohesive group, the less crowding and social overload are experienced. When family members feel warm and close, they have less perception of crowding each other out. This mitigates some of the conditions that are part of crowding.[65]

---

[54]R.J. Greenfield and J.F. Lewis, "An Alternative to a Density Function Definition of Overcrowding," in *Housing Urban America*, ed. Jon Pynoos, Robert Schafer, and Chester W. Hartman (Chicago: Aldine, 1973), p. 168.

[55]Ibid., p. 169.

[56]Alan Booth, "Crowding and Family Relations," *American Sociological Review*, 41 (April 1976), 313.

[57]Ruth H. Smith, Donna Beth Downer, Mildred T. Lynch, and Mary Winter, "Privacy and Interaction Within the Family as Related to Dwelling Space," *Journal of Marriage and the Family*, 31 (August 1969), 562.

[58]Galle, "Population Density and Pathology," 28.

[59]Earl W. Morris, "Mobility, Fertility and Residential Crowding," *Sociology and Social Research*, 61 (April 1977), 375.

[60]A. Chevan, "Family Growth, Household Density, and Moving," *Demography*, 8 (November 1971), 451–58.

[61]Booth, "Crowding and Family Relations," p. 313.

[62]Ibid., p. 318.

[63]Galle, "Population Density and Pathology," 29.

[64]Robert E. Mitchell, "Some Social Implications of High Density Housing," *American Sociological Review*, 36 (February 1971), 27.

[65]Andrew Baum, R. Edward Harpin, and Stuart Valins, "The Role of Group Phenomena in the Experience of Crowding," *Environment and Behavior*, 7 (June 1975), 159.

Privacy both reflects and helps to maintain the status divisions of a group. Privacy has always been a luxury.[66] Doors provide boundaries between ourselves and others, and a wall symbolizes "separation" rather than "separateness."[67] Rules, too, promote privacy.

Two homes with equivalent space and density can differ in quality, space, and design. A poor, bare environment might be more susceptible to the effects of crowding.[68] Also, other factors, such as color or amount of design variation, strongly influence the crowding process.[69]

Much research on density and crowding is still needed. Clearly, culture plays a role. Also, it appears that past experiences with density affect the evaluation and perception of crowding. There are signs that increased density is harmful to both individuals and families. The relationships, however, are unclear and complex.

NEIGHBORHOOD QUALITY Neighborhood quality, as evaluated by the Annual Housing Surveys,[70] is measured by:

1. An overall opinion of the neighborhood by residents.

2. Street conditions.

3. Adequacy of neighborhood services, including public transportation, schools, shopping, and police and fire protection, as well as hospital and health care.

Every year since 1973, about 35 percent of those questioned have rated their neighborhood as excellent and another 45 percent have rated it as good. Black persons consistently rate their neighborhoods lower. The approximate breakdown is as follows: 15 percent excellent, 45 percent good, and 33 percent fair Whether respondents live in the central city, suburbs or a nonurban area also influences their opinion. Whether white or black, central city residents are more likely to criticize their neighborhood than are residents in the other two areas.

Street or neighborhood conditions were rated undesirable by about 75 percent of those surveyed. This evaluation held for central city, suburban, and nonurban residents. However, blacks in central cities more often reported undesirable conditions than blacks in other areas.

Public transportation was reported as adequate by two-thirds of the respondents, with central city residents most satisfied. Schools, shopping, police, and fire protection, as well as hospitals and health care, were adequate for about 85 percent of those surveyed. Suburban residents felt slightly better about neighborhood services than central city or nonurban residents, while blacks felt slightly worse.

[66]Barry Schwartz, "The Social Psychology of Privacy," in *People and Buildings,* ed. Robert Gutman (New York: Basic Books, 1972), p. 155.

[67]Ibid., pp. 160–162.

[68]Steven Zlutnick and Irwin Altman, "Crowding and Human Behavior," in *Behavioral Science and the Problems of Our Environment,* ed. J.F. Wohlwill and D.H. Carson (Washington D.C.: American Psychological Association, 1971).

[69]Andrew Baum and Glenn E. Davis, "Spatial and Social Aspects of Crowding Perception," *Environment and Behavior,* 8 (December 1976), 542.

[70]U.S. Department of Commerce, Bureau of the Census, and U.S. Department of Housing and Urban Development, "Indicators of Housing and Neighborhood Quality," *Annual Housing Survey,* Part B. 1973–1976. (Washington, D.C.: U.S. Government Printing Office.)

Residential Satisfaction

As people move from basic shelter and security needs to fulfillment of higher needs, they become more concerned with housing satisfaction. This concern also includes housing services. In public assisted housing, there is a desire to maximize the welfare of residents receiving the aid. In private housing, builders and developers want to sell the housing they produce and so need to correctly assess its desirability. Also, most buyers expect to be sellers and so want a home that is marketable. All sectors are interested in the process of neighborhood deterioration and abandonment.

Housing satisfaction is not limited to the physical building; it also includes the social, behavioral, cultural, and economic setting.[71] The house is only one factor that determines how satisfied people are.[72]

Housing satisfaction often concerns two areas: the housing itself and the neighborhood.[73] These factors have been found to be highly correlated.[74]

Housing and neighborhood satisfaction are parrallel to the two levels of housing quality measured in the Annual Housing Surveys. Harris postulates that housing satisfaction is related to housing quality.[75] She finds that in general, housing quality significantly affects housing quality satisfaction but is only a small part of overall satisfaction with housing. Race, sex of household head, and marital status do not affect this relationship. However, the effect of housing quality on housing quality satisfaction is weak among families with some college education, high annual income, and with household heads between thirty and forty-four years of age. Galster and Hesser report that the quality of facilities is crucial in determining housing satisfaction,[76] as have earlier researchers.[77] Francescato and his colleagues have compared satisfaction of residents in high-rise and low-rise buildings and found no significant difference in satisfaction levels.[78]

---

[71]For a review of research, see Charles W. Bernhard, Jr., "An Analysis of Residential Satisfaction: Surveys Conducted in Low-Income Settings" (unpublished Master's thesis, Cornell University, 1976), pp. 10–19.

[72]Catherine Bauer, "Social Questions in Housing and Community Planning," *Journal of Social Issues*, 7 (1951), 1–34.

[73]Marc Fried and Peggy Gleicher, "Some Sources of Residential Sattisfaction in an Urban Slum," *Journal of the American Institute of Planners*, 27 (August 1961), 305–15; John Lansing and Robert Marans, "Evaluation of Neighborhood Quality," *Journal of the American Institute of Planners*, 35 (May 1969), 195–99; and George Rent, *Low-Income Housing in South Carolina: Factors Related to Residential Satisfaction*, Southern Cooperative Series Bulletin 197 (Clemson, S.C.: Clemson University, 1975).

[74]Louis Wirth, "Housing as a Field of Sociological Research," *American Sociological Review*, 12 (April 1947), 137–43; Alvin Schoor, *Slums and Social Insecurity* (Washington, D.C.: U.S. Government Printing Office, 1964); Adepoju Onibokun, "Environmental Issues in Housing Habitability," *Environment and Planning*, 5 (August 1973), 461–76; Adepoju Onibokun, "Evaluating Consumers' Satisfaction with Housing: An Application of a Systems Approach," *Journal of the American Institute of Planners*, 40 (May 1974), 189–200.

[75]Christine M. Harris, "The Measurement of Quality in Housing and Its Relationship to Housing Satisfaction," *Housing Educators Journal*, 3 (May 1976), 7.

[76]George C. Galster and Garry W. Hesser, "A Path Analysis Model of Residential Satisfaction," Mimeo. Urban Studies Program (Wooster: Ohio: College of Wooster, May 1977).

[77]Irving Rosow , "Social Effects of the Physical Environment," *Journal of the American Institute of Planners*, 27 (August 1961), 127–33. Onibokun, "Environmental Issues" and "Evaluating Consumers' Satisfaction," 1974.

[78]Guido Francescato, Sue Weidemann, James Anderson, and Richard Chenoweth, "Predictors of Residents' Satisfaction in High Rise and Low Rise Housing," *Journal of Architectural Research*, 4 (December 1975), 4–9.

Since every housing unit is tied to a location, neighborhood satisfaction is closely related to or part of housing satisfaction. Fried and Gleicher report that neighborhood satisfaction increases as people perceive close family and neighborhood ties.[79] In contrast, Lansing and Hendricks and Lansing and Marans have found that neighborhood satisfaction increases as families are seen as *less* close and friendly. Also important is the evaluation of neighborhood condition and noise level.[80] Durand and Eckart conclude that persons in socially uniform neighborhoods are not more satisfied than those in mixed ones.[81] Lansing, Marans, and Zehner have found that people who were satisfied reported how well-kept, quiet, homogeneous, and friendly the neighborhood was.[82] Galster and Hesser report that good public services and friendly neighbors are important; rundown properties, crime, and noise are a detriment.[83] Marital status does not affect neighborhood satisfaction.

[79]Fried and Gleicher, "Sources of Residential Satisfaction." p. 333.

[80]John Lansing and Gary Hendricks, *Living Patterns and Attitudes in the Detroit Region* (Detroit: Regional Transportation and Land Use Study, 1967), and Lansing and Marans, "Evaluation of Neighborhood Quality."

[81]Roger Durand and Dennis Eckart, "Social Rank, Residential Effects and Community Satisfaction," *Social Forces*, 52 (September 1973), 74–85.

[82]John Lansing, Robert Marans, and Robert Zehner, *Planned Residential Environments* (Ann Arbor, Mich.: Institute for Social Research, University of Michigan, 1970).

[83]Galster and Hesser, "Path Analysis Model," pp. 15–17.

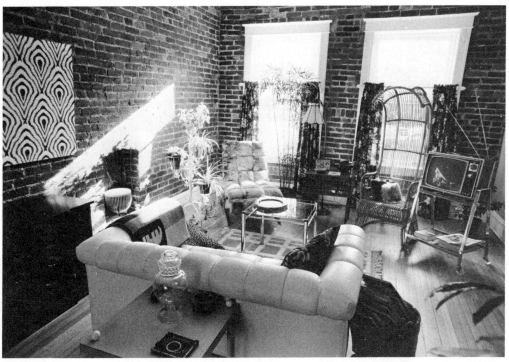

Federal National Mortgage Association

Furnishings within the house enhance satisfaction.

Homeowners are more satisfied with the neighborhood but less satisfied with the housing unit itself. People were also happier in more expensive homes, when the proportion of dilapidated housing dropped, and when higher proportions of people lived in their unit at least five years.

Most housing measures of quality focus on deficiencies. This assumes that the fewer the deficiencies, the higher the quality. Herzberg's work on satisfiers and dissatisfiers indicates that this might not be true.[84] Items that cause dissatisfaction may not necessarily provide satisfaction. Thus, many slum dwellings provide a very satisfying living environment because people have social networks and other ties.

Housing satisfaction or dissatisfaction is a prime factor in the decision to move.[85] Wolpert states that when people reach a threshold of dissatisfaction, they begin to consider moving.[86] The reasons may range from a change in household needs, such as a growing or shrinking family; a change in social or physical conditions, such as neighborhood deterioration; to a change in standards, which may result from a change in social class.[87] Housing dissatisfaction is a necessary but not sufficient condition for voluntary moves. It "pushes" families to begin a search for a new home.[88] The increased benefits gained by moving must outweigh the costs.

Satisfaction with housing is often seen as a link between individual and household characteristics and mobility.[89] Rea found that in any stage of the life cycle, people generally move in order to correct a problem that exists where they now live.[90] Those in the later stages (higher income, larger family, and older household head) focus on neighborhood qualities; those in the earlier stages move because of the housing unit itself. ". . . Where the respondents' present accommodations are an improvement over their last previous accommodations, in terms of type of house, they tend to convey a higher degree of satisfaction with their present accommodations."[91]

According to Rossi, housing is more important as a source of contentment than as a shaper of people's lives.[92] Livability of a housing unit or resident satisfaction can be meaningful only in a relative sense.[93]

---

[84]F. Herzberg, *Work and the Nature of Man* (Cleveland: World, 1966).

[85]Julian Wolpert, "Behavioral Aspects of the Decision to Migrate," *Papers of the Regional Science Association*, 15 (1965), 159–69.

[86]Ibid.

[87]Alden Speare, Jr., "Residential Satisfaction as an Intervening Variable in Residential Mobility," *Demography*, 11 (May 1974), 175.

[88]Rea, "Residential Satisfaction and Intraurban Mobility," p. 2.

[89]Alden Speare, Jr., Sidney Goldstein, and William H. Frey, *Residential Mobility, Migration and Metropolitan Change* (Cambridge, Mass.: Ballinger, 1975), p. 257.

[90]Rea, "Residential Satisfaction and Intraurban Mobility," p. 10.

[91]From "Social System Correlates of Residential Satisfaction," by Adepoju G. Onibokun, is reprinted from *Environment and Behavior*, Vol. 8, No. 3, September 1976, pp. 323–344, by permission of the Publisher, Sage Publication, Inc.

[92]Peter H. Rossi, "Community Social Indicators," in *The Human Meaning of Social Change*, ed. A. Campbell and P.E. Converse (New York: Russell Sage, 1972), pp. 87–126.

[93]D.R. Phillips, "Comfort in Home," *Royal Society of Health Journal* 87 (September/October 1967), 237–46.

Structure Type

An important influence on behavior is the type of housing in which we live. The home is one's individual image to the world. These images are important to most people. The scale of a building may emphasize warmth and humanness or power, awe, and grandeur. Scale may be measured by length, height, bulk, or number. Building details may be in or out of scale.

HIGH-RISE BUILDINGS

Let us examine the effect of tall residential buildings on users, especially children and the elderly. Building characteristics include height, bulk, shape, shadow, noise, traffic, and the number of other tall buildings in the area. These factors, and the building's location, may affect the way occupants respond.

Concerns in high rises were identified by Appleyard and Fishman as:

"1. safety: from fire, earthquake, falling objects, traffic hazards, crime, etc.;
2. stress/comfort: microclimate, noise, glare, shadow, air pollution, places to sit, crowding, other aspects of psychological stress;
3. convenience: changes in pedestrian and auto travel patterns, commuting times;
4. privacy and territoriality: intrusion on neighbors, provision or reduction of public territory through plazas, etc.; availability of building to the public;
5. social interaction: encouragement or disruption of neighborhood cohesion, interest group cohesion, worker morale, etc.; isolation of high-rise inhabitants from the city;
6. visual disruption: disruption through height, bulk, color, shape, scale, detail, blockage of views; "dead" street environments; signs/billboards;
7. symbolism: private versus public symbolism, associations attached to buildings, "dominance," "friendliness," etc.;
8. maintenance: levels of vandalism, cleanliness, trash in surrounding area.[94]

These concerns can be related to the levels of needs which housing provides.

Haber reported what people dislike in tall buildings:[95]

1. Waiting for elevators	65%
2. Lack of greenery	61%
3. Fear of fire	55%
4. Impersonality	52%

Middle-income people complained most about waiting time. More than twice as many whites as blacks missed greenery. More women than men feared fire. Whites felt tall buildings were impersonal more often than blacks. People with children also felt that tall buildings were impersonal. Other dislikes include interior monotony, lack of control over the environment, fear of being stuck in the elevator, isolation, heights and noise, or a belief that the building spoiled the skyline.

---

[94]Donald Appleyard and Lois Fishman, "High-Rise Buildings Versus San Francisco: Measuring Visual and Symbolic Impacts," in *Human Response to Tall Buildings,* ed. Donald J. Conway (Stroudsburg, Pa.: Dowden, Hutchinson, and Ross, Inc., 1977), p. 85.
[95]Gilda Moss Haber, "The Impact of Tall Buildings on Users and Neighbors," in *Human Response to Tall Buildings,* p. 54.

On the other hand, things most often liked in tall buildings included:[96]

1. The view   80%
2. Ability to see far   63%
3. Economical on space   38%

Other likes were aesthetics, convenience, socialization, facilities, prestige, and quietness. It is essentially perceptions and attitudes toward the housing environment, rather than building height, that makes a difference.[97] The social implications of high-rise buildings lie in the user's needs. High rises provide limited social contact and self-expression, and space limits on activities within the home. This is especially important for households with children. Research indicates that high-rise buildings are detrimental to children's behavior.

CHILDREN Children are of particular concern in high-rise buildings because they must explore and socialize close to home. According to Pollaway, "Two factors seem to have the most effect on the child-physical environment situation: the age of the child (i.e., stage of development) and the dwelling type."[98] Children should be planned for when the building is designed. Spaces for the use of small children should be within sight and sound of the home.[99] Parents must be able to supervise play. Apartments need to be soundproof, and noise from outside play areas should not easily enter the apartment. Within the apartment, children need private space as well as common space. Young children in high rises cling more, while older children spend more time away from home.

THE ELDERLY High-rise buildings appear to suit many elderly people well. Nahemow, Lawton, and Howell reported that high rises were "not found to affect an individual's morale, the extent of his or her social contacts either in or out of the buildings or the extent of participation in activities."[100] Elderly persons who dislike high-rise living are likely to have moved in from private houses, are afraid of fire, anxious about the elevator, and concerned about having only one entrance to their apartment.[101]

In general, studies show that a resident's perception of the apartment and building are affected by the floor on which he/she lives, the size of the apartment, and how long he/she expects to live in the building.[102]

SINGLE-FAMILY HOUSE

The detached house affords more privacy and more control than multi-family units. It usually contains more space. Since most owned homes are single-family whereas most multi-family units are rented, the single-family home allows one to be a home owner. More single-

[96]Ibid., p. 47.

[97]Sandra J. Newman, "Perceptions of Building Height: An Approach to Research and Some Preliminary Findings," in *Human Response to Tall Buildings*, p. 192.

[98]A.M. Pollaway, "Children in High-Rise Buildings," *Human Response to Tall Buildings*, p. 150.

[99]Ibid., p. 158.

[100]Lucille Nahemow, M. Powell Lawton, and Sandra C. Howell, "Elderly People in Tall Buildings," in *Human Response to Tall Buildings*, p. 180.

[101]Ibid., p. 180.

[102]Jerald Greenberg and Carol I. Greenberg, "A Survey of Residential Responses to High-Rise Living," in *Human Response to Tall Buildings*, p. 172.

family homeowners are interested in gardening and other home-centered activities than multi-family dwellers.[103] Privacy and child rearing are main concerns for those who prefer a single-family home.[104]

Single-family homes in downtown areas are attractive because of the convenient facilities, such as restaurants, museums, and entertainment, as well as nearness to work. On the other hand, suburban living focuses on the nuclear family and its joint activities.[105] Living in low-density areas, suburbanites see their relatives less often. Most complaints of suburbanites concern their access to recreation, shopping, and work.

U.S. Department of HUD
Playgrounds have an important role in multi-unit developments.

[103]William Michelson, *Environmental Choice, Human Behavior, and Residential Satisfaction* (New York: Oxford University Press, 1977), p. 362.

[104]William Michelson, "Analytic Sampling for Design Information: A Survey of Housing Experience," Proceedings of the 1st Annual Environmental Design Research Association, ed. Henry Sanoff and Sidney Cohn (Raleigh, N.C.: North Carolina State University, Raleigh, 1970), p. 191.

[105]William Michelson, *Man and His Urban Environment: A Sociological Approach* (Reading, Mass.: Addison-Wesley, 1970), p. 92.

The way people behave in different housing types and locations depends largely on the situation in which they find themselves.[106] Different housing types do not appear to attract cerain types of people.[107] Housing influences behavior more than behavior influences housing.[107] People generally prefer the environment in which they live. Their experiences, however, are not necessarily optimal. That is, people cannot know if they are in the best environment if they have not tried other alternatives.

Summary

The living environment affects human behavior. It fulfills a hierarchy of needs, beginning with physical needs and extending to self-fulfillment. Values determine choices made both within and between need categories. The quality of the environment can be assessed in terms of physical standards, functional standards, and housing environment. In terms of physical standards, the U.S. housing stock is gradually becoming newer and larger. The previous problems of lack of plumbing and overcrowding have been greatly reduced, partly because of all the money spent for upkeep and improvement every year. Other measures of housing deficiencies indicate that a majority of units have one or no defects. Neighborhoods are generally rated as highly satisfactory.

Functional standards are related mainly to space and crowding. Space provides status and an indication of life

[106]Michelson, *Environmental Choice*, p. 362.
[107]Ibad., p. 155.

style. It must be defensible. Overcrowding can affect health, family interaction, and behavior. Census definitions of crowding are limited in that age, sex, and other factors related to the use of space are not considered.

Housing type also influences behavior. High-rise buildings seem to fulfill housing needs of the elderly well. They are most likely to negatively influence children's behavior and life style. Single-family homes seem most suited to the nuclear family and its activities.

Terms

additions and alterations permanent additions or changes made to either the inside or outside of the house which increase the enclosed space within it; alternations consist of remodeling or modifying existing space within the house.

construction improvements additions, alterations, and major replacements that increase the value of housing properties.

crowding a large number of people in a relatively small area.

defensible space area which residents feel able to secure and protect.

density the number of individuals per unit of space.

design to conceive or execute.

maintenance and repairs jobs necessary for preventive care and upkeep of a structure, property, or fixed equipment. Represent current costs for maintaining the property rather than further investment.

major replacements complete substitution of a new piece of fixed household equipment, surfacing, or fixed appliances for an old item.

territoriality a persistent attachment to a particular area.

traffic patterns circulation path within the unit that connects each room.

Suggested Readings

Booth, Alan, *Urban Crowding and Its Consequences*. New York: Holt, Rinehart & Winston, 1976.

Freedman, Jonathan L., *Crowding and Behavior*. New York: Viking, 1975.

Hall, Edward, *The Hidden Dimension*. Garden City, N.Y.: Anchor Books, 1969.

———, *The Silent Language*. Garden City, N.Y.: Anchor Books, 1959.

Hinkler, Lawrence E., and William C. Loring, *The Effect of the Man-Made Environment on Health and Behavior*. Washington, D.C.: U.S. Department of Health, Education and Welfare, Superintendent of Documents, U.S. Government Printing Office, 1977.

Human Response to Tall Buildings, Ed. Donald J. Conway. Stroudsburg, Pa.: Dowden, Hutchinson and Ross, Inc., 1977.

Michelson, William, *Man and His Urban Environment: A Sociological Approach*. Reading, Mass.: Addison-Wesley, 1970.

Morris, Earl W., and Mary Winter, *Housing, Family and Society*. New York: John Wiley & Sons, Inc., 1978.

THE HOUSING MARKET

1. WHY AND HOW DO HOUSING MARKETS DIFFER FROM OTHER MARKETS?

2. WHAT IS THE ROLE OF MORTGAGE CREDIT IN THE HOUSING MARKET?

3. HOW IS THE SECONDARY MARKET INFLUENCED BY THE FEDERAL GOVERNMENT?

4. DISCUSS THE HOUSING ABANDONMENT PROBLEM.

5. IS FILTERING A SOLUTION TO HOUSING THE COUNTRY?

In the following chapters, consumption and production of housing will be examined.[1] This chapter analyzes their interdependence—or supply and demand. It establishes a framework upon which the rest of the text elaborates. It is this interdependence that produces the housing market.

The Housing Market

Housing is brought to consumers through the housing market. This market differs from markets for other goods and services because housing is in a fixed location, is durable, and provides services not only from the structure itself but also from the quality of the neighborhood.

Housing markets are local. There is no uniform national housing market, but rather many submarkets or market segments. The housing market may be divided in many ways, including location—with natural boundaries and travel distance—price, structural type, or race. The housing market is also geographically segmented, by natural elements such as rivers or climate. Structural type is another way of dividing the market—single-family versus multifamily. Price may be another dividing line. For example, a household with an income of $10,000 per year does not demand a $100,000 housing unit.[2] Thus,

---

[1]Consumption in this context refers to housing as an economic good that satisfies wants.

[2]Although presumably if quantity is defined correctly, one could view this as demand.

each household is interested in only a small part of the total housing stock.

The market area is affected by local economic conditions, growth in population or demand for housing, and availability of units. Urban and other housing markets differ in structure and operation. Urban areas may have a wider range of choice and prices, more real estate salespersons, and more lenders. Nonurban areas, in contrast, may have fewer restrictions and services. Housing supply may also be more limited. The local market is dynamic, constantly changing in response to demand and supply.

Housing markets distribute the housing stock. This "is not a simple matter of visualizing the kind of dwelling which each type of household should enjoy, or the kind of occupants best suited to each available type of dwelling. It is a problem of compromising intricate needs with inexact resources, measuring out housing benefits and charges in different amounts to different people, settling people physically and resettling them at dissimilar intervals,. . . ."[3]

The housing market is an economic mechanism in which price is generally used to match the supply of housing to the demand. Since it is an *economic* mechanism, certain assumptions are usually made when the theory of housing market operations is discussed. They are:

1. The market is competitive; there are many buyers and sellers, none of whom control the market. Also, buyers and sellers do not collude.

2. Buyers and sellers know everything about the available goods and services, their ability to meet wants, market price, and money income.

3. Products are homogeneous; that is, one may be substituted for another. This is not usually true in housing but is assumed to be so.

4. Resources are mobile; it is easy to enter and leave the market.

These four assumptions are used in most economic analyses. Housing differs from most other goods, since it:

1. Is very expensive.

2. Provides both return on capital and shelter.

3. Tends to appreciate rather than depreciate.

4. Involves legal procedures.

5. Involves high costs for transactions.

6. Lasts a long time.

7. Is bought mainly on credit.

8. Involves buying community services paid for by property taxes.

9. Needs maintenance and repair.

Despite these differences, the economic framework which follows still provides the best method of analyzing how the housing market functions.

Supply and demand curves for a good that is elastic, and under the assumptions made above, are usually visualized as in Figure 4-1. The line DD is the demand for housing. Any point on the line represents the demand for a given quantity of housing at a given price. The movement down the line indicates that as the price of housing decreases, the quantity demand will increase.

---

[3]Wallace F. Smith, *Housing: The Social and Economic Elements,* (Berkeley and Los Angeles, Calif.: University of California Press, 1970), p. 397.

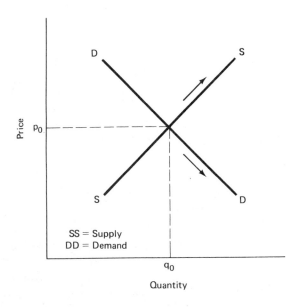

Figure 4-1. The Housing Market.

The line SS represents the supply of housing. Movement up the line indicates that as the price of housing increases, the supply will increase.

The intersection of the two lines (curves) DD and SS establishes the q_0, or quantity of housing, that will be supplied at price p_0. This intersection of the supply and demand curves is the market equilibrium point—that is, demand equals supply.

DEMAND

Housing demand is the quantity and quality of housing a household is willing and able to buy. The household chooses the quantity and quality that yield the greatest satisfaction given its income. Demand depends on the level and distribution of household income, the price of housing and other goods and services, demographic patterns, and household composition, size, and preferences. Further, housing is demanded by government investors as well as households.

Households compare housing packages and prices. They then choose the one that, together with other desired nonhousing consumption, is best for them, given their income and preferences, assets, and expectations (Table 4-1).

Households are always in flux. Changes in income, jobs, and family situations are continual. Households dissolve, expand, and contract.

Increased housing demand in an area depends on in-migration of new residents or the formation of new households. Whether new residents will be attracted to an area depends partly on the economy and employment available. New household formation depends partly on age structure of the population. "The dynamic market in any period is deter-

TABLE 4-1. Demand and Supply Factors in the Housing Market

DEMAND VARIABLES	SUPPLY VARIABLES
Household formation	Construction costs
Migration	Mortgage availability and terms
Price of housing	Rate of new construction
Level and distribution of income	Number of units lost
Liquid assets of households	Federal housing policies
Price of other goods and services	Vacancy rate
Household composition, size, and preference	Maintenance costs

mined by the marginal group who are in the process of making such adjustments."[4]

SUPPLY

The supply of housing consists of both the existing stock, which varies in age, size, and quality, and new units. The lag between demand and the construction of new units is relatively long, but new production is crucial in the supply process. However, since new production is only a small part of the total housing inventory, the supply of housing changes slowly. Certain types of housing may be basically fixed for long periods.

The profitability of new construction is a complex issue. It rises with current rent levels/unit of service and falls when the cost of services and capital rise. In a competitive market, the producers who are right about housing will profit. Speculation—building in anticipation of demand—is a mark of the U.S. housing market. Federal housing policies sometimes subsidize housing production or provide credit for the builder.

---

[4]Sherman J. Maisel, "Rates of Ownership, Mobility, and Purchase," *Essays in Urban Land Economics* (Los Angeles, Calif.: University of California Real Estate Research Program, 1966), p. 76.

MARKET INTERACTIONS

This section will examine the effect of changing demand and supply on the market. First, increased demand will be examined. For example, demand may rise because of a new government subsidy or a large influx of people. In Figure 4-2, DD—the demand—shifts to the right. In the short run, the supply is relatively *inelastic*, so that the price rises from p_0 to p_1. Thus, increased demand with no increase in supply will result in higher prices. This is a somewhat simplistic picture, since many factors are interacting at the same time. On the other hand, suppose the supply of housing increases and demand remains constant. Then the supply curve shifts from SS to SS_1 (Figure 4-3). The quantity of housing has increased from q_0 to q_1, but the price of housing has dropped from p_0 to p_1.

THE ROLE OF GOVERNMENT

Housing markets in the United States are affected by federal, state, and local housing policy and government actions. Housing policy often tries to encourage home ownership. There are many ways to do this. Local tax relief programs for the elderly are one method. Others are

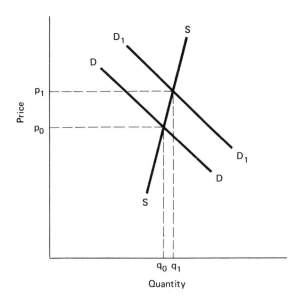

Figure 4-2. Effect of an Increase in Demand for Housing. (*Note:* If the supply was inelastic SS would be vertical.)

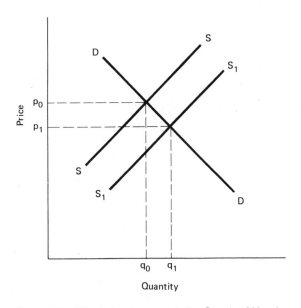

Figure 4-3. Effect of an Increase in the Supply of Housing.

73

detailed in Part III. Government policy also affects housing production by such things as subsidies and monetary policy. Thus, various levels of government may tax housing consumption or production, provide direct or indirect subsidies, or establish regulations that affect the housing market. Government regulations include zoning, building and housing codes, rent control, and labor regulations. Governments may try to affect either supply or demand. For example, there are times when the government supports policies to increase mortgage rates and discourage purchasing that involves borrowing.

Government intervention in the housing market stems in part from the special traits that set housing apart from other markets and the housing goals of society. There are other characteristics that show the need for government intervention. For one thing, basic shelter is necessary for survival. Housing accounts for a large share of household budgets. There is monopoly power in some markets. Finally, information about the details of housing is hard to obtain.[5]

Building codes, one form of government regulation on the housing market, will be examined here. Figure 4-1 assumes that perfect competition exists and that the market is in equilibrium. Building codes would reduce competition by driving out some suppliers. The supply will be not SS but SS_1, so that fewer units will be supplied at a higher price, assuming demand is elastic. If, however, demand is relatively inelastic, as repre-

sented by DD_1, the supply will be reduced from q_0 to q_2 and prices will rise substantially from p_0 to p_2. If building codes have existed for a long time, the market will be in equilibrium at point R. With the building codes removed, the supply will shift to SS.

Research indicates some of the costs of government regulation on housing. In a 1950 study of the effect of codes, Maisel concluded that an increase of less than 1 percent in the cost of new housing could be attributed to "known code inefficiencies."[6] Muth's 1968 econometric analysis of single detached housing suggests that locally modified building codes increase average cost by about 2 percent.[7] However, Johnson concluded that "in large urban areas, it may be possible to achieve on the order of a 10 to 15 percent reduction in direct construction costs (or 5 to 8.25 percent of selling price by Johnson's calculations) . . . if code constraints and restrictive labor practices are removed and if the industry is allowed to produce as efficiently as it knows how."[8] Other evidence suggests that uniform building codes would increase mass production and lower costs.[9] Estimates indicate that if twenty-one "excessive re-

---

[5]Frank de Leeuw, "What Should U.S. Housing Policies Be?" *The Journal of Finance*, 29 (May 1974), 683–98.

---

[6]Sherman J. Maisel, *Housing Building in Transition* (Berkeley, Calif.: University of California Press, 1953), pp. 249–50.

[7]J.A. Stockfisch, *An Investigation of the Opportunities for Reducing the Cost of Federally Subsidized Housing*, Report R-148 (Arlington, Va.: Institute for Defense Analyses, September 1968), p. 8.

[8]Ralph J. Johnson, "Housing Technology and Housing Costs," in *Building the American City*. Paul H. Douglas, Chairman, Report of the National Commission on Urban Problems. (Washington, D.C.: U.S. Government Printing Office, 1968), p. 57.

[9]*Building the American City*, p. 262.

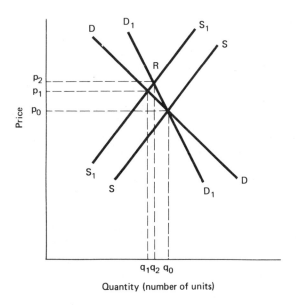

Figure 4-4. Effect of Building Codes on the Housing Market.

quirements" were eliminated, $1,838 would be cut from the costs of a typical $12,000 FHA-insured house. Again, this 15.3 percent reduction in construction costs (or roughly 13 percent in sales price, if 20 percent of the price is the value of the land) represents all twenty-one "excessive requirements"—not all of which are necessarily in effect in any one area.

In analyzing the local housing market, one must consider whether new production is adequate to meet the demand, how and if existing housing is being used, high vacancy rates, abandonment, and overcrowding. Is housing distributed in terms of location, type, price, size, and quality, so that the needs of many households are met? In a housing shortage, everyone who is willing to pay the market price cannot find a housing unit. The market should provide fair and equal service to all.

Housing Mortgage Market

Credit has a major influence in the housing market. The mortgage market influences housing construction in two ways. First, when funds are scarce and the interest rate rises, housing demand declines. This is a signal to builders to cut back on construction. The second factor is the willingness of secondary mortgage market intermediaries to make mortgage commitments. Intermediaries with little money make fewer commitments to builders, whose construction activity is then limited.

Economists suggest that rising *interest* rates encourage households to delay buying a home, while falling rates spur them on. But if market rates rise and are expected to remain at the new level, demand for housing will not be permanently reduced.

75

The housing mortgage market is one of the largest users of borrowed funds in the U.S. economy. This mortgage debt has continued to grow (Figure 4-5). Since World War II, the mortgage debt has increased three times as fast as the total net public and private debt and twice as fast as private corporate debts.[10] Overall, the increase in nonfarm housing mortgage debt accounted for 21 percent of the increase in total outstanding debt.

[10]United States Savings and Loan League Association, *Savings and Loan Fact Book 1976* (Chicago, Ill., 1976), p. 26.

A diagram of the housing mortgage market developed by the Federal Reserve Bank of Richmond (Figure 4-6) shows the major financial sources and users of funds in the market. Supply sources include savings and loan associations, mutual savings banks, commercial banks, life insurance companies, federally sponsored credit agencies, finance and mortgage companies, and real estate investment trusts. Households demand mortgages in order to buy houses, and businesses demand them for building and for multi-family structures.

The amount of mortgage credit de-

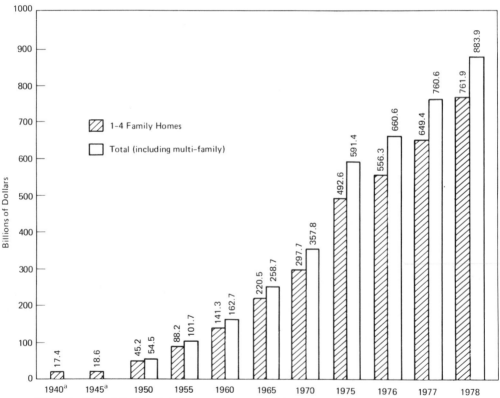

aFigures for 1940, 1945 did not include commercial mortgage debt.

Figure 4-5. Residential Mortgage Debt Outstanding, 1940–1977. [*Source:* U.S. League of Savings Associations, *Savings and Loan Fact Book* 78, Chicago, Illinois 1978, p. 29 and Board of Governors of the Federal Reserve System. *Federal Reserve Bulletin.* Vol. 65. No. 7 July 1979 Table A-41.]

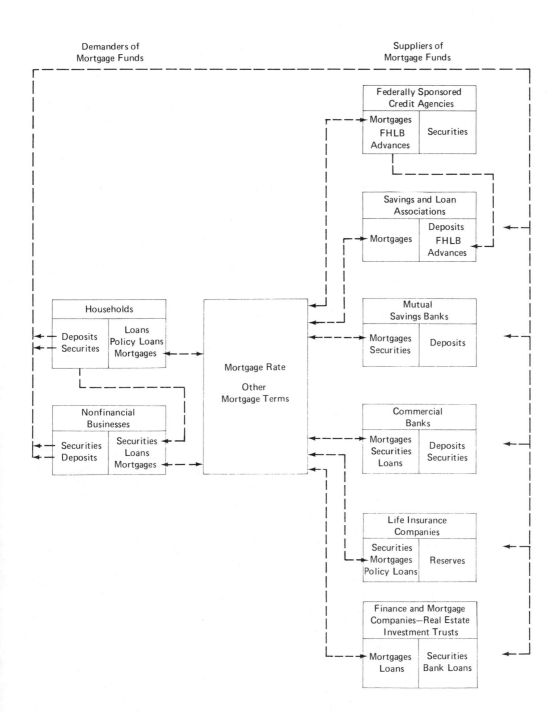

Figure 4-6. The Mortgage Market. [*Source:* Federal Reserve Bank of Richmond, "The Residential Mortgage Market in Recent Years," *Economic Review,* 60, September/October, 1974, p. 5.]

manded or supplied depends largely on the interest rate. This rate, in turn, is influenced by the demand or supply of mortgage credit. When funds are plentiful and demand low, the interest rate drops; when funds are tight and demand high, the interest rate rises. The nonrate mortgage terms, such as *down payment* and maturity, also influence and are influenced by demand and supply.

The demand for mortgage credit in the 1970s has been affected by the growing number of new households. The twenty-five to thirty-four age group is the group responsible for most of this demand. In the early 1970s, the subsidized housing programs added to demand as well. The secondary market also influences demand when it buys mortgages at above-market prices. The private share of mortgage lending normally shrinks during the late stage of economic expansion and during recessions, while the federal government's share rises.

Secondary Mortgage Market

Up to now, we have considered the primary mortgage market, where investors normally use their funds for permanent investment in housing mortgages. Most of these investors are depository institutions—savings and loans, mutual savings banks, and commercial banks.

In the secondary mortgage market, mortgages that have already been issued may be traded. When *lenders* sell their mortgages in the secondary market, they have funds to reinvest in new mortgages. The secondary mortgage market increases the flow of mortgage funds by providing liquidity to primary lenders and by attracting new investors. The ability of the secondary market to match sellers and buyers is a key to its effectiveness. This is limited by the lack of a central marketplace.

Mortgage loans bought in the 1978 secondary market totaled $62.0 billion, an increase of $45.6 billion from 1970.[11] During this period, the secondary market was about one-fourth the size of the primary market. For loans on one- to four-family homes, the largest part (80 percent) of the secondary market, this market was about one-third the size of the primary market.

The secondary market for home mortgage loans is heavily federalized, although the federal role varies with the flow of mortgage funds (Table 4-2). The federal government generally acts to increase funds and moderate mortgage rates. Since the mid-1960s, government-sponsored credit agencies such as the Federal National Mortgage Association (FNMA), Government National Mortgage Association (GNMA), and Federal Home Loan Mortgage Corporation (FHLMC) have accounted for about 15 to 20 percent of mortgage expansion each year—and more than that in periods of escalating interest rates and in at least the early phase of recession. In 1978 the outstanding debt of federal housing agencies was $81.8 billion; included in this total was $43.3 billion in FNMA *debentures*, $3.5 billion in GNMA *securities*, and $3.0 billion in FHLMC banks. A discussion of these agencies' roles in the secondary market follows.[12]

---

[11]*HUD News*, No. 77–373, Dec. 12, 1977, from Quarterly Gross Flow Charts.

[12]*Federal Reserve Bulletin* 65, (July 1979), Table 1.56, A.41.

TABLE 4-2. Percent Distribution of Secondary Market Purchases of 1–4 Family Home Mortgage Loans by Lender Group

QUARTER	COMMER-CIAL BANKS	MUTUAL SAVINGS BANKS	SAVINGS & LOAN ASSNS.	MORTGAGE COMPANIES	FEDERAL CREDIT AGENCIES	FEDERALLY SUPPORTED POOLS	OTHER LENDER GROUPS
1970 I	9.9%	9.6%	10.6%	.5%	52.8%	10.1%	6.5%
II	1.2	12.7	25.9	0.5	45.7	3.5	10.5
III	2.4	9.2	24.8	0.4	41.5	17.6	4.1
IV	2.1	10.9	38.2	0.4	23.3	20.8	4.3
1971 I	8.9	13.3	42.9	2.2	4.1	25.2	3.4
II	6.9	9.5	39.8	1.7	9.6	29.5	3.0
III	4.5	7.4	29.9	3.0	35.8	17.6	1.8
IV	5.2	11.7	34.5	1.9	26.9	15.4	4.4
1972 I	3.6	12.1	38.3	3.3	15.8	24.4	2.5
II	4.9	9.4	40.3	2.7	20.8	17.5	4.4
III	3.2	10.0	36.2	8.7	22.9	16.8	2.2
IV	4.8	11.8	36.7	7.9	19.8	17.7	1.3
1973 I	2.7	13.7	35.9	4.4	24.0	16.4	2.9
II	2.8	9.2	30.1	5.4	26.7	23.2	2.6
III	4.3	5.5	19.7	2.2	49.8	15.8	2.7
IV	6.7	6.0	17.6	12.4	31.8	18.3	7.2
1974 I	2.8	6.3	26.9	10.2	14.1	36.6	3.1
I	2.0	5.7	22.4	2.6	46.3	18.6	2.4
III	0.9	2.9	15.0	1.0	49.4	28.4	2.4
IV	1.1	3.6	20.5	2.2	41.4	25.4	5.8
1975 I	0.6	3.7	23.5	3.1	21.8	43.7	3.6
II	0.9	4.7	25.4	1.3	28.2	37.8	1.7
III	0.7	2.7	21.9	3.1	43.2	26.8	1.6
IV	0.8	3.3	19.5	2.3	40.1	32.1	1.9
1976 I	2.2	3.7	27.5	4.9	25.3	34.8	1.6
II	2.0	4.4	27.5	4.2	24.5	35.6	1.8
III	2.1	4.8	24.9	5.0	21.6	40.5	1.1
IV	1.4	6.6	23.9	6.4	18.5	42.0	1.2
1977 I	5.5	4.1	27.2	5.7	8.0	48.3	1.1
II	2.8	5.7	27.0	5.7	24.1	33.3	1.4
III	2.9	5.5	21.8	7.5	16.4	44.5	1.3
IV	2.4	5.9	20.9	4.8	18.8	44.4	2.7
1978 I	1.7	5.0	18.8	6.4	28.8	36.4	2.9
II	2.0	4.5	18.8	5.3	32.4	36.3	2.4
III	3.1	4.1	15.4	4.3	31.5	37.0	4.6
IV	2.6	4.6	15.5	4.7	28.2	39.6	4.8

Source: Arnold H. Diamond, The Supply of Mortgage Credit 1970–1974 (Washington D.C.: Office of Economic Affairs, Office of Policy Development and Research, U.S. Department of Housing and Urban Development, October 1975), p. 54; HUD News, HUD-No. 78-241 (July 26, 1978), HUD-No. 79-37 (Feb. 13, 1979); and HUD-No. 79-218 (July 10, 1979).

FEDERAL NATIONAL MORTGAGE ASSOCIATION

The Federal National Mortgage Association (FNMA or Fannie Mae) was chartered by the Federal Housing Administration (FHA) in 1938 to provide a secondary market for FHA mortgages. The 1968 Housing and Urban Development Act made FNMA a privately owned corporation. However, the President appoints five of its fifteen directors, and it is generally regulated by the Secretary of

HUD. Within statutory guidelines, the Secretary:

1. Sets FNMA's debt ceiling and the ratio of debt to capital.
2. Sets the maximum rate for its cash dividends.
3. Approves the issuance of all its stock, obligations, and other securities.

The Secretary of the Treasury must approve all debt issues, including the terms and conditions of sale, in order to assure coordination with Treasury debt operations.

During its first ten years, the FNMA bought FHA mortgages when funds were scarce and sold them when funds were abundant. In 1948 FNMA was authorized to buy VA mortgages. The 1970 Emergency Home Finance Act gave FNMA the authority to buy conventional mortgages. In 1975 FNMA entered the field of mobile home financing. It also buys mortgages from mortgage companies, banks and trusts, savings and loan associations, life insurance companies, GNMA, and others. Sellers must meet and maintain FNMA standards and normally continue to service the loans. Sellers must also hold some common stock in the unpaid principal amount of mortgages serviced by FNMA. Other funds for mortgage purchases and operations are obtained from mortgage repayments; sale of debentures, notes, and other obligations; commitment fees; proceeds from mortgage sales; and the difference between interest income and borrowing costs.

Today FNMA is one of the largest financial intermediaries in the mortgage market. It supports mortgage and housing markets when funding is needed.[13] Although FNMA has sacrificed profitability to meet public policy goals, it is still profitable.

GOVERNMENT NATIONAL MORTGAGE ASSOCIATION

The Government National Mortgage Association (GNMA or Ginnie Mae) was created in 1968 by Title III of the National Housing Act. A government corporation within HUD, it supports mortgage market activities that could not be economically carried out by the private market. The Secretary of HUD determines GNMA policies and appoints its officers. The purposes of GNMA are to:

1. Make mortgage money available to those who cannot get decent housing under existing programs.
2. Minimize declines in home building and mortgage lending.
3. Encourage mortgage originators to spend more money on mortgages.
4. Attract new long-term investors to the mortgage market.[14]

GNMA acts by giving mortgage originators commitments to buy mortgages with primarily below-market interest rates; buying and selling these mort-

---

[13]Kenneth T. Rosen, "The Federal National Mortgage Association, Residential Construction, and Mortgage Lending," paper presented at the American Real Estate and Urban Economics Association, New York City, Dec. 30, 1977.

[14]United States General Accounting Office *Government National Mortgage Association's Secondary Mortgage Market Activities*, (Washington, D.C.: U.S. Government Printing Office, Mar. 8, 1977). p. i.

gages; and guaranteeing securities, backed by mortgage pools.

GNMA buys mortgages to support types of housing that are hard to fund and stabilizes mortgage lending. Since 1974, it has been able to buy conventional mortgages on single-family homes as well as FHA and VA mortgages. Funds for this are provided by the Secretary of the Treasury under authorization by Congress. The bulk of FHA and VA mortgages bought are sold to private investors. GNMA subsidizes the difference between the buying and selling prices.

GNMA manages a variety of mortgages and other assets. It also acts as a trustee for pools of mortgages and other government assets owned by itself and other government agencies.

The GNMA stimulates housing construction because:[15]

1. The lender has a purchase commitment and is thus more willing to make the loan.
2. Interest rates paid by homeowners are held to reasonable levels without stifling the flow of investment funds.
3. Discounts are held to a minimum.
4. With a purchase commitment, the builder can obtain construction money and advertise that favorable financing is available.

Processing begins when the builder requests a mortgage commitment and the mortgage originator asks for a GNMA commitment. When the commitment is given, the originator then gives a mortgage commitment to the builder. When a consumer decides to buy a home and asks for a mortgage, the builder arranges financing under the mortgage commitment obtained. The mortgage originator makes the loan to the home buyer, who in turn pays the builder. The mortgage originator may then hold the mortgage, sell it to the GNMA at the commitment price, or sell it to an investor at a negotiated price. If GNMA buys, it will sell the mortgage to an investor at auction to repay Treasury borrowings and absorb the loss on the sale as a subsidy.

To attract new sources of capital into housing, GNMA was authorized in 1968 to implement a Mortgage-Backed Securities program. The program, begun in 1970, guaranteed payment of the principal and interest on securities issued by financial institutions engaged in mortgage lending and based on pools of government-backed mortgages. These securities are backed by the credit of the United States and provide a high yield, ease of investment, and liquidity. Thus, they have attracted money from sources such as pension funds, which have not traditionally invested in mortgages. In November 1977, GNMA reached the $50 billion mark in guaranteeing mortgage-backed securities,[16] compared to about $450 million in 1970. More than 1.8 million homes have been financed through the program.

FEDERAL HOME LOAN MORTGAGE CORPORATION

The Federal Home Loan Mortgage Corporation (FHLMC or Freddie Mae) was created by Title III of the 1970

---

[15]United States Department of Housing and Urban Development, *Annual Report 1975* (Washington, D.C.: Government National Mortgage Association, 1975), p. 15.

[16]*HUD News,* HUD No. 77–349, Nov. 18, 1977.

Emergency Home Finance Act to produce more funding for home mortgages. The FHLMC is a private corporation and a member of the Federal Home Loan Bank System. The three directors of the Federal Home Loan Bank Board, who are appointed by the President, also serve as directors of the FHLMC. The corporation was initially financed by the sale of $100 million in nonvoting common stock to the Federal Home Loan District Banks. Additional funds have come through the sale of bonds and participation certificates.

The FHLMC plays two main roles in supporting the mortgage market. First, it acts as a financial intermediary and mortgage broker by buying mortgages for its own portfolio or for sale to other investors. Second, it attempts to develop a private secondary market for mortgages that will exist independent of government-sponsored support agencies. The FHLMC may buy housing mortgages from any Federal Home Loan Bank, or member bank, the Federal Savings and Loan Insurance Corporation, or any financial institution with deposits or accounts insured by a U.S. agency.

The FHLMC underwrites each conventional mortgage, inspects all multi-family properties, and spot-checks a large percentage of single-family properties. This insures high-quality mortgages. These mortgages are not directly serviced by the FHLMC.

To make mortgage instruments more competitive, the FHLMC has developed and encouraged the adoption of uniform mortgages and promoted standard underwriting procedures. It has also helped to establish an Automated Mortgage Market Information Network (AM-MINET), an electronic link between mortgage buyers and sellers. Subscribers list the terms of a sale or purchase offer. Actual negotiating is done on a personal basis. The objective is to increase the liquidity of mortgage investments by making them easier to buy and sell. As of October 1976, there were 240 subscribers.[17]

The FNMA and FHLMC perform similar functions. They differ in that the FHLMC usually buys conventional mortgages for which there is no secondary market, while the FNMA initially purchased FHA and VA mortgages alone. Not until July 1970 was it authorized to buy conventional mortgages. The two agencies also differ in whom they buy mortgages from; the FHLMC buys mainly from savings and loan associations, the FNMA from mortgage banker associations.

FEDERAL HOME LOAN BANK SYSTEM

The Federal Home Loan Bank System (FHLBS) was established partly to counter the cyclical variations in the flow of mortgage money by supplementing the resources of its member institutions, mainly savings and loan associations. It was created by the Federal Home Loan Bank Act in 1932. Modeled after the Federal Reserve System, the nation was partitioned into twelve districts, each with its own Federal Home Loan Bank. The system is supervised by the Federal Home Loan Bank Board. The three board members are appointed by the President with Senate approval (Table 4-3).

---

[17]United States General Accounting Office, *Government National Mortgage Association's Secondary Mortgage Market Activities*. CED-77-28, Mar. 8, 1977, p. 2.

TABLE 4-3. Federal Home Loan Bank System

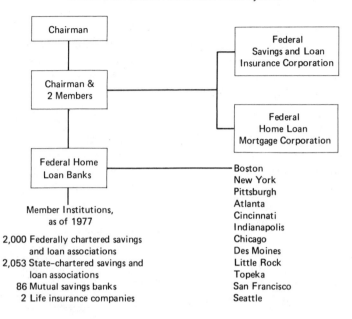

Source: U.S. Department of Housing and Urban Development, *National Housing Policy Review,* based on data from the Federal Home Loan Bank Board; *Savings and Loan Fact Book* (Chicago, Ill.: United States League of Savings Associations, 1978), p. 96.

The FHLBS makes advances or short-term loans to its mortgage-lending member institutions. Advances, financed by the sale of debentures, are usually secured by mortgages as *collateral.* The maximum amount that any FHLBS member may borrow is usually 50 percent of its total savings balances. Advances can be short-term or long-term. Short-term advances mature in twelve months or less and are usually made to cover large withdrawals of deposits. Long-term advances may extend up to ten years and are usually for loan expansion. Thus, the FHLBS serves as a source of funds to equalize seasonal savings inflows and loans. It also lessens the differences between capital-poor and capital-rich areas.

The most important source of funds for the FHLBS is the sale of consolidated obligations in the capital market. Other funds come from the sale of district stock to member institutions, the retained earnings of the institutions, and deposits of member institutions.

Market Imperfections

There are imperfections in the housing market. Major problems include discrimination, redlining, consumer ignorance, and government interference. These keep the market from functioning as it should.

DISCRIMINATION

Discrimination prevents racial or ethnic groups from gaining access to housing. A growing body of literature has examined the impact of race on housing markets. Quigley noted two relationships that are becoming widely accepted:

1. The same housing unit is more expensive in the black ghetto than in the white submarket.
2. The transition from white to black occupancy usually involves an increase in property values.[18]

This statement is supported in studies by: Duncan and Duncan; Ladd; Laurenti; McKenna and Werner; Palmore; Palmore and Howe; Rapkin and Grigsby; and Schietinger.[19] However, Yinger found that white housing prices declined as the proportion of blacks in an area increased.[20]

Studies which support the first relationship include: Duncan and Hauser; James; King and Mieszkowski; Laurenti; McEntire; Muth; Rapkin; Rapkin and Grigsby; Ridker and Henning; and Walzer and Singer.[21] Studies by Bailey[22] and Lapham[23] report contrary findings.

Straszheim reported that discrimination, which keeps blacks out of many neighborhoods, is the most important difference in housing consumption be-

[18]Reprinted by permission of the publisher, from John M. Quigley, "Racial Discrimination and the Housing Consumption of Black Households," in *Patterns of Racial Discrimination, Volume I: Housing,* edited by George M. von Furstenberg, Bennett Harrison, and Ann R. Horowitz (Lexington, Mass.: Lexington Books, D.C. Heath and Company, Copyright 1974, D.C. Heath and Company).

[19]Otis D. Duncan and Beverly Duncan, *The Negro Population of Chicago—A Study in Residential Succession* (Chicago, Ill.: University of Chicago Press, 1957); W.M. Ladd, "The Effect of Integration on Property Values," *American Economic Review,* 52 (September 1962), 801–808; Luigi Laurenti, *Property Values and Race: Studies in Seven Cities* (Los Angeles: University of California Press, 1960); Joseph P. McKenna and Herbert D. Werner, "The Housing Market in Integrating Areas," *The Annals of Regional Science,* 4 (December 1970); 127–133 Erdman Palmore, "Integration and Property Values in Washington, D.C.," *Phylon,* 27 (Spring 1966), 15–20; Erdman Palmore and John Howe, "Residential Integration and Property Values," *Social Problems,* 10 (Summer 1962), 52–55; Chester Rapkin and William Grigsby, *The Demand for Housing in Racially Mixed Areas* (Los Angeles: University of California Press, 1960); and Frederick E. Schietinger, "Race and Residential Properties in Chicago," *Land Economics,* 30 (November 1954), 301–308.

[20]John Yinger, *The Black-White Price Differential in Housing: Some Further Evidence* (Madison, Wis.: Institute for Research on Poverty of the University of Wisconsin, 1975).

[21]Beverly Duncan and Philip M. Hauser, *Housing a Metropolis—Chicago* (Glencoe, Ill.: The Free Press, 1960); Franklin J. James and others, "Race, Profit and Housing Abandonment in Newark," paper presented at the winter meeting of the Econometric Society, Toronto, 1972; A. Thomas King and Peter Mieszkowski, "Racial Discrimination, Segregation, and the Price of Housing," *Journal of Political Economy,* 81 (May/June 1973), 590–606; Luigi Laurenti, *Property Values and Race: Studies in Seven Cities* (Los Angeles: University of California Press, 1960); David McEntire, *Residence and Race* (Los Angeles: University of California Press, 1960; Richard F. Muth, *Cities and Housing* (Chicago: University of Chicago Press, 1969); Chester Rapkin, "Price Discrimination against Negroes in the Rental Housing Market," in *Essays in Urban Land Economics* (Los Angeles: University of California Press, 1966); Chester Rapkin and William Grigsby, *The Demand for Housing in Racially Mixed Areas* (Los Angeles: University of California Press, 1960); Ronald G. Ridker and John A. Henning. "The Determinants of Residential Property Values with Special Reference to Air Pollution," *Review of Economics and Statistics,* 44 (May 1967), 246–57; and Norman Walzer and Dan Singer, "Housing Expenditures in Urban Low-Income Areas," *Land Economics,* 1 (August 1974), 224–31.

[22]Martin J. Bailey, "Effects of Race and Other Demographic Factors on the Values of Single Family Homes," *Land Economics,* 42 (May 1966), 215–20.

[23]Victoria Lapham, "Do Blacks Pay More for Housing?" *Journal of Political Economy,* 79 (November/December 1971), 244–57.

tween blacks and whites.[24] Income is also important, but rising income alone would only increase the price of better-quality housing available to blacks.

Schnare analyzed demographic preferences in relation to housing prices and market segregation. She found that value differences reflect a household's preference in terms of neighborhood mix.[25]

Key concerns in examining reports of housing discrimination are:

1. The definitions of the housing submarket or neighborhood being studied.
2. Quality of housing and neighborhood, services, and amenities.
3. Preferences of blacks and whites.
4. Income.
5. Other demographic characteristics.

REDLINING

When mortgage lenders deny real estate loans or charge higher interest rates for a certain geographic area, the practice is known as redlining. Redlining thus limits the choice of available housing. It also lowers property values as the owners in a redlined area try to sell their homes. When this happens, neighborhood deterioration is increased. For recent legal remedies, see Chapter 13.

CONSUMER IGNORANCE

Buying housing is complex, and buyers often do not completely understand the process. This ignorance hinders a competitive market. Private sellers may also not know what their house is worth, how to sell it, or the kind of contract desired. However, other parties, such as lenders or realtors, should be knowledgeable about local market conditions. (See Chapter 5, for the factors and processes involved in buying housing.)

Externalities

An *externality* is a direct positive or negative effect on one person's welfare as a result of another's activity. Externalities are associated with many activities in the housing market. An increase or decrease in property value resulting from an externality is usually felt immediately only by the owner. After that, the cost is capitalized into the value of the home.

Environmental quality, traffic, airports, and factories are only a few of the things that may influence housing prices. Government action, such as an urban renewal project or a new road, will also have an effect.

An externality may affect land values and housing aspects of real property differently.[26] For example, growing commercialization may make the house less desirable but the land more so for commercial purposes. One externality, housing abandonment, will be examined in more detail here.

[24]Mahlon R. Straszheim, "Racial Discrimination in the Urban Housing Market and Its Effects on Black Housing Consumption," in *Patterns of Racial Discrimination, Vol. 1: Housing,* ed. George M. von Furstenberg, Bennett Harrison, and Ann R. Horowitz, (Lexington, Mass.: Lexington Books, 1974).

[25]Ann B. Schnare, "Racial and Ethnic Price Differentials in an Urban Housing Market," *Urban Studies,* 13 (June 1976), 107–20.

[26]For a theoretical presentation, see Lawrence D. Shall, "A Note on Externalities and Property Valuation," *Journal of Regional Science,* 11 (April 1971), 101–105.

Abandoned housing is vacant housing that is off the market. Both the building and legal rights to the land have been given up. According to Featherman, "Properties vulnerable to abandonment, in areas where abandonment is not yet rife, are most likely to be on streets and in neighborhoods where the housing stock is older and generally either much smaller or much larger than the average house in the neighborhood."[27] Often such properties are storefront residences along commercial strips or on corners of residential blocks. An abandoned building produces negative externalities that affect the use and enjoyment of nearby property. The housing stock is also decreased.

Abandonment occurs in tight housing markets and is sometimes increased by such policies as property taxation and code enforcement.[28] Sometimes it is due to the weeding out of substandard housing; other times to redlining. Tenant vandalism and landlord "milking" of properties are other factors, as are neighborhood stress and interracial tension. Abandoned buildings attract vandals; they may shelter criminal activity or house derelicts. Fires and health hazards are other problems. The depressing effects and expectations of neighborhood deterioration may hasten the process.

All the conditions that lead to aban-donment happen regularly to properties thoughout the housing market. Not every such case causes abandonment. However, the convergence of these events, combined with a weakened market within an area, seem to predispose properties to abandonment.[29]

Nuisance law offers a means of dealing with the harmful externalities of abandonment.[30] Canfield maintains that the owner of an abandoned building that is a health, safety, or fire hazard can be held liable for maintaining a public nuisance. Interference with neighbors' use or enjoyment of their property may also constitute a private nuisance. However, nuisance laws are limited. Owners often cannot pay the damage costs; damages are hard to measure; and litigation costs are high. Still, Canfield notes, "Imposition of liability on the abandoning owner would promote efficiency in the housing market." The owner would be forced to face the costs to society.[31]

Filtering

Housing markets of different income groups are linked by filtering, a way for low-income households to obtain housing. There are two types of filtering. First, a unit may become less valuable or desirable. Second, the unit becomes occupied by poorer and poorer people. The latter is also called residential succession.

One theory is that as new housing units

---

[27]Sandra Featherman, "Early Abandonment, A Profile of Residential Abandonment in Its Early Stages of Development," Papers in Urban Problems, #1, Department of City and Regional Planning (Philadelphia: University of Pennsylvania, March 1976), p. 57.

[28]Richard J. Devins, with Winston O. Rennis and N. Brenda Sims, "The Nature of the Problem," in Where the Lender Looks First: A Case Study of Mortgage Disinvestment in Bronx County, 1960–1970 (New York: National Urban League, 1973).

[29]Featherman, "Early Abandonment," p. 58.

[30]Kenneth S. Canfield, "A Nuisance Law Approach to the Problem of Housing Abandonment," Yale Law Journal, 85 (July 1976), 1130–48.

[31]For another discussion of nuisance law, see James H. Brun, "Abandoned Buildings: Rights and Remedies of Adjoining Landowners," University of Cincinnati Law Review, 44 (1975), 778–95.

are produced, older units filter down to other groups. For this to happen, surplus housing and mobility are needed. If there are no new units, or if older ones are upgraded, then there is no improved housing for households to desire. If households cannot move—whether for economic reasons, a housing shortage, mortgage restrictions, or whatever—then turnover cannot take place. Housing that is available through filtering is usually obsolete, both technologically and stylistically, and physically rundown. Which housing is likely to turn over has been studied by Muth, Brueckner, and Bailey.[32]

Lansing, Clifton, and Morgan concluded that the poor are indirectly affected by the construction of new housing even if they do not occupy the new dwellings.[33] On the other hand, blacks do not benefit from new construction in proportion to their income. The housing market is not divided by family life cycle and social status.

Sands studied chains of moves in two cities in New York State. He found that, starting with new units, most vacancy chains are short, including only one or two existing units, and that income as well as other variables differ little between the family moving in and the one moving out. "As a result, the vacancy chains generated by the most expensive new housing had little effect on the housing needs of low-income families."[34]

---

[32]Richard Muth, "A Vintage Model of the Housing Stock," *Regional Science Association Paper,* Vol. 30, (1973); Jan Brueckner, "The Determinants of Residential Succession," *Journal of Urban Economics,* 4 (Jan. 1977), 45–59; Martin Bailey, "Note on the Economics of Residential Zoning and Urban Renewal," *Land Economics,* 35 (August 1959), 288–92.

[33]John B. Lansing, Charles Wade Clifton, and James N. Morgan, *New Homes and Poor People* (Ann Arbor, Mich.: Institute for Social Research, 1969), 65.

Summary

Housing markets transfer units from producers to consumers. The markets are local due to the fixed nature of housing. They may also be divided by location within the area, price, and structural type. The demand for housing is based on such factors as income, household formation, price of other goods and services, and household composition, size, and preference. The supply of housing depends on such factors as construction costs, mortgage funds, rate of new construction, vacancies, and removals from the stock.

When demand equals supply, the housing market is said to be in equilibrium. Consumers can buy the housing they want at a price they can afford. Producers can build housing at a profit.

Many factors influence market equilibrium. Government regulations limit the activities of market participants.

Credit plays a major role in the housing market. The secondary mortgage market buys mortgages issued by lenders—about one-fourth of all mortgages. Major institutions involved in the secondary market are: Federal Home Loan Bank System, Federal Home Loan Mortgage Corporation, Federal National Mortgage Association, and Government National Mortgage Association.

Terms

budget constraint the entire money income available to be spent.

collude conspire, plot.

---

[34]Gary Sands, "Housing Turnover: Assessing Its Relevance to Public Policy," *American Institute of Planners,* 42 (October 1976), 419–26.

consumption   use of an economic good to satisfy wants.

down payment   the amount of money paid toward the purchase of the house at the closing. Equal to the difference between the sales price and the mortgage loan.

durables   goods with a relatively long life-span.

elasticity   percentage change in quantity demanded in response to 1 percent change in price.

externality   benefit or cost to others that results from activities in the housing market.

inelasticity   unchanging quantity demanded as prices rise.

interest   rent charged for the use of borrowed money, usually a percentage of the principal paid on an annual basis.

lender   issuer of a loan.

utility   satisfaction from a commodity.

Suggested Readings

Arcelus, Francisco, and Allan H. Meltzer, "The Markets for Housing and Housing Services." *Journal of Money, Credit and Banking,* 5 (February 1973), 78–99.

Bagg, Lester H., Carolyn Lebsock, and Richard Lee Ragatz, *The Role of the Absentee Property Owner in Community Development,* ed. Alan J. Hahn and Margaret E. Woods. Cornell Miscellaneous Bulletin. Ithaca, N.Y.: Cornell University, 1973.

Brueckner, Jan, "The Determinants of Residential Succession," *Journal of Urban Economics,* 4, (January 1977), 45–59.

Carliner, Geoffrey, "Income Elasticity of Housing Demand," *The Review of Economics and Statistics,* 60 (November 1973), 528–32.

Coons, Alvin E., and Bert T. Glaze, *Housing Market Analysis and the Growth of Nonfarm Home Ownership.* Bureau of Business Research, Monograph No. 115. Columbus,

Ohio: College of Commerce and Administration, The Ohio State University, 1963.

Courtney, James F., "An Analytical Model of Urban Housing Markets," *Socio-Economical Planning Science,* 8, (1974), 249–56.

deLeeuw, Frank, and Nkanta F. Ekanem, *The Demand for Housing: A Review of Cross-Section Evidence.* Washington, D.C.: The Urban Institute, 1971.

——— and others, *The Web of Urban Housing.* Washington, D.C.: The Urban Institute, 1975.

Duesenbury, J.S., and H. Kisten, "The Role of Demand in the Economic Structures," in *Studies in the Structure of the American Economy,* ed. Wassely Leontief. New York: Oxford University Press, 1953.

Gelfand, Jack E., "The Credit Elasticity of Lower-Middle Income Housing Demand," *Land Economics,* 42 (November 1966), 464–72.

Gillingham, Robert F., *Place-To-Place Rent Comparison Using Hedonic Quality Adjustment Techniques.* BLS Staff Paper #8 Washington, D.C.: U.S. Government Printing Office, 1975.

Kain, John F., and John M. Quigley, "Housing Market Discrimination, Homeownership, and Savings Behavior," *The American Economic Review,* 62 (June 1972), 263–77.

Larkin, Edward W., "Redlining: Remedies For Victims of Urban Disinvestment," *Fordham Urban Law Journal,* 5 (Fall 1976), 83–102.

Lee, Tong Hun, "Demand for Housing: A Cross-Section Analysis," *Review of Economics and Statistics,* 45 (May 1963), 190–96.

———, "The Stock Demand Elasticities of Non-Farm Housing," *Review of Economics and Statistics,* 46, (February 1964), 82–89. 82–89.

Muth, Richard F., "The Demand for Non-Farm Housing," in *The Demand for Durable Goods,* ed. Arnold C. Harberger, p. 96. Chicago: University of Chicago Press, 1960.

Olsen, Edgar O., "A Competitive Theory of the Housing Market," *The American Economic Review,* 59 (September 1969), 612–21.

Reid, Margaret, *Housing and Income.* Chicago: University of Chicago Press, 1962.

Schnare, Ann B., and Raymond J. Struyk, "Segmentation in Urban Housing Markets," *Journal of Urban Economics,* 3 (April 1976), 146–66.

Searing, Daniel A., "Discrimination in Home Finance," *Notre Dame Lawyer,* 48 (June 1973), 1113–44.

Smith, Lawrence B., "A Sectoral Econometric Study of the Postwar Residential Housing Market: An Opposite View," *Journal of Political Economy,* 78 (March/April 1970), 268–78.

Smolensky, Eugene, Selwyn Becker, and Harvey Molotch, "The Prisoner's Dilemma and Ghetto Expansion," *Land Economics,* 44 (November 1968), 419–30.

Stokes, Charles J., and Ernest M. Fisher, *Housing Market Performance.* New York: Holt, Rinehart & Winston, 1976.

Uhler, Russell S., "The Demand for Housing: An Inverse Probability Approach," *Review of Economics and Statistics,* 50 (February 1968), 129–34.

Vaughn, Garrett A., "Sources of Downward Bias in Estimating the Demand Income Elasticity for Urban Housing, *Journal of Urban Economics,* 3 (January 1976), 45–56.

von Furstenberg, George M., Bennett Harrison, and Ann R. Horowitz, *Patterns of Racial Discrimination,* vol. 1, "Housing." Lexington, Mass.: Lexington Books, 1974.

HOUSING CONSUMPTION AND PRODUCTION

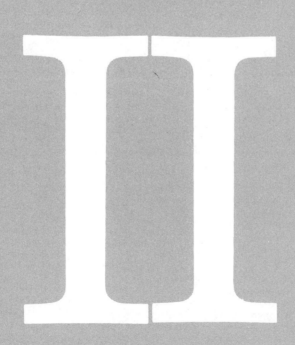

HOME OWNERSHIP

1. WHEN IS HOMEOWNERSHIP THE OPTIMUM CHOICE?

2. WHAT FACTORS INFLUENCE THE TENURE DECISION?

3. HOW DO PURCHASE PRICE AND OCCUPANCY COSTS AFFECT AFFORDABILITY?

4. WHAT IS THE ROLE OF A HOUSING WARRANTY TODAY AND IN THE FUTURE?

Many consumers have the choice between renting or owning housing. This is called *tenure choice* or decision. The United States has a very high rate of home ownership, which has grown steadily.[1] In 1890 only a little over one-third of all nonfarm homes were owned. Since 1950, homeowners have exceeded renters.[2] Today nearly two-thirds of all units are owned.[3] Ownership rates may continue to increase, but at a much slower rate than in the past thirty years.

From 1940 to 1976, the proportion of owned single-family detached homes remained fairly constant: about 85 percent.[4] Further, 40 percent of owner occupied homes were built between 1960 and 1976 and another 21 percent between 1950 and 1959.[5]

[1]The United Nations has issued figures showing that India, Israel, Australia, Mexico, Tunisia, South Korea, the Philippines, Pakistan, and Mongolia have higher ratios of owner-occupancy. *HUD Newsletter,* 8 (December 1977,) p. 2.

[2]Decennial Census data, Bureau of the Census.

[3]U.S. Department of Commerce, Bureau of the Census, *Current Housing Reports,* Final Report H-150-75, and U.S. Department of Housing and Urban Development, *1977 Statistical yearbook,* (Washington, D.C.: U.S. Government Printing Office, 1978) p. 350 and *Annual Housing Survey: 1976.* Part A, "General Housing Characteristics for the United States and Regions," (Washington, D.C.: U.S. Government Printing Office, 1978), p. 1.

[4]U.S. Department of Commerce, Bureau of the Census, *Sixteenth Census of the United States 1940: Housing,* Vol. II, General Characteristics (Washington, D.C.: U.S. Government Printing Office, 1943), p. 10; *1950 Census of Housing,* Vol. I, Part 1, 1953, pp. 1–3; *1960 Census of Housing,* Vol. I, Part 1, 1963, pp. 1–16; *1970 Census of Housing,* Vol. I, Part 1, December 1972, pp. 1–242; *Annual Housing Survey: 1976,* Table A-1, p. 1.

[5]U.S. Department of Commerce, Bureau of the Census, *Annual Housing Survey: 1976,* Table A-1, p. 2.

Most owned homes are single-family units.

This chapter analyzes the factors involved in the decision to rent or buy, the process of buying a home, the legal aspects of ownership, and buyer protection.

Advantages and Disadvantages of Ownership

Both ownership and renting have advantages and disadvantages. The advantage of one form of tenure is often the disadvantage of the other. These advantages and disadvantages can be divided into economic, social, and psychological categories (Table 5-1).

Ownership is an investment. Its value depends on the quality of real estate available, knowledge of the real estate market, degree of risk, liquidity desired, return on capital and capital gain or loss, and income tax situation. Opportunity costs must also be considered; that is, how would the homeowner invest his or her money if it was not invested in the home, and what benefits would accrue? The down payment, for example, could instead be invested in stocks or bonds. These lost gains are part of the costs of ownership.

The following steps will help to evaluate the economic aspects of the available alternatives:

1. *Establish the cost of owning a particular unit.*

   a. Determine the purchase price.

   b. Determine the terms of financing.

TABLE 5-1. Advantages and Disadvantages of Home Ownership

CATEGORY	ADVANTAGES OF OWNERSHIP	DISADVANTAGES OF OWNERSHIP
Economic	Ability to build up equity	Large sum of money often needed for a down payment
Psychological	Interest on the mortgage and property taxes deductible from federal or state income taxes	Possible depreciation in value due to physical deterioration or obsolescence
	Often appreciates in value	High costs of moving
	Freedom to change the environment to meet one's needs	
	Ability to use one's own labor to provide satisfaction and add to the economic value of the home	
	Owned units are usually larger than rented units, with more space	
Social	Family status and pride	Peer Pressure
	Feeling of belonging to the community	

c. Estimate gross and net monthly costs. Gross costs include mortgage payment, property taxes, insurance, maintenance costs, and utilities. To obtain net costs, deduct from gross costs the tax saving received from mortgage interest and property taxes.

2. *Estimate the gain or loss if the house is sold.* The costs of selling the house and the balance owed on the mortgage must be subtracted from the amount received from the sale. Any gain represents a return on equity and appreciation.

3. *Estimate rental costs and savings.* The amount of money available for a down payment and for closing costs but not used in renting may be invested. Estimate returns received over time from investing the money. Remember that interest and dividends are taxable as income. The net amount of money received on the investment is then subtracted from the projected net proceeds of the house sale.

"For short periods of ownership, 1 to 3 years, the costs of buying and selling a house can use up much or all of the equity acquired. Savings not used for down payment and settlement costs by renting, plus the investment return of these savings, in many cases will equal or exceed the net proceeds from buying and then selling a house."[6] For longer periods—ten or twenty years—renters may need to supplement their initial savings with regular monthly deposits to keep up with owners.

From an investment viewpoint, the renter, over time, can spend an amount for rent equal to the difference between his or her investment program and the homeowner's outlay. Of course, the renter may not be able to find housing in a given area for this price. It is very difficult to obtain costs on owned and rented units of the same quality and quantity.

[6]U.S. Department of Labor, Bureau of Labor Statistics, *Rent or Buy? Evaluating Alternatives in the Shelter Market,* Bulletin 1823, (Washington, D.C.: U.S. Government Printing Office, 1974), p. 23.

Factors Influencing the Choice to Own

Many factors influence the decision to buy a home. These include personal preferences and needs, cost, available resources, income, race, household size, composition and stage in the life cycle, education, and occupation, as well as the relative price of homes and tax considerations. Many of these factors change over time. Thus, for various reasons the housing unit may or may not reflect the household's current conditions and needs.

Housing changes are usually related to the life cycle. A single person or couple tends to rent.[7] When children arrive, the couple buys a small house; when more space is needed and income is available, they buy a larger one. Then, when children leave, they rent a smaller apartment. Other motives for moving include occupational change or a desire to improve one's life style, lower housing costs, move to a more convenient location, or move to a prestigious neighborhood. "Household income affects the timing of this sequence of choices and the level of expenditures more than the size of unit occupied."[8]

GENERAL FACTORS

According to Struyk and Marshall, young families with small savings who wish to buy a home usually depend on income increases to provide the down payment.[9] Ownership by elderly households, on the other hand, is generally based on decisions made in the past, often when earnings were higher. These researchers also found that:

1. Occupation influences tenure choice through income and also through social pressure to live as one's peers do.
2. Federal tax subsidies are important in tenure choice only for younger husband–wife households.
3. Family size is important for home ownership in husband-wife households.
4. Family growth and other pressures make home ownership more important for many middle-aged families than for younger ones, and an established earnings record makes financing more feasible.
5. For the wealthiest single white people, permanent income decreases home ownership.[10]
6. The influence of income on the probability of home ownership is different for white and black households.[11]

---

[7]The life cycle as a factor in consumption patterns has been studied by M.H. David, *Family Composition and Consumption* (Amsterdam: North Holland Publishing Co., 1962); J.B. Lansing and J.N. Morgan, "Consumer Finances Over the Life Cycle," in *The Life Cycle and Consumer Behavior,* ed. L. Clark (New York: New York University Press, 1955); J.B. Lansing and L. Kish, "Family Life Cycle as an Independent Variable," *American Sociological Review,* 22 (October 1957), 512–19; and Kevin F. McCarthy, "The Household Life Cycle and Housing Choices," Rand Corporation papers, mimeo (Santa Monica, Calif., 1976), p. 5565.

[8]McCarthy, "Household Life Cycle," p. 34.

[9]Raymond J. Struyk and Sue A. Marshall, "Income and Urban Home Ownership, *The Review of Economics and Statistics,* 62 (February 1975) 24.

[10]Raymond J. Struyk and Sue A. Marshall, "The Determinants of Household Home Ownership," *Urban Studies,* 11 (October 1974), 297–99.

[11]Raymond J. Struyk and Sue A. Marshall, *Income and Urban Home Ownership,* an Urban Institute Paper, 208–19 (Washington, D.C.: The Urban Institute, September 1973), p. 22.

In early research, home ownership was found to depend on the money for a down payment, income available for servicing the loan, adjusted income, and family space needs as determined by family size.[12]

Carliner found that married couples are more likely to own than persons who were never married or are now single.[13] Households that own are more likely to be white than black, older rather than younger, larger and with more income, and in small communities rather than large ones.

Using 1959 data, Duker reported that families in which the wife works, are less likely to own homes and more likely to own lower-valued homes than families in which only the husband works.[14] They also have lower rentals than one-income families of similar income and age. Whether these results are true nearly two decades later is unknown.

Follain and Struyk report these ownership patterns:

1. Increased opportunity as income rises.

2. Less home ownership for black or Spanish households.

3. Increased home ownership rates with age and above-average rates among the elderly.

4. Higher home ownership rates for husband-wife households than for one-person households and unmarried two-person households.[15]

MOBILITY

Recent movers prefer the same type of tenure when moving.[16] About two-thirds of the households with the same head who owned their previous homes moved to another owned home. Households that changed tenure are much more likely to shift from renting to owning than the reverse.

The head of husband-wife families who moved was younger than all husband-wife families. Families that have moved recently are larger in size and have a higher income than owners who did not move.

Recent households that move are less likely than all households to live in single-family permanent homes and more likely to live in mobile homes. About 75 percent of the units occupied by recent mover/owners are single-family homes, compared with 87 percent for all owners. On the other hand, mobile home occupancy accounts for 18 percent of the recent mover/owners, compared to 6.7 percent of all owners. The proportion of units with complete private plumbing facilities is higher for recent movers who own than for all other owners. Generally,

---

[12]John R. Malone, "The Capital Expenditure for Owner-Occupied Housing: A Study of Determinants," *Journal of Business,* 39 (June 1966), 363.

[13]Geoffrey Carliner, "Determinants of Home Ownership," *Land Economics,* 1 (May 1974), 110–12.

[14]Jacob M. Duker, "Housewife and Working-Wife Families: A Housing Comparison," *Land Economics,* XLVI (May 1970), 142.

[15]James R. Follain and Raymond J. Struyk, "Encouraging Homeownership: A Complex Problem Requiring a Non-monolithic Approach," Paper presented at a Joint Meeting of the American Economic Association and American Real Estate and Urban Economic Association, Chicago, August 1978.

[16]U.S. Department of Commerce, Bureau of the Census, *Annual Housing Survey: 1976, United States and Regions,* Part D, "Housing Characteristics of Recent Movers," Series H-150 76D (Washington, D.C.: U.S. Government Printing Office, January 1978.)

recent movers have smaller housing than all occupied units. Among recent homeowners who have moved, the three-or-more-bedroom house is most popular. Recent movers have more valuable homes than all homeowners.

HUSBAND–WIFE ROLES

Husbands and wives play many different roles in the decision to buy a home. Seven elements of the housing decision were examined: decision to move, to rent or to buy; floor plan; style, price, location, and size.

Husbands and wives generally agreed in their perceptions of these varying roles; the exception was the floor plan, for which husbands are more likely to report that their wives dominated. "For every element of the housing decision, a considerable majority of both husbands and wives report that they have equal influence in the decision: When one spouse had relatively more influence in a decision husbands and wives tend to agree that the husband was dominant in the decision to rent or buy and in the price decision, while the wife was dominant in the floor plan, style and size decision."[17] Age, education, length of time married, and income were not found to be closely related to dominance or agreement in the decisions.

GOVERNMENT ASSISTANCE

Home ownership has been promoted by the federal government through tax incentives. These incentives have mainly benefited middle- and upper-income households. Low-income households have been relatively neglected. Federal aid for would-be owners was provided for in Section 235 of the 1968 National Housing Act, but the program did not work as expected. Naive low-income participants had severe problems. Many poorly constructed and poorly rehabilitated homes were bought by unsophisticated buyers at inflated prices.[18]

About 50 percent of the states have programs to assist home buyers. Most of these programs are aimed at moderate-income families who cannot meet financing costs in the private market. For a description of selected programs, see Chapter 12.

Buying a Home

The consumer is faced with many decisions in the buying process, beginning with the type of unit desired and the price he or she is able to pay.

PURCHASE PRICE

Some rules of thumb have been developed to determine the price a consumer can afford:

1. Monthly housing costs should not exceed 25 percent of monthly pay. For example, if take-home pay is $600, housing expenses should not exceed $150.

2. Total monthly costs of housing

---

[17]Gary M. Munsinger, Jean E. Weber, and Richard W. Hanson, "Joint Home Purchasing Decisions by Husbands and Wives, *Journal of Consumer Research*, 1 (March 1975), 60–66.

[18]"Federal Compensation for Victims of the 'Homeownership for the Poor' Program," *Yale Law Journal*, 84 (December 1974), 294–323.

should not be greater than one week's pay.

3. Purchase price should not exceed 2.5 times the annual income.

4. Net income (take-home pay) minus expenses (including savings) equals the amount of money available for housing.

These guidelines are based on the assumption that the percentage of income needed for food, clothing, taxes, transportation, and so on remains relatively stable over time. However, in today's inflationary economy, with prices of goods rising at different rates, these guidelines may not be suitable. The Consumer Price Index (CPI) shows that housing costs rose faster than all items combined but slower than food and slightly slower than medical care. (Table 2-3) Costs of clothing, transportation, personal care, and other goods and services all rose more slowly than housing.

HOME OWNERSHIP COSTS

Housing affordability is directly related to total costs as well as initial price. "Components that account for a large portion of total initial cost can account for major shares of cost increase, even though they increase at less rapid rates than other items."[19] Home purchase prices represent the largest percentage increase in total costs. Thus, they are an important factor in increasing the cost of home ownership.[20]

Median sales prices increased from $23,400 in 1970 to $55,700 in 1978 or 138 percent; average sales prices increased from $26,600 to $62,500 or 135 percent (Table 5-2). New housing must

---

[19] Neil S. Mayer, *Homeownership: The Changing Relationship of Costs, Incomes, and Possible Federal Roles* (Washington, D.C.: U.S. Government Printing Office, January 1977), p. 27.

[20] Ibid., p. 29, and U.S. Department of Housing and Urban Development, *Housing in the Seventies*, (Washington, D.C.: U.S. Government Printing Office, 1974), p. 209.

TABLE 5-2. Sales Price and Percentage Distribution of New One-Family Houses Sold

YEAR	MEDIAN SALES PRICE	AVERAGE SALES PRICE	UNDER $30,000	$30,000 TO $34,999	$35,000 TO $39,999	$40,000 TO $49,999	$50,000 TO $59,999	$60,000 AND OVER
1970	23,400	26,600	71	10	7	8	4a	NA
1971	25,200	28,300	66	11	9	8	6a	NA
1972	27,600	30,500	59	13	11	10	7a	NA
1973	32,500	35,500	41	17	14	15	12a	NA
1974	35,900	38,900	28	19	16	19	17a	NA
1975	39,300	42,600	20	14	18	23	12	13
1976	44,200	48,000	12	11	16	26	16	20
1977	48,800	54,200	7	9	13	24	19	28
1978	55,700	62,500			17b	21	19	41

a Includes houses with sales price over $60,000.

b Includes houses with sales price under $40,000.

Source: U.S. Department of Commerce, Bureau of the Census, *Construction Reports:* "Characteristics of New One-Family Homes," Series C-25; and, "New One Family Houses Sold and For Sale," C 25-79, (April 1979) p. 6.

meet local building codes and zoning requirements. New one-family homes sold in 1970 and 1977 showed certain changes. In 1977 the average price per square foot of floor area for new one-family houses sold, excluding the value of an improved lot, was $25.35; the median price per square foot was $24.75. The average price per square foot has increased 78 percent since 1970 and the median price 77 percent.

Home purchase price and interest rate determine mortgage payments.[21] Property taxes increased from 1970 to 1976, varying from 39 to 87 percent.[22] The former may be more accurate for unsold houses and the latter for homes which changed owners. Fuel and utility costs have risen rapidly since 1970, increasing faster than incomes and all items. Maintenance and repair costs have also increased rapidly from 1970 to 1976. Insurance is the smallest occupancy cost to be discussed. Thus, although it increased rapidly from 1970, its impact is less.

Changes in ownership costs affect first-time buyers, repurchasers, and nonmovers differently.[23] The first-time buyer faces all the cost increases—changes in sales price, interest rate, insurance, maintenance and repairs, and utilities. Thus, the impact of cost increases for single-family houses has been greater for families of average income or less who want to buy homes for the first

time.[24] The family that already owns a home usually benefits from appreciation at the time of its sale even though the new home may cost more and interest rates may be higher. The family that does not move faces increased costs only in household operation. Case reported that "examination of individual case reports indicates that occupancies under five years and over twenty years show extreme variations in average annual costs. This seems to reflect the heavy initial outlays by new owners and the forgetfulness, in reporting expenditures, of long-established occupants. . . ."[25]

SOURCES OF INFORMATION

There are many sources of information on the availability of houses for sale. One primary source is newspapers.[26] Another is the real estate agent or *broker*, who contracts with the *seller* on a *commission* basis to sell the home. The agent will know the area and be able to do some preliminary screening. The agent's contract with the seller may be:

1. *A multiple listing*. All members of the listing service receive notice of the property and may sell it. The com-

---

[21]Other factors play a role, such as down payment and term. See Chapter 6 for a discussion.

[22]For details, see Neil Mayer, *Housing Occupancy Costs: Current Problems and Means to Relieve Them* (Washington, D.C.: The Urban Institute, June 1978).

[23]Ibid.

[24]Bernard J. Frieden and Arthur P. Solomon, with David L. Birch and John Pitkin, *The Nation's Housing: 1975–1985.* (Cambridge, Mass.: Joint Center for Urban Studies of the Massachusetts Institute of Technology and Harvard University, April 1977), p. 103.

[25]Fred E. Case, *Cash Outlays and Economic Costs of Homeownership,* Real Estate Research Program, Bureau of Business and Economics Research (Los Angeles: University of California, 1957), p. 9.

[26]Donald J. Hempel, *The Role of the Real Estate Broker in the Home Buying Process* (Storrs, Conn.: Center for Real Estate and Urban Economic Studies, 1969), p. 3.

mission is split with the listing broker.

2. *An open listing.* Several agencies have the right to sell the property, with the agency making the sale receiving the entire commission.

3. *An exclusive listing.* This gives one agency the privilege of selling the property. This may or may not exclude the owner.

Real estate salespeople who call themselves *realtors* are members of the National Association of Real Estate Boards (NAREB), which establishes standards of conduct and operation and provides educational programs for its members.

Friends, neighbors and employers may know of houses coming on the market or currently for sale. Walks or drives through an area or town can help locate houses for sales and give buyers an opportunity to assess the outside of the house and the neighborhood.

Belkin and his associates studied the length of time a house was on the market (TOM).[27] TOM was defined as the time from the first listing to first deposit receipt. The researchers found "that time on the market is an important descriptor of market behavior."[28] Brokers do a good job of negotiating list price. Within submarkets based on geography, price, and buyer search patterns, a large percentage of properties sold close to list price and within a short time on the market. Also, all homes in a properly priced submarket have an equal chance of being sold the next week regardless of how long they have been on the market. House features are not a good predictor of time on the market, although some house features "were consistently correlated with longer time on the market, indicating consistency in list pricing errors."[29]

KIND OF HOUSE

Another choice that must be made immediately is whether to buy a new or an older house. With an older home, price and value are established and the neighborhood is known. Construction defects are easier to spot since the house has already settled. Landscaping has been done. Depending on age, though, a unit may be due for major repairs, such as roof or heating system replacements. Features of the house may also be dated.

The quality of a new house depends greatly on the reputation of the *builder* and the kinds and quality of materials and workmanship this person is known to use. The length of time a builder has been in business, and satisfaction of previous customers, are two guides to quality. Maintenance costs of a new house are often lower but operating costs are unknown. Often streets, facilities, and houses are seen only on a drawing board, making the neighborhood harder to visualize. But some new homes are covered by one of the Home Owner Warranty Programs (see page 109).

INVESTIGATING THE COMMUNITY

Buying a home includes buying the goods and services of the community as well. The house may be located in a foggy valley, on a windy hill, or near the ocean,

---

[27]Jacob Belkin, Donald J. Hempel, and Dennis W. McLeavey, "An Empirical Study of Time on Market Using Multidimensional Segmentation of Housing Markets," *American Real Estate and Urban Economics Association Journal,* 4 (Fall 1976), 74.

[28]Ibid.

[29]Ibid.

with soil erosion potential. Schools, police, and fire protection are also purchased. The quality and location of health services are important for many people. Taxing and *assessment* policies influence home ownership costs as well as the quality and quantity of services provided.

INVESTIGATING THE NEIGHBORHOOD

In judging the quality of a neighborhood, its physical, social, and economic factors must be considered. Some physical features to keep in mind are location and nearness to work, shopping, schools, public transportation, and recreational facilities; the architecture and quality of housing in the neighborhood; and availability of utilities and public services.

Social factors to consider include age, type, and size of families, cultural and civic interests, and living habits. Information on the extent of development, per-

centage of turnover, taxation and assessment rates, price range of housing in the neighborhood, and zoning or deed restrictions is also important.

Questions a prospective buyer needs to ask include:

1. Are neighbors likely to be compatible with your tastes and life style?
2. Are lots or units arranged to suit the family's life style?
3. Is the area physically attractive?
4. Will nearby sources of noise, smoke, soot, dust and odors affect the environment or endanger the family?
5. Is the area free from hazards, such as gas or oil tanks and streams that might overflow?

INSPECTING THE EXTERIOR

The building should be suited to the surroundings, attractive, and well designed and constructed. The siding should be durable and in good condition. All masonry or brick should be free of cracks. The prospective buyer should check on the kind, age, and condition of any painted surfaces. The roofing material should be known, as well as its age and condition.

Entryways should be sheltered and well lighted. They should be large enough for several persons to enter the house together. Storm doors and weatherstripping reduce energy usage.

The *lot* should be adequate for individual needs. The driveway, walks, patios, and porch should be convenient and well kept. Landscaping makes a home attractive and prevents soil erosion. Trash collection and disposal facilities should be convenient.

INSPECTING THE DWELLING

The interior of the house should be examined carefully by the prospective buyer or by an inspection service. Major areas of concern are size, layout, construction, utility systems, and safety and security.

The size of the home needed depends on family size, activities, and the kinds of furniture and equipment currently owned.

The layout should be logical, with separate areas for living, working, and sleeping. Rooms should be conveniently related to each other—entry to living room, dining room to kitchen, bedrooms to baths. Rooms should be located to take advantage of sun and shade. Outdoor space should be convenient to indoor space.

Housing construction adds to livability as well as to the investment value and economic return. Construction includes carpentry, insulation, freedom from termites, easy-to-care-for materials, and equipment. The functioning of the water, plumbing, heating, and electrical systems is vital. Fireplaces, air conditioning, carpeting, and appliances are often included as part of the home.

INSPECTION SERVICE

In examining the house, prospective buyers use an inspection service, often a firm of engineers or architects. They will provide a written report on the structural and mechanical components of a house. There is a fee, often based on the value of the house.

An inspection report does not establish value; it establishes condition. The Nationwide Real Estate Inspectors Service, in a random sampling of fifty inspection reports of one-family homes, found an average of 5.1 costly defects per home inspected.[30] Defects which occurred in 40 percent or more of the homes inspected were wet basements, roof leaks or deteriorated roofing, drainage and grading problems, and deteriorated hot water systems.

APPRAISAL

An *appraisal* helps the buyer establish the price to pay for a house. It is an expert, impartial opinion of the *market value* of the property based on the factors that make up the current behavior of the local market. The local chapters of the Society of Real Estate Appraisers, American So-

---

[30]Nationwide Real Estate Inspectors Service, Inc., "Study of Major Defects in a Random Sampling of Fifty Inspection Reports of One Family Homes," (New York, 1975).

Cracked foundation.

ciety of Appraisers, American Institute of Real Estate Appraisers, or local financial institutions can help buyers choose an appraiser.

An appraisal report on a residential house will include a method of computation. Many appraisers use two methods: replacement cost and comparative sales

Carefully examine the dwelling interior.

approach. The replacement cost approach establishes value based on what it would cost to replace (build) the housing unit today. The comparative sales approach establishes value based on the selling price of similar dwellings. A third method, capitalization of income, is difficult to apply to owner-occupied housing. The report will also include a brief description and analysis of the property, an analysis of the neighborhood, and comparative sales (if used).

Besides being useful in buying a house, an appraisal may also help an owner to sell a house, protest against property taxes, negotiate with a government agency that is taking the property, and verify damage claims for insurance purposes.

NEGOTIATING THE PURCHASE

Once a house has been chosen, the prospective buyer makes a purchase offer in writing to the seller. The *purchase contract* or *sales contract* is usually written up by a real estate agent or lawyer. The sales contract, also known as an offer, *binder*, or earnest money agreement, is a legally binding document. It specifies down payment; title conveyance; fees to be paid and by whom; deposit amount; conditions under which the buyer or seller may void the contract; date of closing and date of possession; legal description of the property and other items being sold; payment provisions and conditions and names of the parties involved. Everything is negotiable, and considerable bargaining may take place.

Usually a purchase offer depends on the buyer obtaining financing. The transfer of title takes place on the date of closing. The loan process is discussed in Chapter 6.

Legal Aspects

It is important to understand the legal basis for the ownership of housing or *real property*. Throughout recorded history, some nations have recognized individual rights and interest in land. Sources of real property law in the United States vary with location. English, French, and Spanish laws have been influential in different areas.

Real property, or land, is generally defined to include the soil, whatever grows on it, and the space above and below it, as well as any attached permanent structures (Figure 5-1). Any articles attached to real property are known as *fixtures* and may then be considered *realty*. The legal description of real estate must identify the property precisely.

ESTATES

Interest in real property is legally expressed in terms of *estates*. These give the holder the exclusive right to control the property. There are five classes of estates: estates in *fee*; for *life*; for years; at will; and at sufferance. Estates in fee and for life are *freehold estates;* the rest are leasehold estates. The latter will be discussed in the chapter on renting.

An *estate in fee simple* is the highest possible interest to be held in land. It gives the owner unlimited rights over the land.

When the owner dies, the property will be passed on according to the owner's will—or, if no will exists, as state laws dictate. The owner has legal title and exclusive right to possession.

A conventional *life estate* is created by *deed* or will and gives an individual use of the property during his or her lifetime. Legal life estates are created by statutes and include *dower*—life estate to which a widow is entitled; *curtesy*—common-law right of a husband to a life estate in land owned by his wife; and community property—a statutory estate which in some states substitutes for dower or *curtesy*.

TENANCY

An estate may be owned by an individual or shared—for example, by a husband and wife. Individual ownership is known as an estate in severalty. Shared ownership may be by joint tenancy, tenancy by the entirety, or tenancy in common.

Joint tenancy is explicitly stated in a legal document, usually the deed. Each joint tenant (owner) has the same interest and each is considered to own the whole property, subject to the interest of the other owners. All have equal rights to possess and use the property. On an owner's death, the other owners receive his or her share.

Tenancy by the entirety exists only in some states and between husband and wife for property acquired jointly after marriage. Neither spouse may convey his or her interest to another party.

Tenancy in common gives each owner separate, undivided shares in the property which may be sold, pledged, or willed.

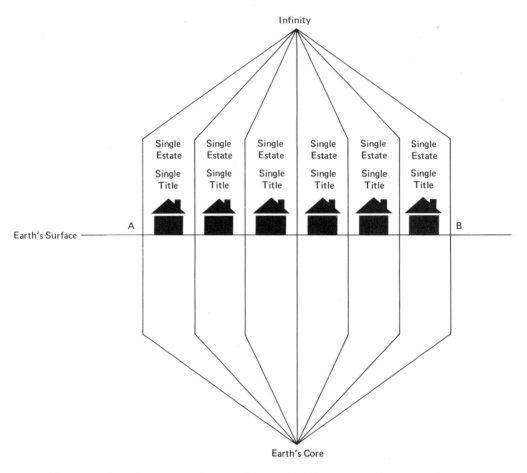

Infinity

| Single Estate | Single Estate | Single Estate | Single Estate | Single Estate | Single Estate |
| Single Title | Single Title | Single Title | Single Title | Single Title | Single Title |

A   B

Earth's Surface

Earth's Core

Figure 5-1. What Real Property Includes. [*Source:* U.S. Department of Housing and Urban Development, *Questions About Condominiums,* HUD-365-F, (Washington, D.C.: U.S. Government Printing Office, June 1974, p. 22.]

OWNERSHIP LIMITATIONS

An owner's use of the property may be limited. One limitation is an *easement,* which gives the right to use some portion of the land to another, often a utility company. Another limitation is a *lien,* which a creditor holds against the property to secure payment of a debt. This may be a mortgage lien, a tax lien, *a mechanics lien,* or a *judgment lien.*

All land in the United States is subject to certain government limitations on ownership:

1. Police power.
2. Eminent domain.
3. Taxation.
4. *Escheat* to the state.

The police power is the community's power to restrict the use of land to protect the well-being of its citizens. It is the legal basis for city planning, zoning, and rent control. Eminent domain is the power of a community to take an individual's property for public use when necessary, by due process and with compensation to the owner. It is used in highway development, urban renewal, and dam development, among others. Property taxes established by communities must be paid; otherwise, the property will be taken and sold to meet the obligations. Escheat provides that land reverts to the state if no heirs can be found. Thus, when buying a home, an owner purchases a bundle of legal rights—to use or not use the property, to lease all or part, to sell or not sell, and to give the property away.

TITLE

The *title* to the property being bought is as important as the house or lot. The title provides evidence of ownership and may vary in quality. A *clear title* is not affected by any liens, spouse's rights, or easements. Before the property changes hands, a *title search* is made to discover problems. A *cloud on the title* or title defect does not necessarily stop the sale. The owner or lending institution may receive an *abstract of title* at the closing.

A *title insurance* policy may be obtained to cover some of the risks. A single premium is paid, usually at the closing. The policy is not transferable. Risks usually covered include: title belonging to someone else; title impaired by defects, liens, or other encumbrances; and lack of access to and from the land. Unmarketability of the title may also be covered. Any problems found in the title search may be noted and excluded from

coverage. Other exclusions may be boundary line disputes, claims, liens, or tax assessments not in public records. Sometimes, for an additional premium, an exclusion may be covered.

Title insurance began in 1876 after a buyer lost his investment in the property because of a lien. The Supreme Court of Pennsylvania dismissed the action to recover the loss, ruling that it occurred without negligence by anyone.

The American Land Title Association, made up of member companies who search, review, and insure land titles, is one of the largest title insurers. Chicago Title and Trust Company is another. In some states, a lawyer guarantees the title.

DEED

The title is conveyed by the *deed*, a written statement transferring title from the *grantor* to the *grantee*. The two major kinds of deeds are:

1. *Warranty deed.* Transfers the seller's rights and warrants the buyer against claims against the title. However, the seller may not be available or be financially capable of meeting the warranty.
2. *Quitclaim deed.* Provides no guarantees by the seller and conveys only such rights as are possessed.

Most deeds are recorded at the courthouse. The *Torrens system* of land registration is also used in many states. Under this system, when the landowner fills out an application, the court may, after appropriate proceedings, order a certificate of title issued.[31] With some exceptions,

---

[31]*Black's Law Dictionary,* rev. 4th ed. (St. Paul, Minn.: West Publishing Co., 1968), p. 1660.

the *Torrens certificate* is proof of the applicant's estate in the land.

Many deeds contain *restrictions* on the use of the property. The restrictions may regulate the type, size, price, use, or location of improvements. There may also be a *reversionary clause* that provides for title to revert to the party imposing the restrictions.

Warranty of Habitability for Home Buyers

The prospective owner can reduce the risk of costly repairs after buying a house. If the buyer is competent to determine technical and structural components, personal inspection may be enough. If not, the buyer can hire a professional inspector. Both of these methods help the buyer decide on the price to offer for the house. Some buyers may choose a warranty or insurance plan which protects them against unexpected repair costs. Inspection and warranty plans are becoming more popular. For this reason, many private and public programs have been developed. They generally include a house inspection before purchase or a warranty.

Since the complexity and cost are greater for a home than for an automobile or major appliance, which have warranties, the need for a warranty on housing is greater. Development, use, and legal support for a warranty of habitability would benefit all buyers and sellers.

LEGAL PROTECTION

During the first half of the twentieth century, the policy was *caveat emptor*: "Let the buyer beware." Since then, according to Kempner, at least seven theories may help the person who buys a defective new home:tort theories of negligence and strict liability, contract theories of breach of express, implied, and statutory warranties; breach of the sales contract, and fraud.[32]

Recent court developments in the implied warranty theory give the first buyer of a new home some legal rights, especially against structural and site defects. Basically, all courts believe that the buyer and the seller do not have the same expertise. Sellers are considered to be more knowledgeable.[33] The courts also recognize that buyers have the right to assume that the house is reasonably fit for use. Some issues which remain unresolved are: What is a reasonable time for defects to show up, and where does the builder's liability stop?

Courts in Ohio, Washington, Illinois, Oklahoma, Colorado, and Louisiana have held that *caveat emptor* does not apply to a house under construction.[34] This ruling has been extended to new houses, first in Colorado and New Jersey, then in other states.[35] In all, at least twenty-three states recognize the existence of implied warranties in the sale of a new house by a

---

[32] Jonathan L. Kempner, "The Home Owners Warranty Program: An Initial Analysis," *Stanford Law Review,* 28 (January 1976), 364.

[33] See Michael B. Bixby, "Let the Seller Beware: Remedies for the Purchase of a Defective Home," *Journal of Urban Law,* 49 (February 1972), 534–64, for a history of cases where the seller is liable and a brief discussion of implied warranty.

[34] Michael Bixby, "Implied Warranty of Habitability: New Right for Home Buyers," *The Clearinghouse Review,* 6 (December 1972), 470.

[35] The states are Alabama, Arkansas, Florida, Idaho, Illinois, Indiana, Kentucky, Louisiana, Michigan, Missouri, North Carolina, Pennsylvania, Rhode Island, South Carolina, South Dakota, Texas, Vermont, Washington, and Wisconsin.

builder-vendor.[36] Still, *caveat emptor* is widespread, and many new home buyers who fail to recognize this have no legal recourse.

Even with legal rights, dollar and time costs may negate action. Each year many construction firms go bankrupt. If all the states enacted implied warranty laws, a maze of court decisions would be unnecessary.[38]

GOVERNMENT PROGRAMS

The 1954 Housing Act required that all new houses bought with mortgages guaranteed by the federal government have a written-one-year builder's warranty.[39] The warranty ensures that a house has been built in "substantial conformity with the plans and specifications." Defects arising from construction that did not conform are the builder's responsibility during the warranty period. There are often differences of opinion on what is a defect and whether the builder substantially conformed to the specifications.

A government program covering *all* housing purchases could force builders to participate, provide more impartiality than an industry program, and be less expensive since it would not be profit oriented. However, government regulation of industry standards and practices has not been very successful. A comprehensive plan could involve substantial economic waste, lag time between a problem and its resolution, and a lot of paperwork. Since such a program would be a political issue, legislation could take years to be enacted. The time needed to set up the program could add further delays.

PRIVATE PROGRAMS

The third alternative is to establish a private insurance program to provide buyer protection. Several plans have already been started.[40] The most widely publicized is the HOW—Home Owner Warranty Program—established by the National Association of Home Builders. The National Association of Realtors (NAR) also offers have protection programs through NAR approved companies: Homestead Inspection Warranty Company, Minnehoma Insurance Company, Certified Homes Corporation, St. Paul Fire and Marine Insurance Company, Triad Home Protection Plan, Pacific Cal-West and American Home Shield. The National Home Warranty Association and the NAR program account for 90 percent of the total U.S. market for warranties on existing houses.[41]

Today only a few home buyers are interested in home warranty programs, and the demand for them is quite sensitive to price. Home buyers prefer plans with inspection, coverage of structural and mechanical systems, and multiyear plans.[42]

---

[36]Bixby, "Implied Warranty," 470.

[37]Kempner, "Home Owners Warranty Program," 368.

[38]Warren H. McNamara, Jr., "The Implied Warranty in New-House Construction Revisited," *Real Estate Law Journal*, 3 (Fall 1974), 136–43.

[39]Housing Act of 1954, Ch. 649, §303, 68 Stat. 642 (1954).

[40]Mathematica Policy Research, Inc., *A Study of Home Inspection and Warranty Programs,* Vol. 1 (Washington, D.C.: U.S. Department of Housing and Urban Development, 1977), pp. 15–16.

[41]Ibid., p. 4.

[42]Ibid., p. iv.

The majority of home owners have no unexpected repair over $100 for the first two years. "Structural and mechanical problems account for approximately 70 percent of all major problems."[43]

PROTECTION: FUTURE DEVELOPMENTS

The protection available to home owners will continue to expand in all three areas—legal, governmental, and private. Both new and older homes will be covered. Other parties involved, such as the financial or sales institutions, may be held partly liable.[44] Standards such as building codes will have to be met in more areas. The following developments support these predictions.[45]

1. In Washington, a builder was held liable even though he was not the vendor because the completed product was unfit for living.
2. In California, a savings and loan institution, along with the builder, was held responsible because of the close connection of the two and the institution's duty to protect buyers from damages caused by major structural defects.
3. In Illinois, a buyer recovered for breach of implied warranty when the house was built in violation of the building code.

The use of implied warranty with older housing presents other problems. The main difference is in the degree of expected quality, which will vary with age, condition, and price. Unless otherwise stated, it is reasonable to expect that major systems such as plumbing, heating, and electricity work properly. With the increase in housing prices and the need for a large downpayment, first time home buyer may desire insurance or warranty protection against unexpected problems. This interest is expected to increase in the future.

Summary

Home ownership is a goal of most Americans. Today almost two-thirds of all U.S. families own their own homes. Many factors—primarily income—influence the decision to own.

In buying a home, one must know about construction, legal specifications, housing markets, and family goals, values, and activities. Currently, there is little protection for the person who makes a poor decision or a "bad buy." There is growing interest, however, in warranty programs for home buyers; limited private and public programs are now available.

Terms

abstract of title a condensed history of the title, together with a statement of all liens, charges, or encumbrances affecting a particular property.

appraisal an estimate of quantity, quality, or value. The process by which property values are obtained; also, the report of the estimated value.

assessed valuation the value placed upon real estate by a government agency for tax purposes.

---

[43]Ibid., p. iv.

[44]For more detail on court cases, see Mathematica Policy Research, Inc., *A Study of Home Inspection and Warranty Programs*, Vol. II, Appendix C (Washington, D.C.: U.S. Department of Housing and Urban Development, 1977).

[45]Bixby, "Implied Warranty," 468–76.

assessment a charge against real estate made by a government agency to cover the proportionate cost of an improvement, such as a street or sewer.

assignment the method or manner in which a right or contract is transferred from one person to another.

binder payment or written statement making an agreement legally binding until a formal contract is completed.

broker an individual or firm that acts as an intermediary in selling and buying real estate. The broker negotiates, contact, and brings together the buyer, seller, and mortgage lender.

builder one who assembles building materials in order to fabricate, erect, or construct, or who oversees building operations.

buyer person purchasing real estate.

binder payment or written statement making an agreement legally binding until a formal contract is completed.

clear title a title free and clear of all encumbrances.

cloud on title a flaw that makes uncertain the validity of a title. A proceeding or instrument, such as a mortgage, tax or assessment, or judgment that, if valid, would impair the marketability of title.

commission the percentage or allowance paid to an agent for transacting business for another person.

contract an agreement between two or more parties to do or not to do a particular thing.

conveyance an instrument by which title or property is transferred from one holder to another.

curtesy the right of a husband to enjoy one-half of his deceased wife's estate in his own right during his lifetime.

deed a document conveying title (evidence of ownership) from one person to another. There are two general types of deed—the quitclaim and the warranty.

deed restriction limitation placed on a deed restricting the use of the land.

dower the right of a wife to one-half of her deceased husband's estate during her lifetime.

earnest money money paid at the time of an initial commitment to buy real estate; makes the contract binding.

easement a right, privilege, or interest in the land of another person which entitles the holder—whether an individual, political subdivision, or utility—to some use, privilege, benefit, or right of way on the lands of another, such as a placement of utility poles, pipelines, or roads thereon, or travel over.

equity the interest or value of real estate over and above the mortgage against it.

escheat the reversion of land to the state.

estate nature and extent of an owner's rights with respect to property and its use.

fee an inherited or heritable estate in land.

fee simple estate sole ownership with clear title of real estate property and right of disposition; largest possible estate in real property.

fixtures property, originally personal, which has become attached to land or a building and is now real property.

freehold estate an estate held in fee or for life.

grantee a person to whom real estate is conveyed; the buyer.

grantor a person who conveys real estate by deed; the seller.

judgment lien designed to make sure that the person who loses a damage suit in court will pay.

lien legal hold on property to satisfy a debt.

life estate holding the rights of ownership during one's lifetime; upon death, the estate reverts to either the owner or the owner's estate.

lot any portion, piece, division, or parcel of land as described in the public records.

marketable title a title not completely clear, yet with only minor objections, which a well-informed and prudent real estate buyer would accept. This is the usual form of title used to transfer real estate.

market value the highest price a willing buyer will pay, and the lowest price a willing seller will accept for property.

mechanic's lien lien imposed on property to ensure that workers, contractors, and suppliers will be paid for work and materials.

option the right to buy or lease a property at a certain price for a designated period, for which right a fee is paid.

plat a precise definition of the boundaries of a piece of real property.

plat book a public record of various recorded plans in the municipality or country.

property the right an individual has in land and chattels to the exclusion of any one else.

purchase contract see *sales agreement*.

quitclaim deed a transfer to the buyer of whatever interest in the property the seller has.

real property ownership of realty that extends for a lifetime or longer, including land, buildings, or things attached thereto.

realtor a real estate agent affiliated with the National Association of Real Estate Boards.

realty land, together with improvements.

recording placing the transaction in the public records at the county courthouse.

restriction a device in a deed for controlling the use of land.

reversionary clause states that if any restrictions are violated, title to the property will revert to the party who imposed the restrictions or to his or her nominee.

sales agreement or sales contract legally binding document that contains conditions and details of a sale.

seller person who conveys real estate.

setback the distance from a lot line which by law, regulation, or restriction in the deed must be left open; the linear distance between the lot line and the buildings or building line.

tax deed a deed given where property has been bought at a public sale for nonpayment of taxes.

title the evidence of a person's legal right to own the property.

title company a company that specializes in insuring title to property.

title insurance protects the buyer or lender against loss of interest in the property due to a defect in the title that might be traced to legal flaws in previous ownerships. The owner's title insurance policy is bought and paid for only once and then continues in force with no further payment. Title insurance policies are not assignable.

title search or examination a check of the title records, generally at the local courthouse, by a title or abstract company or an attorney to establish the seller's right to sell the property and to make sure there are no liens, overdue special assessments, other claims, or outstanding restrictive covenants filed in the records.

torrens certificate a certificate issued by a public authority, known as Register of Titles, establishing title to an indicated owner. Used when title to property is registered under the Torrens system.

warranty deed a deed in which the seller also conveys all claim, right, and title to the property, and warrants the title to be clear except as shown in the deed. The warranty is recognized by law as providing restitution to the buyer for any defects in the title that are conveyed by the seller. In some states, the term "grant deed" is used in place of "warranty deed." There are several forms of warranty deed. See general or special warranty.

Suggested Readings

Burke, Jr. D. Barlow *American Conveyancing Patterns*. (Lexington, Mass.: Lexington Books, 1978).

Carliner, Geoffrey, "Determinants of Home Ownership," *Land Economics*, 1 (May 1974) 109–19.

Davis, Joseph C., and Claxton Walker, *Buying Your House: A Complete Guide to Inspection and Evaluation.* Buchanan, N.Y.: Emerson Books, 1975.

Frieden, Bernard J., and Arthur P. Solomon, with David L. Birch and John Pitkin, *The Nation's Housing: 1975 to 1985.* Cambridge, Mass.: Joint Center for Urban Studies of the Massachusetts Institute of Technology and Harvard University, 1977.

Kempner, Jonathan L., "The Home Owners Warranty Program: An Initial Analysis," *Stanford Law Review,* 28 (January 1976), 357–80.

Malone, John R., "The Capital Expenditure for Owner-Occupied Housing: A Study of Determinants," *Journal of Business,* 39 (June 1966), 359–65.

Marcuse, Peter, "Homeownership for Low Income Families: Financial Implications," *Land Economics,* 48 (May 1972), 134–43.

Mayer, Neil S., *Homeownership: The Changing Relationship of Costs and Incomes, and Possible Federal Roles.* Washington, D.C.: U.S. Government Printing Office, January 1977.

McNamara, Warren H., Jr.,"The Implied Warranty in New-House Construction Revisited," *Real Estate Law Journal*, 3 (Fall 1974), 136–43.

Meeks, Carol B., and Francille M. Firebaugh, "Home Maintenance and Improvement Behavior of Owners," *Home Economics Research Journal,* 3 (December 1974), 114–29.

Munsinger, Gary M., Jean E. Weber, and Richard W.Hanson, "Joint Home Purchasing Decisions by Husbands and Wives," *Journal of Consumer Research,* 1 (March 1975), 60–66.

Pratt, Laurence S., "Home Owner or Tenant? How to Make a Wise Choice," *Economic Education Bulletin,* XVII (December 1977), entire publication.

Severn, Alan, "Home Ownership for the Poor: A Case Study," *Journal of Economics and Business,* 27 (Winter 1975), 186–89.

Struyk, Raymond J., and Sue A. Marshall, "The Determinants of Household Home Ownership," *Urban Studies,* 11 (October 1974), 289–99.

———, "Income and Urban Home Ownership," *The Review of Economics and Statistics,* 62, (February 1975), 19–25.

U.S. Department of Labor, Bureau of Labor Statistics, *Rent or Buy? Evaluating Alternatives in the Shelter Market.* Bulletin 1823. Washington, D.C.: U.S. Government Printing Office, 1974.

RESIDENTIAL MORTGAGE FINANCING

1. WHY ARE ALTERNATIVE MORTGAGE INSTRU- MENTS A MAJOR ISSUE TODAY?

2. WHY DO SOME LENDING INSTITUTIONS HAVE A GREATER ROLE IN HOUSING FINANCE?

3. IS THE CONSUMER PROTECTION LEGISLA- TION RELATED TO HOUSING FINANCE ADE- QUATE?

4. WHAT FACTORS INFLUENCE DELINQUENCY AND FORECLOSURE?

In most cases, a home purchase is financed with a *mortgage*, the pledge of property to a creditor as security against a debt. In the housing area, the house or land is the collateral pledged.

This chapter provides a review of home financing. Various forms of mortgages are discussed. A look at credit sources, both private and public, will help you understand the many institutions and their structure. The process of financing is explained, including key actions, terms, and legal protection, as well as the effects of different down payments, interest rates, and terms.

Conventional mortgages on new and older homes average about 75 percent of the purchase price. Mortgages on new houses usually have slightly longer terms

and lower interest rates than those on older houses (Table 6-1).

From 1970 to 1978 all aspects of home financing—mortgage amount, interest rate, and mortgage *term*—have increased (Figure 6-1). The greatest effect has been on *principal* and interest payments. Median family income has grown more slowly. Annual housing expense as a percentage of net income has jumped from 21.0 to 29.4 percent, a rise of 40 percent.[1] Today larger mortgages are being financed at higher rates, for longer terms

---

[1]Robert J. Sheehan, "Situation in Housing and Trends Affecting the Family," speech given at the National Agricultural Outlook Conference, (Washington, D.C., : U.S. Department of Agriculture, Nov. 19, 1975), p. 5.

TABLE 6-1. Terms on Conventional Home Mortgages in April 1979 by Lender: National Averages

Lender	PURCHASE PRICE (Thousands)	LOAN AMOUNT (Thousands)	LOAN-TO-PRICE RATIO (%)	CONTRACT INTEREST RATE (%)	INITIAL FEE AND CHARGES[a] (%)	EFFECTIVE RATE[b] (%)	TERM TO MATURITY (Years)
Savings and loan associations							
New homes	66.4	49.2	76.0	10.00	1.79	10.30	28.9
Older homes	56.9	42.6	77.1	10.26	1.64	10.55	27.5
Mortgage companies							
New Homes	77.2	60.0	79.9	9.83	1.90	10.16	29.8
Older homes	66.2	52.2	82.0	9.99	2.43	10.40	29.8
Commercial banks							
New homes	69.0	47.3	71.4	10.29	1.10	10.49	26.2
Older homes	70.4	46.7	69.2	10.27	1.20	10.48	25.9
Mutual savings banks							
New homes	70.7	46.3	69.3	9.90	0.78	10.03	27.8
Older homes	58.6	39.5	69.7	9.71	0.58	9.81	25.1

aInclude charges paid by the borrower, or seller, to obtain a loan, except charges for mortgage, credit, life, or property insurance, for property transfer and for title search and insurance.

bIncludes contract rate plus initial fees and charges amortized over a ten-year period.

Source: Federal Home Loan Bank Systems, News, May 9, 1979.

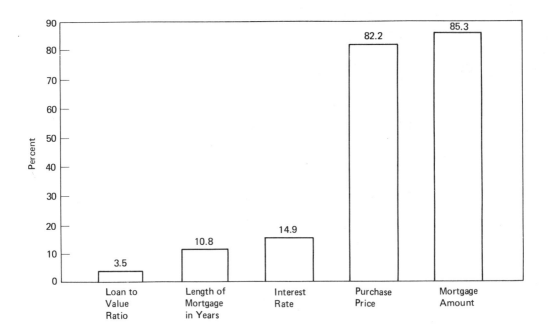

Figure 6-1. Percentage Increases in New Home Mortgage Financing, 1970–1978. [*Source: Federal Reserve Bulletin,* (Washington, D.C.: Board of Governors of the Federal Reserve System), 62, February 1976, A43 and 64; November 1978, A40.]

than in the past. Both the home-building and lending industries are searching for ways to enable more families to buy housing. However, families may also need to be willing to commit a larger income share to this need.

Alternative Mortgage Forms

There are as many possible mortgages as there are ways to repay principal and interest. Early mortgages were arranged for a fee by individuals, often lawyers, for other individuals, such as farmers or businessmen. Eventually, most of the mortgage arrangers joined financial institutions that had money to lend. The

first U.S. association of mortgage lenders, the Farm Mortgage Bankers Association, was formed in 1914. In 1923 it became the Mortgage Bankers Association. At that time, there was little mortgage banking. The loan was usually for 50 or 60 percent of the purchase price, interest rates were high, and the entire principal was due in a lump sum at the end of a short period, often five years. The loan was often renewed at the end of the term.

The Great Depression resulted in numerous *defaults* on mortgages. As borrowers failed to pay the principal or interest, many mortgages were *foreclosed*. Federal government action then brought about a revolutionary change in financing—the amortization of mortgage loans.

AMORTIZED MORTGAGES

Today, almost all mortgages are *amortized*; that is, the mortgage has a fixed rate of interest, a fixed monthly payment, and a stated term. For example, a mortgage may have a 9 percent interest rate, a monthly payment of $250, and a term of twenty-five years. The payments include principal and interest. Since interest is paid only on the unpaid part of the loan, it is largest at the beginning when the outstanding debt is greatest. Near the end of the mortgage term, most of the principal has been repaid. With the loan constantly reduced and the loan fully amortized, a lower down payment and a longer term to maturity can be arranged than were previously possible.

Although amortization makes it easy for households to plan their budgets, inflation and high interest rates present problems. First, as the buying power of the dollar changes, the pattern of payments over time is severely distorted. It starts at a very high level and declines rapidly over the life of the mortgage. This defeats the basic purpose of the mortgage, which is to spread out the cost of home ownership. Young households in a fixed-payment mortgage market may have to wait because earlier payments will take a much larger share of their net income than later payments will (Figure 6-2).

Second, since U.S. financial institutions attract mainly short-term funds, lending on a long basis-term at fixed rates is risky. The supply of funds becomes disrupted and, in extreme cases—as in the recent past—a serious threat to the viability of

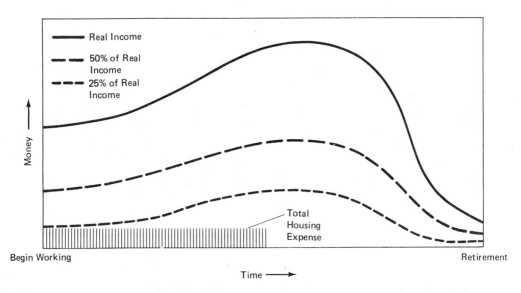

Figure 6-2. Declining Burden of Payments with a Conventional Mortgage. [*Source: "But We Can't Get a Mortgage!" Causes and Cures,* Task Force on Critical Problems, New York State Senate (Albany, N.Y.: May 1975, p. 15.]

thrift institutions. In an expected inflationary period, lenders often charge a higher rate of interest to protect themselves in the future. This immediately raises the cost to borrowers; it may be some time before the borrower's money income reaches a breakeven point.

Although the amortized mortgage has served both borrower and lender well, it is not the only way to finance housing. With a changing economy and varying household situations, no one form is best for all operations and conditions.

INTEREST-ONLY MORTGAGES

A first step in changing mortgage policy was made in February 1974, when the Federal Home Loan Bank Board authorized federal savings and loan associations to grant mortgages with initial payments that were smaller than those needed for amortized loans. Payments during the first five years of the loan cover only the interest. In the sixth year, the mortgage becomes fully amortized. Thus, payments are lower in the early years, when borrowers' incomes may be lower. However, the cost advantage to the borrower decreases as the mortgage term and interest rate increase. Interest-only loans are riskier for lenders during the first five years, since none of the principal is recovered. To offset the risk, the lender might require a larger down payment, thus reducing the advantage to the borrower.

VARIABLE-RATE MORTGAGES

Perhaps the most controversial alternative mortgage form is the *variable-rate mortgage (VRM)*. A VRM allows the interest rate to vary with the market; thus, the rate could go up or down. The VRM can have a fixed term and allow the monthly payments to reflect the interest rate changes. Or the monthly payment could be fixed and the term vary, or some combination could be developed.

The interest rate on a VRM varies according to an index. The index chosen should have proven reliability in moving with home mortgage market interest rates, be beyond the influence of the lending institution, and be explainable to the borrower in clear and simple terms. Suggested indexes include a weighted average yield based on three- to five-year U.S. Treasury securities; the interest rate on savings accounts less some fixed percent, or the prime lending rate.[2]

VRMs are widely used in Great Britain, France, Germany, Italy, Sweden, Australia, and South Africa. Six states—California, Illinois, Massachusetts, South Carolina, Virginia, and Wisconsin—now allow variable-rate or escalator clauses in home mortgage contracts. Three states—Michigan, Pennsylvania, and Vermont—prohibit any changes in mortgage interest rates. The remaining states have no definite policy.[3]

As of May 30, 1979, the FHLBB voted to allow all federally chartered savings

---

[2]For a discussion of the discount rate, prime rate, FHA yield, and U.S. government taxable bond yield, see Candilis O. Wray, "Mortgage Rate Variability and the Housing Market," *Construction Review*, 19 (May 1973), 4–9, and *Variable Rate Mortgage Proposal and Regulation Q,* Hearings before the Subcommittee on Financial Institutions Supervision, Regulation, and Insurance of the Committee on Banking, Currency, and Housing, House of Representatives, 94th Congress, 1st Session, April 8, 9, 10, 1975, p. 206.

[3]Raymond D. Edwards, *Variable Rate Mortgage Proposal and Regulation Q.* (Washington, D.C.: U.S. Government Printing Office, April, 1975), p. 76.

and loan associations to offer VRMs after July 1, 1979.[4]

Several arguments support the VRM concept. First, the flow of funds into home mortgage lending would become larger and more stable. Lending institutions would be more willing to make long-term commitments to mortgage financing because they could expect the rate of return to relate to economic conditions. Today there is little incentive for institutions to lend $50,000 for twenty-five years at 10 percent interest if they can make the same loan a month later at a higher rate of interest or invest in short-term Treasury notes with still higher rates of return. Second, new borrowers will not have to subsidize the lower interest rates that earlier borrowers received. In other words, all borrowers would be paying the same rate, rather than some paying 5 percent and others 10 percent.

However, there are problems. A VRM adds uncertainty to personal management and requires greater flexibility and planning. Money cannot be budgeted so tightly that nothing is left over for an interest rate increase. However, the variable *term* mortgage would not have this disadvantage. The term would lengthen to offset the higher interest costs.

Some VRM proposals would greatly handicap many families. For example, a $50,000 mortgage at 8.5 percent for 25 years starts out at a monthly payment of $403. If, a year later, the interest rate jumps to 9.5 percent, the monthly payment would become about $437. If, in the third year, the interest rate is raised again to 10.5 percent, the monthly payment

then becomes about $472. So, if the interest rate is raised from the original 8.5 percent to 10.5 percent, monthly payments increase by $69. If another 2 percent increase occurs the following 2 years, monthly payments could increase $142 per month over a four-year span. Although incomes for many families will have increased with inflation, a $142 per month housing increase is a large change in only one budget item for families to cope with. On larger mortgages, increases become even greater. Too large a rise in payments could lead to increased mortgage defaults. One proposal to help the VRM borrower is to establish an insurance company that would issue three-year policies against a rise in the interest rate if the borrower's income did not increase proportionately.

Several objections to the VRM have been made. One is that mortgage lenders may be able to manipulate the index. This could be solved by using an outside reference rate which could not be manipulated. However, if a rate based on national averages is used and all institutions are allowed to increase their rates, then average rates will go up.

A second objection is that the VRM is so complicated that borrowers will be unable to understand or realize what it means. Thus, full and fair disclosure is essential if the VRM is to succeed.

The role of the lender should be to bear risk, not to pass it on. This statement when viewed alone seems reasonable, but today's mortgage-lending system shows clearly that lending institutions do not cope well with interest rate risks. Also, as more and more VRMs and other index-type mortgages are used, and deposit rate ceilings are eliminated, the default risks

---

[4]Federal Home Loan Bank Board. *News.* May 30, 1979.

that lenders are willing to undertake should increase. Thus, some borrowers who are now marginal risks might be able to get mortgages under a new system.

Another concern is that VRM mortgages will cause the fixed-rate mortgage to disappear. This is unlikely. Some institutions will specialize in VRM mortgages and flexible-rate deposits, others in standard mortgage contracts financed with long-term fixed-rate deposits. Consumers will be able to choose from among these plans.

The borrower who chooses a VRM mortgage needs more information than one who gets an amortized mortgage. The VRM borrower must know:

1. The initial and maximum interest rate and loan terms.
2. The index used to determine interest rate changes.
3. The interest rate change permitted over time and at any one time.
4. How often the interest rate can change and how the adjustments will be made—whether in the term or the monthly payment.
5. Initial and maximum total monthly payments of principal and interest.

INDEXED MORTGAGES

Another form of mortgage is the *indexed mortgage*, or price-level-adjusted mortgage, or purchasing power mortgage, which allows adjustment of the unpaid principal. Periodically the unpaid principal would be adjusted to the value of the dollars of the original loan. Theoretically this could be a decrease as well as an increase, but with inflation all adjustments would be increases. The adjustment would be based on an external index, such as the cost of living index. Payments are changed whenever the principal is revised. In real terms, payments would remain constant over the life of the mortgage, but in nominal terms they would increase. In real terms, the indexed mortgage actually provides long-term borrowing at a fixed rate and a fixed real payment. Hopefully, if indexed mortgages become a reality, indexed deposits would follow.

Both borrower and lender must be educated to think in real rather than nominal terms. Regulations governing lending institutions and the tax structure will also have to be changed. The indexed mortgage is best for households whose real incomes are expected to rise or those whose wage contracts provide for cost-of-living increases.

According to the New York State Senate Task Force on Critical Problems, the indexed mortgage:[5]

1. Lowers the initial mortgage burden, making home ownership possible for most people.
2. Confronts the problem of inflation.
3. Eliminates the risk of lenders being caught short by allowing matching of deposits and loan maturities.
4. Benefits all parties by reducing costs and risks and possibly stabilizing the housing finance system.
5. Entails some risk to borrowers since they must have at least level real income.
6. Will be hard to introduce because of its novelty.

---

[5]"*. . . But We Can't Get a Mortgage!" Causes and Cures,* Task Force on Critical Problems, New York State Senate (Albany, N.Y., May 1975), pp. 37–41.

The borrower of an indexed mortgage will need to know:

1. When or how often the principal will be adjusted.
2. The index used to make the adjustment.
3. The initial rate of interest.
4. Initial and maximum term.
5. The payment schedule.
6. Advance notification period required.

SHORT-TERM BOND

The short-term bond allows for long-term amortization, but the contract extends for only a short period—say, five years. Every fifth year the loan is renewed at the prevailing interest rate. It is fairly easy to implement but causes some borrower uncertainty. The borrower needs to be aware of terms, payment schedule, prepayment rights, and possible rate of increase.

Short-term bonds are attractive to frequent movers. They are a reality today in some areas. Nearly all single-family mortgages in Canada are of this type.[6]

GRADUATED PAYMENT MORTGAGES

With the graduated payment mortgage, the interest rate remains the same. A payment schedule is worked out when the mortgage is negotiated. Payments may start low and increase or start high and decrease. Lower initial payments would allow borrowers to get a loan for which they would not have otherwise qualified or permit a larger mortgage and thus a larger house. A payment schedule that starts out at a high level and then decreases might be good for a couple looking toward retirement and a reduced income. Variation in the payment makes the mortgage instrument easier to fit the varying needs of borrowers.

In 1977, the Department of Housing and Urban Development (HUD) established a permanent program to insure graduated payment mortgages (GPM). The insurance eliminates the lender's risk and, hopefully, lowers down payment requirements.[7] The plan would increase payments by 3 percent per year until the tenth year. They would start lower than the standard level-payment loan and in ten years would be higher. Variations in the rate of increase and number of years are also being tested.

The borrower would need to understand the payment schedule, be aware that equity buildup depends on this, and know the rate of interest and the term. As of January 1, 1979, federal savings and loan associations were authorized to grant GPMs.[8]

REVERSE ANNUITY

A reverse annuity mortgage (RAM) is a loan secured by real estate that permits borrowers to draw on the equity in their

---

[6]For a discussion, see Donald R. Lessard, "Roll-Over Mortgages in Canada," *New Mortgage Designs for Stable Housing in an Inflationary Environment*, Conference Proceedings (Boston, Mass.: Federal Reserve Bank of Boston, January 1975), pp. 131–41.

[7]U.S. Department of Housing and Urban Development, *HUD News*, HUD No. 78-275, (Washington, D.C., Aug. 21, 1978).

[8]Federal Home Loan Bank Board, *Fact Sheet*, "Questions and Answers about Alternative Mortgage Instruments," Dec. 13, 1978.

homes. The borrower does not pay the lender. Payments are made by the lender or through the purchase of an annuity from an insurance company. The loan becomes due on a specific date—the sale of the property or the death of the borrower. RAMs were authorized by the FHLBB in December 1978.

CONTINGENT APPRECIATION PARTICIPATION MORTGAGES

Contingent Appreciation Participation (CAP) mortgages on single-family homes are also being discussed by lending institutions. A CAP mortgage would allow lenders to share in the appreciated value of the mortgaged property. This gives the lender some protection against inflation. It also provides for adjustment within the mortgage market which would help to stabilize new home construction. The lender's share of the appreciation could be a percentage based on the loan-to-price ratio. A buyer must notify the lender of any improvements made and before resale. If the mortgage is paid off, a method must be worked out so that the lender would get its share.

The borrower should receive a lower interest rate, resulting in lower monthly payments. Also, CAP mortgages require less sophistication to understand than a price-level adjusted mortgage since there are no outside indexes. Issues regarding the rights of fee-simple ownership must be resolved.

Traditionally the homeowner has received all the capital gain from an increase in house value. For many families, this asset is their only source of inflation-generated capital gains. To share this gain with another party may be highly undesirable and could eliminate opportunities to upgrade housing quality over the life cycle.

Along with such common items as rate of interest, loan maturity, payment schedule, prepayment requirements, and foreclosure procedures, the borrower needs to know:

1. How the CAP fee will be determined.
2. The percentage of the loan-to-price ratio the lender will receive.
3. Notification requirements concerning improvements and resale.
4. The method used to determine credit for improvements made.
5. Procedures if the loan is assumed or paid in full.

Disclosure requirements would need to be related to Truth-In-Lending legislation and the Real Estate Settlement Procedures Act.

CONCLUSION

No single form of mortgage can meet every borrower's financing needs. Further, with a choice of mortgages, the decision-making process grows more complicated. There must be full disclosure by lenders, and borrowers must be fully educated as to what the many alternatives mean. The mortgage chosen should meet the borrower's needs as well as those of the lending institution.

Sources of Mortgage Credit

Mortgages can be obtained from savings and loan associations, mutual savings banks, commercial banks, life insurance companies, federally sponsored credit agencies, finance and mortgage companies, and real estate investment trusts (Figure 6–3). The first four sources are long-time suppliers of mortgage credit; the last three are fairly new.

SAVINGS AND LOAN ASSOCIATIONS

The largest source of *conventional* mortgage funds for both single- and multi-family housing is savings and loan associations. These account for over half of all conventional home mortgage

loans.[9] About 87 percent of savings and loan associations assets are in home mortgages.[10] This high percentage is due

[9]Arnold H. Diamond, *The Supply of Mortgage Credit 1970–1974*. (Washington, D.C.: U.S. Department of Housing and Urban Development, 1975), p. 39; U.S. Department of Housing and Urban Development, *HUD News*, HUD No-79-74 (Washington, D.C., May 22, 1979), p. 1; and U.S. Department of Housing and Urban Development, *Tenth Annual Report on the National Housing Goal* (Washington, D.C., n.d.), p. 74.

[10]Federal Home Loan Bank Board, *News*, May 29, 1979. unpaged.

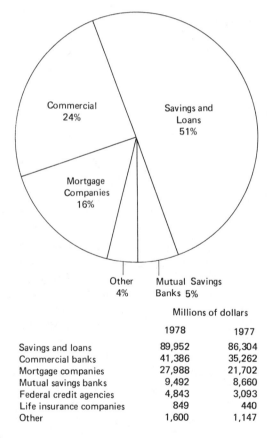

	Millions of dollars	
	1978	1977
Savings and loans	89,952	86,304
Commercial banks	41,386	35,262
Mortgage companies	27,988	21,702
Mutual savings banks	9,492	8,660
Federal credit agencies	4,843	3,093
Life insurance companies	849	440
Other	1,600	1,147

Figure 6-3. Volume of Mortgage Loans Originated, One-to-Four-Family Homes, 1978. [*Source:* HUD News, HUD No. 79-74. (U.S. Department of Housing and Urban Development). March 22, 1979, Table 1.]

to the history and experience of these associations as specialists in housing finance and to the tax advantages they receive from holding mortgages.

Although the interest rate offered by savings and loan associations on deposits is limited by the Federal Home Loan Bank Board, the interest rates on savings accounts are higher than those offered by commercial banks. Thus, savings and loan associations attract savings which can then be loaned on home mortgages.

COMMERCIAL BANKS

In recent years, commercial banks have become more active in the field of mortgage finance. However, they generally keep such lending to a minimum because of other lending opportunities and a desire for liquidity. Commercial banks provide about 24 percent of the mortgage loans.[11] Many of them invest in long-term mortgages as a personal service to their customers, and some specialize in mortgages. Commercial banks usually require lower loan-to-value ratios and shorter maturities than do other mortgage lenders.

In addition to mortgage lending, commercial banks grant many construction and development loans. Their shorter maturity is related more to the banks' need for liquidity and fund availability than is mortgage lending, and their yields are higher.

A commercial bank is under either national or state supervision, depending on its charter. National banks are limited in the amount of money they may lend.

They are allowed to invest either 70 percent of their total time deposits or 100 percent of their capital or surplus funds in mortgage loans other than VA or FHA loans. Mortgage loans must constitute the first lien and be fully amortized by term. If the term is less than thirty years, the loan-to-value ratio may be 90 percent. State banks are supervised by state banking departments or agencies, which generally allow more liberal lending terms.

MORTGAGE BANKING COMPANIES

Mortgage banking companies provide funds for about 15 percent of the mortgages issued.[12] These companies act as intermediaries between lenders, home buyers, and builders. The largest part of their business has traditionally involved *originating* FHA and VA mortgage loans for sale to institutions. But because of the recent growth of private mortgage insurance companies, mortgage bankers are now moving into the field of conventional mortgages.

FHA and VA home loans, coupled with the mortgage bankers' secondary function—document inspection and *servicing* of the purchased loans—create a relatively easy sale investment in mortgages for large investors. The mortgage banking company also channels mortgage money to home buyers in areas where it is needed.

Federal and state supervision of mortgage banking has been minimal. Recently, however, states have begun to adopt licensing laws. Mortgage bankers dealing in FHA loans must be approved by the FHA and can be periodically ex-

[11]*HUD News*, derived from Table 1 and *Tenth Annual Report*, p. 74.

[12]*Tenth Annual Report*, p. 74.

amined and audited by the FHA to make sure that they are well capitalized and can service their loans. While the law does not require the VA to approve lenders, VA regulations ensure that each lender must show the ability to service loans and use good credit judgment.

Mortgage bankers operate by asking for large blocks of single-family and multi-family loans from large institutions. Income comes directly from borrower fees, from servicing fees, and sometimes from the sale of loans; and indirectly from large escrow deposits. Other income may come from activities, such as land development and construction loans, standby commitments, and new cities development.

MUTUAL SAVINGS BANKS

Another source of mortgage funds is mutual savings banks. Almost all of their funds are invested in long-term assets. In 1977, home mortgages made up about 60 percent of these assets, including about 15.0 percent of all federally underwritten mortgages.[13] Savings banks are no longer the largest holders of FHA and VA home mortgages. The expansion of private mortgage insurance companies and the declining importance of FHA mortgages have led savings banks to increase their privately insured conventional mortgage lending.

Mutual savings bank investments in mortgages have been encouraged by the 1969 Tax Reform Act, which provided tax breaks for earnings derived from mortgages. Savings banks tend to have fewer restrictions on their investment policies than do savings and loan associations.

LIFE INSURANCE COMPANIES

Life insurance companies have decreased their mortgage lending over the last twenty years, shifting their funds to corporate debt and equity holdings.[14] In 1950, life insurance companies held about 19 percent of single-family mortgages, but this decreased to only about 2 percent in 1977.[15] Multi-family holdings have remained about the same, with life insurance companies accounting for about 23 percent of the market in 1975, and 20 percent in 1977. One- to four-family mortgages accounted for 53 percent of life insurance company holdings in 1950, but this declined to about 20 percent by 1975.

All life insurance companies are state chartered. They are regulated by the laws of their home states and those states in which they operate. State regulations include limitations on real estate and mortgage loan investments—New York's limitation, for example, is 50 percent—as well as on stock and bond purchases. State regulations also include maximum loan-to-value ratios (generally 66 2/3 to 75 percent) and types of loans. FHA and VA loans are exempt from loan-to-value regulations, however, following FHA and VA rules instead. Life insurance companies are allowed to buy real estate as well as to invest in single- and multi-family mortgages.

---

[13]*1978 National Fact Book of Mutual Savings Banking*, N.Y.: National Association of Mutual Savings Banks, October, 1978.

[14]*Federal Reserve Bulletin* Washington, D.C.: Board of Governors of the Federal Reserve System. Various years.

[15]U.S. Department of Housing and Urban Development. *HUD News*, HUD No. 78-241 (July 26, 1978), Table 8 unpaged.

INVESTMENT TRUSTS

Real estate investment trusts (REITs) and mortgage investment trusts (MITs) act as financial middlemen. They issue equity, debentures, and commercial paper, and borrow with short-term loans to attract funds for investment in real estate. Their greatest impact on housing finance has been in the area of apartment house construction and development loans. REITs pay corporate income taxes only on their retained earnings, provided 75 percent of their income is derived from real estate and 90 percent of their profits is distributed to the shareholders. MITs invest mainly in construction and development loans and long-term mortgages.

PENSION FUNDS

With their tremendous growth over the last fifty years, pension funds may be the largest untapped source of mortgage investment in the United States. Current mortgage investment from pension funds is small. Recently, however, the Government National Mortgage Association has attracted some pension funds for mortgage-backed securities that do not require facilities and staff for portfolio administration. Until mortgages can compete strongly with all other higher-yielding investments, pension funds will probably have little to do with them.

CREDIT UNIONS

In 1977, federal credit unions were authorized to make home loans for up to thirty years and to offer mortgages insured by the FHA.[16]

---

[16]U.S. Department of Housing and Urban Development, *HUD News,* HUD No.-77-387, Washington, D.C., Dec. 26, 1977.

Mortgages are limited to credit union members and cannot exceed 150 percent of the median price of homes sold in the area. A credit union must have at least $2 million in assets to make 30-year loans and is limited to having no more than 25 percent of its total loan dollars outstanding in long-term mortgages. There are some 13,000 Federal credit unions, with some $27 billion in assets which can be expected to offer home mortgages.

Insurers and Guarantors

Both public and private agencies insure or guarantee the payment of mortgages. Thus, they increase the marketability of mortgages by making mortgage investment less risky. Many mortgages can be sold and exchanged on the secondary market with relative safety (see Chapter 4 on the secondary market).

FEDERAL HOUSING ADMINISTRATION

The Federal Housing Administration (FHA) was created by the 1934 National Housing Act. It was authorized to insure home mortgage loans made by private lenders through the creation of a mutual *mortgage insurance* fund. The FHA changed the nature of home financing by offering long-term mortgages with level debt service and low down payments. This resulted in lower monthly payments so that more families with little savings but adequate incomes could qualify for home loans. The FHA works to improve home financing practices, to encourage improvements in housing standards and conditions, and to promote home ownership.

Today the FHA is part of the Department of Housing and Urban Development. It administers many mortgage insurance programs under which lenders are insured against loss in financing first mortgages on single-family homes, on multi-family housing projects, and on loans for repairs or home improvements, including energy-saving solar systems and equipment. The main source of FHA funds is an insurance premium paid by the mortgagor. This premium is 0.5 percent of the remaining principal.

Mortgage limits, down payments, and interest rates all vary. Mortgage limits have risen along with housing prices. This is also true of interest rates—which, however, show short-run variability. Repayment is made in equal monthly installments up to thirty years.

When mortgage interest rates rise above the FHA ceiling rate, lenders acquire FHA loans at a discount. This discount usually takes the form of *points*. Although the mortgagors cannot pay the discount directly, they do so indirectly by paying a higher price for the house. The discount is paid by the seller.

The FHA also administers many programs that do not involve mortgage insurance. These include:

1. Home ownership programs that help low-income families to find housing by making mortgage payments to lenders on behalf of qualified borrowers.
2. A nonprofit sponsor assistance program that lends interest-free money to qualified nonprofit organizations for preconstruction expenses.

Delays in processing, insurance payment delays, and competition from private mortgage insurance companies have contributed to a decline in FHA insured loans. In the future, it is expected that the FHA will supplement private plans—to insure higher-risk mortgages, to help provide housing for lower-income families, and to insure multi-family transactions.[17]

VETERANS ADMINISTRATION

The Veterans Administration (VA) home loan guaranty program began on June 22, 1944.[18] Those eligible include World War II and Korean War veterans, unremarried widows of veterans, and veterans of service after January 31, 1955, who have been on active duty for 180 days. Today the VA operates three programs:

1. The loan guaranty program.
2. The direct loan program when mortgage credit is not otherwise available.
3. Grants for special housing needed by severely disabled veterans.

THE LOAN GUARANTY PROGRAM Almost all VA-guaranteed loans are for single-family homes, mobile homes, and condominium units. The loan amount that the VA will guarantee changes. There is no down payment requirement or guaranty charge. The VA interest rate is set by regulation. Although veterans cannot pay discount points directly, they may do so indirectly by paying more for their homes. The VA appraises each property which is to be the security for a guaranteed loan. Before a loan can be guaranteed, the VA must decide whether the veteran is a good credit risk and has the

---

[17]Robert P. Cunningham, "Requiem for FHA Is Premature," *The Appraisal Journal*, 45 (January 1977), 102.

[18]Robert C. Coon, "The VA Home Loan Program," *HUD Challenge*, VI (December 1975), 10–12.

income to repay the loan. All VA loans must be secured by first liens.

Lenders need not be approved by the VA in order to process loans. VA regulations provide, however, that lenders must show the ability to service loans, maintain good loan accounting records, and determine credit.

VA loans are attractive to lenders and investors because the guaranty reduces the investment risk. In case of default, the VA will settle with the mortgage holder up to a specified amount by allowing interest accrued to the date of foreclose, plus foreclosure expenses. All such settlements are paid promptly in cash after the VA's receipt of guarantee claims. There have been very few claims, amounting to only about 3.6 percent of the number of loans guaranteed.[19]

VA home loans have several advantages for veterans:

1. No down payment is required; thus, the full value of the property may be borrowed.

2. The loan may be repaid in part or in full at any time without penalty.

3. Allowances are made for temporary distress which makes loan payments difficult.

4. Special provisions are made if the borrower is called back to active duty.

5. Repayment terms are equal monthly payments up to thirty years.

6. The veteran has the benefit of VA appraisal services, construction supervision, a builder's warranty, and oversight of the mortgage lender's activities.

DIRECT LOAN PROGRAM The direct loan program extends credit directly to veter-ans to buy, build, repair, and alter homes and farmhouses in rural areas, small cities, and towns where private credit is generally not available. Certain areas are designated as "housing credit shortage areas," and under the direct loan program, veterans apply directly to the VA for a mortgage. The terms are the same as those under the home loan guaranty program, but there is a limit on the amount of the direct loan.

SPECIALLY ADAPTED HOUSING GRANTS
The specially adapted housing grants program helps severely disabled veterans to build or modify their homes. The grant may not be more than one-half of the home's purchase price, with a maximum grant of $25,000.

FARMERS HOME ADMINISTRATION

The Farmers Home Administration (FmHA), part of the U.S. Department of Agriculture, administers the farm credit and rural housing program.[20] Established in 1946, the FmHA began by assisting farmers. Since the 1950s, it has expanded greatly in the scope and volume of services provided. The agency serves all fifty states, Puerto Rico, and the Virgin Islands.

The FmHA emphasizes new construction—homes modest in size and cost. FmHA-financed homes are smaller in size and cost than conventionally financed homes.[21] Most FmHA loans fall into two

---

[19]Ibad., p. 10–12.

[20]Title V of the 1949 Housing Act; Part A, Title III, of the 1964 Economic Opportunity Act; the 1972 Consolidated Farm and Rural Development Act.

[21]U.S. Department of Commerce, Bureau of the Census, and U.S. Department of Housing and Urban Development, "Characteristics of New Housing: 1977," Construction Reports, C25-77-13. 41, 52 August 1978, Washington, D.C.

categories: guaranteed loans and insured loans. In the guaranteed loan program, the FmHA guarantees to limit any loss to the private lender up to a specified percentage. Interest rates are determined between borrower and lender unless established by law. Under the FmHA-insured loan program, loans are originated, made, and serviced by the FmHA. Notes backed by the federal government are then sold to investors, renewing the loan fund. Interest rates for most insured loan programs are determined by the current cost of federal borrowing, but some rates are established by statute.

FmHA loans enable rural residents to obtain decent, safe, sanitary, modest housing at reasonable rates. The applicant's income determines the maximum amount of the loan, and the program is limited to low- and moderate-income families. The funds for loans and grants come from three sources: annual appropriations by Congress, loans from the U.S. Treasury, and private lenders who supply funds for loans insured by the agency. The losses incurred by the interest rate subsidies are financed from general tax revenues.

Besides housing loans, the FmHA offers subsidized housing loans for purchase, construction, and repair; home repair loans; farm labor housing loans and grants; rental housing loans; rent supplements; and self-help technical assistance grants.

PRIVATE MORTGAGE INSURANCE

Private mortgage insurance is issued by private mortgage insurance companies (MIC) and insures the lender against loss. It fulfills a similar function to that provided lenders by the VA or FHA. With the reduced risk, the lender is more willing to invest in higher loan-to-value ratio mortgages. Thus, credit is available to more families. The borrower pays the cost of the insurance premium.

In the United States, private mortgage insurance began in 1885. After many companies went bankrupt during the Great Depression, its use declined. There was some revival after the mid-1950s, but the greatest growth has been since 1971, when the 1970 Emergency Home Loan Financing Act enabled the Federal National Mortgage Association and the Federal Home Loan Mortgage Corporation to enter the secondary market for mortgages covered by private mortgage insurance.[22] Overall, MIC coverage reached about one-sixth of all mortgages in 1973.[23] In 1976, privately insured loans accounted for 13.2 percent of the total volume of mortgage loans.[24] At the end of December 1978, total private insurance on one- to four-family mortgages amounted to $81.1 billion, $17.7 billion more than in 1977.[25]

Mortgage insurance is a young industry, with competition from within and outside. As new companies have been formed, the market shares of older firms have eroded; this shift will continue.[26] Private mortgage insurers also compete with government mortgage insurance and with the fact that lenders rely on their own ability to evaluate and take the risks of mortgage lending. Little reported that "for loan-to-value ratios of more

---

[22]Arthur D. Little, *The Arthur D. Little Study of the Private Mortgage Insurance Industry* (Washington, D.C.: Mortgage Insurance Companies of America, November 1975), p. 3.

[23]Ibid., p. 25.

[24]*HUD News,* HUD No. 77-149 (May 20, 1977), 2.

[25]*HUD News,* HUD No. 79-79 (Mar. 22, 1979), 1.

[26]Little, *Private Mortgage Insurance Industry,* pp. 26–27.

than 95 percent, government insurance currently dominates, while for ratios between 90 percent and 95 percent our best estimate is that government and private insurance share about equally. For ratios between 80 percent and 90 percent, it appears that private mortgage insurance covers about half the total volume, while the other half is self-insured. Loans of under 80 percent of value are insured through MIC coverage only under exceptional circumstances."[27]

Private mortgage insurance companies are regulated by the states in which they operate. Most states grant licenses to mortgage insurers under the insurance codes. Some states are more comprehensive—specifying liquidity requirements, domain, maximum coverage, total liability, dividend policy, reserve requirements, fee limitations, and other factors. In addition to state law, MICs are subject to the requirements of the Federal National Mortgage Association and the Federal Home Loan Mortgage Corporation.

A lender approved by a private mortgage insurance company can apply for insurance on loans when the borrower's credit is good and the lender wants to avoid the risk of property value decline. This usually affects loans with a loan-to-value ratio of 90 percent or higher. The highest loan-to-value ratio on conventional mortgages that the Federal Home Loan Bank Board permits member savings and loan associations to originate is 95 percent. The Comptroller of the Currency restricts national banks to a maximum loan-to-value ratio of 90 percent on such loans. Since private mortgage insurance normally covers the top 20 to 25 percent of a 95 percent loan (it pays 25 percent of the total after foreclosure), the property value would have to decline about 30 percent (5 percent equity and 25 percent coverage) before the lender would actually lose money on the mortgage investment.

The mortgagor usually pays the insurance premium, typically 0.25 percent per year on the unpaid balance of the loan. The actual premium depends on the amount of coverage and the initial loan-to-value ratio. The insurance can be purchased on a five-, ten-, or fifteen-year basis or annually.[28] The policy may be canceled at the discretion of the lender. After the mortgagor has amortized the loan to 60 to 70 percent of its value, the lender will often drop the policy because the risk of losing the principal through foreclosure is then small.

Private mortgage insurance companies can process insurance applications very quickly, usually reporting a decision within twenty-four to forty-eight hours after the application is received. Insurance claims are also processed rapidly. Besides being inexpensive, this speed gives private mortgage insurance companies a strong advantage over the FHA. Also, since there are no administrative interest rate limitations, privately insured mortgages tend to be more attractive than VA or FHA insurance.

CONCLUSION

Savings and loan associations are the major source of mortgage loans on one-to four-family nonfarm homes. Below

---

[27]Ibid., p. 25.

[28]Craig Swan, "Private Mortgage Insurance Companies and Alternative Mortgage Instruments: Attitudes and Practices," mimeo (Minneapolis: University of Minnesota, October 1977), 4.

them, in decreasing order of importance, are commercial banks, mortgage companies, mutual savings banks, and federal credit unions. Less than 1 percent of the loans are provided by state and local credit agencies, life insurance companies, state and local pension funds, and mortgage investment trusts. Thus, the borrower has some idea of the likelihood of financing from a given source. In seeking a mortgage, most borrowers first visit the institution where they do their regular banking. Lenders often try to accommodate their customers.

Mortgage Loan Process

The mortgage loan process involves applying for the loan and receiving a commitment from the lender. A borrower will want to compare purchase terms offered. A *closing* is then held, usually attended by all parties concerned. At the closing the buyer receives title to the property, subject to the lender's claim.

MORTGAGE LOAN APPLICATION

Usually a borrower applies for a mortgage after the purchase offer has been made and accepted. Sometimes a borrower will apply before choosing a house in order to find out how much the lender is willing to loan. After the borrower decides on the type of mortgage desired—conventional, FHA, VA—he or she applies to the lender for a mortgage. The loan application includes:

1. Location, description, and price of the property.
2. Name of the seller, builder, or real estate agent.
3. Indebtedness, if any, against the property.
4. Employment and personal finance information.
5. Credit references.
6. Assets and indebtedness.

Also required are an inspection and appraisal of the property by an appraiser chosen by the lender. The amount an institution will lend depends partly on the appraised value of the house, which may be different from the seller's asking price.

If the lender approves the application, the borrower will receive a letter of *commitment* outlining the terms of the mortgage and authorizing the sale.

MORTGAGE AGREEMENT

The *mortgage agreement* consists of two documents:

1. The mortgage itself, which pledges the property as security against the loan.
2. A *promissory note* or *bond*, which states the repayment terms of the agreement (interest rate, amount and time of payments, and special features) as well as other obligations of the borrower: namely, payment of taxes, keeping the property insured and in good condition, and obtaining the lender's approval before altering the property in any way.

These two documents are signed at the closing of the sale.

Terms of Purchase

In choosing a mortgage, there are three major factors to be considered: *down payment*, interest rate, and mortgage term or repayment period. Other features of the mortgage are also important.

DOWN PAYMENT

The size of the down payment will influence the size of the mortgage. By making the largest down payment possible, a borrower may find it easier to get a mortgage and will have a lower total interest cost resulting from a lower interest rate and a smaller mortgage. On a $60,000 home, with interest at 9 percent and a term of thirty years, the total interest cost is $108,114 with a 5 percent down payment, $91,039 with a 20 percent down payment, and $79,662 with a 30 percent down payment. The down payment should not be so large that it depletes funds needed for closing costs, moving expenses, unexpected emergencies, or day-to-day expenses.

Down payments on conventional loans commonly run between 10 and 25 percent of the appraised value, although insured loans may require only 5 percent. In a tight credit market, the lender may demand a 30 or 40 percent down payment.

An important item which any borrower must consider today is inflation. Although the inflation rate has slowed somewhat, inflation is expected to continue. This means that the borrower pays back the mortgage in cheaper and cheaper dollars. Thus, it may be to the borrower's advantage to make the smallest down payment possible and to obtain the largest mortgate loan available.

INTEREST RATE

The interest rate is an important factor in the cost of housing (Table 6-2). Interest rates vary according to:

1. *The lending institution.* The interest rate includes a rate of return to the institution for the use of its funds. An inflation factor is also included to cover the mortgage period.

2. *Loan risk compensation.* This is the lender's estimate of the safety of the loan as an investment. It varies from loan to loan and is related to the size of the mortgage, the amount of the down payment, and the term.

3. *Conditions of the money market.* When mortgage funds are large and the demand is low, interest rates drop; when funds are low and the demand is high, interest rates rise.

The rising interest payment is the second most important factor in the in-

---

TABLE 6-2. Effect of Different Interest Rates on Payments and Interest Costs of a $60,000 Loan Over a Thirty-Year Period

INTEREST RATE	MONTHLY PAYMENT	MONTHLY INTERESTa	TOTAL INTEREST COST	TOTAL COST
8 1/2	461.35	425.00	106,086	166,086
9	482.78	450.00	113,800	173,800
9 1/2	504.52	475.00	121,630	181,630
10	526.55	500.00	129,560	189,560

aFirst payment.

creased cost of owning a home. Between 1970 and 1978, mortgage interest rates rose, as did purchase prices. Thus, increased mortgage interest payments reflect both rising interest rates and a larger principal. The loan-to-value ratio remained stable during this period. A rise of only 1 percent interest costs more than $15,000 on a thirty-year $60,000 mortgage.

Interest costs can be deducted from federal income taxes and from many state income tax returns. This deduction is a subsidization of costs. Depending on the owner's income and the interest rate, the after-tax cost of interest varies. Table 6-3 shows the effective interest rate, or after-tax cost, of interest paid at varying income levels.

It should be remembered that interest is figured on the balance of the loan. So, early in the mortgage, more is paid on the interest than on the principal. Later, the reverse is true. With inflation and rising housing costs, waiting for interest rates to drop may be costly.

USURY LAWS   Usury laws set a ceiling on interest rates. There are two rationales for usury laws: (1) borrowers of limited means who are unsophisticated and know little about finances are protected from exorbitant interest charges; (2) lenders tend to be noncompetitive, and usury laws restore a competitive-type equilibrium.

Although U.S. usury laws are a carryover from English common law, the United Kingdom repealed its real estate usury laws 120 years ago. Also, in the United States, usury laws vary from state to state. Some states exempt certain classes of lenders, kinds of loans, or sizes of loans. In some states, points and other fees are defined as interest; in others, they are not.

Usury laws may hinder the flow of mortgage funds at a reasonable and competitive rate. When yields on other investments become higher, mortgage money becomes scarce. Usury laws may actually make the mortgage market less competitive. The only sellers in a market

TABLE 6-3. After-Tax Cost of Interest Paid, 1978 For Selected Joint Federal Income Tax Returns

TAXABLE INCOME	7%	8%	9%	10%	11%	12%	13%
Over Not Over							
$ 4,200–5,200	5.95	6.80	7.65	8.50	9.35	10.20	11.05
6,200–7,200	5.81	6.64	7.47	8.30	9.13	9.96	10.79
11,200–15,200	5.46	6.24	7.02	7.80	8.58	9.36	10.14
19,200–23,200	5.04	5.76	6.48	7.20	7.92	8.64	9.36
27,200–31,200	4.48	5.12	5.76	6.40	7.04	7.68	8.32
35,200–39,200	4.06	4.64	5.22	5.80	6.38	6.96	7.54
43,200–47,200	3.64	4.16	4.68	5.20	5.72	6.24	6.76
55,200–67,200	3.29	3.76	4.23	4.70	5.17	5.64	6.11
79,200–91,200	2.94	3.36	3.78	4.20	4.62	5.04	5.46
103,200–123,200	2.66	3.04	3.42	3.80	4.18	4.56	4.94
143,200–163,200	2.38	2.72	3.06	3.40	3.74	4.08	4.42
183,200–203,200	2.17	2.48	2.79	3.10	3.41	3.72	4.03
203,200 & over	2.10	2.40	2.70	3.00	3.30	3.60	3.90

where a maximum price is set are probably those whose average costs are below this price. If economies of scale exist, usury laws may freeze out small lenders.

When market rates are above the usury ceiling, the flow of funds is distorted. Mortgage money will be scarce and lending terms will be restrictive, such as high down payments, a shorter term, or extra fees. The local housing market then becomes depressed.[29] In a really tight market, no conventional mortgage money may be available.

However, some lenders will offer mortgages to maintain good depositor or legislative relations or to encourage the use of other services. Another factor is the percentage of assets which the lender holds in home mortgages and the difference between the usury ceiling and the market rate. Without a usury ceiling, rates are determined by the market. Those who can afford to pay the rate can enter the market.

POINTS To increase the yield on a mortgage, a lending institution may charge points. This often affects government-insured and granted mortgages if the legal interest rate is below the going market rate. One point equals 1 percent of the loan amount.

For example:

Mortgage applied for is	$60,000
4 points charged equals	2,400
Amount of money received by the borrower is	58,600

Amount borrower pays interest on and must pay back is	$60,000

In some states, points are considered interest and are included as such if there is a usury ceiling. In other states, they are not interest. The buyer or seller may pay the points depending on the situation.

REPAYMENT PERIOD

The length of the mortgage *repayment period* affects the size of the monthly payment. The shorter the repayment period, the larger the monthly payment (Table 6-4). On the other hand, the shorter the repayment period, the less total interest paid. Most mortgages are for a term of twenty-twenty-five, or thirty years. The term of the mortgage may differ with the three types of loans. For example, in 1976 mortgage terms for conventional loans averaged twenty-eight years for new houses and twenty-six years for older houses. In contrast, 93 percent or more of VA loans for both older and new houses had a repayment period of thirty years.

FEATURES

In addition to the purchase terms already discussed, there are other features to consider. The prepayment privilege allows the borrower to pay all or part of the mortgage before the term ends. Since most loans are terminated before the end of the payment period, it is important to know what, if any, penalty might be charged. Some state laws limit this pen-

[29]Ernest Kohn, Carmen J. Carlo, and Bernard Kaye, *The Impact of New York's Usury Ceiling on Local Mortgage Lending Activity* (Albany: New York State Banking Department, January 1976), p. 10.

[30]U.S. Department of Housing and Urban Development, *HUD Statistical Yearbook 1977* (Washington, D.C.: U.S. Government Printing Office, 1979), pp. 378, 380.

TABLE 6-4. Effect of Different Repayment Periods on Monthly Payments and Interest Cost for a $60,000 Mortgage at 9 Percent Interest

REPAYMENT PERIOD	MONTHLY PAYMENT	TOTAL INTEREST COST	TOTAL COST
15	$608.56	$ 49,540	$109,540
20	539.84	69,560	129,560
25	503.52	91,060	151,060
30	482.78	113,800	173,800

alty. For example, in New Jersey there is usually a "3-2-1" clause in the mortgage contract allowing the borrower to prepay a set amount per year, often 20 percent. Any amount prepaid over the set sum carries the following maximum penalty: 3 percent of the face amount of the mortgage the first year, 2 percent the second year, 1 percent the third year, and nothing thereafter.

An *open-end mortgage* allows the borrower to increase the mortgage up to the original amount. It is a way to finance repairs and improvements. A package mortgage allows the borrower to include equipment and furnishings in the loan.

CONCLUSION

The factors of interest rate, size of loan, and repayment period must be weighed against each other and compared by the borrower. In the end, the best mortgage is one that provides for a down payment and monthly charges the borrower can afford and includes the desired features.

Closing Procedures

The final step in the purchase or sale of a home is the closing. This is usually a meeting between the buyer and seller, representatives of the lender, the real estate broker if one was involved, and attorneys hired by any and all parties. However, in some parts of the country, an escrow agent holds the transaction, and the buyer and seller do not have a formal meeting. At the closing, certain settlement or *closing costs* and adjustments must be paid. These are the charges and fees incurred in transferring ownership of the home, including charges by the lender for loan processing and by an attorney to examine the title. Closing costs are payable to someone other than the seller. In addition, closing adjustments are made between the buyer and seller for items such as property taxes, which are charged on a pro rata basis. In the following discussion, closing or settlement costs will include costs and adjustments as defined above.

Settlement charges may vary both in type and in total dollar costs. There are several reasons for this:

1. Local laws and customs vary.
2. Lending institution practices and services provided in the sales transaction differ.
3. Responsibility for certain charges varies between buyer and seller and must be negotiated between them.
4. Required closing services and their costs vary with the type of mortgage (conventional, FHA, or VA) obtained.
5. Total closing costs depend on the

buyer's efforts to "shop around" and to bargain with the suppliers of closing services, such as the lawyer, title company, lending institution, and surveyor.

Depending on the state and local area, a buyer may face settlement charges for the title search, title insurance, *attorney's fees,* a *property survey,* a *credit report* obtained by the lender, points, an *appraisal fee,* recording fee, real estate taxes, *state and local transfer taxes, escrow fees,* and mortgage insurance. State or federal laws require many of these items, so that they cannot be avoided.

The seller's closing costs consist mainly of the real estate broker's commission, points if there are any, and the attorney's fee.

Closing costs vary widely across the country.[31] Settlement costs usually increase with the price of the property.[32] The buyer can reduce closing costs by:

1. Negotiating with the seller before signing the sales contract to share costs for some of the items.

2. Seeing if the old survey and an affidavit by the seller may be acceptable instead of a new survey if one is required and no changes have been made since the seller purchased the home.

3. Negotiating with the seller's title insurance company to give a lower or

"reissue" rate if the title was last searched not long before.

4. Comparing the fees or charges made by various lenders.

5. Comparing attorneys' fees and services.

REAL ESTATE SETTLEMENT PROCEDURES ACT

The 1974 Real Estate Settlement Procedures Act (RESPA), as amended, establishes minimum disclosure standards for settlement costs. The law applies to all federally related mortgage loans. This loan is one that is used to finance the purchase of housing property; secured by a first lien; and made by a lender

1. Whose deposits are insured by an agency of the federal government, or

2. Who is regulated by a federal agency, or

3. Who makes or made investments in real estate loans of $1,000,000 in 1974 or 1975 except for agencies or instrumentalities of any state, or

4. The loan is made, insured, guaranteed or supplemented by the federal government; or is in connection with a housing or urban development program administered by a federal government agency; or is intended to be sold to a federal agency operating in the secondary mortgage market.[33]

Some loans are exempted, such as those on twenty-five or more acres, home improvement loans, and loan assumptions.

[31]*Buying a Home: Don't Forget Those Closing Costs,* HUD 342-F(5) (October 1973); "Opening the Window on Closing Costs," *Money,* 4 (June 1975), 50–54.

[32]U.S. Department of Housing and Urban Development, *Report on Mortgage Settlement Costs* (Washington, D.C.: U.S. Government Printing Office, 1972), p. 73.

[33]"Real Estate Settlement Procedures," *Federal Register* (Jan. 9, 1976), 1673–74.

Since June 30, 1976, at the time of a written application for a mortgage, the lender must provide a booklet explaining settlement procedure and a reasonable estimate of the amount or range of charges. A copy of the booklet may also be obtained from HUD. The RESPA law also requires that the borrower be allowed to review the settlement statement one business day before the closing. The borrower may waive this right, and HUD may exempt areas where settlement disclosure is not usually given or where impracticable.

No fee can be charged by the lender for preparing the settlement statement. The lender may mail the information and need supply it to only one borrower. Borrowers can be required to deposit in an escrow account a sum of money up to the amount of escrow charges. Borrowers cannot be required to pay more than one-twelfth of the estimated charges each month.

The RESPA law serves two purposes: (1) to let borrowers know the costs they will face so that they will be able to have the cash needed; (2) to help them understand what they are buying. Enforcement of the law rests with the individuals involved, although the federal agencies involved may check compliance. Thus, the borrower personally must complain to the lender or hire an attorney to prosecute the lender if the information is not provided. A survey by Seidel indicated that RESPA increased loan processing time and costs.[34]

TRUTH-IN-LENDING

The 1969 Truth-in-Lending Regulation requires lenders to disclose the annual percentage rate of interest to borrowers. However, home mortgages are exempted from many other provisions of the act that apply to consumer credit, such as disclosure of exact dollar interest costs. The 1975 Equal Credit Opportunity Regulation, an amendment to Truth-in-Lending, prohibits lending institutions from refusing credit because of an applicant's sex, marital status, race, national origin, religion, age, and receipt of public assistance.[35] A lender cannot ask about plans for having or raising children or assume from the applicants' age that they will become parents. One spouse's income may not be discounted, nor may part-time income be discriminated against or ignored. The probability of continued income is the important issue.

ESCROW ACCOUNTS

Many lending institutions require *escrow accounts* on the home mortgage loans they grant. The money in the account is used to pay the homeowner's real estate taxes, property insurance premiums, and other assessments when they become due. Each month, one-twelfth of the annual total is deposited in the account.

Escrow accounts on mortgages developed as a result of the Great Depression, when many people lost their homes as a result of tax foreclosures. The Home Owners Loan Corporation, created by Congress to take over loans of delinquent

---

[34]Stephen R. Seidel, *Housing Costs and Government Regulations: Confronting the Regulatory Maze.* (New Brunswick, N.J.: The Center for Urban Policy Research, 1978). 280.

[35]Equal Credit Opportunity Act, U.S. Title 15. Sec. 1691 *et seq.*

borrowers, was the first institution to require monthly collection of the annual tax bill. The Federal Housing Administration, also created during the 1930s, requires escrow accounts for property taxes on all FHA-insured loans.

Some state laws require escrow accounts for high-risk mortgage loans. For example, Massachusetts requires an escrow account for all loans greater than 70 percent of the property's estimated value; in New Hampshire the figure is 75 percent.

Recently lenders have been criticized for not paying interest on escrow accounts. The original interest rates paid on savings accounts were so low that interest on escrow accounts was not considered. In fact, some lenders charged a fee for handling these accounts. Today interest rates on savings accounts are higher, and consumers object to lenders having free use of escrow funds. State laws dictate whether and what percentage of interest lenders must pay.

In 1972 the Government Accounting Office (GAO) studied the issue of interest on escrow accounts.[36] It found that 32 percent of escrow operations resulted in a net loss, 10 percent had gross income equal to maintenance costs, and 58 percent had a net profit. Whether (and how much) the financial institution gains or loses from escrow operations depends on the size of the escrow fund, how long it is available for investment, and the nature and yield rate of investment opportunities.

Lenders prefer escrow accounts for two reasons: (1) some borrowers are not able to save for these costs; (2) the accounts assure that a tax lien will not be attached to the property and take precedence over the mortgage. However, many homeowners object to the idea that borrowers cannot budget and pay their taxes and insurance. Still, owners who prefer the escrow system should have it available. When the escrow funds are invested, a reasonable share of the income should be given to the homeowner.

Instead of an escrow account, some lenders have applied escrow deposits against the outstanding principal of the mortgage and then charged funds paid out against the principal; in effect, they have paid interest at the mortgage interest rate. Another alternative is to have the homeowner deposit a sum in an interest-bearing savings account as a pledge to meet tax bills. Finally, rather than continuing for the entire life of the mortgage, limiting the life of an escrow account is more acceptable.

Other Types of Financing

We have discussed the traditional amortized mortgage as well as other types of mortgages. Now let us consider other types of financing. First, instead of originating a mortgage, a borrower may assume one that already exists. In addition, he or she may get a *second mortgage* on the property. Alternately, the borrower may buy the home through a *land contract*. If a home is being built, the borrower may get a construction loan. Each of these loans differs from the types of financing already discussed.

[36]Comptroller General of the United States, *Study of the Feasibility of Escrow Accounts on Residential Mortgages Becoming Interest Bearing* (Washington, D.C.: U.S. Government Printing Office, June 21, 1973).

MORTGAGE ASSUMPTION

Rather than obtaining a new mortgage, a buyer may assume the existing mortgage (the remaining debt) on the house. This is desirable when:

1. The present owner has little equity invested in the house and the down payment required is small. For example, to buy a house priced at $54,00 with a $43,200 mortgage, the buyer assumes the mortgage and, to cover the equity, makes a down payment of $10,800.

2. The interest rate on the existing mortgage is lower than the rate on a new mortgage. Also, closing costs are lower and the sale can be closed more quickly.

However, mortgage assumption must be approved by the lender. When interest rates are high, the lender may hesitate to approve a loan *assumption* with a lower yield.

SECOND MORTGAGE

Besides the first mortgage on the house, a buyer may obtain a second or "junior" mortgage. The second mortgage is a "piggyback" loan on top of the first mortgage and is usually paid back within five years. This type of loan may be needed when a buyer assumes the existing mortgage and must make a large down payment requiring a further loan. For example, to buy a house priced at $54,000 with a $44,000 mortgage, the borrower will need a second mortgage to make a down payment of $10,000 if only $6,000 is available.

A second mortgage is often hard to obtain. According to 1970 census data, only 1.5 percent of all single-family homes had second mortgages.[37] Since 1972, second mortgages have applied to 1 percent or less of all new homes sold.[38] In case of default, the holder of a second mortgage must wait until the first mortgage holder has been paid. Because of this greater risk, the interest rate is usually higher and the loan is for a shorter term. The first mortgage holder often insists on the right to approve a second mortgage because the combined payments may be too high for the borrower to meet, thus causing default. Mutual savings banks and savings and loan associations cannot grant second mortgages. A commercial bank can, but this is unlikely to happen.

LAND CONTRACT PURCHASE

Another way to buy a home is through a land contract. This can be arranged in one of two ways.

1. The seller and buyer make an agreement in which the buyer makes a down payment to the seller, and agrees to make monthly payments and to maintain the property. Should the buyer default, all payments previously made are forfeited and the property reverts to the seller.

2. The seller and buyer make an agreement similar to the one above

---

[37]Census Housing, vol. 5, *Residential Finance*, p. 3.

[38]U.S. Department of Commerce, Bureau of the Census, and U.S. Department of Housing and Urban Development, *Characteristics of New One-Family Homes*, C-25. Yearly.

except that, in case of default, the buyer is entitled to a return of all payments made plus cash recovery of any property improvements undertaken.

The two main reasons a buyer would prefer a land contract are:

1. The buyer does not have a large enough down payment to qualify for a mortgage from a lending institution.
2. For credit or other reasons, the buyer does not meet the mortgage requirements of a financial institution.

Also, since no lending institution is involved, the sales transaction costs less.

The disadvantages for a buyer include:

1. The seller usually holds the title to the land until the contract is completed. For the seller's protection, the contract should state that the title and contract will be placed in escrow.
2. Foreclosure is much easier for the seller in case of default. A buyer should insist that a ninety-day clause, similar to those in most mortgage contracts, be included. This clause states that the seller must wait ninety days before taking possession on a default.
3. The contract should allow the buyer to refinance with a regular lending institution after a certain time— perhaps five or ten years—and thus pay off the land contract. The disadvantage is that the lender may be unwilling to finance because either the buyer or the property still do not meet certain requirements. The sel-

ler may have agreed to a land contract sale knowing that for reasons such as poor location or a deteriorated structure, a regular mortgage would not be offered.

The advantages for a seller include:

1. Tight money markets usually raise the interest rate and down payment required by lending institutions. Young people with a good job may be able to handle higher monthly payments but do not have the large down payment required.
2. A land contract brings monthly money with only a small initial deposit. For sellers who do not need money for a new investment, this monthly check may be a tax advantage or may provide income similar to rental but without the responsibilities of leasing.

The disadvantages for the seller include:

1. The buyer who is a poor credit risk to the lender is probably just as risky for the seller.
2. Just as it is easier for a seller to foreclose with a land contract, it is easier for the buyer to default.

HOME IMPROVEMENT FINANCING

Home improvements can be financed through an open-end mortgage, refinancing an existing mortgage, a home improvement loan which usually involves a second lien on the property, or a personal loan. FHA will insure home improvement loans. In addition, the federal government subsidizes interest rates under its Section 312 rehabilitation loan program (see Chapter 11).

CONSTRUCTION LOANS

A construction loan is a mortgage used to build a home. Such loans made by lending institutions often follow a formula similar to this: 15 percent is given when the subflooring is completed, 45 percent when the roof is on, 25 percent when the walls are finished, and 15 percent when the house is finished. A borrower must compare formulas, procedures, and inspection processes followed by local lending institutions.

MOBILE HOME FINANCING

Financing of mobile homes is changing. Although mobile homes are still treated like consumer property in most states, some lending institutions are beginning to view them as site-built housing. Credit is given through *chattel mortgages* at higher interest rates and for shorter terms than home mortgage loans. The average term and size of the loan has been increasing. More changes can be expected in the future.

Commercial banks, savings banks, and savings and loan associations may make loans for mobile homes. They may lend up to 90 percent of the purchase price of a new or used mobile home for up to twenty years. The term has been increasing. However, the lending institution may ask for more than 10 percent down because:

1. Its policy requires a larger down payment.
2. The institution wants the cash value

of the mobile home to be greater than the loan balance.
3. Money may be tight.
4. The buyer may have a limited credit record, and a larger down payment helps offset the risk involved.

The mobile home dealer usually has sources for financing the unit. The company may have its own financing corporation or the dealer may contact a lending agency and "sell" or "discount" the loan to that agency. Consumer finance companies are another source. Their interest rates are usually higher, and they are limited in the amount they can loan.

The FHA will guarantee loans on mobile homes if the borrower or the mobile home meets its standards. The mobile home must be used as the principal residence for at least nine months of the year. This excludes a mobile home used only for vacations. The borrower must show that the home meets certain standards, including local zoning laws. The mobile home must be built for permanent occupancy, with permanent eating, cooking, sleeping, and sanitary facilities. It must be placed either in a mobile home park approved by the FHA or on a site owned by the borrower. The home must be at least 10 feet wide and 40 feet long or consist of a module(s) having a minimum floor area of 400 square feet. The mobile home must be new or must carry a previous FHA-insured loan.

The amount, term, and interest rate of FHA mobile home loans have changed over time. Down payment requirements are also regulated. Accessory items, transportation, setup charges, and up to five years of insurance premiums on the home may be covered by the loan, and the cost of the site itself. Loans are repaid in equal monthly installments. These are personal loans secured by a *conditional sales contract* or *chattel mortgage* on the mobile home.

Veterans Administration (VA) financing is available to eligible veterans. A VA-guaranteed loan can cover both the mobile home and the land on which it will stand. The maximum loan amount, term, and interest rate change. Accurate information should be obtained from the local VA office.

The FmHA and the Farmers Credit Administration are other possible sources for families in rural areas. Credit unions also offer financing for members, at rates which are often lower than for the other sources discussed.

Delinquency and Foreclosure

A loan becomes delinquent when the borrower misses payments or fails to comply with other terms and conditions of the mortgage, such as maintaining property insurance coverage. After a specified period, often thirty days after the payment was due and not paid, a loan is said to be in default. When this happens, the lender can usually foreclose the loan, selling the home to satisfy the debt.

Delinquency usually results from a loss of income.[39] The buyer cannot make the payments on schedule. Serious loan delinquencies (ninety days or more in arrears) may be caused by: a second mortgage, a high loan-to-value ratio, and the loan type.[40] Loans guaranteed or insured

by the government on the whole had more delinquency than conventionals, although after other factors were controlled, such as loan-to-value ratios and occupation, conventional loans carried higher risks than FHA or VA loans. Older homes were riskier than new homes.[41] Term of maturity, occupation, number of dependents, mortgage payment-to-income ratios, marital status, and region were not important. Borrower age was sometimes important and sometimes not; no firm conclusions could be drawn.

A limited case study by HUD of default counseling in four U.S. cities indicated:[42]

1. Counseling had a strong impact on defaults. Of those referred for counseling, more were current on their payments and were better off after the counseling. In contrast, more of the nonreferrals were foreclosed, and more were late with their payments.

2. Those who were referred but could not be reached or refused counseling did not default. Thus mortgagors who know they are able to bring themselves current tend to refuse counseling or perhaps they could not enter counseling because they were moonlighting or inolved in other self-improvement activities.[43]

3. In a cost-benefit analysis: (a) savings

---

[39]Craig Swan, "Alternative Mortgage Instruments and Mortgage Defaults," mimeo (Minneapolis: University of Minnesota, September 1977). 5.

[40]John P. Herzog and James S. Earley, *Home Delinquency and Foreclosure*, The National Bureau of Economic Research (New York: Columbia University Press, 1970), pp. XVIII, XVII.

[41]George M. von Furstenberg and R. Jeffrey Green, "Estimation of Delinquency Risk for Home Mortgage Portfolios," *American Journal of Real Estate and Urban Economics,* 2 (Spring 1974) 5–19.

[42]U.S. Department of Housing and Urban Development, Office of Program Analyses and Evaluation, *Counseling for Delinquent Mortgagors* (Washington, D.C.: U.S. Government Printing Office, November 1975).

[43]Ibid. p. 19.

to the insurance fund because of foreclosures avoided far outweighed the cost of counseling; (b) future subsidies were about equal to the immediate savings to the insurance fund, although the long-run impact of counseling on the HUD budget was not clear; (c) counseling was considered helpful when federal, personal, and social costs and benefits were included.

We must be careful in drawing these conclusions. The HUD sample was small, counseling programs were of one type only, and the time period studied was short. However, a second HUD study supported these results.[44] Counseling definitely helped to reduce foreclosures, although there were strong differences between cities and agencies.

The lender will usually try to prevent foreclosure when the default is caused by factors beyond the borrower's control. The lender may reduce or suspend the payments for a time, or unpaid taxes, insurance, and interest could be added to the principal and refinanced later. Such actions lessen the financial pressure on the borrower and reduce collection problems for the lender.

However, if it becomes clear that the borrower cannot or will not meet the mortgage payments or terms, the lender may foreclose. Foreclosure is often a long and costly procedure. Sometime, if local law permits, the borrower may give the lender title to the home in return for cancellation of the mortgage and mortgage note. In either case, the lender will need to sell the property. When the sales price received does not equal the cost, the lender may be able to obtain a deficiency judgment against the borrower for the difference.

According to the Mortgage Bankers Association of America, less than .5 percent of total mortgage loans on one- to four-family homes are foreclosed. Conventional loans account about 14 percent of foreclosures; FHA (excluding 235 and 237) loans for 46 percent; FHA 235 and 237 loans for 5.5 percent; and VA loans for 34 percent.[45] Obviously a buyer would not allow his or her home to be foreclosed if it could be sold, the mortgage paid off, and less expensive housing located. Thus, borrowers who are foreclosed must have a negative equity in the home. With low down payments and high interest rates, it takes several years for a borrower to build up enough equity.

Summary

This chapter has examined several aspects of home financing. Different types of mortgages were analyzed, including amortized, interest-only, variable-rate, indexed, short-term bond, graduated payment, and contingent appreciation participation.

The major sources of mortgage credit—savings and loan associations, commercial banks, mortgage companies, and savings banks—were discussed. FHA, VA, and private mortgage insurance programs were covered. The process of obtaining a mortgage loan was

[44]U.S. Department of Housing and Urban Development, Office of Policy Development and Research, *Counseling for Delinquent Mortgages II* (Washington, D.C.: U.S. Government Printing Office, January 1977).

[45]Mortgage Bankers Association of America, *National Delinquency Survey* (Washington, D.C., Feb. 16, 1979). See Chapter 11 for a definition of Section 235 and 237.

outlined, including mortgage features to consider, closing procedures, and federal laws. A discussion of delinquency and foreclosure concluded the chapter.

Terms

acceleration clause a mortgage clause stating that if the buyer fails to make monthly payments or sells the property before the mortgage is paid, the remaining debt becomes due immediately.

amortization payment of a mortgage in equal monthly installments of principal and interest over a designated repayment period.

appraisal fee a charge to establish the value of the property, required by the lending institution.

assumption agreement by the buyer to pay the balance of the existing mortgage on an older home in accordance with the original terms of the mortgage.

attorney's fee amount paid to the buyer's attorney, if one is hired, and also to the lender's attorney. The attorney checks the title and prepares the legal documents.

bond evidences of the amount of borrowed money owed to the lender. See *First mortgage bond*.

chattel mortgage mortgage held by the lender on a mobile home to act as security for the balance due.

closing completion of the purchase of a property. Ownership is transferred from seller to buyer, and the buyer's obligation to begin payment of the mortgage starts.

closing costs also called *settlement costs*. Costs in addition to the price of the house, including mortgage service charges, title search, and transfer of ownership charges.

conditional sale contract a contract between buyer and seller in which the seller retains title until the conditions of the contract have been fulfilled.

conventional mortgage a loan for which the borrower's home is security; not guaranteed or insured by a government agency.

credit report fee a charge by the lending institution to cover costs of checking the buyer's credit worthiness.

default failure of a borrower to make monthly payments on a mortgage.

deficiency judgment a court decision requiring payment of that part of a mortgage debt which is not recovered in the foreclosure sale of a property. For example, if a $20,000 mortgage is foreclosed and the amount received from the sale is only $13,000, the mortgage will have a deficiency judgment for $7,000.

documentary stamps state tax stamps required on a mortgage note and deed. The federal government also requires stamps on a transfer of property.

equity owner's interest in a property; the difference between fair market value and current indebtedness.

escrow account an account set up by the lending institution into which the buyer pays for future taxes, assessments, or insurance premiums.

escrow fees funds usually paid to the lender to be held for taxes or insurance.

first mortgage bond generally issued together with the first mortgage at the closing of the sale. States the repayment terms of the mortgage, the agreement to insure the property, to pay the taxes and assessments, to keep the property repaired, and so on.

foreclosure legal proceedings that deprive a mortgagor of ownership rights when mortgage terms are violated or property taxes not paid. Foreclosure is usually followed by sale of the property to recover the mortgage debt or unpaid taxes.

indexed mortgage a mortgage in which the principal is revalued periodically.

insured loan a loan guaranteed by an agency, such as the FHA, which insures the lending institution against loss on the principal in case of default.

land contract the purchase of property directly from the seller without financing by a lending institution. The buyer usually does not receive the deed to the property until payments on the house are completed.

lien a claim upon a property until a debt is paid.

mortgage a document that pledges the buyer's property as security against a loan.

mortgage agreement consists of the mortgage and the first mortgage bond.

mortgage commitment written notice from the lender stating that specified mortgage funds will be provided.

mortgage insurance guarantees the lender against loss if the borrower fails to make mortgage payments for reasons other than disability or death.

mortgage note see *first mortgage bond.*

mortgagee the lender of the mortgage.

mortgagor the borrower of the mortgage.

open-end clause the provision in an open-end mortgage allowing a mortgagor to borrow more money in the future, usually up to the original loan amount.

open-end mortgage allows the mortgagor to borrow more money in the future without rewriting the mortgage.

origination preparation of the documents supporting a mortgage, such as credit checks and title search.

points a one-time fee charged by the lender at the closing in order to increase the return (profit) on the loan. Each point is equal to 1 percent of the loan. On FHA and VA transactions, the seller must pay the points.

principal the amount of mortgage debt a borrower owes.

promissory note see *first mortgage bond.*

purchase money mortgage given directly to the seller by the buyer (as in a land contract) as part of the purchase price without the involvement of a third party, such as a lending institution.

real estate taxes a charge against real estate by county or city tax authorities, based on some proportion of the property's value.

realtor's fee charge usually paid by the seller to the realtor. Generally some percentage of the gross sales price.

recording fee charge by the local government for recording documents related to the sale.

repayment period length of time given to repay the mortgage.

second mortgage a "piggyback loan," in addition to the unpaid balance of the existing mortgage, on the house the buyer intends to purchase in order to finance the down payment. In case of default and foreclosure, the lender of a second mortgage can recover only after the lender of the first mortgage has been paid.

servicing includes collecting and accounting for monthly payments, maintaining an escrow account, checking insurance coverage, and examining the property.

state and local transfer taxes taxes levied when property changes hands or when a mortgage loan is made.

survey establishment of the boundaries of the property and its area by a surveyor.

tax escrow a fund into which the borrower pays and out of which the mortgagee pays taxes, insurance, and other costs.

tax search a document issued by a local taxing authority stating whether its records indicate any accrued taxes against the property.

term length of time given to repay the mortgage.

variable-rate mortgage mortgage that allows the interest rate to vary over the term.

Suggested Readings

Bruce, Jon W., "Mortgage Law Reform Under the Uniform Land Transactions Act," *Georgetown Law Review,* 64 (July 1976) 1245–89.

Cassidy, Henry J., and Rolando C. Maturana, *Mortgage Adjustment in an Inflationary Economy,* Working Paper #30. Washington, D.C.: Federal Home Loan Bank Board, n.d.

Comptroller General of the United States, *Study of the Feasibility of Escrow Accounts on Residential Mortgages Becoming Interest Bearing.* Washington, D.C.: U.S. Government Printing Office, 1973.

Coon, Robert C., "The VA Home Loan Program," *HUD Challenge* VI (December 1975), 10–12.

Credit Flows and Interest Costs, a study prepared for the Subcommittee on Economic Progress of the Joint Economic Committee Congress of the United States, 94th Congress, 1st Session, Washington, D.C.: U.S. Government Printing Office, March 1975.

Diamond, Arnold H., *The Supply of Mortgage Credit, 1970–1974.* Washington, DC.: U.S. Department of Housing and Urban Development, U.S. Government Printing Office, 1975.

Hall, Florence L., and Evelyn Freeman, "Survey of Home Buyers' and Sellers' Closing Costs," *Journal of Home Economics,* 64 (January 1972), 20–26.

Kidd, Phillip E., "Solid Equity Base Required to Support Expanded Loan Activity," *Mortgage Banker,* 37 (December 1976), 33–36.

Kohn, Ernest, Carmen J. Carlo, and Bernard Kaye, *The Impact of New York's Usury Ceiling on Local Mortgage Lending Activity.* Albany, N.Y.: New York State Banking Department, January 1976.

Little, Arthur D., *The Arthur D. Little Study of the Private Mortgage Insurance Industry.* Washington, D.C.: Mortgage Insurance Companies of America, November 1975.

McDonough, William R., "New Loan Plan Offers Hope in an Inflation," *Federal Reserve Bank of Dallas Business Review* (September 1975), 1–7.

New Mortgage Designs for Stable Housing in An Inflationary Environment, Conference Series No. 14. Proceedings of a Conference sponsored by the Federal Reserve Bank of Boston, U.S. Department of Housing and Urban Development, and Federal Home Loan Bank Board. Boston, Mass.: Federal Reserve Bank of Boston, January 1975.

Rolnick, Arthur J. Stanley L. Graham, and Davis S. Sahl, "Minnesota's Usury Law: An Evaluation," *Ninth District Quarterly,* II (April 1975), 16–24.

Schussheim, Morton J., Statement, Hearing before the Subcommittee on Housing and Urban Affairs of the Committee on Banking, Housing and Urban Affairs, U.S. Senate, 94th Congress, 1st Session, Sept. 23, 24, and 25, 1975.

Spurlock, Hughes H., *Differences in Housing Credit Terms and Usage Between Metro and Nonmetro Areas in the United States 1971.* Agricultural Economics Report #305, ERS. Washington, D.C.: U.S. Department of Agriculture, August 1975.

U.S. Department of Housing and Urban Development, *Mortgage Credit Risk Analysis and Servicing of Delinquent Mortgages.* Office of International Affairs. Washington, D.C.: U.S. Government Printing Office, November 1972.

——, *Counseling for Delinquent Mortgagors,* A Staff Study. Washington, D.C.: U.S. Government Printing Office, November 1975.

U.S. Senate, Committee on Banking, Housing, and Urban Affairs, *Hearings before the Subcommittee on Housing and Urban Affairs on the Committee on Banking, Housing, and Urban Affairs,* statement by David S. Cook. 94th Congress, 1st Session, 1975, p. 386.

OWNERSHIP ALTERNATIVES

1. SHOULD CONDOMINIUMS BE FURTHER REG-
   ULATED?

2. WHAT ARE ABUSES WHICH HAVE EXISTED IN
   CONDOMINIUM DEVELOPMENT?

3. WHAT IS THE ROLE OF COOPERATIVES IN
   SUPPLYING HOUSING?

4. ARE MOBILE HOMES SAFE AND DURABLE?

5. HOW SHOULD MOBILE HOMES BE TAXED?

The majority of American homeowners own a single-family detached house. However, there are other forms of ownership and structural types. The most common of these are *condominiums, cooperatives,* and *mobile homes.* In this chapter, we will examine the characteristics of these alternatives, the legal and tax differences, and the costs involved.

Condominium and Cooperative Production

Condominium and cooperative housing has greatly increased. As of April 1, 1975, there were 1.69 million condominiums and cooperative housing units in the United States.[1] About 75 percent of these were condominiums. More than 85 percent of the condominiums were built since 1970, while 78 percent of the cooperatives existed prior to that date. However, condominiums and cooperatives still account for only about 2.5 percent of all occupied units.[2]

Condominiums accounted for about 15 percent of all units started for sale in 1978 up from the 12 percent of 1977, and 1976, similar to the 16 percent of 1974 but higher than the 5.4 percent of

---

[1]U.S. Department of Housing and Urban Development, *HUD Comdominium/Cooperative Study,* Vol. I (Washington, D.C.: U.S. Government Printing Office, July 1975), p. III-1.

[2]Ibid., p. I-7.

Multi-family units clustered around lake.

U.S. Department of HUD

1970.[3] Conversions of apartment buildings to condominiums during the 1970–1974 period is estimated at about 100,000 units, or 10 percent of new construction condominium activity.[4] Conversion to cooperatives is estimated at 25,000, or 35 percent of new construction cooperative activity.

Of the roughly 15,000 condominium and cooperative projects, about 12,500 are cooperatives, with an average of 100 units per project; the remainder are condominiums, with an average of 150 units per project.[5] "Approximately 25 percent of the current inventory of condominium units represents vacation or 'second' homes."[6]

Condominium and cooperative activity varies greatly by region and state. More than 75 percent of U.S. condominiums are located in the West and South.[7] Nearly 50 percent of all condominiums and cooperatives are in California, Florida, and New York, while ten states—Florida, California, New York, Illinois, Michigan, Pennsylvania, Texas, New Jersey, Arizona, and Maryland—

[3]U.S. Department of Commerce, Bureau of the Census, *Construction Reports*, "Housing Starts," Series C20 (May 1977, May 1979), and U.S. Department of Housing and Urban Development *Condominium/Cooperative Study*, Vol. I, p. IV-26.

[4]Ibid., p. III-13.

[5]*HUD Condominium/Cooperative Study*, Vol. I. p. III-24.

[6]Ibid., p. IV-16.

[7]Ibid., p. III-2.

account for 67 percent of the condominiums and 81 percent of the cooperatives.[8]

In certain markets, condominium construction has replaced multi-family rental units. While in 1974 condominiums accounted for 44.5 percent of building permits for the Washington, D.C., area, up from 7.4 percent in 1970, multi-family rental permits dropped from 39.2 to 6.0 percent in the same period.

Condominiums

"Condominium" means to control (dominium) a certain property jointly with (con) one or more persons. The condominium concept is not new. It was employed by the ancient Romans to solve the same problems faced in the United States today—scarcity and high cost of urban land. Condominiums were also popular in the crowded walled cities of Western Europe in the Middle Ages and again at the beginning of the twentieth century. Both European and Latin American countries permitted condominiums by law.

A condominium is not one particular structural type but may take many forms: a high rise at the beach, a planned community of townhouses in suburbia, or a garden apartment in the city. A rental development may be converted into condominiums. Although the focus here is on residential condominiums, units in commercial buildings, such as medical offices and shopping centers, or industrial complexes may also be owned as condominiums.

[8]Ibid., p. III-17.

LEGAL ASPECTS

Condominiums are created under special state real estate laws that allow individual dwelling unit estates to be established within a larger total estate. Each state, U.S. territory, and Puerto Rico has its own set of condominium laws. The laws, which vary considerably in content and documents required, provide the legal framework for condominiums.

A property owner usually has rights to the land, its minerals, and the air space above it. Condominiums are based on the premise that these rights may be sold or conveyed. A condominium owner buys a set of air rights defined by the walls, floor, and ceiling of a dwelling unit. All the structural, land, and air space outside the various units is common to owners of all the units (Figure 7-1).

The *common areas* and facilities usually include:

1. The land on which the building is located.

2. The foundations, columns, girders, beams, supports, main walls, roofs, halls, corridors, lobbies, stairs, fire-escapes, and entrances of the building.

3. The basements, yards, gardens, parking areas, and storage spaces.

4. The premises for loading by janitors or persons in charge of the property.

5. Installation of central services, such as power, light, gas, water, heating, air conditioning, and incinerating.

6. The elevators, tanks, pumps, motors, fans, compressors, ducts, and in general all apparatus and installations existing for common use.

7. Such community and commercial

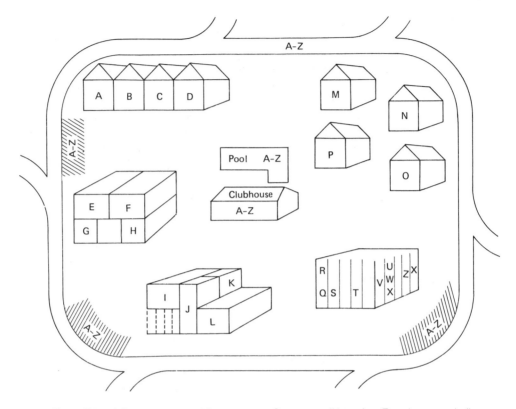

Figure 7-1. A Representation of Condominium Ownership. (*Note:* A to Z each own an individual unit and have an undivided interest in the common elements, including roofs and other structural elements.) [*Source:* U.S. Department of Housing and Urban Development, *HUD Condominium/Cooperative Study*, Vol. III, (Washington, D.C.: U.S. Government Printing Office, July 1975, p. G-10.)]

facilities as may be provided for in the declaration.

8. All other parts of the property necessary or convenient to its existence, maintenance, and safety, or normally in common use.

The master deed or *declaration* is the basic and most important document a condominium owner has. This legal document describes the conditions, covenants, and restrictions on the property. It governs the sale, ownership, use, and disposition of the property according to state law. It specifies the dimensions of each unit and defines the rights and responsibilities of each owner. The deed assigns the tax shares, voting rights, and insurance liabilities. It specifies the *common elements,* such as hallways, land, and recreational facilities, and their regulation. Floor plans and site plans are usually included, and any restrictions on the use of individual units or common areas are stated. Restrictions might exclude commercial establishments, prohibit several families from living in one unit, or prohibit rental.

Part of the master deed establishes the *undivided interest* percentage (ratio of a *unit* to the total of all units). This percentage will affect:

1. The percentage of ownership in common areas.
2. Votes in the homeowners or condominium association.
3. The assessment for maintenance and operation of common areas.
4. Real estate tax assessment.
5. The amount of money a lender will loan.

The formula may be specified by state law and may be based on the property's original value, the size of the unit, equal shares, or market value.

Usually the agreement of all owners is needed to change the declaration. When the declaration is recorded, it extends the state condominium laws to the property.

To administer the common elements and govern the condominium's development, an owners' association is formed; each unit owner is automatically a member. When the association starts to function is very important. The association develops a set of *bylaws* to govern the property's day-to-day operation. The bylaws specify the responsibilities of the owner and the board of directors. Details on the use and maintenance of common areas, budget, charges, provision for property management, rules for recreation, and insurance provisions are also spelled out. Avenues of recourse against owners who fail to pay fees are specified. It is important for the condominium buyer to know what is part of the declaration and what is part of the bylaws. Bylaws can usually be changed by a majority vote.

Rules or restrictions regarding the condominium development are generally included in the bylaws and should be weighed carefully by a prospective buyer.[9] For example, not all condominiums allow children, and some do not allow pets. The planting of outside shrubs may be prohibited.

The homeowners association should decide how the development should be managed.[10] Some projects allow for the hiring of a professional manager, who is responsible to the association and whose duties are specified in the bylaws or the declaration. Other condominiums are managed by the association itself, and problems are solved by the group or governing board. Professional management is often preferred for its efficiency, particularly if the project contains more than fifty units.

The contract provision which underlies the project will affect the owner's satisfaction. The advice of a lawyer experienced in condominium sales may be invaluable. Any resale restrictions should be carefully considered; they will not exist with federally insured (FHA or VA) condominiums. The person buying a condominium as an investment should be sure that the right to rent is clear.

PURCHASE CONSIDERATIONS

A prospective condominium owner should thoroughly investigate the history of the developer and his or her sources of money. The builder's integrity is

---

[9]F. Scott Jackson, "How Homeowners Associations Solve Their Enforcement Problems," *Real Estate Review*, 18 (Spring 1978), 80–86.

[10]For a discussion of management arrangements, see William D. Sally, "The Special World of Condominium Management," *Real Estate Review*, 15 (Fall 1975), 110–15.

paramount and may determine the project's success or failure for the owner. The developer needs enough capital to complete the development. What is the risk of loss before occupancy or prior to closing? In case the developer goes bankrupt, down payments should be deposited in an escrow account to protect the buyer against loss. If the developer retains ownership of any units, the number and time period should not permit him or her to control the owners association.

Often a condominium development is built in phases (Figure 7-2). The prospec-

tive buyer should know what the development will look like if not every phase is completed. The amount of land that will belong to the owners is also important. The number of units built per acre will affect density, privacy, and use of facilities. If the building or project is poorly planned, much privacy may be sacrificed.

As with a single-family house, quality construction of the condominium and common facilities is very important. An appraisal by an independent construction engineer or real estate appraiser trained

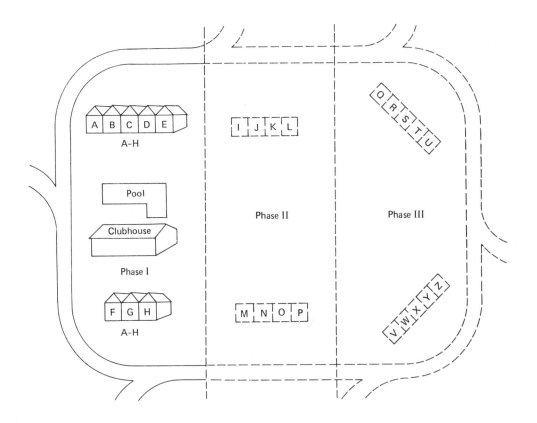

Figure 7-2.   Phase Development of a Condominium. [(*Source:* U.S. Department of Housing and Urban Development, *HUD Condominium/Cooperative Study*, Vol. III, (Washington, D.C.: U.S. Government Printing Office, July 1975, p. G-11.)]

USDA Soil Conservation Service/Photographer—Henry Richardson

Soil slippage on a supersaturated hillside of marine clay threatens to undermine house along subdivision south of Alexandria.

to evaluate construction is often a good idea. This is especially necessary when older apartments are being converted to condominiums.

The cost of the unit itself is important to any buyer.[11] The price increase of condominiums between 1972 and 1974 was relatively moderate, with the median price rising 10 percent over the period, or about 3 percent per year. The number of units priced below $20,000 is small; two-thirds of all units studied were in the

---

[11]Data on price are available from annual surveys of NAHB members; *Professional Builder Magazine;* the 1973 HUD survey of unsold homes; and the results of a survey of homeowners associations.

$20,000–$40,000 range. The higher-priced units are concentrated in the South and the West, while lower-priced units are most prevalent in the North Central region. For 1973, condominium units were the most expensive form of housing, costing 30 percent more than single-family homes on the basis of price per square foot of living area. This may seem to contradict notions of savings, but the condominium may include other amenities not found in single-family units.

The average size of condominium units, as reported in the 1974 NAHB survey, was 1,256 square feet, compared

153

with 1,282 square feet in 1973. This compares with an average size for new single-family housing of 1,695 and 1,660 square feet, respectively. Arthur D. Little, Inc., had previously estimated that the average size of all housing units in the U.S. inventory today is 1,300 square feet.[12] Thus, condominium units in projects now being built are slightly smaller than the U.S. average. In addition to having fewer square feet than single-family homes, condominium units have fewer rooms.

A condominium buyer purchases not only a housing unit but also services and maintenance. Thus, while condominium units are generally smaller than traditional single-family homes, and tend to cost more per square foot, much of this difference is theoretically made up by the amenities provided. For prospective buyers, project plans should be complete and available, including information on all common facilities. Nearly 80 percent of the projects surveyed by HUD included swimming pools. Other popular amenities were recreation rooms (58 percent), separate storage space (54 percent), laundry facilities (43 percent), and covered parking (43 percent).[13] In general, projects in the South and West have a more complete amenity package than those in the Northeast and North Central regions. Golf courses (6 percent), day care centers (2 percent), and medical facilities (2 percent) were reported for only a small fraction of the projects.

For most buyers, financing is important. Financing from the VA and FHA is available for some condominiums. Set-tlement or closing costs are paid by the condominium buyer, just like the purchaser of a single-family home. Debt responsibility is less with condominiums than with cooperatives. Because each owner has the deed to a specific piece of property, he or she is not responsible when other owners in the project default or do not make tax or mortgage payments on time.

Maintenance costs, which vary greatly for each project, are spelled out in the contract. If the fee includes the upkeep of recreational facilities or utility service, such as water, it will be higher. If a manager is hired by the owners association, his or her salary is included. Also, any insurance premiums on policies for the entire project are prorated among all owners. Monthly fees are lower in condominiums where streets are maintained by the city or there is municipal garbage collection. Part of the monthly fee should be set aside to cover major maintenance costs (sinking or *reverse fund*). For an older condominium, or one converted from rental apartments, previous maintenance records may indicate possible large repairs in the immediate future.

Common expenses include:

1. All sums lawfully assessed against the homeowners by their association.
2. Expenses of administration, maintenance, repair, or replacement of the common areas and facilities.
3. Expenses agreed upon as common expenses by the association.
4. Expenses declared common expenses by the declaration or the bylaws.

What is included in the maintenance fee

---

[12]Arthur D. Little, as reported in *HUD Condominium/Cooperative Study,* Vol. I, p. III-27.

[13]*HUD Condominium/Cooperative Study,* Vol. I, pp. III-29.

greatly influences the cost of condominium ownership.

Rising maintenance costs with inflation present problems. Evidence of these costs should be given to the prospective buyer. Unscrupulous salespeople have sometimes underestimated the living costs, and owners have found that their payments are not enough to maintain the common areas.

INSURANCE

Separate ownership within a larger condominium project creates many insurance problems, such as overlapping policies, gaps in coverage, and uncertainty on the part of individual owners and their association. In particular, there is the problem of liability insurance.[14] Some projects carry liability insurance on common areas; other delegate it to individual owners. The risk and extent of individual liability and the right to sue the corporation are not always specified in project bylaws. Further, assessments of payment after a lawsuit are not always clear. The New York State law regulating condominiums requires fire and property damage insurance but says nothing about liability coverage.

Insurance may consist of coordinated unit-owner policies, an association master policy, or some combination. A coordinated owner policy is specified in the declaration, with the coverage each owner must carry and a procedure for periodically filing proof of compliance with the association. Under an association master policy, the individual owner would insure personal property and any improvements made. The master policy would then contain subpolicies for unit owners. There are administrative problems involved in amending the master policy as subpolicies are changed. The best method will probably involve either a management association or a set of trustees who will insure all units under a single policy. The trustees would be authorized to negotiate all loss adjustments. Mortgagees would receive a certificate as proof of coverage. Each unit would be insured on its value based on price. The amount of the premium would probably correspond to the owner's percentage interest in the common areas.

If more than one unit is lost, who is reimbursed, the association or the individual owners? If the association decides not to rebuild, the policy should contain a clause to repay the owners as if there were a total loss.

The association needs liability coverage on all owners anywhere on the premises and on employed personnel. It should also have workmen's compensation and employers' liability, as well as fidelity bonds to cover loss of money or securities due to dishonesty, acceptance of worthless money orders, and forgery, including check forgery.

FRACTIONAL TIME PERIOD OWNERSHIP

Fractional time period ownership (FTPO) of condominiums—owning a condominium for part of a year—is one of the latest developments. Its main use is in recreational or second-home resort areas.[15] For successful ownership, the documents must ensure:

---

[14]For a discussion, see Patrick J. Rohan, "Perfecting the Condominium as a Housing Tool: Innovation in Tort Liability and Insurance," *Law and Contemporary Problems,* 32 (Spring 1967), 305–18.

[15]The Resort Timesharing Council of the American Land Development Association, Washington, D.C. prepares a Directory and Consumers Guide.

1. The specific time period of use, which is binding on all present and future owners.

2. Expense proration.

3. Management agreements.

4. Rules of occupancy.

New laws are needed to specify the kind of estate being bought and to cover non-payment of taxes, mortgage, or owner fees, and owner neglect.[16]

Ownership costs are two-tiered. One set of costs is based on the value of the unit, including such items as property taxes and insurance. The other set is based on the period of use and includes such items as utilities and recreational fees.

In a FTPO condominium, good management is important. Duties of the manager may include:

1. Repair, maintenance, and furnishing of the rent.

2. Payment of taxes, assessment, insurance, utilities, and legal and accounting services, as well as the cost of recreational privileges for the unit.

3. Discharge, contest, or protest liens or charges affecting the unit.

4. Adoption and enforcement of rules regarding the possession, use, and enjoyment of the unit by the owners.

5. Obtaining legal and accounting services needed to operate the unit and enforce the declaration by bylaws.

6. Assessing and collecting payment from the owners for the above costs.[17]

REGULATION OF CONDOMINIUMS

Today condominiums are regulated by state laws and federal agencies. States requirements vary greatly. The federal agencies involved have limited and specific concerns.

FEDERAL REGULATION Four federal agencies have certain regulatory powers over condominiums. Two agencies of the Department of Housing and Urban Development are involved. First the *Federal Housing Administration (FHA)* insures the mortgages of approved condominiums. However, less than 5 percent of condominium loans are so insured, either because of stringent guidelines or because the red tape involved discourages developers from applying.[18] Second the *Office of Interstate Land Sales Registration* can require full disclosure in some sales or transactions across state lines.[19] However, the conditions are rare, and the Office actually has little to do with condominiums.

Because more and more people are buying condominiums as an investment, the *Securities and Exchange Commission (SEC)* is becoming involved. The Commission is particularly concerned if the condominium is managed as a resort for

---

[16]For details, see Alan M. Roodhouse, "Fractional Time Period Ownership of Recreational Condominiums." Reprinted by permission from the "Real Estate Law Journal," Summer 1975, Volume 4, Number 1, 35–60. Copyright 1975, Warren, Gorham and Lamont Inc., 210 South Street, Boston, Mass. All rights reserved.

[17]Roodhouse, "Fractional Time Period Ownership," pp. 35–60.

[18]U.S. Department of Housing and Urban Development, *HUD-FHA Condominiums: Their Future* (Washington, D.C., August 1975).

[19]U.S. Department of Housing and Urban Development, Office of Interstate Land Sales Registration Condominium and Other Construction Contracts, Docket No. N-74-219 *Federal Register* (Feb. 28, 1974), 7824–25.

profit while the owner is absent. In this case, the owner is using the condominium not only for recreation but also to earn a return. Full disclosure and registration with the SEC are mandatory for condominiums bought for investment. Few companies now sell condominiums as investments.

Generally, a condominium must be registered with the SEC if:[20]

1. The units, along with any rental arrangement or similar services, are offered and sold to a buyer who wishes to make a profit via the management efforts of a promoter or his or her agent.

2. The buyer is offered a share in a rental pool. In the typical rental pool, the condominium promoter or some third party contracts to rent the unit when the owner is not using it. The rents and expenses of all the units are combined and each owner receives his or her share, regardless of whether the unit was rented.

3. The buyer must make the unit available for rental for some part of the year, must use an exclusive rental agent, or is otherwise restricted in the use or rental of the unit.

If a developer covered by SEC regulations fails to register and deliver a prospectus, the buyer has the right to rescind the contract and claim a refund with interest within one year—in some cases, as much as three years—from the time of purchase.

---

[20]Securities and Exchange Commission, "Guidelines as to the Applicability of the Federal Securities Laws to Offers and Sales of Condominiums or Units in Real Estate Development," Release No. 5347 (Washington, D.C., Jan. 4, 1973), p. 3.

Finally, the *Federal Trade Commission (FTC)* is concerned with deceptive or unfair practices and has the power to outlaw them. The FTC is now investigating possible deceptions arising from condominium marketing practices, direct-mail campaigns, and purchase contracts. This investigation also covers undisclosed limitations on ownership. Through test cases in court, precedents will be set for future condominium regulations.

FUTURE FEDERAL REGULATION   More federal regulation of condominiums may be on the way; comprehensive regulation is now being studied by Congress. One vital area is disclosure, especially of the legal arrangements and responsibilities involved in buying and owning, a full description of the unit, costs, and terms of any financing offered by the developer.

A second area of concern is minimum consumer protection standards, which developers would have to meet. These would include such items as the right to have deposits held in escrow; a warranty; and control over the project's management at a specified time. The buyer may also be allowed to revoke or void the contract under certain conditions, and to sue any developer who gives insufficient or false information or practices other forms of fraud. One controversy has been over whether HUD or the buyer should be responsible for enforcement.

States are encouraged to enact and enforce laws on condominium purchases and sales at least as strict as proposed federal laws. Thus state governments, rather than the federal government, would be responsible for regulating condominiums. This change was made because it was felt that the fine efforts of some states to regulate condominiums should not be wasted.[21] Furthermore, because the sale of land has long been considered part of state and local law rather than federal law, state enforcement meets federal requirements and means less reliance on federal bureaucracy. On the other side, according to Shank, "the major argument against state regulation of condominium development is that most states have failed to keep pace with the market."[22] Finally, regardless of who is responsible, there is always concern about whether regulation will protect consumers and correct inequities or whether more confusion, delays, red tape, and higher costs will result.

UNIFORM CONDOMINIUM ACT . The many differences in state laws make it difficult for national lenders and the buyer who moves to a different area to assess condominium documents and financing arrangements. In an attempt to standardize laws, the National Conference of Commissioners on Uniform State Laws has developed a Uniform Condominium Act.[23] The act covers the creation, allocation, and termination of condominiums, management, time share ownership, and protection of buyers, including rights to cancel, conversion, warrant, administration, registration, and disclosure.

---

[21]For a discussion of state regulation of condominiums and major legal provisions in New York, Florida, Virginia, and Washington, D.C., see Benjamin Jones, *State Regulation of Condominiums,* BFA 75 (Lexington, Ky.: The Council of State Governments, 1975).

[22]Andrew G. Shank, "Better Condo Laws Needed on All Government Levels," *Mortgage Banker,* 36 (August 1975), 40.

[23]National Conference of Commissioners on Uniform State Laws, *Uniform Condominium Act,* Discussion Draft (Chicago, July 31–Aug. 6, 1976).

CONCLUSION

Condominiums are an ownership alternative that is increasingly attractive to Americans. Concern over suburban sprawl and rising housing prices are two of the factors involved.

The declaration and bylaws must be reviewed by prospective buyers in addition to the traditional deed, zoning, structural, and neighborhood concerns of the single-family property owner.

New federal and state laws will improve disclosure and provide consumer protection. Thus, buyer satisfaction should improve.

Cooperatives

A housing *cooperative* consists of one or more units—owned, operated, or managed—by a group of persons on a nonprofit basis. The U.S. cooperative housing movement began with the pioneer tradition of building each other's homes. By the 1800s there were a few cooperative financing and insurance efforts. However, cooperative housing as it is today did not begin until about 1920. Two early efforts were those of the Finnish Home Building Association in Brooklyn, New York, and the Amalgamated Clothing Workers of America, in Manhattan and then the Bronx.[24] Many cooperatives failed during the Depression. In 1942, the enactment of Section

---

[24]U.S. Department of Housing and Urban Development, *Cooperative Housing in the U.S.A.,* HUD-331-1A (Washington, D.C.: U.S. Government Printing Office, February 1972), p. 1.

216 of the Internal Revenue Code, which gave cooperative owners a tax deduction for part of their expenses, revived interest in cooperatives.[25] Between 1945 and 1950 trade union-sponsored cooperatives made important progress. After government insurance became available, cooperatives grew even more. However, since 1970, growth has slowed as condominiums have become more popular.

Cooperative units may be detached, semidetached, rowhouse, or multi-family (Figure 7-3). The cooperators may be stockholders in a corporation that holds title and issues leases, or beneficiaries under a trust agreement, with title being vested in a trustee.[26]

The most common form of cooperative is the nonprofit housing corporation. Articles of incorporation and bylaws are

[25]"Cooperative Housing Corporations and the Federal Securities Laws," *Columbia Law Review,* 71 (January 1971), 119.

[26]For details, see Edwin Yourman, "Some Legal Aspects of Cooperative Housing," *Law Contemporary Problems,* 12 (Winter 1947), 133.

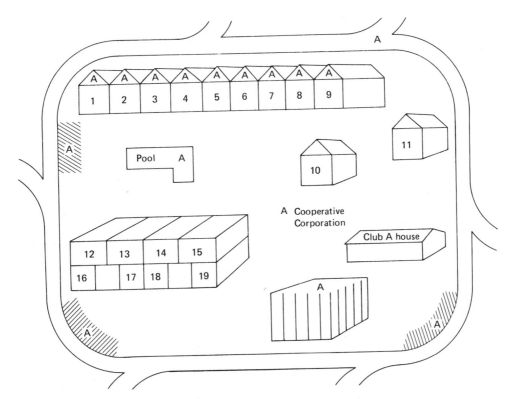

Figure 7-3. Cooperative Ownership by a Corporation. (*Note:* A cooperative is usually composed of a single type of building. Numbers indicate stockholders in cooperative corporation A, which owns title to all structures, streets, and community facilities.) [*Source:* Adapted from U.S. Department of Housing and Urban Development, *HUD Condominium/Cooperative Study,* Vol. III, (Washington, D.C.: U.S. Government Printing Office, July 1975, p. G-10.)]

specially designed so that the corporation can be owned and operated by its member-stockholders. Cooperative members own shares in the corporation based on the value of the apartment they live in. Each owner has a fractional interest in the corporation and an exclusive right to a particular living unit. The owner usually pays a monthly charge that includes mortgage payments, taxes, maintenance and repair costs as well as corporate operating expenses.

LEGAL ASPECTS

In contrast to condominiums, no laws specifically govern the way a cooperative is formed. However, since most cooperatives are corporations, corporate law must be followed. The documents must be filed with the state, and after approval the corporation is officially in business. A housing cooperative must usually file one other document—the *proprietary lease*. The basic legal documents of the cooperative are the corporate charter and the bylaws, including the proprietary lease. A prospective buyer should have a lawyer examine all these documents as well as the stock certificates.

The corporate charger states the purpose of the corporation and must follow state regulations. It usually contains the legal name of the corporation; the law that governs the charter; the operation, value, class, and number of shares of stock; the designation of legal representatives of the corporation, the number and qualification of the board of directors and officers, plus their selection and duties; how votes are allocated; and meeting and quorum requirements.[27]

Cooperative bylaws are similar to condominium bylaws. They clarify how the cooperative will be run and establish rules and the form of government and administration.

The bylaws usually include the proprietary lease, which is similar to an ordinary rental lease. It explains the legal obligations of the tenant and the corporation. Unlike a rental lease, the term of a proprietary lease is longer. There is no provision for fixed rent, and maintenance charges are included. The lease should be the same for all tenants.

Voting rights of each stockholder are specified. Often it is one vote per living unit. Sometimes voting privileges depend on length of residence or paid-up membership. Often a couple has one vote between them.

The owner of a cooperative does not have fee simple title to the individual unit. Title to the property is vested in the corporation. Often the individual's equity cannot be used as security.

The corporation has a blanket mortgage on the property which makes it responsible to repay the mortgage. The members have no personal liability for the mortgage and cannot be forced to make payments. However, if foreclosure occurs, the members lose their homes.

The cooperative owner may be liable for all debts of the corporation and for the unpaid assessment of other owners up to the value of the individual unit. If bankruptcy occurs, claims of creditors come before those of cooperators. Thus, the cooperative's financial condition is important. This joint liability discourages the growth of cooperative housing.

PURCHASE CONSIDERATIONS

Many of the purchase considerations for cooperatives are similar to those of single-family homes and condominiums,

---

[27]Patrick E. Kehoe, *Cooperatives and Condominiums* (New York: Oceana Publications, 1974), pp. 21–22.

especially those related to physical structure, neighborhood, services and location. Therefore, these items will not be discussed here. In a new cooperative, it is important to know how many units have to be sold before the plan will be declared effective or abandoned. In an existing cooperative, one should know what percentage of the total units are leased and if any are in default.

Most cooperatives have the right to approve incoming members. This protects the interests of current members. Some cooperatives limit their membership by income, or by family size or type, such as adults only. Others limit members' rights to make structural changes.

Subleasing should be permitted only for the short-term absence of a member, if at all. The length of the sublease agreement and the amount of payment should be determined by the cooperative. To allow subleasing on any scale would result in absentee ownership.

Members in a cooperative community have the right to use and occupy all facilities at reasonable rates.[28] They also have an obligation to help make the policy decisions that regulate the operation of the coop. At a minimum, each member should vote on the issues that come before the annual meeting, including the election of the board of directors. Participation may also include serving as a board member or active membership on a committee. As a co-owner, a member must help to establish the coop's financial policies and to act as a trustee for future occupants. Cooperative members are bound to obey the rules and to comply with the bylaws. They may be penalized for any breach of the bylaws or any serious infringement on the rights of other members. The board of directors may have to revoke membership if it is continually violated.

COSTS

The initial cost of stock in a cooperative is similar to the down payment a prospective single-family home or condominium buyer makes. According to the National Association of Housing Cooperatives, there are three approaches to the initial membership payment.[29] One plan does not increase this payment over time. It calls for the purchase of a small membership share, usually $50 to $500, which has no relation to the value of the living unit. This share is refunded, less any amounts due for charges when the member leaves the cooperative. A second plan has a limited payment increase. The initial payment grows over time according to a formula. In the third plan, the membership share is sold at the market price.

The monthly charges that cooperative members pay are often called carrying charges. These include the mortgage payment, utilities, maintenance and repair, contributions to the reserve fund, and corporate operation. Because of the nonprofit nature of most cooperatives and the volume of goods or services purchased, these monthly costs are often lower than could be achieved by an individual buyer alone. A prospective buyer should carefully examine what is included in the monthly charge, how the charge is paid, and the likelihood of increases. An annual audit should be available to all members.

Stock allocation is important to the

[28]*Cooperative Housing: People Helping Each Other,* (Washington, D.C.: National Association of Housing Cooperative, Nov. 19, 1976), unpaged pamphlet.

[29]Ibid.

prospective buyer. A schedule of allocations for all apartments will show that the price of a prospective buyer's unit has been fairly determined.[30] In the usual allocation formula the proportion of shares per unit reflects the value of each unit as a percentage of the entire cooperative. Not only does the price of each unit depend on the number of shares given it, but carrying charges and other obligations and rights depend on the amount of stock held.

As with condominiums, cooperative associations must maintain enough reserves to protect the cooperative and its members' interests. These usually include a general operating reserve and a reserve to replace parts of buildings and equipment as they deteriorate. With such reserves, members are less likely to be billed for unexpected special charges.

There have been abuses in cooperative housing at times, such as:

1. Retention of majority shareholder votes by the sponsor.
2. Overpricing.
3. Long-term management contract at an inflated price.
4. Coercion to convert rental units to a cooperative.
5. Underestimation of costs.
6. A balloon mortgage on an inflated purchase price.

Federal aid to cooperatives includes mortgage insurance, subsidies for low-income residents, and below market interest rate (BMIR) programs.[31] State laws such as the New York Mitchell-Lama Law, have spurred new cooperatives through long-term loans to developers and tax abatement privileges.

CONCLUSION

Cooperative housing involves joint ownership of a development on a nonprofit basis. It has a longer history than condominiums and is governed by corporate law rather than special cooperative laws. Members own everything jointly and are jointly responsible for all liabilities up to the value of the individual unit.

Mobile Homes

Today's mobile home has changed dramatically from the early house trailer, which could be towed by the family car. The mobile home is among the largest one-package consumer products produced. It offers "instant" housing, an attractive feature in areas with a housing shortage. However, in some urban areas, mobile homes are not feasible and in others they are zoned out. Mobile homes come in *single* or *multiple sections*.

The number of mobile homes used for living increased from 2 million in 1970 to 3.63 million in 1976.[32] Mobile home shipments have grown in relation to housing starts. Reported shipments in 1960 were 8 percent of conventional single-family production, 18 percent in 1965, and 33 percent in 1970. They de-

---

[30]David Clurman and Edna L. Hebard, *Condominiums and Cooperatives* (New York: Wiley-Interscience, 1970). p. 183.

[31]For details, see ibid., pp. 199–217.

[32]Manufactured Housing Institute, *Quick Facts* (Arlington, Va., May 1977) p. 8; *Annual Housing Survey: 1976,* Part A, Series H-150-76 (February 1978), p. 14.

clined to 21 percent in 1975 and 16 percent in 1978.[33] Bloom notes that "an important factor handicapping the recovery of mobile home shipments was the high delinquency and repossession rates of the proceeding years."[34] However, in 1976 mobile homes accounted for 96 percent of the sales of new single-family homes under $20,000 and 76 percent of those under $30,000.[35] In 1977, mobile homes accounted for 67% of new single family homes under $35,000. A general shortage of rental housing in nonurban areas, the advantages of low initial costs, and the willingness of local governments to permit mobile homes all helped market growth.

Further, from 1952 to 1978 about 6.2 million homes were shipped; thus, about 2 million units are not permanent residential units.[36] Undoubtedly many of the smaller earlier homes have either been demolished, or are being used as vacation homes, or are on the dealer's sales list. But what happens to older mobile homes is not really known.

PURCHASE CONSIDERATIONS

All mobile homes built after June 15, 1976, must meet HUD's minimum and uniform standards. These standards cover body and frame construction, plumbing, heating, and electrical systems. Fire-retardant materials are required near the furnace, water heater, and cooking range. Energy conservation is considered in the insulation needs of homes manufactured for different climates. Safety requirements include two exterior doors far apart, at least one egress window in each sleeping room, smoke detectors, and tie-down systems. A label(s) in a conspicuous place indicates compliance. Prior to June 15, 1976, forty-six states required compliance with the Mobile Home Standard established by the National Fire Protection Association and the American National Standards Institute.

National Bureau of Standards

Mobile homes must meet federal insulation standards.

Unlike the other forms of housing discussed, mobile homes may have a limited useful life. Estimates vary greatly, and the newer homes are expected to last longer than earlier models. One study estimates the average life as fifteen years.[37] However, in 1970, 17 percent were one year old, 36 percent were five years old, 23 percent were ten years old, 17 percent

[33]U.S. Department of Commerce, Bureau of the Census, "Housing Starts," *Construction Reports.* C-20-79-3 (May 1979).

[34]David E. Bloom, "Housing Activity in the Recent Recovery," *Survey of Current Business,* 56 (September 1976), 15.

[35]*Quick Facts,* May 1977, p. 7 and June 1978, pp. 3–4.

[36]U.S. Department of Housing and Urban Development, *1977 HUD Statistical Yearbook,* HUD-338-6-UD (Washington, D.C.: U.S. Government Printing Office, December 1978), p. 369 and *Manufacturing Report* (Arlington, Va.: Manufactured Housing Institute, December 1978), n.p.

[37]Werba Shiefman et al., "The Mobile Home Market," *Appraisal Journal,* 40 (July 1972), 391.

were 15 years old, and 7 percent were twenty or more years old.[38] In the 1976 Annual Housing Survey, mobile homes two years old or less accounted for 31 percent of the mobile homes reporting age; those two to six years old, 30 percent; those seven to eleven years, 15 percent; and the rest were older.[39]

Mobile homes, like automobiles, have been thought to depreciate over time. Depreciation is a decrease in the value of the home. It is a "hidden cost"—one not seen by the buyer. Mobile homes depreciate because they are viewed as a durable good, which is traded or resold due to obsolescence. However, whether a mobile home depreciates or appreciates depends on the quality of its construction, the care given it, and its location.

There is evidence that double wides across the nation appreciate.[40] In addition, in California single wides have been found to appreciate 16 percent a year and double wides 20 percent.[41] Inflation has contributed to the increase in mobile home resale value.

Mobile home purchases are unique in that most are bought from a dealer, who plays an important role in consumer satisfaction. It is often the dealer's aid, service, and care that make the choice a satisfying one. The retailer's responsibility continues after the sale, so that services provided and satisfaction received are important. In contrast to other housing purchases, new mobile homes have a warranty or guarantee that specifies both the dealer's and the manufacturer's responsibilities.[42]

The warranty will state:

1. Items covered under the warranty.
2. Whether there are separate guarantees for specific items in the unit, such as refrigerator, range, or water heater, and what each one covers. Appliance certificates should be dated and kept. If the appliance manufacturer requires that they be registered, this should be done.
3. The time limits on each guarantee.
4. Who is responsible for servicing a broken or damaged item—the dealer or the manufacturer—and the charge, if any, for labor.
5. What routine servicing is covered.
6. Any other requirements or conditions that must be met.

The unit and accessories should be chosen with the same care as any prospective housing purchase. The interior should meet the consumers' life style and needs.

Mobile homes have grown wider and longer over time. Thus, ten-foot wides came into mass production in 1955, 12-foot wides in 1962, and 14-foot wides in

[38]U.S. Department of Commerce, Bureau of the Census, *Subject Reports* Final Report HC(7)-6, *Mobile Homes* (Washington, D.C.: U.S. Government Printing Office, 1973).

[39]U.S. Department of Commerce, Bureau of the Census and U.S. Department of Housing and Urban Development, *Annual Housing Survey,* "General Housing Characteristics," Part A, Series H-150-76A, (Washington, D.C.: U.S. Government Printing Office, 1978), p. 14.

[40]E.R. Haas, "Mobile Home Analysis—The Double Wide Perspective," mimeo (Indianapolis: Datapraise, Inc., January 1979).

[41]Jan L. Rosenbaum, "Price Appreciation in Mobile Homes Sold in Southern California During the First Four Months of 1978," memorandum (Riverside, Calif.: Fleetwood Enterprises, Inc., October 1978).

[42]For a discussion of the legal aspects of mobile home warranties, see Mark Summers, Frederick D. Fahrenz, and David C. Shepler, "Housing—Mobile Homes—Some Legal Questions," *West Virginia Law Review,* 75 (June 1973), 401–6.

1969. In 1975, 43 percent of mobile homes were 14 feet wide, up from 16 percent in 1971.[44] Overall mobile homes have increased in size from 684 square feet in 1969 to 1,105 square feet in 1977. Double wides or multisectionals accounted for 30 percent of shipments in 1977.[45] The interior living space of a 24 x 60 foot double wide is 1,440 square feet, close to the square footage of the average site-built home.

Prices of mobile homes have risen with the increase in size. Even so, however, they are increasing at a slower rate than the price of the site-built home. In 1977, the average price was $13,000 for single sections, $20,350 for multi-sections, and $15,200 for all sizes.[43] In 1977, the price per square foot was $13.75, including furnishings but excluding land, plus setup costs, steps, skirting, and anchoring. This is compared with $24.75 per square foot for single-family site-built homes.

In addition to size, prices depend on the quality of materials, workmanship, and furnishings. Most mobile homes have a base price with options added. New mobile homes are usually sold fully furnished. The consumer can usually omit, exchange, add, or special-order furnishings. Price often includes transportation to the site and setup. The price of a home may be lower if it is a discontinued model, if it is last year's model, or if the manufacturer has gone out of business. A new dealer may sell at a lower price to get established. A dealer who is moving may sell at a lower price rather than move stock.

Several studies have reported on what people like and dislike about mobile homes (Table 7-1). Economy and low maintenance were two of the strongest advantages. Most of the unfavorable comments dealt with construction.

SAFETY   In choosing any form of housing, safety is an important concern. Much attention in the past focused on the need for improved safety features in mobile homes. The new federal standards on construction and safety are a step in this direction.

The National Fire Protection Association reports that human acts and omissions, such as misusing a gas range to provide heat, are equally responsible for fires in both mobile and conventional homes. However, mechanical failure or malfunction contribute to more fires in mobile homes. The sources were heating and cooking equipment in nearly 60 percent of the fires in mobile homes, compared to about 32 percent in conventional homes.[46] In a National Bureau of Standards report, fire hazard near the kitchen range was reduced by installation of a range hood and 1/4 inch asbestos millboard.[47]

Each bedroom in a mobile home must have an approved smoke detector. Persons should be able to escape from every bedroom, usually through a window,

---

[43]*Quick Facts*, 1978, p. 4.

[44]U.S. Department of Housing and Urban Development, *HUD News*, HUD No. 76-86 (Mar. 17, 1976), p. 1.

[45]*Quick Facts* (1978), p. 4.

[46]*A Study of Mobile Home Fires*, NFPA No. FR-75-2 (Boston: National Fire Protection Association; 1975), p. 2.

[47]Edward K. Budnick and David P. Klein, *Evaluation of the Fire Hazard in a Mobile Home Resulting from an Ignition on the Kitchen Range*, NBSIR 75-788, Interim Report (Washington, D.C.: Center for Fire Search, National Bureau of Standards, February 1976), p. 20.

TABLE 7-1. Mobile Home Characteristics

STUDY	FAVORABLE CHARACTERISTICS		UNFAVORABLE CHARACTERISTICS	
Spurlock 1972	Mobility	19.6%	Poor construction	14.3%
	Low maintenance	12.8%	Unsafe in stormy weather	11.8%
	Low utilities	10.2%	Deteriorates too fast	11.2%
	Equipped home quickly	11.4%		
Smith 1975	Economical to heat	61.5%	(Maintenance problems)	
	Low maintenance	30.0%	Leaky roof	30.0%
	More economical than other types of houses	5.7%	Pipes freeze	12.3%
Owens-Corning 1974	More economical than other types of houses	73.0%	(Initial maintenance problems) Doors didn't close/stuck	22.0%
	Desire for ownership	64.0%	Plumbing	21.0%
	Low maintenance	48.0%	Electrical problems	15.0%
	Mobility	36.0%	Roof leaked	14.0%
	Retirement home	21.0%	Furnace/heating	11.0%
Owens-Corning 1969	Low maintenance	29.0%	(Initial maintenance problems)	
	More economical	25.0%	Plumbing problems	38.0%
	Mobility	18.0%	Furnace/heating	25.0%
			Doors didn't close/stuck	15.0%
			Electrical problems	11.0%
			Roof leaked	10.0%
			General complaints	
			Living area too confined	24.0%
			Lack of storage	15.0%
			Poor construction	5.0%
Greenough 1976	Low maintenance	18.0%	(Initial maintenance problems)	
	Easy to clean	16.0%	Doors didn't close/stuck	14.0%
	Economical	12.0%	Windows leaked	11.0%
	Mobility	3.0%	Roof leaked	8.0%
			Doors leaked	7.0%
HUD 1968	Small cost of obtaining and living	44.5%		
	Mobile home style of living	49.0%		
	Mobility[a]	17.0%		
	Only housing available	8.0%		
	Head's occupation requires frequent moves	14.5%		

[a]Only 20 percent have moved since buying their mobile home.

Sources:

Focus on the Mobile Home Market (Toledo, Ohio: Owens-Corning Fiberglas Corporation, 1970).

Greenough, Jeanne, "Mobile Home Consumer Study" (Ithaca, N.Y.: Cooperative Extension, Cornell University, 1976).

Smith, Frances, "1975 Survey of Mobile Home Owners and Renters" (Delaware County, N.Y. 1975).

Spurlock, Hughes, H., "Mobile Home Situation in Washington County, Arkansas, 1972" (Fayetteville, Ark.: Agricultural Experiment Station, University of Arkansas Division of Agriculture, 1974).

The New Mobile Home Market (Toledo, Ohio: Owens-Corning Fiberglas Corporation, 1974).

U.S. Department of Housing and Urban Development, *Housing Surveys, Part 2* (Washington, D.C.: U.S. Government Printing Office, 1968).

without going past the furnace. All equipment, such as the furnace, water heater, and dryer, should be properly vented with individual cutoff valves. Information on fuel storage and ignition temperature should be permanently attached.

"Next to fire, wind is a primary cause of death, injury, and property damage in mobile homes."[48] After studying wind loads, McGehan determined that HUD criteria are fairly adequate, with some increases needed in the uplift loads. He recommends additional tie-down straps near the middle of the structure.

USED MOBILE HOMES The purchase of a used mobile home is final; there is no warranty from the former owner. Financing may be more difficult, with a higher down payment and shorter term required by the lender. A used mobile home should be checked out completely—construction, wear and tear, operation of appliances, and plumbing and heating systems. Past utility bills can provide a clue as to how well the home is insulated or sealed. The certificate of title must be transferred to the new owner's name. A HUD study of used mobile homes concluded:[49]

1. State construction and safety standards rarely apply to used mobile homes and do not assure their soundness.

2. State inspection requirements and procedures for used mobile homes are inadequate.

3. State standards and procedures for disposal of used mobile homes are inadequate.

4. The 1974 National Mobile Home Construction and Safety Standards Act will probably have an indirect effect on state standards and inspection procedures for used mobile homes. It will probably have no effect on the ultimate problem of disposing of used mobile homes.

SITE SELECTION

After deciding to buy a mobile home, the next problem is where to place it. A location should be chosen as carefully as the home and financing. There are three possible kinds of locations: an owned lot, a rented space in a *mobile home park*, or a purchased lot in a *mobile home subdivision*. The dealer is one source of information on locating a site, especially if he or she is not trying to fill a park. About 23 percent of mobile homes are placed on individually owned property, while 49 percent are located in groups of six or more units.[50]

Many state laws require that every mobile home lot have a pad designed for the support and placement of the home. Also, there must be some means of securing the home against uplift, sliding, rotation, or overturning.

INDIVIDUAL LOT An individual site for the mobile home should be attractive, with good soil and drainage. It must not

[48]Frederick P. McGehan, "How Fares the Mobile Home in Wind, Fire and Energy Use?" *Dimensions*, 60 (December 1976), 18.

[49]U.S. Department of Housing and Urban Development, *Report on Used Mobile Homes* (Washington, D.C., August 1975), p. 4.

[50]U.S. Department of Commerce, Bureau of the Census, and U.S. Department of Housing and Urban Development, *Annual Housing Survey: 1976*, Part A, Series H-150-76A, (Washington, D.C.: U.S. Government Printing Office, 1978), p. 14.

Mobile home—Convenience inside, relaxation outside.

violate local community regulations. Health requirements for water, sewer, and zoning regulations must be followed. Some communities require tie-downs. The cost of the lot and property taxes must be paid. A well, septic system, tie-downs, and utility connections all add to ownership costs. The average development cost per site varies from $3,500 to $5,500 or more, without land.[51]

MOBILE HOME PARKS   There are more than 24,000 mobile home communities in the United States. They provide more than 1.8 million spaces for mobile homes, with many new parks opening and existing parks expanding each year. The

trend is toward larger developments of twenty-five acres or more, with an average of 150 to 175 sites.

A park should be carefully chosen after several visits at different times of day and in bad weather as well as good. The opinion of both residents and management should be checked, as well as the reputation of the manager/owner. Sometimes parks are limited to certain types, styles, and widths of homes. The prospective buyer should get approval in writing to locate his or her home in a particular park *before* buying it.

Park rents vary depending on the type and age of the park, lot size, location, convenience, services offered, and availability of other park spaces in the area. Rents range from $50 to $200 per

---

[51]*Quick Facts,* 1978, p. 9.

month, with most between $80 and $150.[52] Services usually provided by the park include:

1. Water with an individual shutoff
2. Sewage disposal
3. Electricity
4. A fuel source
5. Telephone connections at each stand
6. Refuse collection and storage
7. Snow removal
8. Lawn care
9. Laundry facilities

Location and landscaping factors are similar to those of single-family homes. Thus, 5 to 8 percent of the park should be open space for recreation. Play areas for children under ten years of age should be protected from traffic and parking and kept clean. Other facilities, such as tennis courts, a swimming pool, and a community center, may be available.

Some states require and many park owners will offer a lease.[53] (See the section on leases under "rental" for what is included in a lease.) A mobile home lease should clearly specify the rules for park residents, such as lot and home care, mowing, opportunity for planting temporary or semipermanent plants or trees, and other yard-related activities.

Many states have laws prohibiting entrance fees and oppressive rules and regulations, such as requiring all services to be bought from the park owner or paying the park owner a commission when the home is sold.[54] The mobile home occupant should obtain a copy of the regulations for his or her state.

MOBILE HOME SUBDIVISION A small but growing number of mobile homes are being placed in subdivisions. Here, each family owns its lot and the mobile home and often pays a fee for upkeep. Within the subdivision, the lot size and orientation of the home are important. A permanent foundation may be provided, or the buyer may need to supply it. The subdivision may limit the size or age of the house and additions to it. Not every community has a subdivision for mobile homes.

MOVING THE MOBILE HOME

Most mobile homes are moved only once, from the factory to the buyer's lot. Less than 2 percent are ever moved.[55] The move to the first site is usually handled by the dealer. Later moves require a firm that specializes in moving mobile homes. To locate a mover, the Yellow Pages for the nearest major city is a place to start. The mover should be insured and bonded to protect the home in transit and should be able to produce preplanned routing and scheduling.

Mobile home manufacturers must meet state requirements for state permits, escort vehicles, signs, routes, flagging, and warning lights. Complying for inter-

---

[52]*Quick Facts*, 1978, p. 9.

[53]New York State law requires that tenants have the opportunity to sign a year's lease.

[54]Robert S. Hightower, "Mobile Home Park Practices: The Legal Relationship between Mobile Home Park Owners and Tenants Who Own Mobile Homes," *Florida State University Law Review*, 3 (Winter 1975), 103–26.

[55]Walter L. Benning, *Statement*, HUD National Conference on Housing Costs (Washington, D.C., Feb. 25–27, 1979), p. 3.

National Bureau of Standards.

Mobile home ready for delivery.

state shipment of a 12-foot-wide mobile home costs about $50 to $100.[56]

The Interstate Commerce Commission (ICC) regulates interstate moves. Most states also regulate the moving of mobile homes on state highways. Local governments usually control county and town roads. The federal government requires the carrier to file evidence of insurance. Additional personal property insurance may be useful.

Moving costs are based on the length and width of the mobile home as well as the number of miles the home must be moved. Interstate rates are on file with the ICC. Any problems or complaints regarding authorized motor carriers should be filed at the nearest ICC office. Moving costs include basic transportation cost, flagging services, tolls, and permits. Not included in the blanket fee are costs that may result from structural or tire failure of the mobile home, blocking and unblocking, and unhooking and hooking up of utilities.

After the move, including the first one,

the home should be checked for damage, including such hidden damage as the settling of insulation material behind wall panels.

TAXATION

One of the most hotly debated issues, and a major concern for many communities, is taxation of mobile homes. When mobile homes first appeared in the late 1920s, they were considered *personal property* and taxed as such. However, with increasing size and decreasing mobility, they have often been declared real estate.[57]

There are four major types of taxes on mobile homes: special privilege or use tax, real property tax, a license fee, and personal property tax.

The privilege tax approach allows the government to tax the mobile home owner for municipal services, regardless of whether such services actually apply to the mobile home. Since the privilege tax is a special tax imposed only on the mobile home, the assessment and enforcement procedures used can be tailored to this form of housing. Thus, the problem of using assessment procedures that apply to other types of property but are inefficient and unjust when used for a mobile home is eliminated.[58]

Local property taxes are *ad valorem* taxes; that is, the tax is based on the assessed value. Problems arise because of difficulties in assessing mobile homes. The assessment practices used include:

[56]William D. Glauz, Barrie M. Hutchinson, and Donald R. Kobett, *Economic Evaluation of Mobile and Modular Housing Shipments by Highway* (Washington, D.C.: U.S. Department of Transportation, Federal Highway Administration, April 1974), p. 216.

[57]For a discussion of whether a mobile home is a vehicle or a dwelling, see James H. Carter, "Problems in the Regulation and Taxation of Mobile Homes," *Iowa Law Review,* 48 (Fall 1962), 16–58.

[58]Donald Lee Mrozek, "Comment: The Search for an Equitable Approach to Mobile Home Taxation," *De Paul Law Review,* 21 (Summer 1972), 1034.

1. Number of square feet times standard valuation per square foot.
2. Flat charge regardless of size or condition.
3. Charge based on length alone.
4. Assessment based on *Blue Book* valuation.

Usually conventional home assessment is related to market value. (For a more detailed discussion on real property taxes, see Chapter 12.) Real property taxes are not regarded as fees for a service.

A license fee on a mobile home is a charge for its registration, usually as a vehicle. There may be one set charge for all mobile homes, or the charge may be assessed on some measure of value, usually purchase price less depreciation.

The variation in taxing methods often leads to unfair and unequal treatment. A mobile homeowner may be paying more or less than his or her fair share of community costs. Sometimes mobile home occupants are excluded from benefits such as veterans' or senior citizens' exemptions. Local communities may not receive their share of tax revenues depending on the tax or distribution method.

ZONING

Should mobile homes meet special zoning requirements or should they be treated as any other housing unit? Zoning laws limit the location of mobile homes within the community as well as set conditions for their establishment and occupancy. Zoning regulations for mobile homes must be reasonable and part of an overall plan.[59] Mobile homes cannot be

banned entirely or be treated in an arbitrary manner.

CONCLUSION

The mobile home provides housing for many American families. Its quality, size, and use have grown over time, and with them the need for well-sited and planned parks or subdivisions.

Comparison of Ownership Alternatives

In summary, the various forms of home ownership—single-family, condominium, cooperative, and mobile home—are compared. All of the alternatives may not exist for any single consumer, and financial conditions may place some of them beyond reach even if they exist in the local area (Table 7-2).

The single-family homeowner is personally responsible for all aspects of ownership and receives any benefits derived from it. A condominium owner is responsible for items related to the individual unit and also for common elements and fees. A cooperative member, as an owner of the entire development in common, is responsible for all items as a corporate member. The mobile homeowner in a park is responsible for items related to the home, but the park owner is responsible for grounds and facilities upkeep. Taxes may be assessed on the park owner rather than the resident.

FUTURE

Condominiums and cooperatives will continue to grow, due to scarcity of land in desired locations, increased demand

---

[59]Shepard's Citations, Inc., *Shepard's Mobile Homes and Mobile Home Parks* (New York: McGraw-Hill, 1975), p. 185.

TABLE 7-2. Comparison of Single-Family, Condominium, Cooperative, and Mobile Home Ownership

ITEM	SINGLE-FAMILY	CONDOMINIUM	COOPERATIVE	MOBILE HOME IN A PARK
Ownership	Owner has individual title to the unit	Resident owns the unit, plus a share of the common elements	Resident owns a share of the corporation	Owner has title to unit but rents land
Equity	Owner's interest in the unit increases in value as the mortgage is paid off and from market value appreciation	Owner's interest in the unit increases in value as the mortgage is paid off and from market value appreciation	Value of a membership certificate increases after the down payment as the member contributes monthly toward payment of the corporate mortgage	Ownership interest increases in value as the mortgage is paid off
Extent of Responsibility	Owner personally responsible for mortgage, taxes, maintenance and utilities	Personally liable for mortgage, taxes, and upkeep of the unit. Default on maintenance charges may obligate others. Default on mortgage by one owner will not involve others	Corporation is liable. Default by one member may force others to make up the deficit	Owner responsible for loan, upkeep on unit and rent payments. Taxes often part of park rent. Park owner responsible for grounds and facilities upkeep
Voting	Not applicable	The number of owner votes usually represents the proportional value of the unit to the total units	Each member usually has one vote	Owner may be a member of a tenants' group, in which case he or she has one vote
Closing or Settlement Costs	Costs include price of the unit, title search, attorney fees, credit check, mortgage transfer tax. Charges are paid each time a unit is resold	Costs include price of the unit and its undivided interest in the common estate, mortgage service charge, title search, insurance, and transfer of ownership charges paid each time the unit is resold or refinanced	Costs include price of the corporate property, mortgage service charge, title search, insurance, and transfer of ownership charges paid when the cooperative first buys the property. Only a small transfer fee is charged to transfer future membership in the cooperative	Costs will include a credit check and any local tax or lending charges. Since a mobile home loan is often a consumer loan, closing costs are lower.
Escrow Funds	Part of the down payment may be held in escrow before the closing. After the sale, payment for taxes may be col-	The down payment is held until the condominium project is recorded on the property and titles are con-	Subscription of down payments must be held unused until the viable cooperative is assured. Transfer of member-	A deposit on the mobile home may be held in escrow until the transfer of ownership is complete

	lected by the lender and deposited in an escrow account	veyed to each buyer. Escrows are usually used for each resale. The deed is held in escrow until all conditions of the sale (including any prepayments) have been met	ship funds are sometimes escrowed until the transfer is complete	
Monthly Costs	Owner pays own mortgage, utility, and other monthly costs	Percentage of common estate costs. Any mortgage payments on the individual unit are paid separately, as are those assessed on the unit	Proportionate share of all costs, including mortgage	Owner pays own mortgage, utility, and other monthly costs, plus park rent
Improvements and Maintenance	Owner responsible	Determined by board of directors with consent of residents (usually a simple majority) for improvements over a specified minimum value. Consent of mortgagee holding more than a specified number of mortgages may be required	Determined by board of directors. Membership approval may be required for expenditures over a specified minimum	Owner responsible for own improvements. Park owner responsible for park grounds and facilities
Resale of Units	Usually no limitation on right of resale	No limitation on right of resale except hat in some instances the right of first refusal must be given to the condominium	Applicants screened by tenant committee. Those not satisfactory to majority cannot buy	Park owner/operator may have some control over who buys
Resale Financing	Buyer must take out mortgage to finance resale	Buyer may take out mortgage to finance resale	Mortgage cannot be obtained to finance resale. Recently, however, many banks have begun granting "coop loans," which are similar to mortgages except that they carry higher interest rates than most mortgages	Buyer must obtain a loan to finance resale. Interest rates are higher than on conventional mortgages

Sources: Partly adapted from U.S. Department of Housing and Urban Development, *Condominiums, Their Development and Management* (Washington, D.C.: Office of International Affairs, September 1972). p. 71, and *Condominiums—The New Home Ownership* (White Plains, N.Y.: Westchester County Department of Planning, December 1973), pp. 3–4.

for owned housing, more families without children, and the need to conserve energy. Mobile homes will supply most of the lower-cost housing provided by private industry. Multi-sectionals will assume a growing share, and more areas of the country will see subdivisions of manufactured housing develop.

Terms

ad valorem taxes   taxes based on assessed value.

blue book valuation   average market value of an unused mobile home.

bylaws   operating guidelines that specify organization of the board of directors, the officers and their duties, and the calling of meetings.

chattels   personal property, as compared to real estate.

common area or common estate   joint ownership with other fee owners of all land and areas within the structures that are not individually owned units. The interest is defined by a percentage of the total area but not actually divided into individual parts.

common elements   see common area.

common profits   the balance of all income, rents, profits, and revenues from the common areas and facilities remaining after the common expenses have been deducted.

condominium (development or project)   the real property, including structures and community facilities, as recorded under condominium law.

condominium association, association of owners, condominium association board of directors, or council of co-owners   the governing body of a condominium, elected by and from among the owners when titles are conveyed to the individual owners by the grantor. Its authority to operate comes from the declaration. It must govern according to the bylaws.

condominium map   the floor plan, site plan, or parcel map that shows the layout of the units and their dimensions.

cooperative   joint ownership by an organization to provide housing for its members on a nonprofit basis. A corporation holds title to the land, buildings, and other facilities. Each stockholder receives a unit, with the cost of the stock in direct proportion to the unit's value. Monthly payments are determined by the owner's proportionate share of mortgage interest and principal, taxes, insurance, and maintenance of the whole project.

declaration   document containing conditions, covenants, and restrictions governing the sale, ownership, and use of a condominium.

expandable sections   one or more rooms that fold or telescope into the principal housing unit when being moved and that can be expanded at the site to provide more living space. Each section adds 60 to 100 square feet to the room in which it is located.

homeowners association   all of the unit owners acting as a group in accordance with the declaration and bylaws to administer the project.

master deed   see declaration.

membership certificate   a certificate (like stock) showing evidence of ownership in a cooperative corporation. Rights under the certificate are usually governed by personal property laws.

mobile home   a structure, movable in one or more sections, that exceeds either 8 feet in width or 32 feet in length. Built on a permanent chassis and designed to be used as a dwelling, with or without a permanent foundation, when connected to the required utilities. Contains plumbing, heating, air conditioning, and electrical systems.

mobile home community   planned housing development for mobile homes with local management of operations. Community services and utilities are provided for use by all occupants. Often recreational facilities, streets, sidewalks, and laundry areas are also included.

mobile home condominium a housing development similar to a mobile home park, except that the land area and facilities are held in common, with only the space occupied by the mobile home itself individually owned.

mobile home development a generic term that refers to mobile home parks, subdivisions, and condominiums.

mobile home parks an area of land under one ownership where two or more spaces for mobile homes are rented, with its operations managed and various facilities provided for common use.

mobile home subdivision similar to a mobile home park, but with spaces or lots generally sold as sites for mobile homes.

multi-section mobile home consists of two sections combined horizontally at the site which still retain their individual chassis for possible future movement.

personal property movable property.

proprietary lease an agreement similar to an ordinary rental lease that explains the rights and responsibilities of the tenant and the corporation. The lease is long term and does not provide for fixed rent, but administrative charges are specified.

reserve funds (replacement) funds held in escrow from monthly payments to replace common elements, such as roofs, at some future date.

sectional home a manufactured home of two or more modular units that are moved separately to the home site, where they are put on a foundation and joined to make a single house.

undivided interest see common interest.

unit value ratio a percentage determined by dividing the appraised value of a unit by the total value of all units. The percentage determines the percentage value of the common estate attached to each unit, the percentage of votes each owner has in governing the common estate, and the percentage of total operating costs each unit owner must bear.

single section mobile home one 8 or more feet wide and 32 or more feet long. See mobile home.

Suggested Readings

Bair, Frederick H. Jr., "Mobile Homes—A New Challenge," *Law and Contemporary Problems,* published by Duke University School of Law, 32 (Spring 1967), 286–304.

Bartke, Richard W., and Hilda R. Gage, "Mobile Homes: Zoning and Taxation," *Cornell Law Review,* 55 (April 1970), 491–526.

Berney, Robert E., and Arlyn J. Larson, "Micro-analysis of Mobile Home Characteristics with Implication for Tax Policy," *Land Economics,* 42 (November 1966), 453–63.

Cloos, George W. and Edward W. Burgells, Jr., "Mobile Homes and the Housing Supply," *Federal Reserve Chicago, Business Conditions: A Review* (November 1972), 2–16

Clurman, David, and Edna L. Hebard, *Condominiums and Cooperatives.* New York: Wiley-Interscience, 1970.

Cooke, P.W., L.P. Zelenka, and H.K. Tejuja, *Mobile Home Construction Standards Adopted by State Regulatory Programs—An Analysis,* NBSIR 75-680. Washington, D.C.: National Bureau of Standards, March, 1975.

Drury, Margaret J., *Mobile Homes: The Unrecognized Revolution in American Housing.* New York: Praeger, 1972.

Dwyer, Jeffry F., "Protecting the Rights of Purchasers of Condominium Units," *Fordham Urban Law Journal,* III (Spring 1975), 475–89.

Gibson, Constance B., *Policy Alternatives for Mobile Homes.* New Brunswick, N.J.: Center for Urban Policy Research, Rutgers University, 1972.

Glauz, William D., Barrie M. Hutchinson, and Donald R. Kobett, *Economic Evaluation of Mobile and Modular Housing Shipments by Highway.* Washington, D.C.: U.S. Department of Transportation, Federal Highway Administration, Office of Research, April 1974.

Goldblatt, Abraham, and Charles B. Pitcher, "Mobile Homes—A Growing Force in the

Housing Sector," *Construction Review,* 18 (September 1972), 4–8.

Goldstein, Charles A., "Negotiating for a Cooperative Apartment," *Real Estate Review,* 1 (Spring 1971), 75–83.

Hodes, Barnet, and Gale G. Robertson, *The Law of Mobile Homes,* 2nd ed. New York: Commerce Clearing House, 1964.

Kenyon, Paul, "Insuring the Condominium," *The Practical Lawyer,* 19 (November 1973), 13–26.

McVey, Lanel, and David R. Murchison, "Federal Securities Regulation of Condominiums: A Purchaser's Perspective," *Georgetown Law Journal,* 62 (May 1974), 1403–27.

Miller, Walter W., Jr., "Cooperative Apartments: Real Estate or Securities?" *Boston University Law Review,* 45 (Fall 1965), 465–505.

Mobile Home Industry. New York: Practicing Law Institute, 1973.

"Mobile Homes: Tin Boxes or a Housing Solution?" *Appalachia,* 4 (May-June 1971), 1–17.

Mobile Homes—The Low-Cost Housing Hoax, Report by the Center for Auto Safety, New York: Grossman Publishers, 1975.

"Mobile Home Issue," *Banking,* Journal of American Bankers' Association, LXX (October 1978), 118–26.

National Association of Housing Cooperatives, *Cooperative Housing: A Consumer Guide.* Washington, D.C., 1976.

Newcomb, Robinson, and Max S. Wehrly, "Mobile Home Parks: Part 1, An Analysis of Characteristics," Technical Bulletin 66, Washington, D.C.: Urban Land Institute, 1971.

———, "Part II, An Analysis of Communities," Technical Bulletin 68. Washington, D.C.: Urban Land Institute, 1972.

Norcross, Carl, *Townhouses and Condominiums.* Washington, D.C.: Urban Land Institute, 1973.

Pielert, J.H., W.E. Green, Jr., L.F. Skoda, and W.G. Street, *Performance of Mobile Home Data Acquisition and Analysis Methodology,* NBSIR-75–641. Washington, D.C.: National Bureau of Standards, 1975.

Shepard's Citations, Inc., *Shepard's Mobile Homes and Mobile Home Parks.* New York: McGraw-Hill, 1975.

Street, W.G., W.E. Greene, Jr., J.H. Pielert, and L.F. Skoda, *A Compilation of Problems Related to the Performance of Mobile Homes,* NBSIR 75–690. Washington, D.C.: National Bureau of Standards, April 1975.

U.S. Department of Commerce, Bureau of the Census, *Subject Reports Final Report HC (7)-6 Mobile Homes.* Washington, D.C.: U.S. Government Printing Office, 1973.

———, "Cooperative Housing in the U.S.A.," *HUD International Brief,* HUD 331-1a. Washington, D.C.: Office of International Affairs, February 1972.

———, *Transcript of Hearings on Condominiums and Cooperatives.* Washington, D.C.: Feb. 10-11-12, 1975.

———, *HUD Condominium/Cooperative Study.* Washington, D.C.: July 1975.

———, *Report on Used Mobile Homes.* Washington, D.C.: Housing Production and Mortgage Credit—Federal Housing Administration, August 1975.

U.S. House of Representatives, *Condominium Development and Sales Practices.* Hearings before the Subcommittee on General Oversight and Renegotiation of the Committee on Banking, Currency and Housing, 94th Congress, 2nd Session, Feb. 18, 19, May 19, 22, 1976.

———, *Report on Condominium Sales Practices.* Report by the Subcommittee on General Oversight and Renegotiation of the Committee on Banking, Currency and Housing, 94th Congress, 2nd Session, July 1976.

RENTAL HOUSING

1. HOW HAS THE LANDLORD TENANT RELA-
   TIONSHIP CHANGED OVER TIME?

2. DISCUSS THE PROS AND CONS OF LEGAL
   REMEDIES TO TENANT PROBLEMS?

3. IS RENT CONTROL DESIRABLE?

4. WHAT DOES A HOUSING WARRANTY MEAN
   FOR TENANTS? LANDLORDS?

About 35 percent of all housing in the United States is rented. Within this category, the percentage of rented single-family homes decreased from 53 percent in 1940 to 28 percent by 1976. A higher proportion of rental units are in buildings with more than ten apartments, with the greatest growth in buildings with fifty or more. In 1976 about 43 percent of all rented units had been built before 1939. Only 12 percent had been built between 1950 and 1959, and 21 percent between 1960 and 1970. The median number of rooms in renter-occupied units was 4.0 from 1940 to 1970.[1]

This chapter consideres the rental process, the legal foundation of renting, and consumer protection laws. Major social issues in regard to renting are also identified.

Landlord-Tenant Relationships

Renting involves a relationship between a *landlord*, who owns property and rents it, and a *tenant*, who rents. A good relationship depends on both parties acting responsibly. To understand the nature of the relationship and the problems of today's tenants, let us put the issue in historical perspective.[2]

---

[1]U.S. Department of Commerce, Bureau of the Census and U.S. Department of Housing and Urban Development, *Annual Housing Survey: 1976*, "General Housing Characteristics" Part A, Series H-150-76 (Washington, D.C.: U.S. Government Printing Office, 1978), pp. 1–31.

[2]For a detailed history, see Jean C. Love, "Landlord's Liability for Defective Premises: Caveat Lessee, Negligence, or Strict Liability," *Wisconsin Law Review*, 49 (1975), 19–61.

The landlord-tenant relationship depends largely on real property law, or the law relating to land. It is a very old, complex legal area that has become highly developed and refined over the years. Tradition, as well as legislation, strongly supports the landlord. Recently tenants have questioned the justice of this situation and actively worked to change it. Change has come slowly, but legislative and court decisions are beginning to shift the tenant's way.

The landlord-tenant relationship has been based on the landlord as owner of real property and the tenant as an individual who wants to possess and use it. The first tenants were serfs or small farmers renting land to till; the building on the property was little more than four walls and a roof, of minor importance. Renting, then, was based on the social, economic, and common law relationship between a poor tenant farmer and a wealthy landowner or landlord. This concept remained unchanged until the Industrial Revolution. But even after the rise of tenement housing, when renting involved space rather than land, the legal status of tenants remained based on the transfer of land.

Early laws defined not the rental relationship but construction standards and housing codes. Only recently have legislatures and courts looked at the rental relationship and seen leases as contracts with rights and responsibilities for both parties. Previously, the common law concept of "rent for possession" prevailed and still prevails in many places. Under common law the tenant is obligated to pay rent, at the risk of eviction, regardless of the condition of the unit. Also, unless there is a clear agreement, a lease contains no implied warranty of habitability. The person in possession of the property must repair and maintain it, and a lease defines interest in real estate rather than mutual obligations.

Because common law saw the lease as a transfer of real property, *caveat emptor* became not only a tenant watchword but also part of the law governing the landlord-tenant relationship. The courts are only now starting to recognize the plight of the modern tenant, who lacks the skills and knowledge to evaluate the premises. Recent legal changes in the landlord-tenant relationship are discussed later in this chapter.

The Rental Process

The rental process is similar, in some ways, to the process of buying a home. The would-be renter first sets priorities on items desired and decides what can be afforded. Then the search for a unit begins.

The would-be renter has all the information sources of a home buyer, plus one more—a rental referral agency. Apartment referral agencies list and advertise for landlords, describing the size, cost, and location of different units. This information is available for a fee. The would-be renter must be careful to determine how the fee is set, if enough information is given, and whether there is any guarantee that one will find a place. Some states, such as Colorado and New York, have requirements that agencies must meet.[3] A prospective renter should choose with the same care as a

---

[3]Becky Bilderback and Carol B. Meeks, "Apartment Referral Agents," *Human Econology News Service*, 4 (Ithaca, N.Y.: Cornell University, July 1977), 4.

homeowner, so as to be reasonably satisfied and avoid another possibly costly move. The unit should be conveniently located, in good condition, and with reasonable safety and security.

Although consumers expect most products to have some guarantee of quality and performance, the agreement between landlord and tenant, even if written, is no warranty or guarantee. It is a contract the renter must pay. However, the landlord now has much greater responsibility for the condition of the premises leased.

WARRANTY OF HABITABILITY

A *warranty of habitability* is an implied promise by the landlord that the rented property is fit for human occupation. This warranty runs from the beginning of the lease though the lease term. What is "fit for human habitation" often means the standards set by the local housing code, although specific statutory standards may apply. The District of Columbia court in *Javins* v. *First National Realty Corporation* established the warranty of habitability, with the local housing code

General Electric Co.—Re-entry & Environment Systems Division.

A garden apartment complex in Memphis, Tennessee.

as a measure.[4] The same case also held that leases on residential property should be governed by the principle of ordinary contracts. Other courts following suit include New York, Hawaii, Wisconsin, Colorado, New Jersey, Illinois, Iowa, California, and Massachusetts.[5] Today warranty of habitability is legally recognized in twenty-six states and the District of Columbia (Table 8-1).

According to Abbott, the warranty of habitability:

1. "abolished caveat emptor by making the landlord responsible for latent and even patent defects which existed at the incep-

[4]*Javins* v. *First National Realty Corporation, Federal Reporter,* 2nd Series, 428, F2d, 1970.

[5]Louis B. York, "Landlord Tenant Caveat Emptor Implied Warranty of Habitability in Residential Leases" *New York Law Forum* 21 (May 1976), 613.

National Housing Partnership/Photographer—Joshua Freiwald.

All Hallows Gardens, San Francisco, California.

TABLE 8-1. Landlord-Tenant Legislation Adopted by States

State	LEGISLATION				
	Warranty of Habitability[a]	Housing Receivership[b]	URLTA[c]	Repair and Deduct[d]	Retaliatory Eviction[e]
Alaska	X		X	X	X
Arizona	X		X	X	X
California	X			X	X
Colorado				X	
Connecticut		X	O		X
Delaware		X	X	X	X
District of Columbia	X				X
Florida	X		X	X	
Georgia					
Hawaii	X		X	X	X
Idaho			O		
Illinois	X	X	O	X	X
Indiana		X	O		
Iowa	X				
Kansas	X		X		
Kentucky	X		X	X	X
Louisiana	X			X	
Maine	X				X
Maryland					X
Massachusetts	X	X		X	X
Michigan	X	X	X	X	X
Minnesota	X	X			X
Missouri	X	X			
Montana				X	
Nebraska	X		X	X	X
New Hampshire					
New Jersey	X	X		X	X
New Mexico	X		X		
New York	X	X			X
North Carolina			O		
North Dakota				X	
Ohio	X	X	X	X	X
Oklahoma				X	
Oregon	X		X	X	X
Pennsylvania			O		X
Rhode Island	X	X	O		X
South Dakota				X	
Tennessee			X		X
Vermont			O		
Virginia	X		X	X	X
Washington	X		X	X	X
Wisconsin	X	X	O		X

X—adopted.

O—introduced in legislature.

[a]Samuel Bassett Abbott, "Housing Policy, Housing Codes and Tenant Remedies: An Integration," *Boston University Law Review,* 56 (January 1976), 12.

[b]Richard E. Blumberg and Brian Quinn Robbins, "Beyond URLTA: A Program for Achieving Real Tenant Goals," *Harvard Civil Rights-Civil Liberties Law Review,* 11 (Winter 1976), 23.

[c]Ibid., 3, and John M. McCabe, Legislative Director, National Conference of Commissioners on Uniform State Laws, Correspondence, (June 15, 1976).

[d]Ibid., 11.

[e]Ibid., 14 and 15.

tion of the tenancy and affected habitability

2. abolished the no-repair rule by imposing a duty to repair upon the landlord throughout the term of the tenancy.
3. changed the independence of the convenant to pay rent from the convenants respecting the condition of the premises, or implied in law, to interdependence."[6]

RENTAL COSTS

Most tenants pay *rent* to the landlord for the use of the premises. Rent is usually money, although it may also take the form of services. Rent for any unit is related not only to the size and location of the unit but also to maintenance, quality of the neighborhood, and extras such as air conditioning, swimming pool, or party room. Rent also includes the landlord's cost of financing, property taxes, and insurance.

The CPI component for rent increased 48.9 percent between 1970 and 1978. From 1970 to 1976, the median monthly rent rose 54 percent, from $108 to $167. (Home ownership costs, in contrast, increased 77 percent from 1970 to 1978.) A distribution of rental costs can be seen in Figure 8-1. There are some indications—reduced supply of rental housing, increased legal requirements on landlords, and increased demand as a result of high home ownership costs—that rents will eventually catch up with the cost of owning a home.

In addition to rent, many tenants have separate utility bills and sometimes decorating or maintenance costs. ". . . Data for

unfurnished rental units in metropolitan areas in 1973 (85% of all metropolitan rental units) show 86% paying separately for electrictiy, and 75% of gas users and 21% of users of other fuels paying separately for them."[7]

The best protection against rent increases is a long-term lease. The renter should know what the rent includes—whether utilities, parking, garbage disposal, snow removal, recreational facilities, or other amenities.

Are rent increases related to better quality in rental units? One measure can be obtained for the 1960–1970 period by analyzing the median rent paid in 1960 and 1970 for the same apartment. The median rent actually paid has risen by much more than the median rent required for the same apartment. This increase is because of quality improvement.

"For all renters, for example, the quality improvement according to this measure was $23, or 27 percent, from 1960 to 1970. In general, quality improvements have been least for households headed by elderly persons, or for single-person elderly households, although such calculations indicate that even these groups have had improvements of at least 15 percent during the decade."[8] The relatively small rent increases and the improved quality for renters are especially important because there are more renters in lower-income groups.[9]

---

[6]Samuel Bassett Abbott, "Housing Policy, Housing Codes and Tenant Remedies: An Integration," *Boston University Law Review*, 56 (January 1976), 10.

[7]Neil Mayer, "Housing Occupancy Costs: Current Problems and Means to Relieve Them" (Washington, D.C.: The Urban Institute, June 1978), p. 15.

[8]U.S. Department of Housing and Urban Development, *Housing in the Seventies*, (Washington, D.C., 1974), p. 234.

[9]Ibid., p. 236.

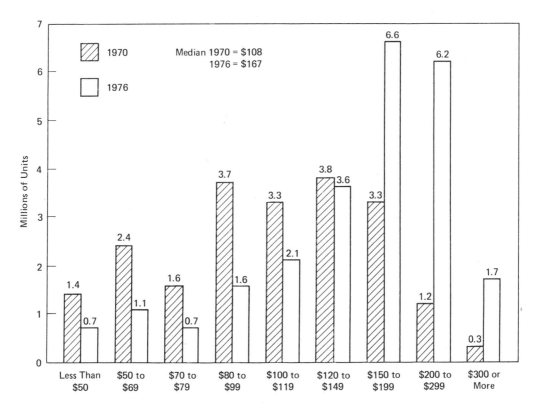

Figure 8-1. A Comparison of Rental Costs, 1970–1976. [*Source:* U.S. Department of Commerce, Bureau of the Census, and U.S. Department of Housing and Urban Development, *Annual Housing Survey: 1976,* U.S. and Regions: General Housing Characteristics, Part A, Series, H-150-A, February 1978, p. 12.]

INSURANCE

Most landlords have insurance that covers rental property but not the tenant's personal belongings. A tenant should obtain a renter's policy insuring personal possessions against dangers such as fire and lightning, wind and hail, explosion, riot, smoke, vandalism, and theft. The policy also usually provides personal liability protection and medical payments to others.

The cost of the policy depends on such factors as the value of the property, the amount of protection desired, the extent of protection, the location, and the type of building. The cost for the same coverage may vary among insurance companies, so comparison shopping is important to assure the best "buy."

Rental Agreements

Rental situations differ with the rental agreement involved. In general, there are three types: tenancy under a lease, at will, or at sufferance. Tenancy under a *lease* involves a written agreement between landlord and tenant which gives the tenant exclusive possession of the premises for a definite period of time.

Under tenancy *at will*, the tenant rightfully possesses the premises under an arrangement other than a lease. It can occur:

1. When the landlord allows the tenant to take possession, with the only agreement (oral or written) being the amount of rent.
2. When the landlord-tenant agreement does not specify a definite term.
3. When the tenant "holds over" after the lease has expired if the landlord accepts payment of rent.

Tenancy *at sufferance* involves holding possession of the premises without right. The tenant is liable to the landlord for the reasonable value of the property for as long as he or she lives there. The tenant is entitled to no more than a reasonable time to remove personal belongings. Tenancy at sufferance arises as soon as "true" tenancy ends.

LEASES

A *lease* is a legal document of property rental specifying the landlord's and tenant's responsibilities. Many problems can be prevented if the tenant and landlord discuss these issues before any agreement is made. The lease also sets the amount of the rent for the term of the lease unless there is a clause allowing increases. A

National Housing Partnership.

Cumberland Court, Harrisburg, Pennsylvania.

lease also commits the tenant to pay rent for the term of the lease.

LEASE PROVISIONS   A lease should contain the following provisions:

1. Date of signing.
2. Complete names of landlord and tenant.
3. Location of rental unit, including apartment identification.
4. Length of lease terms—both beginning and ending dates.
5. The amount of the rent.
   a. When and where the rent is due.
   b. Penalty, if any, for late payment.
   c. When the rent can be raised (e.g., taxes increased, water assessment raised).
   d. What utilities, if any, are included in the rent.
6. Extra charges, if any, for parking, storage, recreational facilities, and so on.
7. Who pays for repairs and maintenance; what happens if damage results from tenant negligence.
8. Amount of security or damage deposit if required.
   a. What the deposit covers.
   b. When it will be returned.
   c. Conditions for refund.
   d. Provision for payment of interest.
9. Provisions for subletting.
10. Are multiple lessors jointly or separately obligated?
    (If tenants are "jointly and severally" responsible for paying rent, each tenant is responsible for the total rent payment.)
11. When the landlord can enter the unit.
12. Rules about pets and guests.
13. Limit on number of occupants, if any.
14. Special equipment allowed, such as musical instruments, boat, or snowmobile.
15. If furnished or unfurnished:
    a. If furnished, the lease should list everything provided. The tenant should check the list carefully to avoid hard feelings and accusations later.
    b. Condition of the items provided should be noted in writing and signed by both landlord and tenant.
    c. Which if any items in a furnished apartment belong to the current occupants.
16. Provisions for terminating the lease at the end of its term.
    a. Lease may continue on a month-to-month basis.
    b. Renewal option available.
    c. Automatic renewal or extension of lease for another year.
17. Provisions for terminating the lease before the term ends.
    a. Military clause—allows service people to terminate the lease if they are transferred.
    b. If lessee is transferred to another locality in connection with employment.
    c. If property (building) is damaged.
    d. Nonpayment of rent.
    e. Is there a penalty for leaving before the lease is terminated?
18. Parties to a lease may stipulate an amount to be paid in compensation if the lease is violated.

DANGER CLAUSE   The following clauses may create problems for the tenant and should be avoided if possible:

1. The landlord is not liable for repairs.
2. The landlord can cancel the lease if he or she sells the property, is "dissatisfied with the tenant's behavior," or feels the tenant's behavior is immoral.
3. The tenant agrees to pay all attorney's fees, including the landlord's.
4. The tenant waives the right to a jury trial.
5. The tenant agrees to obey rules not yet written or to pay possible extra rent.
6. The landlord has the right to enter the apartment at any time.
7. The tenant agrees that no one else will live in the apartment. "Live with" versus "visit" should be clearly specified.
8. The tenant agrees that any improvements made belong to the landlord.
9. The tenant agrees that the premises are fine as is.
10. The tenant agrees to show the premises to prospective buyers or renters without a definite time span specified (e.g., thirty days before vacating). Items of importance to the tenant may not be included in a lease at all; this omission is as important as the above clauses.

ACTION After reading the lease, the tenant should mark all objectionable clauses and try to have them removed as well as add the missing provisions that are desired. All agreed changes should be in writing and initialed by both landlord and tenant on all copies. Each person signing the lease should keep a copy of it. If rules or other provisions from another document are included as part of the lease, the renter needs to know what these are and keep a copy of them. An attorney should be consulted if the lease is complex, involves a lot of money, or is for a long time, such as three or more years. Oral additions to a written lease are generally not binding. A tenant should not assume that a landlord will not enforce any of the lease provisions; the same is true for the landlord.

RENTING WITHOUT A LEASE

Many tenants rent housing without a lease. Rent is usually paid weekly or monthly. The tenant and landlord have a verbal agreement as to the rights and responsibilities of each party. The disadvantage of renting without a lease is that over time, memories become vague and disputes may arise. Further, the rent can be raised at any time.

SECURITY DEPOSITS

Special attention is given to the subject of *security deposits*. A security deposit protects the landlord's investment and encourages the tenant to live up to the lease. It guarantees that the tenant will leave the premises in good condition. A landlord usually may keep money from the security deposit only to cover the actual cost of damages. It is a good idea for the tenant to obtain a receipt. Security deposits are sometimes held in interest-bearing accounts; this depends on state law.

Problems arise in the return of security deposits because leases are vague about the conditions under which the deposit, or part of it, will be returned. Since a security deposit is designed to recover the costs for returning the premises to the *same* condition as when the tenant moved in, tenant and landlord should jointly inspect the premises *upon occupancy* and jointly sign a checklist of the condition at that time. This should be part of the lease.

SUBLETTING

If a tenant can no longer remain and the landlord will not void the lease, the tenant must *sublet* or continue to pay rent for the rest of the lease. Subletting is the transfer of part interest in property. Thus, the original tenant gives up the right to live in the unit to another person.

If the landlord will not sign a new lease with the prospective sublettee—and is often not required to—then the original tenant is still responsible for complying with the lease, even though someone else lives there. Thus, the tenant should have a written sublease agreement with the subletter, identical to the original lease, so that the new person has the same obligations as the original tenant.

An apartment or house can usually be sublet unless the lease forbids it. When subletting, the tenant should personally check the sublettee's credentials and obtain as large a security deposit as possible. If the sublettee is paying the landlord directly, the sublettor should check to see that each payment is made. This prevents a notice that the subletting tenant has skipped and that the original tenant now owes several hundred dollars in back rent.

Tenant Protection

There are many groups and legal *remedies* to help the tenant or landlord deal with problems that cannot be resolved by discussion. Local agencies such as the hous-

ing department, building department, health department, or fire marshal may be contacted. A human rights problem may be taken to a state agency or to HUD.

The following sections explain some of the remedies available to tenants. These should be judged in terms of how quickly the problem is solved, how appropriate the remedy is, how widely it can be applied, and how easy it is to use.

REPAIR AND DEDUCT LAWS

Repair and deduct laws permit a tenant to repair certain conditions if the landlord has been notified and failed to act in a reasonable time. The cost of the repairs is deducted from rent payments; usually this is limited to a specific dollar amount or a multiple of the monthly rent.[10] Repair and deduct has been adapted by statute or judicial decision in twenty-two states.

From the tenant's perspective, repair and deduct has certain limitations. The tenant must finance the repairs and may have trouble getting workmen and recovering the money spent. The landlord may claim that the repair was not legitimate. The tenant may be liable if the repair was poor or the service overcharged. If the court decides that the costs are unreasonable, the tenant may lose the money spent.

The availability, quality, and price of repair services may all limit the usefulness of repair and deduct. Also, it is limited to an individual tenant making repairs on his or her own unit. Often the amount that can be deducted and the number of times any one tenant can do

---

[10]Abbott, "Housing Policy," p. 57.

this are limited. The tenant, out of ignorance, may not notify the landlord and may not wait the required time before making the repair. Thus, the tenant faces losing the dollars spent.

From the landlord's perspective, repair and deduct has problems too. The landlord may be able to get the job done cheaper. Also, the condition and cause are hard to determine after a repair is made. The landlord can avoid these problems by responding promptly when a complaint is made. Weitzman reported that repair and deduct laws did not have a noticeable impact on rent levels or on the quality or quantity of rental housing.[11] Earlier, Hirsh and his colleagues reported similar results.[12]

RENT WITHHOLDING

Rent withholding is a legal remedy that authorizes a tenant to deposit rent in an escrow account with a court or an escrow agent. While paying into the account, a tenant cannot be evicted for nonpayment of rent. Often the landlord may draw on funds held in escrow to remedy the complaint.

Rent withholding allows tenants to join together to have common areas repaired. It makes the landlord responsible for the work and does not limit the cost of repairs since the landlord usually has more resources than an individual tenant. At the same time, the escrow payments are security for the rent.

Rent withholding does not guarantee repair, and a stubborn or lazy landlord may delay indefinitely. Unprofitable buildings may be abandoned rather than repaired.

RENT ABATEMENT

Rent abatement allows the tenant to stop paying part or all of the rent when the unit is not livable. A landlord cannot receive full rent until the repairs are made and is not entitled to full back rent. A tenant using rent abatement runs the risk that a court will declare the action unwarranted and that he or she will face rent costs, moving costs, and court and legal fees.[13]

HOUSING COURTS

In many cities, housing courts have been established to deal only with housing problems.[14] In most situations, civil rather than criminal cases are heard. Housing courts act to remove violations and improve the housing stock rather than to punish the landlord. The courts may take the following actions: impose and collect fines for housing code violations; make emergency repairs; order enforcement of housing standards; set up rent withholding by tenants; and handle eviction and other suits by landlords against tenants. Housing courts, with their emphasis on correction, will play an increasingly important role in the future.

Housing courts must be able to re-

---

[11]Phillip Weitzman, "The Impact of Repair and Deduct Legislation," *Clearinghouse Review,* 11 (April 1978), 985.

[12]Werner Z. Hirsh, Joel G. Hirsh, and Stephen Margolis, "Regression Analysis of the Effects of Habitability Laws Upon Rent: An Empirical Observation on the Ackerman-Komesar Debate," *California Law Review,* 63 (September 1975), 1139.

[13]Ibid., 1108.

[14]Housing courts have been established in the following places, among others: Boston, Pittsburgh, New York City, Springfield, Mass., Detroit, Baltimore, St. Louis, and New Orleans. Many other communities have a housing calendar or specified time when housing cases are tried.

spond quickly and have a staff knowledgeable about housing. Their usefulness to tenants also depends on who can bring cases before the court. If only government bodies can do so, the process will be slower and the results reduced.

HOUSING RECEIVERSHIP

In housing receivership, the court appoints an administrator to manage the rental property. It is a complex task with legal, economic, and political problems. Rent is usually deposited with the receiver until the code violations are corrected. The receiver can be a private party, a social service agency, or a municipality. If rental income does not cover the repairs, some laws allow a lien to be placed on the property. Once housing conditions are repaired, control of the building and any money left over are returned to the owner. Receivership requires tenant participation and cooperation in caring for the building. It is a tenant remedy in thirteen states (Table 8-1). Receivership may be the most costly remedy to the landlord since it affects the entire building.[15]

RETALIATORY AND CONSTRUCTIVE EVICTION

Tenant protection from landlord retaliation is provided in twenty-six states (Table 8-1). The tenant activities which are allowed and the forms of retaliation prohibited vary among the states. However, in each jurisdiction, tenants who report code violations are protected. In a majority of the states, retaliatory rent increases and decreases in services are pro-

hibited where tenant activity would have been a valid defense to eviction.

Under constructive eviction, the tenant's duty to pay rent ends when the landlord fails to provide a livable place.[16] This is a change from earlier times, when a tenant had to pay rent whether or not the place was livable. However, there are two problems. If there is a housing shortage, a tenant may have trouble finding another place that is affordable. Further, if too many tenants move, the landlord may abandon the property, depriving the remaining tenants of a place to live.

TENANT-MORTGAGEE NEGOTIATING STRATEGY

Tenants may involve the mortgagee in rehabilitating a deteriorated building. If the tenants follow a rent withholding or abatement practice, the landlord may not be able to pay the mortgage, which could lead to default. Thus, the mortgagee may be willing to declare a temporary moratorium on mortgage payments. The landlord must agree to an extension of the mortgage loan. This strategy makes the property more valuable, and the new funds obtained may be sufficient for major repairs. Whether a mortgagee is willing to cooperate depends on the market for the building in question.

Rental Issues

There are several remaining areas of concern for tenants and landlords. Four issues are highlighted here.

---

[15]Hirsh and others, "Regression Analysis," p. 1112.

[16]Frank J. Parker, "Must the Residential Landlord Run for Cover?" *Real Estate Review*, 6 (Spring 1976), 76–80.

UNIFORM RESIDENTIAL LANDLORD AND TENANT ACT (URLTA)

The Uniform Residential Landlord and Tenant Act was drafted by the National Conference on Uniform State Laws in 1972 (amended 1974) and recommended for enactment in all states.[17] Purposes and policies of the act are:

1. To simplify, clarify, modernize, and revise renting laws and those concerning the rights and obligations of landlords and tenants.
2. To encourage landlords and tenants to maintain and improve the quality of the property.
3. To make landlord-tenant law uniform among the states.

Major provisions of the act include:

1. Terms and conditions of a rental agreement, such as where and when rent is due, and security deposit requirements.
2. Prohibition of acts such as agreement by the tenant to give up rights or pay the landlord's attorney's fees.
3. Designation of the rental agreement as a contract, with the tenant's obligation to pay rent and the landlord's to maintain the premises.
4. Tenant obligations, including reasonable use and care of the unit and equipment.
5. Landlord obligations, including

maintenance, security deposit, and liability specifications.
6. Tenant and landlord remedies.

Major revisions to the original include:

1. Protection against landlord retaliation if the tenant organizes or joins a tenants union.
2. Injunctive relief for the tenant if the landlord fails to meet obligations.
3. Establishment of a basis for granting the warranty of habitability.

Whether the URLTA is progressive or regressive depends on the situation in any given state. Thus, it should not automatically be supported. It has been adopted with variations in thirteen states and introduced in the legislature of ten others (Table 8-1).

TENANT COUNCILS

Tenant councils, associations, or organizations are groups of tenants who have joined together to fulfill a common need or to reach a goal, such as repairs of common areas. A National Tenant Organization was founded in 1969 and publishes a newsletter for tenants and tenant groups.

Tenant councils may do many things, including advising management of tenant needs, problems, and views; helping tenants to solve their problems; improving living conditions; arranging day-care and recreational programs for young and old; and creating and staffing safety and security programs. To be most effective in meeting tenants' needs, the council should be organized and operated by the tenants themselves. The officers and

---

[17]National Conference of Commissioners on Uniform State Laws, *Uniform Residential Landlord and Tenant Act* (Chicago), August 1972; amended August 1974.

Village Green, garden apartment development in Mobile, Alabama.

committees should be elected by the tenants.

From the management's viewpoint, a tenant council can improve the housing environment and provide a means for communication. By understanding the limits under which management must operate, tenant councils and continuing tenant participation may avoid conflict and problems in operations.

From the tenants' viewpoint, an organization can accomplish what one person alone may not be able to do. It can also be a catalyst, help the residents know one another, and improve the decision-making process. Improved landlord-tenant relations and a better living environment are all possible.

HUD encourages tenant councils in low-income public housing. HUD's history of tenant participation began in 1968, with its statement of social goals for public housing, including a larger role for tenants. Now, tenants can be appointed to the Public Housing Authority Board of Commissioners, develop tenant councils and organizations for program development, and take part in modernization projects. Issues concerning tenant participation include funding of the organization, methods for settling disputes, and defining what is effective tenant participation.

SECURITY DEPOSIT FOR LANDLORDS

It has been proposed that landlords pay security deposits. A set sum of money would be deposited for each unit to ensure the landlord's immediate repair of an emergency condition. The city would hold the funds in an interest-bearing account. If the landlord fails to respond to an emergency, such as supplying heat, the city would step in and correct the

situation using this fund. The landlord would be required to replace the deposit or the city could sue. Deposits would not be pooled. The landlord would be allowed to appeal the situation, and the tenant would need protection against retaliatory rate increases or eviction. The definition of what constitutes an emergency is also important. A Landlord Security Deposit Act was first adopted in Ridgefield, New Jersey, in 1972.[18]

RENT CONTROL

One way communities can regulate the price of rental housing is by rent control. It was first used in the United States during World War I and was revived again in World War II.[19] In 1942 Congress enacted the Emergency Price Control Act.[20] In 1947 it extended rent control and required that preference be given to veterans in the sale and rental of new housing.[21] The Housing and Rent Acts of 1948 and 1949 continued to extend both rent control and veterans' preference in new housing.[22]

The Housing and Rent Act of 1950 extended rent control until December 31, 1950, except in areas that had earlier declared, by referendum or resolution of their government, that continued rent control was necessary. Later this act was

[18]Richard E. Blumberg and Brian Quinn Robbins, "The Landlord Security Deposit Act," *Clearinghouse Review,* 7 (November 1973), 411.

[19]John W. Willis, "A Short History of Rent Control Laws," *Cornell Law Quarterly,* 36 (Fall 1960), 54–94; Edith B. Drellich and Andree Emery, *Rent Control in War and Peace* (New York, N.Y.: National Municipal League, 1939).

[20]Public Law 421, 77th Cong. (Jan. 30, 1942).

[21]Public Law 129, 80th Cong. (June 30, 1947).

[22]Public Law 464, 80th Cong. (Mar. 30, 1948); Public Law 31, 81st Cong. (Mar. 30, 1949).

extended to April 30, 1953.[23] On that date, Congress passed the Housing and Rent Act of 1953, which allowed federal rent controls to expire on July 31, 1953. The expiration date was extended to April 30, 1954, in critical defense housing areas.[24] The tenant movement of the late 1960s again increased interest in rent control. Rent control exists today in several states, among them New York, New Jersey, Massachusetts, Connecticut, Maryland, Maine, and Washington, D.C. On a national scale, the Nixon Administration froze rents for ninety days in 1971 and restricted annual rent increases for thirteen months following.[25]

Rent control is generally used when a large share of the population cannot obtain reasonable quality housing at affordable rents. There are several issues involved in rent control:[26]

1. Are housing costs really affordable?.

2. How fairly and efficiently are the costs and benefits distributed?

3. What is the impact on other housing policy goals?

The effectiveness of rent control depends on how inflated rents are and what methods are used to determine rent increases. Rent control does provide for adjustments in rent. Usually it gives the landlord a "fair return." This "fair return" must be attractive enough to encourage continued investment in rental property and should reflect the rate paid by other investments with comparable rates. Formulas used to calculate rent increases may be based on the Consumer Price Index, the landlord's operating costs, some percentage of market or assessed value. In addition, rent increases for hardship cases are usually allowed. Rent control almost always limits the amount of rent increase from one lease to another or one year to another.

Rent control is often unfair to both tenants and landlords. It favors long-term residents over new ones or those who must move frequently. Over time, occupants of rent-controlled units may have higher incomes and lower rents than those of free-market units. However, Olsen found that on the average, occupants of rent-controlled apartments are poorer.[27] Roistacher reported that if rent control were removed, 77 percent of projected rent increases would fall on households with incomes under $10,000.[28] Rent control also allows for black marketing and thus may favor persons with enough cash to pay the entrance fee. Landlords of rent-controlled units may have more requirements and lower profits than those with uncontrolled units. Olsen found that rent-controlled tenants in New York City consumed 4.4 percent less housing service and 9.9 percent more nonhousing goods than uncontrolled tenants.[29] "There is nothing approaching equal treatment of equals among the beneficiaries of rent

[23]Public Law 880, 81st Cong. (Dec. 20, 1950); Public Law 8, 82nd Cong (Mar. 23, 1951); Public Law 96, 82nd Cong. (July 31, 1951); Public Law 429, 82nd Cong. (June 30, 1952).

[24]Public Law 23, 83d Cong. (Apr. 30, 1953).

[25]Monica R. Lett, *Rent Control* (New Brunswick, N.J.: The Center for Urban Policy Research, 1976), p. 5.

[26]Emily P. Aktenberg, "The Social Utility of Rent Control," in *Housing Urban America,* ed. Jon Pynoos and others (Chicago: Aldine, 1973), p. 437.

[27]Edgar O. Olsen, "An Econometric Analysis of Rent Control," *Journal of Political Economy,* 80 (November/December 1972), 1094.

[28]Elizabeth A. Roistacher, "The Removal of Rent Control Regulation in New York City," American Economic Association meeting, December 1977.

[29]Olsen, "Rent Contrl," 1094.

control."[30] Olsen also estimated the mean net benefit for each family in 1968 to be $213, or 3.4 percent of their income, for a total benefit of $270 million. In contrast, the cost to landlords under rent control was $514 million. In addition, about $7 million was spent administering the program.[31] Moorhouse found that rent control lowers the optional level of maintenance during a period of inflation.[32]

Black concluded that little new rental housing will be built in Washington, D.C., until rent control is lifted or changed to insure that investment in new housing is competitive with other forms of investment.[33] Rent control in one community may affect market prices, building activities, and residents' location in an entire area.

Rent control is only a short-term solution. In the long run, it can decrease investment interest in leasing, cause poor maintenance and abandonment, create a black market for rent-controlled housing, and possibly lead to more government regulation. Because of its explicit control of individual property rights, it is often controversial.

Summary

Rental of housing has decreased as home ownership has increased. The rental process is somewhat similar to the home ownership process in many ways. Instead of a purchase contract and a mortgage, the majority of renters have a lease that spells out the rental terms.

In most early legislation, the landlord was favored. However, this is changing with the use of warranty of habitability statutes and other forms of tenant protection, such as repair and deduct, rent withholding, rent abatement, housing courts, and housing receivership.

Major rental issues are tenant councils and their role in rental housing, rent control, and establishment of a uniform landlord-tenant act.

---

[30]Ibid., 1096.

[31]Ibid., 1094.

[32]John C. Moorhouse, "Optimal Housing Maintenance Under Rent Control," *Southern Economic Journal*, 39 (July 1972), 104.

[33]J. Thomas Black, "Prospects for Rental Housing Production under Rent Control: A Case Study of Washington, D.C." (Washington, D.C.: The Urban Land Institute, 1976).

Terms

accepting of premises lease term stating that the tenant accepts the premises "as is"; may mean that the tenant has no way to force the landlord to correct defects.

assignee person to whom interest is transferred.

assignor person transferring an interest.

assignment transfer of an interest.

automatic renewal clause provision in a lease that extends the term automatically upon expiration.

caveat emptor "Let the buyer beware."

constructive eviction tenant's decision to leave rented unit and not pay the rent if the landlord interferes with the tenant's use, enjoyment, or possession of the premises.

contract agreement.

covenant a binding agreement between two parties.

discrimination unfair treatment of one person or group compared with others.

dispossess to remove a person from land.

duty to repair lease clause that specifies who is responsible for repairs.

ejectment form of eviction.

eviction depriving a person of possession of real property.

improvement alteration, addition, or change to property.

injunction court order compelling or forbidding certain actions.

joint and several liability when several persons occupy a rental unit, the responsibility of each person for payment of the total rent.

judgment a decision or opinion of the court after hearing the case.

landlord one who owns and leases real property to a tenant.

lease agreement (contract) between tenant and landlord.

lessee tenant.

lessor landlord.

liability legal responsibility.

multi-family dwelling one that provides living quarters for more than one family.

parties persons involved in a legal contract; a lessor and lessee under a lease.

quit to leave or vacate.

remedy a legal means to reduce grievances.

rent consideration, usually money, that a tenant pays a landlord for use of the premises.

rent abatement suspension of the tenant's obligation to pay rent.

rental apartments those built or bought by the owner as an investment. From the rent tenants pay, the owner pays expenses and obtains a profit.

rent escrow fund into which the tenant pays for repairs or improvements.

rent withholding procedure by which a tenant places rent in escrow in an attempt to force the landlord to live up to the lease.

security deposit financial guarantee to the landlord that the tenant will leave the premises in good condition on moving.

subletting transferring part interest in property; the original tenant gives his or her right to live in the unit to another person.

tenant one who rents property from a landlord.

waiver relinquishment of a right, privilege, or protection.

Suggested Readings

Abbot, Samuel Bassett, "Housing Policy, Housing Codes and Tenant Remedies: An Integration," *Boston University Law Review,* 56 (January 1976), 1–146.

Arnault, E. Jane, "Optimal Maintenance under Rental Control with Quality Constraints," *American Real Estate and Urban Economics Association Journal,* 3 (Summer 1975), 67–82.

Berger, Curtis J., *Housing Cases and Materials,* American Casebook Series. St. Paul, Minn.: West Publishing, 1969.

Blumberg, Richard E., "Retroactive Rent Abatement: A Landmark Tenant Remedy," *Cleaninghouse Review,* 7 (October 1973), 323–26.

———— and Brian Quinn Robbins, "Beyond URLTA: A Program For Achieving Real Tenant Goals," *Harvard Civil Rights–Civil Liberties Law Review,* 11 (Winter 1976), 1–47.

————, ————, and Kenneth K. Baar, "The Emergence of Second Generation Rent Controls." *Clearinghouse Review,* 8 (August 1974), 240–49.

Briggs, Bruce B., "Rent Control Must Go," *New York Times Magazine,* Apr. 18, 1976, pp. 19–31.

Burghardt, Stephen, Ed., *Tenants and the Urban Housing Crisis,* Dexter, Mich.: The New Press, 1972.

Crim, Sarah K., "Rent Control Seminar Yields Much Controversy, Few Answers," *Mortgage Banker,* 30 (March 1976), 34–37.

Grampp, William D., "Some Effects of Rent

Control," *Southern Economic Journal,* 16 (April 1950), 425–47.

Hillman, Robert A., "Judicial Expansion of Tenants' Private Law Rights: Implied Warranties of Habitability and Safety in Residential Urban Leases," *Cornell Law Review,* 56 (January 1971), 489–506.

Lett, Monica, R., *Rent Control.* New Brunswick, N.J.: The Center for Urban Policy Research, Rutgers—The State University of New Jersey, 1976.

Marcuse, Peter, "The Rise of Tenant Organizations," in *Housing Urban America,* ed. John Pynoos and others. Chiacgo: Aldine, 1973.

Mattox, Joe L., "Housing Courts Answer to Problem Tenants," *Journal of Property Management,* 41 (January–February 1976), 29–32.

Moskovitz, Myron, "Retaliatory Evictions—the Law and the Facts," *Clearinghouse Review,* 3 (May 1969), 4–6, 10.

Robbins, Brian Quinn, "The New Oregon Landlord-Tenant Act and the Uniform Residential Landlord and Tenant Act—A Comparison," *Clearinghouse Review,* 7 (October 1973), 327–28.

Rodwin, Lloyd, "Rent Control and Housing," *Social Research,* 27 (September 1950), 302–19.

Rose, Jerome G., *Landlords and Tenants.* New Brunswick, N.J.: Transactions Books, 1973.

———, "Landlords and Tenants: Do They Have a Future?" *Real Estate Review,* 3 (Summer 1973), 327–28.

Rutzick, Mark C., and Richard L. Huffman, "The New York City Housing Court: Trial and Error in Housing Code Enforcement," *New York University Law Review,* 50 (October 1975), 738–97.

Shenkel, William M., "Rent Control: A Critical Review," *Journal of Property Management,* 39 (May/June 1974), 101–10.

Sternlieb, George, and Robert W. Burchell, *Residential Abandonment: The Tenement Landlord Revisited.* New Brunswick, N.J.: Center for Urban Policy Research, Rutgers University, 1973.

Strum, Brian J., "New Trends in the Landlord-Tenant Relationship," *Real Estate Review,* 4 (Summer 1974), 125–30.

HOUSING THE ELDERLY

1. SHOULD HOMEOWNERSHIP BY THE ELDERLY BE ENCOURAGED OR DISCOURAGED BY GOVERNMENT POLICY?

2. WHAT KIND OF ADJUSTMENTS DO THE ELDERLY MAKE IN HOUSING?

3. HOW DOES DESIGN ENHANCE THE LIVING ENVIRONMENT OF THE ELDERLY?

4. WHAT IS ROLE OF HEALTH CARE FACILITIES IN HOUSING THE ELDERLY?

The elderly have different physical needs and resources than the population as a whole. This chapter describes the elderly demographically and then deals with issues to be considered in providing and choosing housing for them.

The Elderly in America

Although aging is continual, it is different for every individual. "Demographically, however, aging is defined essentially in terms of chronological age, on the assumption that for large populations the aging process, functional age, and physiological age follow the chronological age closely."[1]

Roughtly 1 out of 10 persons in the United States is sixty-five years of age or more today, compared to 4 out of 100 in 1900. The elderly population is increasing faster than the population as a whole. From 1900 to 1978, the elderly population rose almost 707 percent, the total population about 302 percent.[2]

Part of this increase is due to the rising birth rate in the late 1800s and early 1900s. Another reason is the large immigrant population that entered the United States before World War I. A third factor is increased life expectancy. Even as the proportion of the elderly population has grown, so has the average age within the group. In 1900, the proportion seventy-five years and over was 29 percent; by

---

[1]U.S. Department of Commerce, Bureau of the Census, "Demographic Aspects of Aging and the Older Population in the United States," *Current Population Reports:* Special Studies, Series P-23, no. 59 (Washington, D.C., May 1976), p. 1.

[2]U.S. Department of Commerce, Bureau of the Census, "Estimates of the Population of States, by Age: July 1977- 1978," *Current Population Reports,* Series P-25, No. 794, March 1979. Table 1, p. 2.

1978 it had risen to 38 percent.[3] The greater concentration of the elderly at higher ages affects the health and living arrangements of the various population groups.

The elderly are not evenly distributed across the United States. States with relatively large older populations (over 12 percent) include Florida, Arkansas, Nebraska, South Dakota, Iowa, and Missouri (Table 9-1). Such states have lost many younger people to other areas. When this happens, the elderly are usually left behind and the age distribution becomes "older." On the other hand, a few states have had an influx of retirees to swell the aged population.

States with a lower share of older residents either have populations with relatively high fertility (Georgia, Louisiana, New Mexico, Utah, and South Carolina) or have received more younger inmigrants from other states (Maryland and Nevada).

Florida and Nebraska illustrate different forces that may result in similar proportions of the elderly. In 1970, 14.6 percent of Florida's population and 12.4 percent of Nebraska's were sixty-five years or over. Between 1960 and 1970, however, the aged population increased by almost 80 percent in Florida but by only 12 percent in Nebraska. The situation in Florida is explained by inmigration of the old; in Nebraska it is caused by the exodus of the young and the longevity of the remaining population.

In terms of numbers, the largest states have the most people over sixty-five. These include New York and California, followed by Pennsylvania, Florida, Illinois, Texas, and Ohio. These seven states together account for about 45 percent of the over-sixty-five population.[4] Most of the elderly (55 percent) live in major cities, while another 40 percent live in smaller communities and 5 percent on farms.[5] This relationship will change in

TABLE 9-1. States with the Highest and Lowest Percentages of Populations Aged 65 and Over, 1978

HIGHEST		LOWEST	
State	Percentage	State	Percentage
Florida	17.6	Alaska	2.5
Arkansas	13.4	Hawaii	7.4
Iowa	13.1	Utah	7.8
Nebraska	12.9	Nevada	8.3
Missouri	12.9	Wyoming	8.5
South Dakota	12.9	New Mexico	8.6
Rhode Island	12.8	Colorado	8.7
Kansas	12.6	South Carolina	8.8
Oklahoma	12.4	Maryland	8.9
Pennsylvania	12.4	Virginia	9.1

Source: U.S. Department of Commerce, Bureau of the Census, "Estimates of the Population of States by Age: July 1977–1978," Current Population Reports: Series P-25, no. 794 (Washington, D.C., March 1979), pp. 2, 3.

[3]U.S. Department of Commerce, Bureau of the Census, "Estimates of the Population of the U.S. by Age, Sex, and Race 1976–1978," Current Population Reports, Series P-25, No. 800. April 1979, Table 1, p. 6.

[4]Ibid., p. 16.

[5]Raymond J. Struyk, "The Housing Situation of Elderly Americans," (Washington, D.C.: The Urban Institute, November 1976), p. 10. Source of data is 1973 Annual Housing Survey.

the future as those who moved to the suburbs after World War II enter the sixty-five age or over group.

The elderly are not evenly distributed according to race and sex. Elderly women outnumber elderly men by a large margin, and the gap is widening. In addition, a large number of these are widows.

The black population has a much smaller proportion of elderly (7.8 percent in 1978) than the white population (11.5 percent in 1978).[6] This difference results from the higher black fertility rate, the

[6]U.S. Department of Commerce, Bureau of the Census, "Estimates of Population by Age," p. 6.

Office of Human Development Service, Administration on Aging, U.S. Department of Health, Education, and Welfare.

The elderly prefer to remain in their own homes and neighborhoods.

relatively high death rate of blacks at younger ages, and the large immigration of whites prior to World War I.

The elderly generally have less formal education than younger adults. This reflects both the values and opportunities of the past. By 1990, it is expected that about half the aged population will be high school graduates, and beyond that point even more education as today's young adults age.

The median income of the elderly is below that of the population as a whole. The sex of the family head makes an important difference for elderly families. Families headed by women sixty-five years and over have higher median incomes than all female-headed families; but families headed by men over sixty-five have much lower median incomes compared to male-headed families under sixty-five. When income is related to the number of persons in the family, the picture improves greatly, regardless of whether the family is headed by a man, woman, black or white. While the proportion of older men who continue working has decreased, the proportion of older women who work is holding steady.[7] Retirement benefits (Social Security and public and private pensions) are the most prevalent and important source of income for the elderly. For elderly couples with a household head over sixty-five years, retirement payments provide at least half the income for the majority of couples. For individuals, this figure rises to nearly two-thirds of total income. About 95 percent of all elderly Americans are eligible for Social Security benefits in pensions or aid.

Income derived from wages is second in importance to the elderly, and that from assets in real estate and investments is third. However, only 7 percent of aged couples, and even fewer individuals, obtain all their income from wages, and less than 25 percent of elderly couples earn as much as half their incomes. The fourth-ranking source of income is public assistance.

Income limits housing options. Murray reported that low-income elderly persons are more likely to live with relatives than those with higher incomes.[8]

Poverty rates, which control for size, composition and household location, are perhaps a better guide than income to the economic situation of the elderly. Poverty rates for older blacks are about double that of whites.

Housing Status

The housing needs of the elderly must be given special attention. The majority of elderly persons live with their family; less than 5 percent live in institutions—about 1 million persons in 1970 (Table 9-2). In the 85 and over age group, one in five live in an institution. About eight out of ten of these were in homes for the aged; another one out of ten were in mental hospitals and residential treatment centers.[9] The other 1 percent were hospital

---

[7]Ibid., p. 50.

[8]J. Murray, *Living Arrangements of People Aged 65 and Older: Findings from the 1967 Survey of the Aged,* Report No. 4, Social Security Administration, (Washington, D.C.: U.S. Government Printing Office, 1971).

[9]U.S. Department of Commerce, Bureau of the Census, "Social and Economic Characteristics of the Older Population: 1974," *Current Population Reports* Series P-23, no. 57 (Nov. 1975), p. 9.

TABLE 9-2. Percent of Elderly Men and Women in Various Living Arrangements, 1970

LIVING ARRANGEMENT	MEN	WOMEN
Family	79	59
Alone	14	35
Living with a nonrelative	3	4
Institution	4	4

Source: Leon Bouvier, Elinore Atlee, and Frank McVeigh, "The Elderly in America," Population Bulletin 30 (1975), 16.

patients because of physical problems or residents of correctional and other institutions. About twice as many women as men were in institutions. Living arrangements reflect such factors as marital status, income, availability of housing choices, family ties, and a desire for independence.

Although most of the elderly are not institutionalized, many are alone. Their life styles range from swinging single to isolated living death. Reality is somewhere in between. Results from a number of small surveys indicate that those in good health prefer to live independently rather than with relatives.[10] However, family networks are important.

According to Witkowski, the elderly greatly improved their housing situations from 1960 to 1970. The proportion of elderly-headed households living in standard-quality housing rose from 80 to 92 percent. Rent-income ratios decreased from 24.1 to 21.9 percent for two-or-more-person households.[11]

Struyk found that overall, elderly-headed households live in smaller, lower-quality housing than other American households.[12] The elderly in rural areas are housed much more poorly than city dwellers. There are sharp differences in the quality of basic systems—piped water and adequate heating—as well as general physical condition of the structure. The urban elderly, however, often live in neighborhoods which they feel have serious problems.

TENURE

Ownership is an important indicator of economic well-being for the elderly. Earned income drops off with retirement so that income-yielding assets become more important. On the whole, a larger proportion of older than younger Americans own their own units (Table 9-3). This is not surprising, since the ownership ratio tends to increase with age. In urban areas, the proportion of owner-

[10]L. Rosenmayr, "Family Relations of the Elderly," Journal of Marriage and the Family, 30, (November 1968), 672–80; J. Stenhouwer, "Relations Between Generations and the Three-Generation Household in Denmark," in Social Structure and the Family: Generational Relations, ed. E. Shanas and G. Streib (Englewood Cliffs, N.J.: Prentice-Hall, 1965), pp. 142–62; E. Shanas, D. Townsend, H. Wedderburn, P. Friis, P. Milhoj, and J. Stenhouwer, Old People in Three Industrial Societies (New York: Atherton Press, 1968); H.Z. Lopata, Widowhood in an American City (Cambridge, Mass.: Schenkman, 1971).

[11]Sanford A. Witkowski, Abstract: "Response of HUD to the Housing Needs of Senior Citizens." Transcript of a hearing by the Subcommittee on Housing and Consumer Interests, Select Committee on Aging, House of Representatives, 94th Congress, 1st Session (Washington, D.C., Sept. 25, 1975).

[12]Struyk, "Housing Situation," pp. 4–5.

TABLE 9-3. Percent of Persons Living in Their Own Units, 1970

HOUSEHOLD	PERCENT
All households	67.1
60 or older	72.4
60–64	74.2
65–74	72.0
75 or older	70.7

Source: U.S. Department of Housing and Urban Development, *Older Americans, Facts About Incomes and Housing,* HUD-359-S (Washington, D.C.: U.S. Government Printing Office, October 1973), p. 18.

occupants and owned units is smaller than in rural areas.

Among older owners, some 85 percent of the homes were debt free in 1971.[13] Although the major expenses are property taxes and repairs, housing continues to be the largest single expense, accounting for 34 percent of the retired couple's budget. Thus, in a very real sense, the elderly are house poor.[14] In 1971 about 8.1 percent of their income went for real estate taxes[15] compared to 3.4 percent for the total population.

Elderly renters pay about 35 percent of their income for housing. Among those seventy-five years and older, this increases to 48 percent.[16] The number of elderly renter households that spend more than 30 percent of their income is greater than the number of homeowner households; government subsidies should be directed to the elderly renter.[17]

However, the ratios of house value and rent to income imply that home-owning older Americans are wise to remain homeowners as long as their physical ability permits. If a change in tenure is made, the decrease in standard of living tends to be greater the later the change is made.[18]

Tax relief programs for the elderly are popular and growing in number, type, and scope.[19] Most offer only modest benefits and have limited outreach efforts with complex rules, forms, and procedures. An Abt study reported that property tax relief is likely to:

1. Improve housing conditions for some of the elderly by increasing their buying power.

2. Provide poorly focused assistance because much of the aid goes to families and individuals who are not normally considered needy.

[13]U.S. Department of Housing and Urban Development, *Older Americans, Facts About Incomes and Housing,* HUD-359-S (Washington, D.C.: U.S. Government Printing Office, October 1973), p. 17.

[14]Morton Leeds, "Housing Directions for the Elderly," in *Housing for the Elderly,* ed. Richard H. Davis, Margaret Audet, and Lawrence Baird (Los Angeles, Calif.: Ethel Percy Andrus Gerontology Center, University of Southern California, 1973), pp. 13–23.

[15]U.S. Department of Commerce, Bureau of the Census, *Real Estate Tax Data by Home Owned Properties in the U.S. and Region,* Supplementary Report HC(51)-17 (Washington, D.C.: U.S. Government Printing Office, 1973).

[16] U.S. Senate, *Developments in Aging: 1976,* Special Committee on Aging Report No. 95-88, 95th Congress, 1st Session (Washington, D.C.: U.S. Government Printing Office, 1977), p. 53.

[17]Raymond J. Struyk, "The Housing Expense Burden of Households Headed by the Elderly," *The Gerontologist,* 17 (October 1977), 447–52.

[18]HUD, *Older Americans,* p. 20.

[19]Abt Associates, Inc., *Property Tax Relief Programs for the Elderly: An Evaluation,* (Cambridge, Mass.: U.S. Department of Housing and Urban Development, Office of Policy Development and Research, November 1975), p. 1.

3. Be very expensive if the plans of the more generous states are followed.
4. Have little effect on housing prices.
5. Have a noticeable impact on voting behavior of the general population but not on elderly voters.[20]

MOBILITY

Mobility here refers to a change of residence within a twelve-month period. In general, older persons move less often, out of choice as well as economic considerations. In 1970–1971, 91.2 percent of the elderly in the United States did not move; of those who did, most remained within the same county. Only 1.4 percent moved to another state. Owners were more reluctant than renters to move, Langford reported in a 1960 study of Old Age Survivor Insurance beneficiaries.[21]

The 1976 Annual Housing survey relates mobility to tenure.[22] That is, 2.9 percent of elderly homeowners moved, while for renters the future was 12.4 percent. All elderly-headed households had a mobility rate of 5.7 percent.

Living patterns in both rural and urban areas show this domestic stability. A higher proportion of elderly people, compared to the general population, live outside the SMSAs, remaining where they lived during their working years. In urban areas, older people tend to be con-

centrated in the inner cities. This is related to the price of housing, availability of public transportation and other services, and length of residence. As suburbs age, their percentage of elderly residents will increase too.

Where older persons live is related to:

1. *Family and social attachment.* Those who have strong local ties move less than those who have family and friends in other communities.
2. *Health and climate.* Poor health may either hinder mobility or act as a spur to change climates.
3. *Home ownership.* Here the pattern is mixed. As a fixed asset, a home tends to keep a person in an area. If sold, however, it provides the income to move elsewhere.[23]

Other factors affecting location are residency—rural, suburban, or urban—at the time of retirement, job opportunities, income, work status, previous occupation, need for safety, and education.

The loss of occupation or income, deterioration of the senses or health, and the loss of a spouse may cause an older person to change housing or living arrangements. Newman studied the changes in housing and living arrangements made by persons over sixty at retirement, death of a spouse, and with permanent physical or mental disability.[24] She found that such changes are more likely to be considered or discussed if there is a serious physical or mental

[20]For more detail see Chapter 12.

[21]Marilyn Langford, "Community Aspects of Housing for the Aged," Research Report No. 5, (Ithaca, N.Y.: Center for Housing and Environmental Studies, Cornell University, 1962).

[22]U.S. Department of Commerce, Bureau of the Census and U.S. Department of Housing and Urban Development, *Annual Housing Survey,* 1976, Part D, "Housing Characteristics of Recent Movers," (Washington, D.C.: U.S. Government Printing Office, January, 1978), p. 2.

[23]Steve L. Barsby and Dennis R. Cox, *Interstate Migration of the Elderly* (Lexington, Mass.: Lexington Books, 1975), p. 10.

[24]Sandra Newman, *Housing Adjustments of Older People* (Ann Arbor, Mich.: Institute for Social Research, University of Michigan, March 1975).

disability. The death of a spouse or retirement causes fewer changes.

In the case of disability, if the spouse is not alive when the disability occurs, and if the disabled person is white, changes in housing or living arrangements are much more likely to be considered. The disabled person is more likely to be institutionalized than moved to the home of a relative if the spouse is alive when the disability occurs and if the child who makes the decision has a fairly high family income.

Widowed women are less likely to move than widowed men (for females, 76.9 percent of reports indicate changes made; for males, 91.3 percent). This may suggest that a surviving wife cares for herself, but if she dies first, other arrangements must be found for her husband.

Most changes made by retired persons involve moves to a different environment—a more pleasant climate, a smaller house, or closer to friends and relatives. This is not the case for either deaths or disabilities. A large proportion of changes made when the spouse dies indicate a move by the survivor to the home of a relative, usually a child. In the case of a permanent, serious disability, the disabled person either moves to a nursing home or lives with a child.

In the second phase of her study on housing adjustments of older people, Newman reported that whether a parent lives with a child is affected not by the child's income but by the parent's health. Most older people living with their children need little care.[25]

Even when the older person voluntarily changes housing, there are stressful factors, such as:

1. Leaving a home bought with one's own earnings.
2. Leaving a neighborhood to which one has belonged for a long time.
3. The loss of feelings and memories evoked by the constant association with home, neighborhood, and neighbors.
4. Inability to move certain possessions to the new home.
5. Learning how to work new appliances.
6. Meeting new neighbors and making friends.
7. The need to adjust one's living style to accommodate management and other tenants or family.
8. Adjustment to the new pathways, sights, sounds, and physical resources of the new neighborhood.[26]

Carp concluded that the right housing and living arrangements not only increased the psychological and social well-being of the elderly but also extend their life and improve their health.[27] In terms of Maslow's need hierarchy, the improved living environment attained by moving increases satisfaction and reduces stress.[28]

[25]Sandra Newman, James Morgan, Robert Marans, and Leon Pastalan, *Housing Adjustments of Older People: A Report of Findings From the Second Phase* (Ann Arbor, Mich.: Institute for Social Research, University of Michigan, October 1976).

[26]M. Powell Lawton, *Planning and Managing Housing for the Elderly* (New York, John Wiley & Sons, Inc., 1975), pp. 246–47.

[27]Frances M. Carp, "Impact of Improved Living Environment on Health and Life Expectancy," *The Gerontologist*, 17 (June 1977), 247.

[28]Ibid., 248.

Design of the Housing Environment

In designing housing for older persons, it is critical that their special needs and life style be kept in mind.[29] The right housing will provide many benefits and require little care. It will not only give shelter but also security, privacy, freedom, and convenience. The environment should allow the person to express personal tastes and preferences. Most important, it should make older persons feel good about themselves.

It has been found that the healthiest retirees are those who find activities in their social environment that help them triumph over handicaps, lift their morale, bring friends to them, and expand their feeling of well-being. To be home, it must provide a quality of home life.

Planners must be sensitive to individual differences in the community. The fifty-five-year-old, the seventy-year-old, and the ninety-year-old person cannot be treated the same. They differ in culture, education, experience, and points in the aging process. Based on these expected differences in the elderly population, choices must be provided.

In general terms, the environment of the older person should:

1. Provide for private, semiprivate, and public activities.
2. Provide for maintenance of basic physical and safety needs.
3. Consider perceptual behavior; this may require larger, more noticeable visual and audio guides.

[29]Robert J. Obenland, *Behavioral Factors for Elderly Housing Design,* April 1976, and *Design Options for a Continuum of Care Environment,* August 1976 (Washington, D.C.: U.S. Department of Health, Education, and Welfare).

4. Recognize problems with memory and orientation and increase environmental signals to decrease the effect.
5. Promote effective participation.
6. Provide a variety of choices in promoting social behavior so as to maximize freedom of choice for a social life, as well as physical privacy and anonymity.

ENVIRONMENTAL NEEDS

Older people spend a great deal of time in their own units. Thus, color, texture, lighting, and form can do a lot to alter their moods and feelings. Color should be pleasing—generate a feeling of happiness; decrease feelings of loneliness or depression; be well related to the amount of light available; and enhance the furnishings. Creative results cost no more than dull colors.

Color and design can help aging people maintain their orientation. For example, if different levels in a building have different-colored walls, a tenant is given an immediate signal as to location. Different plants, pictures, or other design guides can also help. Insets, projections, and hardware on doors can further help people to remember where they are and where they live.

Light and color combined stimulate and influence people's actions and affect the appearance of objects. Lighting can make people feel important by creating a pleasing atmosphere. Good lighting can make a room bright, cherry, and gay, and bring peace of mind. "Good" lighting refers to the right kind of light where it is wanted and needed.

The failing eyesight of many older persons must be considered in choosing or designing housing. Ample light should be provided on steps and walks, in hallways, and in all rooms. For safety, light switches that can be reached from a wheelchair should be placed at all entrances to a room and at the top and bottom of stairways. Luminous cover plates for switches also make them easier to locate. Task-oriented lighting is important—for example, in food preparation, reading, sewing, hobbies, and inside closets. Fixtures should be easy to clean and bulbs easy to change. Fixtures should be mounted so that climbing is unnecessary. Multi-story developments need emergency lighting for all corridors and fire escape stairs. Many needs of the elderly are similar to those of handicapped persons.

THE BUILDING

Entrances, for both the building and individual units, must be carefully considered. Entrances should be easy to enter—for a frail person, one with a bag of groceries, one who uses a cane or walker, and one with arthritic hands. Doors should be easily closed by a person in a wheelchair without too much maneuvering. The entrance should be covered and well lit, possibly with another light at the keyhole. Ramps rather than steps are good, with no or low thresholds and handrails. There should be a horizontal mullion on glass doors. The doorbell should be tuned to the hard-of-hearing. Individual apartment doors need peepholes. As a convenience, locks on front and rear doors and building entrances should be master-keyed to prevent the need for many keys.

The lobby is a natural focal point of a building. It is a social center, a traffic center, and a visual area that should provide places to sit, walk, play, observe, and a place to buy small items. Also, the manager should be able to check activities in the lobby. A gay, decorative lobby in a warm place will attract the residents. A pay telephone that can be used from a wheelchair is desirable, as is a large-face clock with oversize numerals. If they are well located, both the tenant mail area and a reception desk staffed by tenants or volunteers will increase social interaction.

Steps and stairways can be dangerous for a person of any age. These factors are especially important: no steepness, rises and treads of uniform height and width, handrails on both sides with ends that will not catch clothing, nonslip treads, no protruding tread nose that will catch the toe of a handicapped person, and short flights of stairs with landings rather than a single long flight.

To prevent falls, all floors should be smooth and even. Nonskid backs or pads should be placed on scatter rugs. Carpets should be smooth at the edge, durable, fireproof, with a short pile and minimum padding for wheelchair movement.

Windows should be safe and easy to operate from a wheelchair, from crutches, or with arthritic or otherwise impaired hands. They should be easy to clean from the inside and outside. Sitting and looking out of the window are important; windows should be low enough to see out from a sitting position but still a safe height. Floor-to-ceiling windows are costly to drape, impossible to use when sunlight is coming from that direction, and unsafe. Inside sills for plants, books, and knicknacks are also appreciated.

Bodily warmth becomes more important as one gets older. A heating system should distribute 75 to 80 degrees evenly in every room. Radiators should be shielded to prevent burns. Portable room heaters can be hazardous; they should be avoided if possible.

INTERIOR DESIGN

The inside of the dwelling unit should be designed so that the person can move through it simply and directly, with as few turns as possible. Abrupt changes in height should be avoided. The living unit should preferably be on one floor. Split levels are undesirable; they present architectural barriers and are unsafe.

A sense of space needs to be emphasized. The floor plan should be designed for the special needs and preferences of the elderly, such as use of aids for movement. Many of them like a living area separate from the kitchen and sleeping area. A dividing screen or movable closet may make the arrangement more flexible. Sound-reducing materials and buffer zones are good.

The bathroom should be near the sleeping area and the access route clear of furniture. One door or window (at least 24 inches wide and no more than 36 inches above the floor, according to safety experts) should be in the sleeping area in case of fire. Screens and storm windows should be movable from the outside. There should be a night light, telephone, or emergency call button that can be reached from the bed and the floor. The bedroom should be sensibly located in relation to other areas of the building—for example, not back to back with the recreation area.

Most older people need generous storage space for their many possessions. Stretching, bending, or climbing should be minimized. Storage areas placed between hip and eye level are the easiest to use.

In the bathroom, good location, arrangement and furnishings are important to prevent falls, burns or scalds, and poisoning. Prosthetic bathing design should be emphasized. Important factors to consider in bathroom design for the elderly are: enough space to maneuver a wheelchair; an emergency call button within reach of the shower and lavatory; and no sharp edges. Doors should be designed to be opened from the outside. If the door opens inward, it may be impossible to reach a person who has fallen and is blocking the entrance.

Kitchen appliances should be easy to use and to clean. An oven at waist level is desirable, and a side-opening oven is easier for a person in a wheelchair. Controls at the front of the range are safer for the elderly; otherwise, sleeves may create a fire and safety hazard. A light over the range makes seeing easier, as do large numbers or letters on controls.

Work arrangements in the kithen should include at least one counter built low for work in a sitting position; the oven at waist level to avoid stooping or excessive reaching; an unbroken work triangle between range, sink, and refrigerator; ability to work at the sink in a wheelchair; direct access to the outside; and ample space to prepare and eat meals.

Housing Alternatives
for the Elderly

As a person ages, the services needed in relation to housing change. Since the elderly population is quite varied, a broad range of services and environments are needed. Services provided in connection with different housing choices are discussed here.

Keeping one's possessions is important.

Community services are generally classified as preventive, supportive, rehabilitative, and sheltered care. In general, preventive services are designed for the healthiest elderly persons; supportive services are for those with a disability that can be reduced by the service; rehabilitative services train people with severe dis-

PREVENTIVE SERVICES	SUPPORTIVE SERVICES	REHABILITATIVE SERVICES	SHELTERED CARE SERVICES
Planned housing	Medical or visiting nurse services	Community mental health center	Congregate housing
Advocacy or consumer involvement actions groups	Home health aides	Rehabilitation hospital	Institutional day care
	Homemakers	Sheltered work shop	
Shopping facilities	Hot meals		
Employment opportunities	Meals on wheels		
Volunteer programs	Multiservice senior center		
Recreation center	Family service agency		
Safe escort services	Legal aid		

abilities who may permanently improve; and finally, sheltered care service provides relatively permanent support for those least able to care for themselves.[30] The following list indicates services in the different categories:

Institutional housing for the elderly falls into three categories: residential, service or personal-care oriented, and health oriented.

RESIDENTIAL FACILITIES

Residential facilities are for the relatively self-reliant and independent elderly person, with extra safety features. They may be called retirement hotels, golden-age villages, or housing for the elderly. The staff is generally limited. Extra services such as meals, laundry facilities, and light housekeeping help may be available at an extra charge. Residents usually live in their own apartments, but the complex has a central lounge and other rooms for socializing and recreation. This type of facility maximizes individual freedom and privacy.

In retirement communities, participation in social activities is expected and may be the most important single criterion of adjustment; the same is true of the elderly who live in homes for the aged.[31]

SERVICE OR PERSONAL CARE FACILITIES

Besides safety features, service-oriented housing provides aid on a day-to-day basis. Residents usually live in

[30]M. Powell Lawton and Thomas O. Byerts, eds., *Community Planning for the Elderly* (Springfield, Va.: National Technical Information Service, U.S. Department of Commerce, 1974), p. 15.

[31]Ruth Bennett and Lucille Nahemow, "Institutional Totality and Criteria of Social Adjustment in Residences for the Aged," *Journal of Social Issues,* 21 (October 1965), 44–78.

Congregate eating facilities provide an opportunity for natural socialization.

studio apartments or rooms, often without cooking facilities, since meals are served in a central dining room. The supportive services help residents maintain an independent way of life.

Service-oriented housing is also called: homes for the aged, adult homes, congregate-care facilities, rest homes, domiciliary-care units, sheltered-care for the aging, and retirement homes. In addition, some retirement hotels may be certified to offer this type of service.

Residents are assured of meals and sociability and freed from housekeeping. There are common lounge and recreation areas. Most projects have an infirmary with personnel qualified to control and administer medication. In case of

emergency, someone is usually on call twenty-four hours a day.

HEALTH-ORIENTED FACILITIES

Health-oriented facilities stress care and treatment, and persons are admitted on a doctor's recommendation. There are three types of health-type residences for older people: health-related or intermediate care; skilled nursing homes, also called convalescent homes, extended care facilities, or skilled-care facilities; and hospitals.

INTERMEDIATE CARE FACILITIES (ICFs) These may provide regular medical nursing, social, and rehabilitative services, in addition to room and board for people who cannot live independently. ICFs are for those who need less nursing care than that provided by extended-care facilities. ICFs may choose to become part of the Medicaid program.

SKILLED NURSING FACILITIES (SNFs) These provide continuous nursing service on a twenty-four-hour basis for convalescent patients. Registered nurses, licensed practical nuses and nurse's aides provide services ordered by the patient's doctor. Emphasis is on medical nursing care, with restorative, physical, occupational, and other therapies also provided. This type of facility has both Medicare and Medicaid programs.

Nursing homes must be licensed in all states. Every state except Arizona requires the administrator to have a license.[32] Nursing homes must meet state and federal fire safety codes. The code considered best is the Life Safety Code of the National Fire Protection Association. A fire safety inspection should be conducted at least once a year. SNFs and ICFs that choose to participate in either Medicare or Medicaid must meet the National Fire Protection Association Life Safety Code.

Perhaps the toughest standards are those of the Joint Commission on Accreditation of Hospitals (JCAH), an independent accrediting agency. The JCAH standards are supported by the two leading national associations of nursing homes—the American Nursing Home Association, which represents mainly proprietary homes, and the American Association of Homes for the Aging, which represents the nonprofit institutions—as well as the American Hospital Association and the American Medical Association. JCAH accreditation is strictly voluntary on the part of nursing homes.

From 1960 to 1976 the number of nursing homes increased 140 percent, the number of beds 302 percent, and total spending for nursing home care 2,000 percent. In contrast, proportion of older persons increased only 23 percent.[33] Medicaid payments represent 50 percent of all nursing home revenues.

Hospitals are the third type of health care facility that provide diagnoses, acute care, therapy, and intense nursing and medical care.

Choosing a Congregate Housing Facility

Whether a congregate facility is chosen by the elderly person or someone else, there are many factors to consider. The facility's location and its nearness to businesses and services are important. Many facilities have eligibility requirements. Some have long waiting lists. Others accept only single persons, while some also accept couples.

The previous sections on design of housing for the elderly and type of congregate facility deal with the physical and health aspects of housing. In addition, social, regulatory, safety, and economic features and sponsoring organization should be considered.

SOCIAL ENVIRONMENT

The social environment in the facility is important. The way residents spend their days should be comfortable for the new

[32]"How to Choose a Nursing Home," *Changing Times,* 28 (January 1974), 35–39.

[33]U.S. Senate, *Developments in Aging: 1976,* p. 43.

entrant. Facilities and equipment for hobbies make the housing more attractive for many. Staff members should be friendly yet efficient. The facility should give one a warm, comfortable feeling.

REGULATORY POLICIES

Rules and regulations should protect the individual's freedom and privacy without being too restrictive. Rules also specify when a resident must give up the living unit, such as when income changes or when more services are needed. They specify what happens to a living unit shared by two people if one person must leave.

SAFETY FEATURES

The safety features of the facility are very important. Materials should be fire resistant. Smoke detectors and a sprinkler system increase safety. A twenty-four-a-day communication system is desirable. Auxiliary power for the elevator and for emergency lighting should be provided.

Yaffe reported that all elderly tenants saw themselves as safer in their apartments than did the managers.[34] That is, 96 percent of 202 tenants and 95 percent of public housing tenants said they felt safe in their apartments, while only 90 percent of 202 managers and 88 percent of public housing managers shared this feeling.

[34]Silvia Yaffe, "The Physical Security of Tenants in Federally-Assisted Housing for the Elderly," *Fourth Report, National Survey of Housing for the Elderly, 1971* (Philadelphia, Pa.: Philadelphia Geriatric Center, January 1974), p. 6.

SPONSORSHIP

Sponsorship of housing facilities for the elderly may influence one's choice, although sponsorship alone is not an indication of the quality of service provided. Sponsorship may be classified as government, voluntary, and proprietary. Each of these is described below.

GOVERNMENT OR PUBLIC   The state, county, or local municipality may sponsor facilities and programs. Public housing is generally based on economic and personal need. Since there may be rent supplements or rent adjustments based on assets and income, these facilities may rent at slightly less than some voluntary or proprietary facilities.

VOLUNTARY OR NONPROFIT   Voluntary or nonprofit facilities are run by churches or religious groups, fraternal and charitable organizations, or trade groups. Because of their endowment and favorable tax status, they may be able to offer services at lower cost. Some provide special benefits to wives and families of persons with certain qualifications. Others offer financial aid depending on one's income or assets.

PROPRIETARY   The majority of housing programs for the elderly are run on a profit-making basis. A proprietary facility may be managed by the owner or owners or may be run by an administrator. Proprietary facilities, like the other two sponsorship types, vary in their costs and services.

COSTS

Facilities vary greatly in terms of their charges. Some of the costs to be expected are:

1. *Rent:* the basic charge for the living unit, which may or may not include utilities.

2. *Services fee:* charges for meals, cleaning, laundry, and any help or extras.

3. *Application or processing fee:* an amount ranging from $5 to $1,500, paid when the application form is submitted. This fee may not be refunded even though the application is rejected.

4. *Initial payment:* an initial sum charged by a facility, ranging from $500 to over $10,000, which may or may not be applied to rents or service fees. Some facilities offer residents a trial living period ranging from a few weeks to several months. During this time, the resident may decide to leave and will have the initial payment returned. After this time, the initial payment is not refundable.

5. *Membership or club fee:* a charge for extra facilities, such as a clubhouse or golf course, or to attend certain events.

Newman reported that in 1976, the average cost per month for nursing home care was $514, compared to a 1973–1974 figure of $479.[35] Older people in nursing homes paid these fees mainly with Social Security benefits and income or savings.

The *life lease* or *life contract* arrangement specifies a sum to be paid based on the applicant's life expectancy. In turn, the older person is guaranteed lifetime occupancy. A life lease does not provide operating services or health care, and the unit cannot be left as a legacy.

Sources of financial aid include Medi-

care, Medicaid, and private insurance. Medicare covers care in a skilled nursing facility on a formula basis. Restrictions include physician certification, an approved facility, and entry requirements. The local Social Security Administration office can provide details on current requirements.

Medicaid rules and payments vary considerably. Usually they fund nursing home care for low-income people.

There are many other payment plans, including cooperative arrangements. The prospective resident should take specific questions to an attorney. With the attorney's help, the resident will be able to review his or her financial assets and make a reasonable decision.

Some facilities also provide rent supplements opportunities to work part time, or put off paying some monthly charges. The person may also qualify for elderly public housing. The local housing authority, the Social Security Office, the social services office, or office for the aging can supply more information.

HOUSING CHOICES

Researchers have studied the housing choices of elderly people, focusing on feelings of satisfaction or alienation and behavioral changes.

SATISFACTION The elderly are more likely to be satisfied with their housing than the population as a whole.[36] Carp evaluated a group of elderly persons who moved into low-cost housing in San An-

---

[35]Newman and others, *Housing Adjustments of Older People,* p. 107.

[36]M. Powell Lawton, "The Housing Problems of Community-Resident Elderly," HUD-497-PDR, Vol. 1, *Occasional Papers in Housing and Community Affairs* (Washington, D.C.: U.S. Department of Housing and Urban Development, Office of Policy Development and Research, December 1978).

tonio, Texas, after one year and again after eight years of residence. She found that satisfaction increased with the move and after eight years.[37] The physical conditions were an improvement over their previous housing and continued to be valued. Gossip and lack of privacy were reported by 30 percent as the worst problems. A comparison group who did not move either remained at their original satisfaction level or became more unhappy over the eight years.

Brody, Kleban, and Liebowitz studied three groups of elderly people: those who moved into intermediate housing, those who moved into other facilities, and those who remained in the same housing.[38] All three groups were interviewed at the start of the study and six months later. The results: Those who wanted to move and did so were more satisfied with their living arrangements and their apartment. They also enjoyed life and social contacts more. Neighborhood satisfaction increased for both sets of movers.

ALIENATION   Although *alienation* is in part associated with aging, it may be enhanced by the environment.[39] Dudley and Hilley found that residents in homes for the aged were more alienated than those in other types of facilities.[40] Alienation re-sulted, in part, from restrictions on the residents' choices. Larson studied elderly persons who moved into public housing in two Vermont towns. He found that "the greater the similarity between the type of housing to which an individual is accustomed and the public housing into which he moves, the lower the level of alienation." There was less alienation for those accustomed to living in multiple dwellings but more for those who were used to a single-family unit. Larson also found that contact with friends and relatives especially after a move into public housing, helps to decrease the sense of alienation.[41] Visiting with other tenants is also helpful.

BEHAVIORAL CHANGES   Lawton studied tenants before and one year after a move into congregate and traditional elderly housing. Residents in the congregate housing were served a hot midday dinner in a common dining area, had an activity program, and had nursing and physical services available. After one year in the traditional housing environment, residents showed increased participation in activities, social interaction, and activities such as keeping up with the news, spending time outdoors, and following personal interest. In the congregate housing, residents showed improved morale, loner status, and housing satisfaction. Thus, Lawton concludes, other behavioral changes were seen in the traditional housing environment, whereas residents' feelings or emotional status improved in the congregate housing.[42]

---

[37]Frances M. Carp, "Long-Range Satisfaction with Housing," *The Gerontologist,* 15 (February 1975), 68–72, and "User Evaluation of Housing for the Elderly," *The Gerontologist,* 16 (April 1976), 102–11.

[38]Elaine M. Brody, Morton H. Kleban, and Bernard Liebowitz, "Intermediate Housing for the Elderly: Satisfaction of Those Who Moved In and Those Who Did Not," *The Gerontologist,* 15 (August 1975), 305–56.

[39]Charles J. Dudley and George A. Hilley, Jr., "Freedom and Alienation in Homes for the Aged," *The Gerontologist,* 17 (April 1977), 143.

[40]Ibid., 144.

[41]Calvin J. Larson, "Alienation and Public Housing for the Elderly," *International Journal of Aging and Human Development,* 5 (Summer 1974), 224–25.

[42]M. Powell Lawton, "The Relative Impact of Congregate and Traditional Housing on Elderly Tenants," *The Geronotologist,* 16 (June 1976), 237–42.

A HUD study on congregate housing reported that the congregate elderly needed an environment that provides both independence and support services if needed.[43]

Housing for the Handicapped

Housing for the handicapped must compensate for the functional difficulties created by the handicap. Disabilities may include loss of sight or hearing; lack of coordination; limited stamina; difficulty in moving the head, lifting, reaching, bending, turning, sitting, or kneeling; difficulty in handling or fingering; reliance on walking aids; or the inability to use arms or legs. Most handicapped persons living in a single-family units have removed the doors or other features that hinder their mobility and adapted kitchen and bathroom facilities.

[43]Urban Systems Research and Engineering, Inc., *Evaluation of the Effectiveness of Congregate Housing for the Elderly* (Washington, D.C.: U.S. Department of Housing and Urban Development, October 1976).

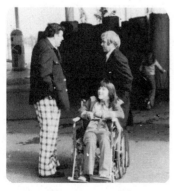

U.S. Department of HUD

Architectural barriers often exist for people in wheelchairs.

Many communities are providing more and more congregate housing and shared or group homes that meet the needs of handicapped persons. Technological advances also compensate for some functional problems.

Most of the preceding discussion on housing selection can be applied to housing by or for the handicapped.[44] Essential design elements that need to be added or modified are: (1) communication systems, (2) barrier-free circulation, (3) smooth, nonslip flooring, (4) protected walls, (5) easily operable windows, (6) adaptable kitchen cabinets, (7) central laundry facilities, (8) garbage/trash chutes, (9) adapted bathrooms, (10) accessible outlets and controls, (11) signals

[44]Marie McGuire Thompson, *Housing for the Handicapped and Disabled, A Guide for Local Action* (Washington, D.C.: The National Association of Housing and Redevelopment Officials, March 1977); Testimony and recommendations before the HEW Architectural and Transportation Barriers Compliance Board, *Freedom of Choice, Volumes I and II* (June 1975); President's Committee on Employment of the Handicapped, Architectural Barriers Subcommittee, Washington, D.C. Excellent sources of information on removing architectural barriers in the environment are: Stephen A. Kliment, *Into the Mainstream—A Syllabus for a Barrier-Free Environment* (Washington, D.C.: American Institute of Architects, 1735 New York Avenue, N.W., 1975); *Housing the Handicapped,* The Central Mortgage and Housing Corporation, Ottawa, Canada, revised 1975; *Standards for Residential Facilities for the Mentally Retarded,* 5th printing, (Chicago, Ill.: Joint Commission on Accreditation of Hospitals, 875 North Michigan Avenue, 1975); President's Committee on Mental Retardation, Washington, D.C., has several documents on the importance of appropriate housing for retarded persons; *The Right to Choose* (Arlington, Tex.: National Association for Retarded Citizens, 1973); Irving Dickman, *No Place Like Home: Alternative Living Arrangements for Teenagers and Adults with Cerebral Palsy* (New York: Professional Services Program Department, United Cerebral Palsy Associations, 66 East 34th Street); *Study and Evaluation of Integrating the Handicapped in HUD Housing* (Washington, D.C.: U.S. Department of Housing and Urban Development, May 1977).

and controls adapted for sensory disabilities in public areas, (12) pull-type and lever handles, (13) spaces that permit wheelchair circulation and furniture placement, and (14) secured entrances that can be opened by the disabled.

Summary

Persons aged sixty-five and over often face lower incomes and decreasing physical capabilities. Most of these persons, however, continue to live in their own homes. Less than 5 percent of the elderly live in institutions.

In developing facilities for the elderly, structural and service needs as well as health, social, and economic features must be kept in mind.

Terms

accommodation fee a lump sum paid prior to admission and guaranteeing occupancy for a specified time.

alienation social-psychological feeling of being powerless, uprooted, and isolated.

congregate housing housing for the elderly that provides meals and usually other services as well. It is a noninstitutional living environment.

entrance fee a lump sum paid for assuring occupancy in a residence; club type facility. An additional monthly charge is required for services and maintenance.

founders fee a lump sum usually paid at the time of entrance and guaranteeing life occupancy for the resident. Sometimes the payment includes health care. An additional monthly charge is required for services and maintenance.

homemaker service a program providing for a specially trained person who enters and helps to manage a household. A homemaker is prepared to cook, clean, shop, and do other chores. She is usually supervised by a social work agency, which makes sure that the older person gets the services required. She may come in daily or a few days per week, depending on the need.

initial payment partial payment made at the beginning toward the total sum contracted for in life lease or founders' fee agreement. The remainder may be paid monthly or annually, or in later lump sums.

life care a guarantee to the resident for his or her lifetime; includes living quarters, food, personal care, and sometimes health care, in return for a stipulated amount, often the resident's total assets, which is held in escrow until the resident's death. No extra monthly charges are required.

life contract see *life lease*.

life lease a sum paid prior to and guaranteeing lifetime occupancy; determined by actuarial tables based on life expectancy, plus estimated operating costs. There is an additional monthly charge for services and maintenance.

meals-on-wheels a portable meal service providing one or more hot meals per day to persons unable to leave their own homes or prepare their own meals. This may be done on a commercial or nonprofit basis.

membership fee a payment similar to an entrance fee, by which a person receives the right of occupancy, joins a residence-club type housing, and is entitled to use its facilities. There is an additional monthly charge for services and maintenance.

residence-club type nonhousekeeping living quarters (usually without cooking facilities) in which units vary from single rooms and suites to cottages; and which have central facilities for dining, housekeeping, and other services provided by the management. Hotels, residence club, and motel-type housing may fall within this area.

shopper service a service in which purchases are made at the request of or on behalf of persons unable to do their own shopping. These services are provided by businesses or volunteer organizations.

visiting nurse service a program through which nurses visit persons in their own homes to give professional nursing care when needed. A visiting nurse organization, a hospital home care program, a family agency, American Red Cross, or public health department provides such services.

Suggested Readings

Balkema, John B., *Housing and Living Arrangements for Older People: A Bibliography.* Washington, D.C.: The National Council on Aging, 1972.

Carp, Frances M., "Long-Range Satisfaction with Housing," *The Gerontologist,* 15 (February 1975), 68–72.

———, "User Evaluation of Housing for the Elderly," *The Gerontologist,* 16 (April 1976), 102–11.

Davis, Richard H., Margaret Audet, and Lawrence Baird, eds., *Housing for the Elderly.* Los Angeles, Calif.: Ethel Percy Andrus Gerontology Center, University of Southern California, 1973.

Diamond, Beverly, ed., *Furniture Requirements for Older People.* Washington, D.C.: National Council on Aging, 1963.

Gold, Jacob G., and Saul M. Kaufman, "Development of Care of Elderly: Tracing the History of Institutional Facilities," *The Gerontologist,* 10 (Winter, 1970, Part I), 262–74.

Lawton, M. Powell, "Planner's Notebook: Planning Environments for Older People," *AIP Journal,* 36 (March 1970), 124–29.

———, *Planning and Managing Housing for the Elderly.* New York: John Wiley & Sons, Inc., 1975.

———, Robert J. Newcomer, and Thomas O. Byerts, eds., *Community Planning for an Aging Society.* Stroudsburg, Pa.: Dowden, Hutchinson and Ross, Inc., 1976.

Newman, Sandra, *Housing Adjustments of Older People.* Ann Arbor, Mich.: Institute for Social Research, University of Michigan, 1975.

———, James Morgan, Robert Marans, and Leon Pastalan, Housing Adjustments of Older People: A Report of Findings from the Second Phase. Ann Arbor, Mich.: Institute for Social Research, University of Michigan, 1976.

Pastalan, Leon A., and Daniel H. Carson, eds., *Spatial Behavior of Older People.* Ann Arbor, Mich.: Institute of Gerontology, University of Michigan—Wayne State University, 1970.

THE HOUSING INDUSTRY

1. HOW DOES FIRM SIZE AFFECT THE PRODUC-
TION OF HOUSING?

2. WHAT HAS CAUSED SHIFTS IN MATERIALS,
LAND AND LABOR COSTS?

3. NEW HOUSING PRICES ARE INCREASING.
HOW HAVE HOUSING CHARACTERISTICS
CHANGED?

4. IS THERE A SHIFT IN MATERIALS USED IN
CONSTRUCTION?

Although the amount of new housing each year is small, the construction industry has a strong impact on the U.S. economy. To understand the kind of housing produced and the policies developed, we must look at the industry itself. The housing construction industry is so huge that building 700,000 units involved more than 1 million worker-years. A second factor is the value of new construction put in place. In 1978 this amounted to $202.2 billion, 18.5 percent more than the 170.7 billion for 1977. The total value of new construction in constant (1972) dollars was 4.3 percent more in 1978 than in 1977, or $114.9 billion and $110.2 billion, respectively.[1] New private housing

construction amounted to $89.3 billion in 1978, an increase of 4.3 percent over the $85.6 billion reported in 1977. In constant dollars, the value of new one-family homes was $34,424,000 in 1978, the highest year since 1972 (Table 10-1). In constant dollars, the value of two-or-more-unit structures has declined in the past several years but is showing a small increase.

Every firm that produces housing or materials for it is part of the housing industry. This includes home builders, contractors, manufacturers, mobile home producers and dealers, building product manufacturers, distributors of materials, and subcontractors. The state of the housing industry is crucial to the amount, kind, location, and cost of housing produced.

---

[1] U.S. Department of Commerce, Bureau of the Census, *Construction Reports*, "Value of New Construction Put in Place," Series C-30-79-3, March 1979, issued May 1979, Table 3, p. 6.

TABLE 10-1 Value of New Private Housing Construction (Seasonally Adjusted Annual Rate) in Millions of Dollars, 1970-1978

Year	IN CURRENT DOLLARS		IN 1972 DOLLARS	
	1 unit	2 or more units	1 unit	2 or more units
1970	14,754[a]	9,518[a]	18,945[b]	11,523[b]
1971	22,202[a]	12,864[a]	25,442[c]	15,179[c]
1972	27,632	17,247	27,632	17,247
1973	30,649	19,438	27,851	17,690
1974	26,293	14,351	21,619	11,873
1975	27,423	6,986	20,776	5,315
1976	40,049	7,228	28,207	5,092
1977	54,550	10,596	34,079	6,636
1978	62,527	12,964	34,424	7,142

Source: U.S. Department of Commerce, Bureau of the Census, Construction Reports, "Value of New Construction Put in Place," C-30-79-3, March 1979, issued May 1979, p. 6.

[a]April 1976, C30-76-4, p. 4.
[b]May 1977, C30-77-5, p. 21, (for Dec. 1970).
[c]May 1977, C30-77-5, p. 22, (for Dec. 1970).

New One-Family Houses Sold

One important indicator is the number of houses sold. About 816,000 new one-family houses were sold in 1978—slightly less than the 819,000 units sold in 1977 and 21 percent more than the 646,000 sold in 1976 and 14 percent more than the 718,000 sold in the peak year of 1972.[2] The ratio of houses sold to houses for sale is a guide to the backlog of homes on the market and a signal to builders. A low ratio, for instance, either indicates overbuilding or shows that houses are selling very quickly and more may be needed (Figure 10-1).

The relationship of new one-family homes started for sale in any year to the number of homes sold that year is com-plex. The number of new homes sold in any year includes both homes started in a prior year and homes to be built the following year. On the other hand, data on new one-family homes started for sale in any year include only homes started in that year. Some of these homes could already be sold, and some will remain unsold at the end of the year.

Characteristics of new homes have changed during the 1970s. New homes sold in 1977 were larger than homes sold in 1970. Fewer homes under 1,600 square feet were sold; the growth was in homes between 1,600 and 2,400 square feet. In 1977, homes that sold for under $30,000 were usually less than 1,600 square feet; those over $50,000 usually had more than 2,000 square feet; and most homes between $30,000 and $50,000 ranged from 1,000 to 2,000 square feet. By 1977 the percentage of homes being sold with one or one-and-one-half baths had declined from 1970.

[2]U.S. Department of Commerce, Bureau of the Census, Construction Reports, "New One-Family Houses Sold and For Sale," Series C-25-79-2, April 1979, p. 6.

*Higher ratio means slower sales

Figure 10-1. Ratio of Homes for Sale to Homes Sold (Seasonally Adjusted), 1971–1978a. [(*Source:* U.S. Department of Commerce, Bureau of Census, *Construction Reports,* "New One-Family Homes Sold and For Sale," Series C25, Issues C25-74-1, January 1974, p. 3 through C-25-75-5; July 1975, p. 3, C25-77-10; October 1977 (December 1977); and C25-78-12, December 1978 (February 1979), p. 3.)]

In 1977 houses selling for under $30,000 were more likely to have one or one-and-one-half bathrooms, whereas those over $30,000 were more likely to have two or more bathrooms. Data show that 40 percent of all buyers want two baths, 29 percent want one-and-one-half baths, and 22 percent want two-and-one-half baths.[3]

Between 1970 and 1977, there was a slight decline in the percentage of four-bedroom homes sold and a slight increase in the percentage of three-bedroom homes sold. In 1977 houses that sold for under $30,000 generally had three bedrooms; this was also true of homes between $30,000 and $50,000 (78 percent). Of those between $50,000 and $60,000, 67 percent were three-bedroom and 28 percent were four-bedroom homes; those $60,000 and over were generally four-bedroom homes. A *Professional Builder* survey reported that about 54 percent of the buyers want three bedrooms and another 29 percent want four bedrooms, while builders are supplying 70 percent three-bedroom homes and 24 percent four-bedroom homes.[4]

In 1977, 92 percent of the new one-family houses sold included a range in the sales price; 88 percent gave a dishwasher but only 11 percent a refrigerator.[5] The biggest change since 1970 was in the number of homes with a dishwasher included in the sales price. Then only 42 percent of the homes sold had a dishwasher, 85 percent a range, and 10 percent a refrigerator. At the

---

[3]"PB's Consumer Builder Survey," *Professional Builder* 42 (January 1977), 149.

[4]Ibid., 140.

[5]"New One-Family Houses," p. 3.

upper end of the sales prices, both a range and a dishwasher were usually included in both years. Central air conditioning was featured in about 50 percent of the homes above $30,000 in 1970 and 60 percent in 1977.

The percentage of new homes sold with fireplaces increased between 1970 and 1977. In 1977 homes under $30,000 usually had no fireplace; about 37 percent of the $30,000 to $40,000 homes sold had one fireplace; and 66 percent or more of those above $40,000 had one or more fireplaces.

Between 1970 and 1977, gas as a fuel source declined in new one-family homes sold and electricity increased. There was also a slight increase in the use of oil. In 1977, over 50 percent of the homes over $60,000 used gas for heat, whereas those under $50,000 generally used electricity. Of all homes sold, 91 percent had central heating and 8 percent had electric baseboard, panel, or radiant heat.

In 1977 more homes sold had garages; fewer were sold with carports or no garage. In 1977, 80 percent of all homes had a garage. A *Professional Builder* survey reported that about 70 percent of home buyers wanted a two-car garage.[6]

The number of new one-story homes sold declined between 1970 and 1977. There was a slight increase in the number of split-level homes, but the greatest increase was in two-story-or-more homes. In 1977, most homes under $30,000 were one story; as price increased, the house was more likely to be two-story or split level.

Median lot size in 1977 was 9,870 square feet. Lot size was related to the price of the house. Houses selling for under $50,000 had a median lot size under 10,000 square feet; more expensive houses had larger lots.

Housing Construction

Housing construction has been defined as consisting of four phases:

1. *Preparation:* land to be developed is identified and plans are drawn up.
2. *Production:* the site is prepared, financing is arranged, and the housing is built. Seasonality—cold, rain or snow, and wind—hinders this part of the construction process.
3. *Distribution:* the unit is marketed.
4. *Servicing:* the unit is repaired and maintained.[7]

The preparation phase may involve buying the land. Development plans may need local approval. An environmental impact statement may be required. Zoning may have to be changed to accommodate the proposed use.

Production of the unit involved not only building the housing unit but also preparing the land and providing services like sewage, water, and utility connections. Production involves coordination of men and materials so that the work proceeds smoothly.

The distribution or marketing phase may involve an open house or display of model homes to prospective buyers, ad-

---

[6]"PB's Consumer Builder Survey," *Professional Builder*, 42 (January 1977), 139.

[7]The Report of the President's Committee on Urban Housing, *A Decent Home* (Washington, D.C.: U.S. Government Printing Office, Edgar F. Kaiser, Chairman, 1968), p. 14.

A soil scientist examines the soil, identifies it, and draws its boundaries on an aerial photograph.

vertisements, and special promotions for local salespeople. A large developer may have a packet of promotional literature and a scale model of the entire area for review. Competition with other developments and existing markets influence marketing behavior.

Once the unit is bought, maintenance and repair as well as remodeling are part of the owner's responsibilities. Goods and services must be bought. In times of rising costs for new housing, the demand for changes in older housing may increase and compete with materials and goods for new construction.

Housing construction involves land, labor, and materials. The role of each is described in the following sections. Financing is also important, but its relationship to production is defined in other chapters.

LAND

Land is a major part of housing cost. The supply of land is somewhat fixed, although swamps can be filled in and arid areas irrigated. The supply of developable land is limited by public facilities—especially water and sewers—and by land use controls.

Land cost depends on the price of raw land, land development costs, and the amount of land used for each unit. Land use regulations and lot size requirements affect these costs. Other legal constraints—convenants, easements, and title encumbrances—will also affect land use. Aesthetics—climate, water, view, noise, odors, and pollution—increase or decrease the land's value.

According to a congressional report, land costs increased 56 percent between 1970 and 1975.[8] The average lot value increased from $4,800 in 1970 to $8,900 in 1976 (Table 10-2). However, the median percent of the value of the lot as a percent of sales price rose from 16.9 percent in 1970 to 18.5 percent in 1976. An increase in lot size may be one reason for this change.

[8]U.S. Department of Commerce, Bureau of the Census, *Construction Reports*, C-25-73-13, July 1974, p. 110; C-25-74-13, August 1975, p. 101; and U.S. Congress, *Ninth Annual Report on the National Housing Goal*, Message from the President of the United States, House Document No. 95-53, 95th Congress, 1st Session (Washington, D.C.: U.S. Government Printing Office, 1977), p. 92.

Land price is a major factor in determining how the land will be used. Differences in price reflect topography, accessibility, and amenities such as schools, parks, and shopping and health services. Other services, such as roads, water supply, sewage, drainage, and other utilities, turn raw level land into land suitable for housing. Price is also a reflection of the demand for land.

Local government action plays a major role in land supply. Limitations on such things as sewers or roads prevent development. Zoning or other special ordinances are also restrictive. Property tax practices sometimes work to keep raw land off the market and at other times may force its sale. The U.S. Government Accounting Office concluded that site improvement requirements could be reduced in most communities with typical savings of $1,300. Street width and street thickness could be reduced, as could sidewalk width, material, and thickness, and driveways. The type and size requirements of pipes, pipe materials, and manholes in water and sewer systems

TABLE 10-2. Median and Average Land Costs and Percent of Sales Price, 1970–1976

YEAR	MEDIAN VALUE OF LOT	AVERAGE VALUE OF LOT[a]	MEDIAN %OF VALUE OF LOT AS A % OF SALES PRICE	AVERAGE VALUE OF LOT AS A % OF AVERAGE SALES PRICE
1970	$4,100	$4,800	16.9	18.3
1971	4,400	5,200	17.1	18.3
1972	4,700	5,500	16.9	18.1
1973	5,400	6,200	16.2	17.6
1974	5,800	6,500	16.2	16.9
1975	b	7,500	17.6	b
1976	b	8,900	18.5	b

[a]Lot is an improved piece of land supporting new one-family homes sold.

[b]Information no longer available.

Source: U.S. Department of Commerce, Bureau of the Census, *Construction Reports*, "New One-Family Houses Sold and For Sale" C-25-13 (July 1974), p. 110; C-25-74-13 (August 1975), p. 101.
Tenth Annual Report on the National Housing Goal, U.S. Department of Housing and Urban Development, no date. Appendix C, p. 55.

could be decreased. Large lot width requirements, a local review and approval process, land dedication requirements, and expenses such as development, utility and building fees are other items that could be trimmed.[9]

Fiscal problems of local governments, as well as higher environmental standards, will continue to limit services for raw land. Thus, not only the overall supply of land but especially land for higher density housing may be limited. Alternately, city land for high rises may be unattractive to live in or very difficult to develop.

Site development costs, too, have been steadily increasing. Higher and more costly standards are part of the reason. Also, some of the costs formerly paid for by the community have been shifted to the developer. Site development may include the costs of grading and clearing, construction of on-site and off-site streets, installation of on-site or off-site utilities, storm sewers, land for community facilities such as schools and parks, and other assessments.

A Home Owner and Lease Development Program (HOLLD) has been proposed to reduce the rising costs of land acquisition, use, transfer, and financing.[10] To achieve this goal, the fee simple title to selected land areas is placed in trust with a state-chartered local HOLLD authority. The land is then leased to individuals on a long-term basis. In this way, land and building costs are separated.

LABOR

The construction industry employs about 4 million workers.[11] Always somewhat erratic, the recent unemployment rate in construction has been high—20 percent in 1976, 13 percent in 1977, but declining to 10.6 percent in 1978 (Figure 10-2). The accuracy of labor statistics is affected by the high rate of leaving and entering the market, as well as seasonal variation. "The supply of labor to construction is quite sensitive to aggregate labor market conditions and the supply of skilled labor to homebuilders is sensitive to the availability of other construction work."[12]

In 1978 the average hourly earnings in contract construction was $8.65, for an average 36.9-hour weekly rate of $319.[13] From 1970 to 1978, average weekly earnings have increased 61 percent and the average work week has decreased 1 percent.[14] With 1967 as a base year equaling 100, the hourly earnings index for contract construction in 1978 was about 207.6.[15] This is lower than for most other

---

[9]U.S. General Accounting Office, *Why Are New House Prices So High, How Are They Influenced by Government Regulations and Can Prices Be Reduced?* CED78-101 (Washington, D.C.: Comptroller General of the United States, May 11, 1978).

[10]For details, see James M. Brown, "The Home-Owner's Land-Lease Development Program: A Proposal for Reducing the Land-Related Costs of Housing," *The American University Law Review*, 23 (Fall 1973), 55–117.

[11]U.S. Department of Labor, Bureau of Labor Statistics, *Monthly Labor Review*, 101 (April 1979), 78, 82.

[12]Craig Swan, "Labor and Material Requirements for Housing," *Brookings Paper on Economic Activity* (Washington, D.C.: The Brookings Institution, 1971), p. 357.

[13]Contract construction—contractors primarily engaged in the erection of buildings, general contractors in heavy nonbuilding construction, and special trade contractors. U.S. Department of Commerce, *Construction Review*, 25 (February 1979), 60–61.

[14]U.S. Department of Labor, Bureau of Labor Statistics, *Monthly Labor Review*, 102 (June 1979), 69.

[15]Ibid., 72.

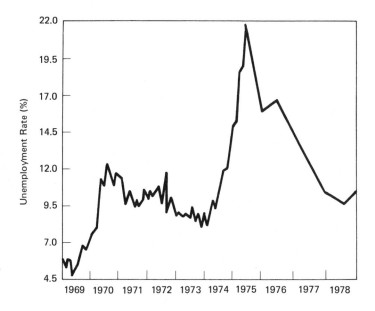

Figure 10-2. Unemployment Rate in Construction (Seasonally Adjusted), 1969–1978. [(*Source:* U.S. Congress, as prepared by the Bureau of Labor Statistics, *Employment and Earnings* (Washington, D.C.: U.S. Department of Labor, June 26, 1976; *Monthly Labor Review,* 101 (July 1978, 58; 101 (January 1978), 58; 100 (January 1977), 78; 99 (January 1976), 90; (April 1979), 82.)]

production or nonsupervisory workers. Wages also vary within the building industry. Usually plumbers, bricklayers, and electricians are the most highly paid; carpenters and plasterers are next; followed by painters and, finally, building workers.[16]

The National Commission on Urban Problems has analyzed labor costs for multi-family buildings.[17] Labor costs account for about 40 percent of construction costs and vary with the job. Labor costs are 20 to 25 percent of steel or concrete costs, 60 percent of masonry costs, and 75 percent of painting and decorating costs.

For conventional homes, construction costs break out as follows: 40 percent for labor; 38 percent for materials; and 22 percent for overhead, operating expenses, and profit. For mobile homes, the comparable figures are 12 percent, 66 percent, and 23 percent.[18] The much lower labor cost in mobile home manufacturing is the result of assembly line techniques and semiskilled labor.

Labor costs affect the price of housing. Wage and price increases in construction

[16] U.S. Department of Housing and Urban Development, *1977 HUD Statistical Yearbook* (Washington, D.C.: U.S. Government Printing Office, December 1978), p. 375.

[17] National Commission on Urban Problems, *Building the American City* (Washington, D.C.: U.S. Government Printing Office, 1968), p. 424.

[18] U.S. Department of Housing and Urban Development, *Housing in the Seventies,* (Washington, D.C.: 1974), p. 224.

U.S. Department of HUD.

Town House Parks. These are systems houses erected in one day by National Homes Corporation in Chicago, Illinois.

probably have their greatest impact on the size of units started.

CONSTRUCTION MATERIALS COSTS

Construction material costs have risen faster than prices in general, although slower than land costs. Demand for construction materials was stimulated by new housing starts in 1977 and 1978. Mobile home production was an important component of demand as were expenditures on repair and improvements. The increase in retrofit work related to energy conservation should continue to add to demand.

Supply factors also had a role in the rise of building product prices. Cost increases were related to energy, transportation, raw material and labor inputs. Many basic building products are energy intensive, including cement, birch, clay, glass, gypsum board and steel. Fuel price escalation has significantly added to transportation costs.

According to the Bureau of Labor Statistics wholesale price index, prices of all construction materials doubled since 1967 (Table 10-3). Recent increases are averaging 9 percent per year, below the 16 percent of 1973 but considerably

TABLE 10-3. Indexes of Prices of Selected Construction Materials (1967 = 100)

MATERIAL	1970	1972	1974	1976	1978[a]
All construction materials	112.5	126.6	160.9	187.7	228.3
Lumber and wood products					
Lumber	113.7	159.4	207.1	233.0	322.4
Plywood	108.5	130.7	161.1	187.0	235.6
Paint and paint materials					
Prepared paint	112.4	118.0	145.7	174.4	192.3
Paint materials	101.4	104.1	152.3	189.8	212.7
Metal products					
Structural shapes	115.3	134.6	179.0	227.1	226.4[b]
Hardware N.E.C.	109.5	117.3	136.1	166.1	200.4
Plumbing fixtures and brass					
fittings	112.5	119.7	149.1	174.1	199.1
Heating equipment	110.6	118.2	135.0	158.0	174.4
Nonmetallic mineral products					
Window glass	116.1	128.2	158.4	206.4	172.8
Concrete ingredients	114.6	126.9	148.7	186.7	217.7
Concrete products	112.2	125.6	151.7	180.1	214.0
Structural clay products					
(ex. refractories)	109.8	117.3	135.2	163.5	197.2
Asphalt roofing	102.9	131.2	196.0	238.3	292.0
Gypsum products	100.0	114.7	137.6	154.4	229.1
Insulation materials	123.1	136.9	156.5	212.6	c
Miscellaneous products					
Building paper and board	101.2	106.4	123.5	133.8	187.4
Hard surface floor coverings	101.0	104.5	125.8	162.6	116.3[d]

[a]The Wholesale Price Index is now called the Producer Price Index, and measures average changes in prices received in primary markets of the U.S. by producers of commodities in all stages of processing.

[b]Fabricated structural metal products.

[c]No longer available.

[d]1975 = 100.

Source: U.S. Department of Labor, Bureau of Labor Statistics, Wholesale Prices and Price Indexes through 1976; Produce Price Indexes for 1978.

larger than most years since World War II.[19] Rosen noted that "both output and prices of materials tend to fall during contractions and rise during expansions of housing activity."[20]

The prices of some construction materials have risen faster than the total. Lumber and wood products costs are highest, followed by asphalt roofing, metal products, insulation, and portland cement.[21] On the other hand, hardware, water heaters, heating equipment, clay and gypsum products, building paper and board, and hard-surface floor coverings have increased much more slowly than other items.

[19]Charles B. Pitcher, "Building Materials Output and Price Developments, 1975, '76," U.S. Department of Commerce, Bureau of the Census, *Construction Review,* 22 (October 1976), 4; *Construction Review,* 24 (May/June 1978), 46.

[20]Kenneth T. Rosen, "Preliminary Measurements of Cyclical and Seasonal Fluctuations in Housing Construction," Working Paper No. 18 (Cambridge, Mass.: Joint Center for Urban Studies of the Massachusetts Institute of Technology and Harvard University, February 1973), 20.

[21]U.S. Department of Housing and Urban Development, *1977 HUD Statistical Yearbook* (Washington, D.C., December 1978), p. 376.

The shift to single-family homes has raised the demand for lumber. These homes require about three times the amount of lumber as a multi-family unit.[22] Since 1975, lumber prices have been affected by restricted logging on federal timber land controlled by the Bureau of Land Management and the U.S. Forest Service. Imports from Canada have helped to fill the need.

The strength in home building has resulted in rising demand for masonry products especially brick and cement both of which were in tight supply during some periods recently. Prices of these products are sensitive to energy and transportations costs. However, concrete use in precast walls, floors, and ceilings has increased. Plastic is now used in some areas for plumbing, baths, siding, and as insulation. The use of steel has increased, but only in a limited way in housing. Glass and aluminum are two other popular home building materials.

With increasing energy costs, development and promotion of housing products will focus on materials that provide the best insulation and on energy-efficient equipment. Building material producers are themselves affected by rising energy costs. Major fuel users such as producers of cement, brick and other clay products, gypsum board, and some insulation materials have to cope with higher fuel prices, costs for backup fuel systems, and uncertain supplies. Petroleum is used as a raw material in asphalt roofing and paving, plastic products, and paint. The cost of moving building materials goes up as fuel prices rise.

Many building material industries are also affected by air and water pollution standards, which require expensive control equipment, building codes, safety and fire standards. Further, housing construction and other types of construction are related. Thus, growing demands for materials and labor by all types of firms may raise prices and cause short-term shortages.

SINGLE-FAMILY HOUSING How does this picture of rising costs affect the single-family home. In the fourth quarter of 1970, total construction costs were $13,188.75, compared to $18,040.10 in the fourth quarter of 1974—an increase of 36.8 percent.[23] The largest increases were in masonry (94.1 percent), lighting fixtures (94.1 percent), and hardware (107.5 percent). The latter two items added together, however, accounted for only about 2 percent of the construction costs in 1974. Other items increasing 50 percent or more were concrete, lumber, hardwood flooring, electric wiring, and incidental costs. Gutters were the only item that cost less (-7.1 percent). In 1974, the largest construction costs were for lumber (16.9 percent), millwork (10.2 percent), carpentry labor (10.2 percent), plumbing (8.7 percent), and concrete (8 percent).

In 1977 labor and materials for the new single-family home were estimated to be 46.7 percent of the unit's total cost (Figure 10-3) or down from 54.6 percent in 1969. Land accounted for 25 percent, financing 10.8 percent, and builder's

[22]Council on Wage and Price Stability Report, October 1977, as reported in U.S. Department of Housing and Urban Developemnt, *Final Report of the Task Force on Housing Costs* (Washington, D.C., May 1978), p. 47.

[23]National Association of Home Builders, *Construction Components Cost Data*, as reported in Neil S. Mayer, *Homeownership: The Changing Relationship of Costs and Incomes, and Possible Federal Roles* (Washington, D.C.: Congressional Budget Office, January 1977), p. 31.

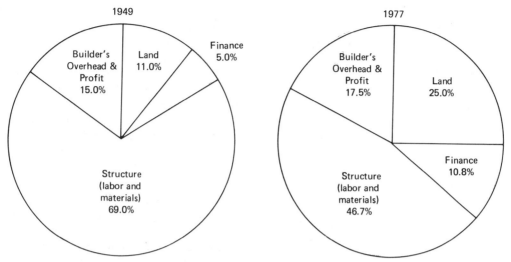

Figure 10-3. Component Costs for New Single-Family House, 1949 and 1977. [*Source:* U.S. Department of Housing and Urban Development, *HUD News,* HUD No. 78-175, (Washington, D.C.).]

overhead and profit 17.5 percent. Land and financing costs increased as a proportion of total costs. In contrast, 1949 labor and materials costs were 69 percent, land 11 percent, finance 5 percent, and builder's overhead and profit 15 percent.

MULTI-FAMILY HOUSING   In a 1976 Bureau of Labor Statistics study, materials and supplies made up over 40 percent of the construction costs for multi-family housing.[24] Stone, clay, glass, and concrete products represented over 20 percent of the materials and supplies costs. Lumber and wood products were the next most important materials, followed by manufactured metal products.

Costs of building materials as a percentage of total costs were similar for multi-family and single-family housing.

However, equipment costs were higher for private multi-family housing, indicating the more capital-intensive nature of multi-family construction.[25]

Multi-family housing required different materials from single-family housing. Lumber and lumber products were more important in the single-family home, while metal products were used more in multi-family housing. Stone, clay, and glass products were used similarly in single-family and multi-family housing.

IMPROVEMENTS AND REPAIRS   One of the bright spots for building materials demand was the improvements, alterations, and repairs market. During 1978, housing property owners spend $37.5 billion for upkeep and improvements. Of this, $26.3 billion was spent by owner-occupants of one- to four-unit properties, while the remaining $11.2 billion was

[24]Joseph T. Finn, "Materials Requirements for Private Multi-Family Housing," *Construction Review,* 22 (April 1976), 4–10. Survey results are based on a sample of eighty-nine projects completed between July 1, 1970, and Aug. 1, 1971, in twenty-two SMSA's.

[25]Finn, "Materials Requirements," 7.

spent by owners of rental properties. Spending for improvements ($24.5 billion) included $3.7 billion for additions and $8.4 billion for alterations and $8.0 billion for major replacements.[28] Additions and alterations outlays have soared to record levels in both current and constant dollars, with further gains expected.[26]

TECHNOLOGY

Technology has not had a major impact on U.S. housing production. Some emergency industrialized housing was built in World War I, with prototypes at the 1933 Chicago Exposition.[27] During the 1930s, small local companies tried using concrete molds. Foster Gunnison started one of the early prefabricated housing factories. "The Gunnison house is assembled from standard, interchangeable plywood panels, plastic-bonded, filled with mineral-wool insulation, bolted together at the building site."[28] This was one of the first housing packages. Attempts in the late 1940s and early 1950s by the Lustron Corporation to produce industrialized housing resulted in bankruptcy. Again in the mid-1950s, Monsanto tried mass-producing housing.

In May 1969, HUD initiated Operation Breakthrough to increase housing production. Twenty-one housing system producers were chosen to design and build systems on nine sites.[29] In 1973 HUD reported that innovations in site planning and housing technology exist at all nine sites, with major benefits in such nonhardware areas as building code modernization and labor relations.[30] The units included single-family detached homes and low-, mid-, and high-rise structures. Delivery distances ranged from 12 to 2,700 miles. Materials included wood, steel, concrete, and polyester. The housing systems used in Operation Breakthrough varied widely in terms of earlier development or use. Some systems were modifications of current housing products, while others were barely off the drawing board.[31]

Technology has not worked in housing as in other areas partly because the product cannot be easily tested. Heavy capital costs are also involved in setting up plants. Building and housing codes limit mass-produced housing.

Oster and Quigley studied the ways in which regulations limit changes in house building.[32] They suggest that the education of the chief building official, union power, and the relative size of housebuilding firms in the local construction industry help determine whether costcutting innovations will be accepted. In addition, wealthier areas, presumably more exclusive suburbs, are more likely to prohibit such techniques. Labor costs do not seem to be a factor. The state of the local housing market—as measured by unionization and firm size—and the

---

[26]U.S. Department of Commerce, Bureau of the Census, *Construction Reports*, "Residential Alterations and Repairs," C50-78-A (April 1979), 1, 2.

[27]Karl G. Pearson, *Industrialized Housing* (Ann Arbor, Mich.: Institute of Service and Technology, University of Michigan, 1972), p. 8.

[28]Harwood F. Merrill, "A Keystone for a Nickel," *Forbes* (Apr. 15, 1940), 12.

[29]U.S. Department of Housing and Urban Development, *Operation Breakthrough* (Washington, D.C., March 1970), p. 4.

[30]U.S. Department of Housing and Urban Development, *1973 Annual Report*, HUD-329-2-U (Washington, D.C., 1973).

[31]*Operation Breakthrough*, p. 14.

[32]Sharon Oster and John M. Quigley, "Regulatory Barriers to the Diffusion of Innovation: Some Evidence from Building Codes," in *Research and Innovation in the Building Regulatory Process* (Washington, D.C.: U.S. Department of Commerce, National Bureau of Standards, June 1977), pp. 113–35.

professionalism of local regulators—as measured by education, background, and professional contacts—affect the rate of technical progress in housing construction.

However, mass production of parts used in housing construction has grown in these areas: trusses and panels for floors, ceilings, and walls; mechanical cores, such as an entire kitchen or bath; and individual plumbing and electrical cores. Housing packages are also growing in use. These packages include *panelized housing, modular housing,* sectional housing, and precut housing.

Custom and catalog manufacturers offer a huge array of products and services. "Custom" manufacturers prefabricate a home or building to the buyer's specifications; "catalog" manufacturers produce a limited number of homes, as listed in their catalog. Architects have usually designed the catalog homes, and manufacturers have tested a prototype.

In another area, production has also been improved by construction aids. Some of the most common aids are automatic gun nailers, panel cranes, and adhesives and adhesive guns. In the management area, computers may be used in scheduling, pricing, purchasing, and sales.[33]

Off-site construction, such as production of housing parts, does reduce the labor cost per unit because skills are more finely divided. Also, less time is lost and costs are lower since weather is not a factor. Thus, efficiency is increased, reducing construction time. This, in turn, will help reduce interest paid on borrowed money. These factors should reduce the cost of the unit to the consumer.

National Bureau of Standards.

Installation of 2 x 6 floor joists.

FUTURE HOUSING A preview of future structural changes can be seen in the "Tech House" in Hampton, Virginia.[34] Included are solar heating, a waste water reclamation system, computer-directed air conditioning, a seismic burglar alarm, and a tornado detector. The house is built to lower energy use and to increase safety.

Characteristics of the Housing Industry

SIZE OF FIRMS

Of the roughly 127,000 home builders in the United States, the small builder accounts for 80 percent of residential construction.[35] The number of firms indicates how easy it is to enter and leave this market. This ease provides flexibility, which is especially important given the volatile nature of housing production.

---

[33]*Housing in the Seventies,* p. 200.

[34]"Tech House: An Experiment in Future Living," *Consumers' Research Magazine* 60 (August 1977), 41.

[35]The Annual Report of Housing's Giants' *Professional Builder,* 46 (July 1979), 118.

Small builders allow for more custom work and can produce a few units each year in a small town or rural area.

Builders of all sizes—small, medium, and large—are similar in many respects.[36] All reported an average net profit of about 9 percent in 1978, while about 4 percent in each size category reported a net loss. Cost breakdowns are similar, although largest firms had lower materials and labor costs but higher overhead and marketing costs. Time needed to complete a housing unit increases with company size. Small-volume builders spend about four months on the average constructing a home, while the largest ones take about five months. Bigger builders tend to use more components in building. About 25 percent of builders in each size category built only single-family units.

A housing giant is a firm with revenues of more than $10 million, mainly through house building. This includes single-family and multi-family housing, panelized and modular housing, and mobile home manufacturers but excludes those that build only high rises. These firms control the production of many units and are more likely to develop or adopt new materials, products, or techniques. They also help to stabilize housing industry.

From 1970 to 1978, the number of housing giants rose from 253 to 487, or 92 percent. In 1974 there were 568 giants. There was a 16 percent decline from 1976 to 1977 and another 17 percent decline in 1977 but then remained stable in 1978. However, in 1977 the 487 existing companies retained the 19.6 percent share of the total shelter market shared by the 419 companies in 1976. Certain companies that were no longer giants still had revenues of $5 million or more; some went backrupt; and others drastically reduced their building operations or went out of business. Thus, even in large construction firms there is high risk and turnover. There is also a continual small turnover in the top ten firms in total dollar volume although 1978 was remarkably similar to 1977. In 1978, in order of decreasing dollar volume, the top ten companies were: Centex Corporation, United States Home Corporation, GDV Inc. (which holds three individual giants—Wood Brothers, Guerdon Industries, and General Development Corporation), Lincoln Property, Ryan Homes, Kaufman and Broad, Weyerhaeuser, Skyline Corporation, National Housing Partnership, and Fleetwood Enterprises.[37] Centex is the only company that has been in the top-ten listing since the data on giants were first compiled in 1967.

The giants increased the percentage of both dollar and unit volume in for-sale housing. In 1978 their total dollar volume was $23.8 billion, up 19 percent from 1977. This exceeded the industry's best year—1974, with $20.1 billion. Thus, larger firms sometimes increase their dollar volume in a recession, whereas during expansion small firms grow.

Distribution of earnings among the housing giants has changed somewhat from 1970 to 1978 (Table 10-4). The percentage of earnings from low-rise multi-family units built for the builder's own investment greatly decreased, as did the percentage of earnings from townhouses and *quads*. Condominiums in-

---

[36]Ibid., 125.

[37]Ibid., 132.

TABLE 10-4. Percent Distribution of Sales Volume for Housing Giants

	1970[a]	1971[b]	1972[c]	1973[d]	1974[e]	1975[f]	1976[g]	1977[g]	1978[h]
Single-family detached	24.1	24.9	25.1	23.3	25.3	30.7	34.4	37.0	40.1
Townhouses, quads, condominiums	6.7	8.1	12.0	14.4	14.0	15.6	12.0	13.1	14.3
Mobile homes	14.2	14.6	14.6	13.9	13.8	11.8	12.4	12.0	11.4
Low-rise Multis for sale to investors	11.2	11.1	11.7	10.5	8.4	5.6	6.5	6.8	5.7
Low-rise multis for own investment	13.6	11.6	7.5	7.1	3.8	4.0	4.3	4.6	4.2
Modular/prefab.	4.1	5.1	4.7	4.9	6.6	6.1	5.8	5.2	5.3
High-rise multis	2.5	2.5	3.2	3.2	3.1	1.8	2.0	1.6	1.7
Nonresidential constru.	7.7	6.6	5.4	5.8	6.4	6.1	5.0	3.6	4.2
Gross rental revenue	5.9	4.7	5.0	5.4	6.4	8.4	7.3	6.5	
Land sales	4.2	4.5	4.3	5.4	5.0	4.5	4.0	3.3	13.1[i]
Miscellaneous	5.8	6.3	6.5	6.1	7.2	5.4	6.1	4.4	

Source: Annual Report of Housing Giants, July issues. Each year's report covers building activities of the previous calendar year.

[a] *Professional Builder,* 36 (July 1971), 85.

[b] *Professional Builder,* 37 (July 1972), 101.

[c] *Professional Builder,* 38 (July 1973), 70.

[d] *Professional Builder,* 39 (July 1974), 82.

[e] *Professional Builder,* 40 (July 1975), 66.

[f] *Professional Builder,* 41 (July 1976), 64.

[g] *Professional Builder,* 43 (July 1978), 163.

[h] *Professional Builder,* 46 (July 1979), 135.

[i] No longer available by separate categories.

creased, as did earnings from single-family detached homes. The distribution of number of units between the types of housing is similar to the earnings trends.

In large-scale building, capital is substituted for labor, especially in the use of large power tanks and equipment. However, for capital return, units must be produced each year. Whereas labor will be hired only if building is going on, capital is owned. The more equipment owned, the more fixed costs a builder has.

Large-scale builders may also save on materials since they buy in volume. Thus, they may be in a better bargaining position with unions and the government. They can hire their own lawyers, designers, architects, and accountants. Finally, materials and work practices may be more standardized than in smaller firms.

The 1960s and early 1970s saw increased development of large-scale projects.[38] The climax of this trend was the new town. These developments included a mix of land uses and amenities. The 1974 recession halted the trend and highlighted the problems of large-scale developments: complexity, high risk, and need for capital. Large-scale developments are more efficient in terms of public service and infrastructure costs; they promote innovations in design and operation. Schemes to encourage large-scale developments include coordinated permitting, planning urban development

[38]Donald Priest and others, *Large-Scale Development Benefits, Constraints, and State and Local Policy Incentives* (Washington, D.C.: The Urban Land Institute, 1977), p. 10.

ordinances, and designation of areas as development areas.

MANUFACTURED HOUSING INDUSTRY

The manufactured housing industry is only about fifty years old. In 1929, Arthur G. Sherman established the Detroit-based Covered Wagon Company, the first large-scale producer of trailer coaches. It was followed by the Silver Dome Company of Detroit, the Palace Corporation of Flint, Michigan, and the Schult Corporation of Elkhart, Indiana (which still bills itself as the mobile home capital of the world). Although by 1936 house trailer manufacturing was one of the fastest-growing U.S. industries, neither the Ford Motor Company nor General Motors Corporation entered the field; they believed the market potential was too small. In 1936 the American Automobile Association estimated that there were 250,000 trailers housing one million people. One year later, the industry's sales totaled $17 million.[39]

---

[39]"Manufactured Homes Meet Modern Housing Demands" (Arlington, Va.: Manufactured Housing Institute, n.d.), p. 1.

U.S. Department of HUD.

Housing project.

However, even in 1940 the industry was producing only 10,000 units a year. During World War II, the federal government bought trailers to house defense workers and military personnel, thus boosting the industry. During the postwar years, when an acute housing shortage occurred, the number of retailers quadrupled between 1945 and 1951; 85,000 units were sold during one peak year. By 1956, 200 trailer manufacturers had produced 125,000 units in two years. FHA financing of mobile home park construction and insuring of loans up to 60 percent of the value of the park made mobile homes more acceptable. The Mobile Home Manufacturers Association (MHMA) furthered this trend when they officially dropped the name "trailers" in favor of "mobile homes."

The industry grew in the 1970s, with giants emerging as smaller manufacturers were absorbed by competition and high costs. The approval of a mobile home code by the American National Standards Association and the National Fire Protection Association gave some protection to the mobile home buyer in most states. By 1966 most mobile homes were stable rather than mobile, and within the next few years accounted for 40 percent of all new single-family homes sold at any price.

As the 1970s began, sales neared the $3 billion mark. In 1971, 334 firms produced mobile homes from 700 factory sites. In 1977, there were about 200 firms with 550 factory sites, for an estimated retail value of $4 billion. The top twenty-five firms produced 62 percent of all mobile homes.[40] Although the top producers are nationwide, plants are operated regionally. However, distribution and retailing are not concentrated. A large and increasing number of these manufacturers are now building sectional or modular units as well.

"Production of manufactured homes today represents nearly 30 percent of the entire new single family housing market, and 73 percent of all single family homes sold for less than $30,000. They are larger (as much as 1,500 square feet of living space) and more luxurious than those of only eight years ago."[41]

The mobile home and prefab industries are combining by the gradual integration of multisection mobiles and modular (sectional homes). The modular unit is produced to conform to statewide or local codes, whereas the mobile home must meet federal construction and safety standards.

PERFORMANCE OF THE BUILDING MATERIALS INDUSTRY

Activity in the building industries is measured by the Census Bureau every five years, most recently in 1972. The performance of each building material industry can thus be gauged. Several types of performance are considered: value added per worker-hour, capital spending, value of shipments, and percent of payroll. Value added per worker-hour averaged $12.58 for the 40 building material industries surveyed, compared with $12.26 for all 115 industries surveyed. New capital spending per employee averaged $1,479 for the building materials industries and $1,335 for all industries. The total value of shipments in the 40 building materials industries ac-

---

[40]*Housing in the Seventies*, p. 187.

[41]"Manufactured Homes Meet Modern Housing Demands," 3–4.

Riding the nation's rails from Avon, New York to Corinth, Mississippi are 56 modules or 14 townhouses, built by Stirling Homex Corporation of Avon.

counted for 8 percent of all manufacturing industries; they had 9 percent of all manufacturing employment, 9 percent of total production workers, and paid over 8 percent of the total payroll.[42]

In the building materials industries, those with the greatest percentage increase (20 percent or over) in number of companies since 1963 were: hard surface floor coverings, steel wire and related products, building paper/board, cement, vitreous plumbing fixtures, fabricated structural metal, and metal sanitary ware. The greatest decrease in number of companies was in ceramic tile, sawmills and planing mills, heating equipment (except electric), structural clay products, concrete block and brick, gypsum products, mineral wool, prefabricated metal building and miscellaneous metal work industries, and brick and structural clay tile.[43] The changes in the number of companies

---

[42]C.B. Pitcher, "The 1972 Census of Manufacturers: Performance of 40 Selected Building Material Industries," *Construction Review,* 22 (May 1976), 4–7.

[43]Ibid., 5.

within these industries provide another clue to the use of materials in construction, the demand for the material, and the profitability of meeting that demand.[44]

CONSTRUCTION FIRM FAILURES

The instability of the building industry can be seen by the number of construction firms that fail each year (Figure 10-4). In 1978, 1,204 firms failed, with

---

[44]See *Construction Review* for changes in industries and prices.

liabilities totaling about $3.3 million. Although liabilities were higher in 1975, even more firms failed in the early 1960s.

Failures by home builders increase consumer costs for housing. This is especially true for those who have bought a home that is not completed. Consumers, in turn, demand more regulation and protection, which increases housing costs to all. Also, building firms and lending institutions that have uncollectible debts for materials bought by bankrupt construction firms must pass this on as increased cost.

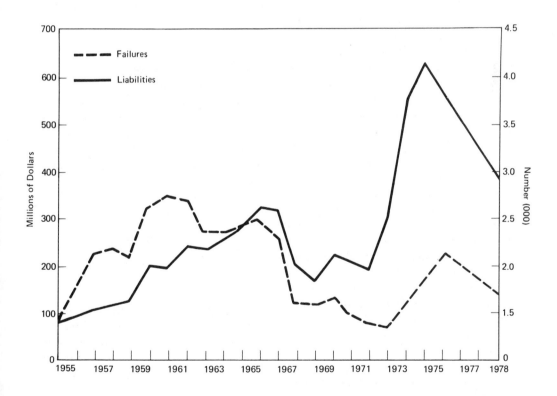

Figure 10-4. Construction Firm Failures and Liabilities, 1955–1976. [*Source:* Dun and Bradstreet, Inc., "Business Economics, Monthly Failures" data compilation by NAHB Economics Department, adapted from U.S. Congress, *Current Economic Situation and Outlook for the Housing Industry,* Joint Economic Committee, 94th Congress, 1st Session (June 26, 1975), p. 12.]

In the short run, low construction activity results in underutilized capacity, bankruptcies, and unemployment. In the long run, the home building industry is less efficient because of these wide fluctuations. The industry attempts to minimize fixed costs by being less capital-intensive and by demanding a high rate of return on the capital invested. Less is invested in personnel training, and workers are prevented from changing their craft or moving to another geographic area.

INDUSTRY ASSOCIATIONS

One of the organizations of the housing industry is the National Association of Home Builders (NAHB). The NAHB is one of the largest and most influential trade organizations in the country. As of June 1977, 87,349 members were affiliated with 650 state or local associations.[45] The members provide about 85 percent of all housing starts. The NAHB gives its members a variety of services. High on the list is participation in a broad range of government activities, including testifying at hearings for laws favorable to builders. Members also receive management and marketing aids, economic reports, and mortgage market information. There are educational programs and research reports. Obviously the NAHB is interested in supplying housing; it encourages government subsidy programs for housing production and reduced regulations on firms.

The Producers' Council is the national association for the manufacturers of quality building and construction products. Its members comprise manufacturers of construction products—steel, brick, concrete, roofing, interior furnishings, and equipment.[46] The council has chapters in 48 major-market cities and more than 200 satellite cities throughout the country, influencing the quantity and quality of housing produced. These chapters provide a means of updating industry firms on materials and technology to increase efficiency, lower costs, and improve profits.

The National Association of Home Manufacturers was formed in 1943 to improve housing technology and quality.[47] In 1978 it had about 200 members. Activities include supporting or opposing laws or regulations that affect the cost of homes; improving management and production skills of members; and providing information and educational programs on manufactured housing.

The Manufactured Housing Institute is a trade association with members that manufacture or supply materials or services needed in manufacturing mobile and modular homes. It provides services to its members similar to NAHB but in support of manufactured housing.

Summary

This chapter has examined the housing industry. Attention was given to the housing giants, those firms with revenues in excess of $10 million; and performance and failures in the industry. Material,

---

[45]Letter from Amanda P. Leech, National Association of Home Builders, Washington, D.C. June 6, 1977.

[46]The Producers Council, Inc., 1717 Mass. Ave., NW, Washington, D.C. 20036.

[47]NAHM's 1978 Guide to Manufactured Homes, 1 Virginia: Falls Church, (January 1978).

land, labor, and technological trends were presented.

For the future, continued consolidation of firms, price increases, and shifts in construction materials seem indicated. Energy conservation will be important. Thus, good insulating materials will be in demand, while those that require a lot of energy to produce will continue to increase in price. There will be new developments in land usage and rights.

Terms

manufactured housing a complete housing structure assembled in a plant and used as a permanent dwelling. The house, built in single or multiple sections, has a foundation or chassis so that it can be transported to its site.

manufactured housing subdivision a popular new concept which allows people to buy building lots designed to accommodate manufactured houses. Today, construction of such subdivisions follows local codes, and services are provided by the local municipality instead of by the developer.

modular housing factory-produced unit used alone or in combination with other units after it is erected at a building site.

panelized housing factory-produced panels that are combined on site to form a structure.

quads structures that contain four housing units.

value added per worker-hour amount that a worker adds to an item's worth in an hour.

Suggested Readings

Brown, James J., "The Home-Owner's Land-Lease Development Program: A Proposal for Reducing the Land-Related Costs of Housing," *The American University Law Review*, 23 (Fall 1973), 55–117.

Finn, Joseph T., "Materials Requirements for Private Multi-Family Housing," *Construction Review*, 22, (April 1976), 4–10.

Pearson, Karl G., *Industrialized Housing*. Ann Arbor, Mich.: Institute of Service and Technology, University of Michigan, 1972.

Pitcher, Charles B., "Building Product Prices and Output—an Overview," *Construction Review*, 24 (August/September 1978), 4–12.

——— and Franklin E. Williams, "Building Materials Outlook for 1976," *Construction Review*, 22, (January/February 1976), 2–3.

Rabb, Judith and Bernard Rabb, *Good Shelter: A Guide to Mobile, Modular, and Prefabricated Houses, Including Domes*. New York: Quandrangle/The N.Y. Times, 1975.

"Trade Union Discrimination in the Pittsburgh Construction Industry," in *Housing Urban America,* ed. Irwin Dubinsky, Chicago: Aldine, 1973, pp. 376–91.

U.S. Department of Housing and Urban Development, *An Analysis of Twelve Experimental Housing Projects*, ST/MP-98. Washington, D.C., June 1969.

Williams, Franklin E., "Building Materials for Residential Construction in Colonial America," *Construction Review*, 22, (July 1976), 5.

HOUSING POLICIES

III

FEDERAL HOUSING POLICIES

1. SHOULD HOUSING CONSUMPTION OR PRODUCTION BE SUBSIDIZED?

2. IS PUBLIC HOUSING A PROGRAM OF THE PAST? WHAT ALTERNATIVES ARE THERE?

3. ARE HOUSING ALLOWANCES THE WAVE OF THE FUTURE?

4. HOW DO COMMUNITY DEVELOPMENT PROGRAMS AFFECT HOUSING?

5. DISCUSS CATEGORICAL PROGRAMS VERSUS BLOCK GRANTS

Federal housing policies must be viewed both historically and in their political, social, and economic context. The federal role in housing is extensive and complex. This chapter provides a brief history and highlights major federal housing programs.

Federal housing policy deals with both production and consumption. Objectives in housing production include strong, stable housing construction; available mortgage money and controlled interest rates; and attracting private capital to housing production. Objectives in housing consumption include reduced housing costs; better-quality housing; aid to special groups, such as low- and moderate-income families, or the elderly and handicapped; and improved inner cities or rural areas.

Government aid in these areas can take many forms:

1. Noncash assistance, such as providing land for home sites and giving technical or supervisory help.
2. Mortgage insurance or loan guarantees.
3. Interest subsidies to builders or consumers.
4. Subsidy of capital development costs.
5. Direct cash payments to occupant families, public agencies, private organizations, or property owners.

A subsidy changes the use of resources in the private sector of the economy. It may operate by offering rewards for certain activities. Housing program subsidies affect both production and consumption. Income subsidies for housing should lead to long-range changes in the housing stock. "A housing subsidy will increase consumption of housing services and

U.S. Department of HUD.

HUD Office, Washington, D.C.

necessarily cause the housing stock to grow."[1]

In looking at housing policy, we need to consider who benefits, who does what, for what purpose, and at what cost to whom. Table 11-1 lists the major federal housing acts and executive orders pertaining to housing.

The two major federal agencies that administer housing programs are the Department of Housing and Urban Development (HUD) and the Farmers Home Administration (FmHA). HUD, the newer agency, was created in 1965 to consolidate federal housing activities into a Cabinet-level department. Its activities are guided by (1) a responsibility to maintain and promote economic stabilty, (2) a social obligation to help those in need, and (3) an emerging interest in how the country's communities develop.[2] HUD is the principal federal agency responsible for programs on housing needs and

[1]Henry J. Aaron, *Shelter and Subsidies: Who Benefits from Federal Housing Policies?* (Washington, D.C.: The Brookings Institution, 1972), p. 48.

[2]Ibid, p. 1.

TABLE 11-1. Major Federal Legislation and Executive Orders Authorizing Housing Programs (Chronological Order)

ACT	PUBLIC LAW NO.	TITLE	SECTION	FOCUS
National Housing Act, 1934	73-479	I	2	Mobile homes loan insurance and property improvement loan insurance
		II	203	Mortgage insurance for one- to four-family homes
			203(h)	Disaster housing
			203(i)	Mortgage insurance for low-cost homes in outlying areas
			203(k)	Insurance for major home improvement loans of homes outside of urban renewal areas
	81-475 as amended by H.A. 1950	II	207 (1950)	Mortgage insurance for constructing, buying, and rehabilitating cooperative housing
	83-560 as amended by H.A. 1954	I	220 (1954)	Mortgage insurance for constructing or rehabilitating rental housing in urban renewal or code enforcement areas for moderate or middle-income families
	83-560 as amended by H.A. 1954	I	221	Mortgage insurance for new or rehabilitated homes and rental housing for displaced families or low- or moderate-income families
		II	221(d)(2) (1954)	Mortgage insurance for home purchase by low- and moderate-income families. Mortgage limits are lower than Sec. 207
			221(d)(3) (1954)	Mortgage insurance for nonprofit sponsors and limited dividend corporations for rental housing for displaced or low- or moderate-income families with mortgages bearing below-market interest rates (BMIR) and bought by the GNMA under its special assistance program
			221(d)(4) (1954)	Mortgage insurance for rental or cooperative housing for low- and moderate-income families
	89-754 as amended by Demonstration Cities and Metropolitan Development Act of 1966	III	221(h) (1966)	Mortgage insurance for buying and rehabilitating housing for resale to low-income families with BMIR financing
		I	222	Mortgage insurance for homes for servicemen
	90-448 as amended by Housing and Urban Development Act of 1968	I	223(e) (1968)	Mortgage insurance for buying or rehabilitating housing in declining neighborhoods
		II	223(f) (1974)	Mortgage insurance for buying or refinancing existing multi-family projects in older, declining neighborhoods

TABLE 11.1. Continued

ACT	PUBLIC LAW NO.	TITLE	SECTION	FOCUS
			231	Mortgage insurance for constructing or rehabilitating senior citizens or handicapped rental housing
			232	Mortgage insurance for new or rehabilitated nursing homes and intermediate care facilites
			233	Mortgage insurance for experimental housing
			234	Mortgage insurance for constructing or rehabilitating condominiums
	90-448 as amended by Housing and Urban Development Act of 1968		235 (1968)	Interest subsidy on loans to low-income families for the purchase of new, existing, or rehabilitated housing
	"	II	236 (1968)	Interest rate subsidy for mortgages on rental and cooperative housing
	"	II	237	Mortgage insurance and home ownership counseling for poor credit risks
	"	II	240	Mortgage insurance on purchase of fee simple title
		II	241	Insured supplemental loans on multi-family housing projects
		III		Government National Mortgage Association
		VIII	809	Mortgage insurance for armed services housing for civilian employees
			810	Mortgage insurance for armed services housing in impacted areas
		X		Mortgage insurance for land development and new communities
		XII		Urban property protection and reinsurance
U.S. Housing Act of 1937				
HUD-Assisted Homeownership Management Program				
Low-Rent Public Housing	75-412	I	10(c)	Low-rent public housing
89-117 as amended by the Housing Act of 1965		I	23 (1965)	Leasing of housing from private owners by local housing authorities to provide low-rent housing units
Housing Act of 1949	81-171	I		Urban renewal projects loans and grants
		V	502	BMIR loans for buying or improving rural homes
			504	1 percent loans for minor repairs of homes owned by extremely low-income families ineligible for 502 loans.
			514	BMIR loans for building or rehabilitating housing for domestic farm labor

245

TABLE 11.1. Continued

ACT	PUBLIC LAW NO.	TITLE	SECTION	FOCUS
			515	BMIR loans to nonprofit sponsors of low-income rural rental housing
			516	Grants to states, localities, or groups to build housing for domestic farm labor
			521	BMIR loans to cooperative-owned and managed rural housing
	89-117 as amended by Housing Act of 1965	I	115 (1965)	Grants for rehabilitating housing in urban renewal or code enforcement areas
			116	Grants for demolition of unsafe structures
			117	Grants for code enforcement
Housing Act of 1954 as amended by Title IV Housing and Community Development Act of 1974	83-560	VII	701	Comprehensive planning assistance, urban planning research and demonstration
	93-383		702(b)	Urban-systems engineering
Housing Act of 1959	86-372	III	314	Grants for demonstration urban renewal projects
		II	202	Direct loans for rental housing for elderly or handicapped persons
Housing Act of 1961	87-70	II	207	Grants for demonstrations of new or improved ways of housing low-income families, including handicapped persons
Housing Act of 1964	88-560	III	312	Rehabilitation loans at low interest rates to owners of housing in code enforcement and urban renewal areas
Department of Housing and Urban Development Act, 1965	89-117	I	101	Rent supplements; payments directly to the sponsors of low-income housing making up the difference between one-fourth of the tenants' income and market rentals.
Demonstration Cities and Metropolitan Development Act of 1966	89-754	I X	1010 & 1011	Model Cities Urban research and technology
Housing and Urban Development Act of 1968	90-448	I	106(a)	Assistance to nonprofit sponsors
		I	106(b)	Counseling
				Seed money to nonprofit sponsors or public housing agencies to cover early planning expenses of project to house elderly, handicapped, or lower income persons
		IV		New communities
		VII		Government National Mortgage Association
		XI		Urban property protection and reinsurance
		XIII		Flood insurance
		XIV		Interstate land sales

246

TABLE 11-1. Continued

ACT	PUBLIC LAW NO.	TITLE	SECTION	FOCUS
Civil Rights Act of 1968 Civil Rights Act of 1866 and 1964	90-284	VIII		Equal Opportunity in Housing
Housing and Urban Development Act of 1970	91-609	V		Research and technology
		VI		Crime insurance
		VII		Urban growth and new community development
		I		Community development block grants
		II	8	Assisted housing
				Lower-income rental assistance, payments on behalf of lower-income tenants directly to owners of private dwellings or through public housing agencies, to make up the difference between the fair market rent for a unit and the amount the tenant is required to pay (15–25% of adjusted income)
		III		Mortgage credit assistance
			244	Coinsurance
			245	Experimental financing
		VIII		Miscellaneous
			802	State housing finance agency coinsurance
			809	National Institute of Building Sciences (NIBS)
			810	Urban homesteading
			811	Counseling
			315	GNMA conventional tandem authority
Emergency Home Purchase Assistance Act of 1974	93-449			
Emergency Homeowners' Relief Act	94-50	I		Standby authority to prevent mortgage foreclosures
Housing and Community Development Act of 1974	93-383	I	213(a)	Brooke Amendment
		II		Community development block grants
		VI	8	Lower-income rental assistance subsidies; mobile home construction and safety standards
Housing and Community Development Act of 1977	95-128	VIII	801	Community Reinvestment Act of 1977 to encourage financial institutions to meet credit needs of local communities

community development. Most of its efforts are concentrated in urban areas.

The FmHA was created in 1935 to serve low-income farmers. In the 1960s and 1970s it was transformed into a multifaceted credit arm for rural development, with a strong interest in housing. Of the $12.25 billion advanced for housing in its first forty years, the FmHA has spent more than $11.5 billion since its insured loan authority began in 1965. Its housing credit service is now more than $2 billion annually, producing well over 100,000 living units a year.[3] The FmHA operates through a nationwide system of about 1,750 county offices, easily accessible to rural communities.

Historical Overview

One of the first federal activites in housing were congressional hearings on slums and blight in the 1890s. These hearings helped to dramatize housing problems. In 1892 Congress authorized the Secretary of Labor to investigate slums in cities of 200,000 people or more.[4] Since only $20,000 was given for the study, the results were limited. In 1908, the first Presidential Commission to evaluate slum conditions was formed.

After that, there was little federal activity in housing until World War I. On March 1, 1918, Congress authorized the U.S. Shipping Board and the Emergency Fleet Corporation to provide housing for shipyard employees who were facing a serious housing shortage.[5] Loans were given to real estate companies incorporated by the ship-building concerns. As a result, housing projects were constructed in twenty-four areas, totaling 9,000 houses, 1,100 apartments, 19 dormitories, and 8 hotels. Congress also established a Bureau of Industrial Housing and Transportation in the Department of Labor to house war workers.[6] The Bureau worked through the U.S. Housing Corporation, which was created by Executive Order of the President.[7] The Bureau built and managed twenty-five community projects composed of more than 5,000 single-family dwelling units, in addition to apartments, dormitories, and hotels. In addition, the U.S. Housing Corporation considered and handled rent grievances. After the war, all housing was sold to private owners, with the exception of certain units that were transferred to other government agencies.

In 1921 Congress funded a new Division of Building and Housing in the National Bureau of Standards, which had been established in 1901.[8] A Senate committee in 1920 stated that the housing shortage must be solved by private business rather than the government.[9] Thus, another lull in federal activity followed; housing legislation now rested with the states.

In the Great Depression of the early

[3]U.S. House of Representatives, *Equal Opportunity in Rural Housing*, Serial No. 51, Hearings before the Subcommittee on Civil and Constitutional Rights of the Committee on the Judiciary, 2nd Sess., 94th Congress (July 20–23, 1976), p. 154.

[4]Public Resolution 52–22.

[5]Public Law 65–102, Chapter 19.

[6]Public Law 65–149, Chapter 74, and Public Law 65–164.

[7]Executive Order No. 2985A, Oct. 29, 1918.

[8]31 Statutes of the United States, p. 1449, Chapter 872, Mar. 3, 1901, and Public Law 67–18.

[9]U.S. Congress, *Reconstruction and Production*, 66th Congress, 3d sess., Senate Report 829 (Washington, D.C., 1921), pp. 2–3.

1930s, the United States was faced with the collapse of the residential financing system and the need to create jobs. In 1931 a White House Conference on Home Building and Homeownership was convened by President Herbert Hoover. The conference helped to shape many of the key features of federal housing policy in this decade. Recommendations included broadened home ownership; a strong credit system for better protection of both homeowners and lending institutions; improved planning and zoning; better homes at lower costs through improved technology; and rehabilitation of old homes.

Congress then began a broad attack on housing problems. On July 22, 1932, the Federal Home Loan Bank Act was enacted.[10] It established twelve regional federal home loan banks financed by government capital and bonds. The banks were to advance money secured by first mortgages to member institutions.

On July 21, 1932, Congress passed the Emergency Relief and Construction Act, which authorized the Reconstruction Finance Corporation (RFC) to make loans to corporations to build low-income housing or to reconstruct slum areas.[11] These loans were subject to state and local laws on rents, charges, capital, and rate of return and were to be self-liquidating. Under this law, two loans were made by the RFC. One was for $8 million to finance Knickerbocker Village in New York City; the other was for $155,000 to finance rural homes in Ford County, Kansas.

On June 13, 1933, the Home Owners Loan Act was passed and, three days la-

ter, the National Industrial Recovery Act.[12] The latter authorized the Public Works Administration to use federal funds to finance low-cost housing, slum clearance, and subsistence homesteads. On July 8, 1933, President Franklin D. Roosevelt appointed a Federal Emergency Administration of Public Works to carry out this program.[13] The Home Owners Loan Corporation, authorized under the former act, had the power to buy mortgages threatened with foreclosure.

The 1934 National Housing Act established the Federal Housing Administration (FHA) to insure long-term home mortgage loans made by private institutions.[14] More broadly, the purposes of the act were to: improve nationwide standards, stimulate employment and industry, and improve the financing system. Direct federal construction of low-rent housing projects resulted.

In 1935 Congress passed the Emergency Relief Appropriation Act, which set aside funds for public works, including $450 million for housing.[15] The Works Projects Administration and the Bureau of Labor Statistics in the Department of Labor did a combined construction survey to aid public works planning. The survey included housing projects. A major policy statement about housing was made in the 1949 National Housing Act,[16] which established the right to "a decent home and a suitable living environment for every American

---

[10]Public Law 72–304.

[11]Public Law 72–302.

[12]Public Law 73–43; Public Law 73–67.

[13]Executive Order No. 6198.

[14]Public Law 73–479.

[15]Public Resolution 11, 74th Congress, Apr. 8, 1935.

[16]Public Law 171, 81st Congress, July 15, 1949.

family." The act also strongly encouraged private enterprise to fulfill the demand for housing. In addition, it authorized federal aid in clearing slums and blighted areas. Title V of this act extended aid through the FmHA to enable farmowners to obtain decent, safe, and sanitary dwellings for themselves, their workers, and their tenants.

For the first time since the 1930s, a Republican administration was able to influence housing with the Housing Act of 1954.[17] Actually, it made few major program changes, but it did attack many smaller problems and needs of special groups. This act required local governments to develop a "workable program" for community development as a condition of funding. Urban redevelopment programs now included rehabilitation of existing structures. The financing system was revised, FHA mortgage terms were liberalized, special attention was given to mortgage insurance programs for housing for displaced families, and the FNMA was restructured.

The 1959 Housing Act authorized direct federal loans to nonprofit sponsors of rental projects for the elderly and handicapped (Section 202).[18] This was the first time the government had recognized the need to subsidize persons marginally above public housing levels; it also affirmed the role of private industry in housing development.

Housing legislation in the 1960s featured direct and indirect subsidy programs with an emphasis on special groups, such as elderly and low-income persons. The 1961 Housing Act introduced the BMIR mortgage insurance program [Section 221(d)(3)] and authorized the first subsidy to finance operating costs of housing projects.[19] FmHA programs were extended to all rural residents.

The 1964 Housing Act extended the subsidy for elderly families displaced by urban renewal projects and authorized housing rehabilitation loans to meet either local housing code standards or urban renewal plan objectives.[20]

The Department of Housing and Urban Development (HUD) was created in 1965,[21] bringing housing programs to a Cabinet level. The 1965 Housing Act also established two more subsidy programs: the rent supplement program and the Section 23 leasing operation.[22] These programs served low-income people without the stigma attached to concentrated public housing. Rehabilitation grants were given to low-income homeowners in urban renewal areas.

In 1966 a new approach to housing and urban problems began with the Demonstration Cities and Metropolitan Development Act.[23] This act authorized the "Model Cities" program, which gave cities great discretion in planning, developing, and carrying out programs to improve the physical environment, increase the supply of low- and moderate-income housing, and provide vital health and welfare services. Also that year, BMIR loans were given to nonprofit sponsors to rehabilitate property for resale to low-income families.

In the late 1960s, two presidential

---

[17]Public Law 560, 83d Congress, Aug. 2, 1954.
[18]Public Law 86–372.

[19]Public Law 87–70.
[20]Public Law 88–560.
[21]Public Law 89–174.
[22]Public Law 89–117.
[23]Public Law 89–754.

commissions—the National Commission on Urban Problems (the Douglas Commission) and the President's Committee on Urban Housing (the Kaiser Commission)—helped shape federal housing policies. The Douglas Commission recommended more housing assistance to the poor; the Kaiser Commission called for 26 million new and rehabilitated housing to be constructed during the years between 1968 and 1978.

Both of these recommendations became part of the 1968 Housing and Urban Development Act.[24] A national production goal was established. Subsidies of interest rates were enacted under Section 235 for homeowners and under Section 236 for multi-family rental units. Section 238 also established a special risk pool for mortgage insurance and Section 223(e) for insurance in "older, declining urban areas."

The most important part of the 1969 Housing and Urban Development Act was the Brooke Amendment, which limited rents charged by local housing authorities to 25 percent of the tenant's income.[25]

The next year, 1970, was a watershed year in housing. The Housing and Urban Development Act set up the experimental housing allowance program, authorized payment for structural defects to Section 235 homeowners, established a cost formula for public housing construction, and set up the New Community Development Corporation in HUD.[26] The 1970 Uniform Relocation Assistance and Real Property Acquisitions Policies Act established a consistent basis for payments to

families displaced by federal programs.[27] The Emergency Home Finance Act allowed the FNMA to buy conventional mortgages, established the Federal Home Loan Mortgage Corporation, and authorized mortgage interest subsidies for middle-income homeowners.

The majority of federal housing programs were halted in 1973 by the Nixon moratorium. The 1974 Housing and Community Development Act revived some of the programs and instituted some new ones—Section 8, urban homesteading, and the establishment of mobile home construction and safety standards.[28] The 1974 Emergency Home Purchase Assistance Act extended the GNMA's purchases to conventional mortgages.[29] The Emergency Homeowners Relief Act gave the GNMA standby authority to prevent mortgage foreclosures.

On July 2, 1975, President Gerald Ford signed into law the highly compromised Emergency Housing Act.[30] This law extended Section 312 and authorized HUD on a standby basis to coinsure or make repayable mortgage relief payments up to $250 per month for two years for families facing foreclosure.

On August 3, 1976, President Ford signed into law the Housing Authorization Act.[31] This act primarily allocated funds and extended programs. Extensions were given to Section 235, 236, and 312 programs. Subsidies given under federal housing programs were excluded

---

[24]Public Law 90–448.

[25]Public Law 90–448.

[26]Public Law 91–609.

[27]Public Law 91–646.

[28]Public Law 93–383.

[29]Public Law 93–449.

[30]Public Law 94–50.

[31]Public Law 94–375, 12 USC 1701, 90 Stat. 1067.

in determining supplemental security income. Eligibility provisions were changed in the Section 8 program to include traditional public housing under certain conditions and to single nonelderly persons.

In the mid-1970s federal legislation was geared toward consumer protection. In 1974 the Real Estate Settlement Procedures Act[32] and HUD's Office of Consumer Affairs and Regulatory Functions were established.

The Housing and Community Development Act of 1977 amended the 1974 act.[33] It expanded the role of citizen participation in the Community Development Block Grant program (CDBG) and required that housing needs be identified in the CDBG plan.

The Housing and Community Development Act of 1978 amended and extended federal housing, community, and neighborhood programs.[34] A National Neighborhood Reinvestment Corporation was established to implement and expand activities started by the Urban Reinvestment Task Force.

Thus has federal housing policy evolved. The earliest concerns were slum conditions, followed by public housing, growth of financing programs, producer subsidies, and later, consumer subsidies. Most recently, federal housing actions have focused on consumer protection.

The following sections detail the major housing programs outlined above. Attention is focused on consumer subsidy programs, producer programs, and community development programs.

---

[32]Public Law 93–533.
[33]Public Law 95–128.
[34]Public Law 95–557.

Major Housing Programs

PUBLIC HOUSING

The public housing program combines federal and local dollars to provide housing for low-income families. The program began as an effort to provide jobs in the 1930s.

CONSTITUENTS The constituents of public housing have changed over time. Originally the program was designed for families who wanted to improve their housing but could not afford private rentals; a limited number of welfare recipients received housing aid. In the 1940s, the program was redirected to provide housing for war workers. After 1949 it was changed again, this time to help poor families. According to Aaron, "the number of public housing residents is about one-tenth of the poor, but not all public housing residents are poor."[35] The 1974 Housing and Community Development Act established a distinct group: Very low income was defined as income not exceeding 50 percent of the median family income for the area.[36] At least 20 percent of all units in a project created under the 1974 act must be occupied by very-low-income families. The median income of all families in public housing in 1977 was about $3,691, compared to $12,000 for all U.S. families.[37]

---

[35]Aaron, *Shelter and Subsidies*, p. 108.
[36]42 U.S.C.A. 1437a(2) Supp. 1975.
[37]U.S. Department of Housing and Urban Development, *HUD Statistical Yearbook*, 1977, (Washington, D.C.: U.S. Government Printing Office, 1978), pp. 245, 248, 346.

Elderly tenants had a median income of $2,928.

To avoid concentration of low-income families, public housing must have an economic mix of tenants.[38] Further, a housing authority must receive in total rentals from all public housing families residing a sum equal to at least 20 percent of the combined incomes of all tenants.[39] These policies encourage the LPHA to admit tenants in the higher low-income ranges.

The policy of promoting an economic mix of families in public housing can be justified on the theory that the poorest families, as well as those with severe social problems, can benefit from the role models provided by more stable, higher-income families. "It also may be desirable to disperse the poor over wider geographical areas, rather than forcing their concentration in urban slums where they present a highly visible target for public opprobrium and official neglect."[40]

About 97 percent of public housing units have been occupied since 1970. Whites account for about 39 percent. The proportion of elderly rose from 38 percent in 1970 to 45 percent in 1977.[41] Benefits rise with family size but decline per person.[42] Benefits also vary across cities. The more needy do seem to benefit

more than others, but the elderly do not receive extra benefits.

LOCAL HOUSING AUTHORITIES The city government creates a local housing authority to build public housing and to obtain federal subsidies. In 1971 all states except Wyoming had enacted enabling laws to allow local authorities to make public housing contracts.[43] In 1971 there were 2,930 local housing authorities in the United States.[44] Only 173 of these managed 1,000 or more units; another 114 controlled between 500 and 1,000. The large-scale public housing projects which are considered typical exist only to a small degree.

A housing authority may also exist at the county level. In addition, there are consolidated or regional housing authorities to serve several municipalities or counties. Thus, six kinds of housing authorities are permitted under state law: state, regional, consolidated, county, municipal, or a cooperative agreement.[45]

FEDERAL SUPPORT The first federal subsidies for public housing were designed to cover only capital costs. Maintenance and operating costs were to be paid from rent received. However, by the 1960s inflation and maintenance needs had made the system unworkable. Congress responded by providing operating costs subsidies up to a maximum of $120 per

---

[38]42 U.S.C.A. Sec. 1437d(c) (4) (A) Supp. 1975.

[39]42 U.S.C.A. Sec. 1437g(b).

[40]"The Housing and Community Development Act of 1974—Who Shall Live in Public Housing?" *Catholic University Law Review*, 25 (Winter 1976), 320–41.

[41]*HUD Statistical Yearbook 1974 and 1977*, pp. 169, 170, 233, 235.

[42]Michael P. Murry, "The Distribution of Tenant Benefits in Public Housing," *Econometrica*, 43 (July 1975), 771–88.

[43]Aaron, *Shelter and Subsidies*, p. 111.

[44]George R. Genung, Jr., "Public Housing—Success or Failure," *The George Washington Law Review*, 39, (May 1971), 735.

[45]For a description of what each state permits, see Stephen Butler and Susan Peck, *Alternative Low-Income Housing Delivery Systems for Rural America* (Washington, D.C.: Housing Assistance Council, February 1974), pp. 15–16.

year per unit if occupied by elderly tenants.[46] Since this was too little, Congress in 1969 removed the dollar limit and specified that no tenant's rent would exceed 25 percent of adjusted gross income.[47] Insufficient funding is still a problem.

Tenant eligibility is determined by statute and local rule. HUD finances capital improvements in public housing to raise living conditions, correct physical defects, and improve operating efficiency and costs.[48] In the 1978 fiscal year, about 800 public housing authorities received about $474.7 million.[49]

With all the money being spent, how do the tenants themselves feel about public housing? Genung reported a concern with unsightliness of the buildings, poor productive authorization levels and maintenance, and unresponsive bureaucrats.[50] Other problems were related to poor social services and security. In 1978 HUD instituted a Public Housing Urban Initiatives Program, for those with 1,250 or more units under management, to aid large projects with rehabilitation, management, and security.[51]

In addition to traditional public housing, two other programs deserve mention. In the Turnkey method, public housing authorities invite proposals from developers to meet specific housing needs. "The authorities then commit themselves to buy the projects on completion, when the developer turns over the key. HUD has found this method is substantially more efficient than the conventional approach."[52]

The Section 23 program permitted the LPHA to lease housing from private owners and rent it to lower-income tenants.[53] The LPHA pays the difference between 25 percent of the tenants' income and the market rent. This program was replaced by the Section 8 Lower Income Rental Assistance Program.

RENTAL ASSISTANCE

In addition to public housing programs, rental assistance programs include the Section 101 rent supplement program, Section 236, and the most recent program, Section 8.

RENT SUPPLEMENTS This program provides federal payments to reduce rents for certain low-income persons.[54] HUD pays rent supplements on their behalf to multi-family housing owners of new or rehabilitated units insured by the FHA. The payment is the difference between 25 percent of a tenant's adjusted income and the fair market rent determined by HUD. The subsidy is limited to 70 percent of the fair market rent of any unit.

---

[46]Housing Act of 1961, Public Law 87–70, Sec. 203, 75 Stat 149.

[47]Housing and Urban Development Act of 1969, Public Law 91–152, 83 Stat 379.

[48]U.S. Housing Act of 1937, Public Law 75–412, as amended by Section 7(d); Department of Housing and Urban Development Act of 1965, Public Law 89–174; U.S. Department of Housing and Urban Development *HUD Programs,* (Washington, D.C.: U.S. Government Printing Office.) HUD-214-4-PA, May 1978, p. 37.

[49]*HUD Programs,* p. 37.

[50]Genung, "Public Housing," 742–52.

[51]*HUD Newsletter* (Washington, D.C., July 24, 1978).

[52]U.S. Department of Housing and Urban Development, *HUD News,* No. 76-431 (Washington, D.C., Nov. 24, 1976), 2.

[53]*HUD Programs,* p. 35.

[54]Housing and Urban Development Act of 1965, Public Law 89–117, Sec. 101.

HUD may pay the supplements for a maximum term of forty years. Eligibility is limited to low-income households that qualify for public housing and are either elderly, handicapped, displaced by government actions, victims of national disaster, occupants of substandard housing, or headed by a person serving on active military duty.[55] New rent supplement contracts are no longer available since the program was suspended in January 1973. Today the program is amending contracts and converting 236 rent supplements to 236 *deep subsidy* assistance.

Owners of housing units insured under Sections 221(d) (3), 231, 236, and 202 may apply for rent supplements. The most popular program has been Section 221(d) (3).[56] This enabled low- and moderate-income families to rent standard housing. Nonprofit organizations, limit-dividend corporations, and cooperatives, as well as some public agencies, were eligible. Interest rates were low, and the FHA insured both the construction and a permanent loan.[57] The locally determined maximum income for public housing became the minimum income needed for 221(d)(3) housing. The maximum equaled the median family income in the local community. Priorities in admitting families were given to the displaced, the elderly, and the handicapped.

SECTION 236   The Section 236 program of Rental and Cooperative Housing aid for lower-income families provides for mortgage insurance, interest reduction, and operating subsidies to reduce rents.[58] Originally HUD insured multi-family mortgages and paid interest subsidies to lenders. The reduction in interest kept monthly rents low and thus made the housing affordable for lower-income households. Beginning in 1974, HUD has paid additional subsidies to cover operating costs since tenants contribute no more than 25 percent of their adjusted income. The program was suspended in January 1973; current activity consists of honoring commitments made before the moratorium. Through June 1977, 4,217 projects with 460,188 units were insured for over $7.6 billion.[59] Sponsors included nonprofit corporations, cooperatives, or private builders who, after construction, sell the units to nonprofit corporations or cooperatives, or to limited-profit corporations. There is a limit on the amount of the mortgage as well as a percent limitation.

Section 236 is the foremost example of government aid for privately developed and financed rental housing. It was effective in providing housing for moderate-income households during a period when moderate-priced rental housing was shrinking rapidly.[60] The U.S. Comptroller General urged its revival and continuance. Households aided by the Section 236 program are different from those helped by other multi-family subsidy programs. They are smaller and

---

[55]*HUD Programs*, p. 32.

[56]Section 221(d)(3), National Housing Act of 1934, Public Law 73–479, as amended by Housing Act of 1954, Public Law 83–560.

[57]*HUD Programs*, p. 27.

---

[58]Section 236, National Housing Act 1934, Public Law 73–479 as amended by Section 201 Housing and Urban Development Act of 1968, Public Law 90–448; *HUD Programs*, p. 31.

[59]*HUD Programs*, p. 31.

[60]Comptroller General of the United States, *Section 236 Rental Housing–An Evaluation with Lessons for the Future* (Washington, D.C., January 1978), p. ii.

have higher incomes than public housing tenants. They tend to be younger and are more likely to earn most of their incomes than to receive welfare, retirement pensions, or other assistance.[61]

The 1974 Housing and Community Development Act permitted payment of a subsidy to tenants to cover increased rents caused by rising tax and utility costs.[62] The program was never implemented, and HUD became involved in litigation as tenants tried to enforce its enactment. As part of the settlement in a class action suit by 236 tenants, HUD has agreed to pay the amount credited to the 236 Rental Housing Assistance Fund as of September 30, 1977, for distribution.[63] Final approval will come after a March 1979 hearing.

SECTION 8   As part of the 1974 Housing and Community Development Act, a new program of housing aid known as Section 8 came into being.[64] Section 8 provides the difference between the housing costs a family can afford and the cost of standard housing in an area. To be eligible, a tenant's income must not exceed 80 percent of the median income of the area. But at least 30 percent of the families assisted under Section 8 must be very-low-income families at the time of initial rental; that is, their incomes must be less than 50 percent of the median for the area. Tenants pay no more than 25 percent of adjusted income toward rent.

Housing units may be new or rehabilitated as well as existing. They must meet certain code standards and rent criteria. Landlords must agree to lease provisions. The existing housing must be inadequate, as determined by HUD, before new or rehabilitated units qualify. Sponsors include nonprofit as well as profit organizations, public housing agencies, or state housing finance agencies. When existing housing is used, the local public housing agencies certify the tenants, inspect the units, and contract with the landlords for payment of their share. HUD establishes a rent schedule by area, unit, and structural type that limits the amount to be spent. In 1977, the Section 8 program was the major federally subsidized program available.

In a 1976 report to Congress, the U.S. Comptroller General reported a need to improve administration and increase activity. Major problems included rents that may be too low, unavailability of acceptable standard units for rents specified, and regulations that keep developers, landlords, and tenants from participating. As of September 30, 1976, private developers were building and rehabilitating only about 10,000 units; only about 1,306 were occupied.

HUD officials report the advantages of Section 8. These include: avoiding concentrations of lower-income persons, giving them freedom of choice to find housing, and serving a broad range of incomes.

The Comptroller General criticized the program for its limited success. He claimed that developers had trouble obtaining financing; owners were reluctant to participate because payments were too low; and some communities felt that their allocations were too low and concen-

---

[61] Ibid., p. iii.

[62] U.S. Department of Housing and Urban Development, *Consumer Notice*, "Settlement Agreement," in *Underwood* v. *Harris*, n.d.

[63] *Underwood* v. *Harris*, U.S. District Court for the District of Columbia.

[64] Housing and Community Development Act of 1974, Public Law 93–383, amended U.S. Housing Act of 1937.

trations were too high.[65] In analyzing costs of the Section 8 and 236 rental housing program, the Comptroller General concluded that Section 8 existing units cost less than Section 8 or 236 new units. Section 8 is also more flexible.[66]

The Congressional Budget Office reported that for four programs that assist low- or moderate-income households, the Section 8 existing housing program is least expensive. Section 236, public housing, and Section 8, new construction, cost more because they not only assist families but also support housing construction.[67]

HOME OWNERSHIP ASSISTANCE

Most of the programs that have helped families and individuals to buy homes are insurance programs; that is, the federal government insures the borrower's loan. Specific programs are designed for poor credit risks, for those who buy housing in a declining neighborhood, or for other groups. The most widely recognized mortgage insurance program is Section 203(b)—the FHA. Properties must meet all applicable FHA Minimum Property Standards, but there are no special qualifications for borrowers. Anyone with a good credit record who can make the down payment and shows the ability to meet the mortgage can be approved. This program is available in both rural and urban areas.

SECTION 235 Mortgage insurance and interest subsidies to low- and moderate-income home buyers are provided under Section 235.[68] The buyer must pay 20 percent of adjusted income on monthly mortgage payments and make a down payment of 6 percent (including closing costs). The applicant's adjusted income must not exceed 95 percent of the area's median income. There is no restriction on assets. Adjusted income is based on family size and on factors such as construction costs and unusually low median income areas—for example, one person, 67 percent; two persons, 76 percent; three persons, 85 percent; four persons, 95 percent; five persons, 101 percent; six persons, 107 percent; seven persons, 113 percent; and eight or more, 119 percent.[69] Mortgage limits are $25,000 for a three-bedroom unit and $29,000 for a four-bedroom unit. In high-cost areas, these amounts may be increased by $4,000.

The subsidy is attached to the house, not the occupant. Profit-oriented builders may produce units. Over an eight-year period, 478,353 units have been insured, with a value of about $8.6 billion.[70] Section 235 assistance payments are also available to help lower-income families join a cooperative association that operates a housing project with a mortgage insured under Section 213, or to buy a condominium under Section 234. On a limited basis in selected areas, a buyer-oriented counseling program, Home-

[65]Comptroller General of the U.S., *Major Changes Are Needed in the New Leased-Housing Program,* ED-77-19 (Washington, D.C., January 1977), pp. 54, 68.

[66]Comptroller General of the U.S., *Comparative Costs of the Department of HUD's Section 8 and 236 Rental Housing Programs,* RED-75-349 (Washington, D.C., April 1975), p. 18.

[67]Congressional Budget Office, *Housing Assistance for Low- and Moderate-Income Families,* (Washington, D.C.: U.S. Government Printing Office, February 1977), p. xiv.

[68] Section 235, National Housing Act of 1934, as added by Section 101, Housing and Urban Development Act of 1968, Public Law 90–448.

[69]U.S. Department of Housing and Urban Development, *HUD News,* HUD No. 76-42 (Nov. 19, 1976), Washington, D.C., p. 6.

[70]*HUD Programs,* 1978, p. 17.

ownership Counseling (Section 235/237), designed to promote and protect the interests of the home buyer, is available.[71]

THE FmHA   Under the FmHA Section 502 program, families in rural areas are helped to buy homes. Housing units must be moderate, in a population area of less than 10,000 or, in some cases, less than 20,000. There are income limits, and the borrower must be ineligible for a conventional mortgage. Little or no down payment is required.

MAINTENANCE AND REHABILITATION

Because some people have bought homes under federal programs that were not structurally sound, Congress enacted a program of compensation for substantial defects.[72] Homes bought between August 1968 and August 1976 under Section 235, Section 203, or Section 221(d)(2) with critical defects existing when the mortgage commitment was made fell under this program. From March 1975 to July 1976, 12,659 valid claims were submitted for an average payment of $900.[73]

Section 115 rehabilitation grants are for the repair and improvement of owner-occupied houses of eligible families. These grants are designed to bring the housing up to urban renewal specifications under the local housing code.[74]

Grants of up to $3,500 are available but cannot exceed the cost of repairs and improvements. If a person's income is too high, the grant pays the difference between the total cost and the amount that can be financed by a Section 312 loan. Section 115 grants have been superseded by the Community Development Block Grant Program and are available only in areas that still have funding from earlier times.

Section 312 loans are direct federal loans of up to $27,000 at 3 percent interest. They are given to home owners in urban renewal areas, concentrated code enforcement areas, or areas marked by local governments for public improvements. The loans are also available to participants in the Section 810 Urban Homesteading Demonstration Program. By financing rehabilitation, basically sound structures are preserved. From 1964 through September 30, 1977, $471 million was loaned.[75]

Section 504, the Rural Housing Repair Program, allows low-income owners to finance repairs for their houses. Funds are limited to repairs or improvements that will correct health and safety hazards. Recipients must be unable to obtain financing under the FmHA Section 502 home ownership program. Loans of up to $2,500 are available for repairs or $3,500 if the repairs involve plumbing facilities such as a bathroom, septic tank, or kitchen; the repayment period is ten years. Loans under $1,500 may be secured with a promissory note; larger loans require a mortgage.[76]

Community Development Block Grant

---

[71]U.S. Department of HUD, *Section 235 (i) Homeownership for Lower Income Families, HUD Program Guide,* for builders, sponsors, lenders, and sellers, HPMC-FHA G 4441.31 (Washington, D.C., April 1972).

[72]National Housing Act of 1934, Section 518(b), Public Law 73-479, as added by the Housing and Community Development Act of 1974, Public Law 93-383.

[73]*HUD Programs,* 1977, p. 22.

[74]Housing Act of 1949, Section 115, Public Law 81-171.

[75]*HUD Programs,* 1977, p. 5.

[76]Housing Act of 1949, Section 504, 81-171.

Maintenance and rehabilitation needs receive some federal support.

(CDBG) funds may be allocated to rehabilitation programs; more than 1,500 localities are participating.[77] Aid may be in the form of a direct grant or loan, a *conditional grant* or *forgivable loan*, a partial loan or grant, subsidization of the interest or principal, or guarantee. Eligibility requirements are determined locally.

HOUSING ALLOWANCES

Housing allowances are grants to lower-income families to be spent on housing. This strategy influences the demand for housing and allows families to make their own choice. A housing allowance differs from unrestricted cash assistance, since the subsidy involves requirements such as minimum housing standards.

The housing allowance concept as part of national housing policy has been debated since the 1930s. There have been legislative hearings on "rent certificates," as housing allowances were termed.[78]

---

[77]U.S. Department of Housing and Urban Development, *A Guide to Housing Rehabilitation Programs* (Washington, D.C., August 1978), pp. 1–3.

[78]U.S. Congress, House Committee on Banking and Currency, *To Create Housing Authority*, 75th Congress, 1st Session, HR-5033, S-1685, 1937; U.S. Congress, Senate Subcommittee Housing and Urban Redevelopment of Special Senate Committee on Post War Economic Policy and Planning, *Post War Economic Policy and Planning*, 78th Congress, 1st Session, S. Res. 102, Part 6, 1945; U.S. Congress, Subcommittee of Senate Committee on the District of Columbia, *Investigation of the program of the National Capital Housing Authority*, 78th Congress, 2nd Session, S. Res. 184, Part 1, October 1943, January/February, 1944; and U.S. Congress, Subcommittee of Senate Committee on the District of Columbia, *Investigation of the Program of the National Capital Housing Authority*, 78th Congress, 2nd Session, S. Res. 184, S-1699, Part II, February 1944.

The 1953 Report of the President's Advisory Committee on Government Housing Policies and Programs considered the concept but rejected it in favor of the conventional public housing program.[79] The 1965 Housing and Urban Development Act enacted rent supplement and leased housing. Thus, housing policy shifted toward the idea of an allowance. In 1968, the President's Committee on Urban Housing recommended that the housing allowance approach be tried on an experimental basis.[80] In 1970, Model Cities agencies in Kansas City, Missouri, and Wilmington, Delaware, undertook small-scale demonstrations.[81] In the 1970 Housing Act, Congress authorized a national experiment to test policy questions.[82] Some issues of concern are:[83]

1. What is the effect of housing allowances on the housing market, including price and supply? What if there are so few vacancies in an area that housing choice is limited?

2. What kinds of families participate?

3. Do the families that participate buy more housing? Do they make changes in the other goods they buy? Which ones and what kinds of changes?

4. What kind of administrative process is needed? What kind is most efficient? What formula works best?

5. How does a requirement of a standard unit affect the participation and the market?

The Experimental Housing Allowance Program (EHAP) consists of three parts:

1. A Demand Experiment to observe how allowances are used by program participants.

2. A Supply Experiment to investigate the effects on housing markets and prices.

3. An Administrative Agency Experiment to assess different administrative procedures.

In selected communities, housing allowances are given to families who cannot afford a decent home in a suitable living environment. To be eligible, a person must meet the income requirements and choose or live in a unit that meets housing standards or rent guidelines.

Participation in EHAP has been affected by awareness of the program, perception of a "welfare" stigma, and the anticipated size of allowance payments.[84] Minority enrollment rates were higher than nonminority rates. Elderly households were less likely to enroll than all households. Welfare families enrolled

[79]President's Advisory Committee on Government Housing, Report 1953, *Government Housing Policies and Programs* (1953), pp. 261–63, 323–30.

[80]President's Committee on Urban Housing, *A Decent Home* (Washington, D.C.: U.S. Government Printing Office, 1969), p. 7.

[81]Arthur Solomon and Chester G. Fenton, "The Nation's First Experience with Housing Allowances: The Kansas City Demonstration," *Land Economics,* 50 (August 1974), 213–23; and U.S. Department of Housing and Urban Development, *First Annual Report of the Experimental Housing Allowance Program* (Washington, D.C.: Office of Policy Development and Research, May 1973).

[82]U.S. Department of Housing and Urban Development, *Housing Allowances: The 1976 Report to Congress,* Office of Policy Development and Research, (Washington, D.C.: U.S. Government Printing Office, February 1976).

[83]Carol B. Meeks, "Review of the Housing Allowance Program," *The Journal of Consumer Affairs* 10 (Winter 1976), 208–23.

[84]David B. Carlson and John D. Heinberg, *How Housing Allowances Work* (Washington, D.C.: The Urban Institute, February 1978), p. x.

more often than others; the reverse was true for the working poor. About half of all participating families met the housing requirements at the time of enrollment. All were able to pay smaller percentages of preallowance incomes for rent.

Any housing allowance program must determine whether housing prices will increase while housing quality remains the same. As of 1977–1978, there was no evidence of program-induced price inflation. Part of the reason was the relatively low participation rate and the small increase in housing expenditures.[85]

In analyzing the program, both management costs and cost of the transfer payment were considered. Changes in management procedures have affected the cost of bringing families in and maintaining them in the program.

The three EHAP experiments will continue to be analyzed. Whether a housing allowance program will be adopted on a national level is still under review.

COMMUNITY DEVELOPMENT

Community development programs are closely related to housing and in many cases include aspects of housing. Programs that involve housing are highlighted here.

MODEL CITIES Title I of the 1966 Demonstration Cities and Metropolitan Development Act enacted the Model Cities program, a comprehensive attack on social, economic, and physical problems in selected slum and blighted areas.[86] Grants and technical aid were available to help cities carry out this program. The grants were designed to supplement

other aid. Cities were required to coordinate resources and to involve neighborhood residents in planning, monitoring, and evaluating five-year plans. Activities included housing as well as physical improvements of the environment. Cities and towns of all sizes were eligible. When the program was superseded by the Housing and Community Development Act of 1974, 145 cities had been funded for $22 million in planning grants, $2.5 million in operating funds, and $29.5 million in technical aid.[87]

URBAN RENEWAL In 1954 the Housing Act of 1949 was amended to include an Urban Renewal Program of federal aid to eliminate blight in certain urban areas.[88] Urban renewal goals included eliminating blight and slum conditions, making the central city more competitive with the suburbs, and making central city governments financially stronger. Federal grants paid two-thirds of the net cost for cities with populations over 50,000 and for areas designated as economic development areas by the Department of Commerce. Planning activities, land acquisition and clearing, construction of new buildings as well as rehabilitation of old ones, and public improvement such as streets, sidewalks, utilities, and preservation of historic structures were all eligible activities. The Urban Renewal Program was superseded by the 1974 Housing and Community Development Act. As of June 30, 1976, grants paid out and reserved for future repayment or urban renewal notes included $61.4 million for community renewal, $333.3 million for

[85]Ibid., p. xv.
[86]Public Law 89–754.

[87]HUD Programs, 1978, p. 8.
[88]Public Law 81–171, as amended by the Housing Act of 1954, 83–560.

code enforcement, and $10.4 million for demonstration projects.[89]

COMMUNITY DEVELOPMENT BLOCK GRANTS
The 1974 Housing and Community Development Act was designed to develop communities with decent housing and a suitable living environment and to expand economic opportunities, mainly for persons with low or moderate incomes.[90] Many of the programs discussed above were superseded by this act, which generally combines their purposes, objectives, and eligible activities. The act tries to build upon the individual program strengths. It increases the flexibility and certainty of federal aid while relating it more closely to local needs and goals.

HUD awards "block" grants to local governments to fund a wide range of community development activities, including the activities previously conducted under Model Cities, urban renewal, neighborhood development grants, rehabilitation loans, and urban beautification and historic preservation grants. Priorities are determined locally, but communities must estimate their lower-income housing needs and address them in the overall plan to receive their grant. Cities and urban counties (populations of at least 50,000 and 200,000, respectively) are guaranteed an amount (entitlement) based on need. Need is determined by a formula that takes into account population, poverty, and overcrowded housing. Smaller communities may compete for the funds available. Matching funds are not required. For a three-year transition period, local governments that took part in categorical

grant programs but did not qualify for block grants were funded at a level to complete projects underway. Housing-related activities that may be funded include code enforcement, clearance and rehabilitation of buildings and improvements, increased access for the elderly and handicapped, relocation costs, and disposal of real property.

In March 1978, HUD issued the final regulations for Community Development Block Grants (CDBG) for small cities.[91] Communities chosen for funding will be those with the greatest need, as shown by poverty and substandard housing, and that deal adequately with locally determined needs of low- and moderate-income persons. Local plans must do one or more of the following:

1. Support realistic and attainable strategies for expanding low- and moderate-income housing opportunities.

2. Promote dispersal of lower-income housing.

3. Promote more rational land use.

4. Provide more economic opportunities for low- and moderate-income persons.

5. Rehabilitate public facilities that affect public health or safety, especially for low- and moderate-income persons.

Communities may also apply for single-purpose grants.

A required local housing aid plan is a major change in federal housing and

---

[89]*HUD Programs*, 1978, p. 13.
[90]Public Law 93—383.

[91]U.S. Department of Housing and Urban Development, "Community Development Block Grants: Eligible Activities," *Federal Register*, Part III (Mar. 1, 1978), p. 8482.

community development policy. The plan must survey the housing stock and assess the aid needed by lower-income persons, including the elderly, the handicapped, large families, and displaced persons. The plan must also specify a realistic annual goal for the number of dwelling units needed, including: (1) relative proportions of new, rehabilitated, and existing units, and (2) the sizes and types of housing projects and aid best suited to local lower-income residents. In terms of the location of proposed housing, community revitalization, greater housing choice, dispersal of low-income persons, and availability of public facilities must be considered.

In 1978 HUD's new regulations made the CDBG program more responsive to the needs of low- and moderate-income persons.[92] HUD specifies that if a town, city, or urban county submits a plan for funds which budgets at least 75 percent of its block grant to benefit low- and moderate-income residents, the plan will be accepted. Plans that use less than 75 percent of their funds for the poor will be subject to review. This is to ensure that the program benefits mainly low- and moderate-income persons. Applications which do not do so may have their plans disapproved or funds reallocated. These new regulations limit somewhat the freedom given to communities by block grants.

URBAN HOMESTEADING Homesteading allows people to receive title to land for little or no cost except construction of a housing unit or rehabilitation of one and a period of occupancy. Homesteading in America dates back to the pre-Revolu-

tionary era, when future Virginians were given free land to develop.[93] In 1862, Americans could receive 160 acres in the West for a $26 fee and a five-year residency period.

The Depression of the 1930s revitalized interest in homesteading. Section 208, Title 2, of the 1933 National Industrial Recovery Act gave loans and purchase help to *subsistence* homesteads. The three main programs were for communities of part-time farmers, resettlement of submarginal farmers, and colonies with newly decentralized industry.

Urban homesteading exists as both federal and city programs. It involves buying an abandoned inner-city house, bringing it up to code requirements, and an occupancy period that varies with the program. The fee itself is also variable. The objective is to make previously unattractive units available at little or no cost.

The average rehabilitation cost for the first 118 properties restored was $5,600 per unit. The average homesteader and his or her family spent more than eleven work weeks of their own time on repairs. Homesteaders have a mean income of $12,300 and an average family size of 3.3 persons. They tend to be younger than other local residents and more optimistic about the future of their neighborhood.[94]

NEW COMMUNITIES "New communities" or "new towns" have been of interest in

---

[92]*Federal Register* (Mar. 1, 1978), pp. 8450–74.

[93]For a detailed history of homesteading, see James W. Hughes and Kenneth D. Bleakly, Jr., *Urban Homesteading* (New Brunswick, N.J.: The Center for Urban Policy Research, Rutgers University, 1975).

[94]U.S. Department of Housing and Urban Development, *HUD News*, HUD-No. 77-361 (Washington, D.C., Nov. 29, 1977). For more detail, see *Evaluation of the Urban Homesteading Demonstration Program*, U.S. Department of Housing and Urban Development, October 1977.

the Western world since Ebenezer Howard promoted "garden cities" for England in 1898. During the 1920s, Radburn, New Jersey, and Sunnyside in Queens, New York, were built as new towns by private sponsors. Then, during Franklin D. Roosevelt's administration, "greenbelt" towns in Maryland, Ohio, and Wisconsin were built under government direction to generate jobs and provide communities for moderate-income families. The federal government also

U.S. Department of HUD.

New communities, Columbia, Maryland.

built new towns at Los Alamos, New Mexico, Oak Ridge, Tennessee, and Hanford, California, during World War II in connection with its atomic weapon development program. Park Forest, south of Chicago, and Columbia and Reston in the Washington, D.C. area are examples of more recent new communities.

The federal government strongly supports the development of new communities. They are seen as a means to conserve land resources, minimize transportation problems, increase housing choices, and promote economic development. The government's role is crucial. Few private firms have the capital to invest in new communities and the ability to wait a long time before receiving a return on their investment.

Federal action on new communities began with Title X of the 1965 National Housing Act, which provides a mortgage insurance program. Insurance covered up to 50 percent of land costs and 90 percent of improvement costs. Little activity was generated under this act since the buyer still needed a large amount of equity.

Therefore, Title IV of the 1968 Housing and Urban Development Act was passed. It provided loan guarantees for further costs and authorized other grants for items such as water and sewers. Title IV was little more successful than Title X. Continued concern with city growth and development led to Title VII of the 1970 Housing and Urban Development Act. This extended the guaranteed aid and authorized grants for new communities undertaken by private or public developers. "Eleven new community projects eventually received loan guarantee assistance ranging from $5 million to the stat-

utory limit of $50 million."[95] Two other developers received loan guarantee aid under Title IV.

Unfortunately, national economic conditions led to serious financial problems. Developers had heavy front end costs, and the government did not use new towns as a way of channeling growth. HUD is now evaluating results to date and trying to correct some of the problems noted.

The New Towns Intown (NTIT) program focuses on redeveloping or revitalizing part of existing communities. The NTIT scale should be determined by development potential of an area rather than by physical blight, social conditions, or available vacant land. The aim is to create a viable community. The new town intown should include a wider area than a typical Urban Renewal project or Model Cities neighborhood. Size should depend on the requirements of central city modernization and should consider: (a) type and location of public service systems and facilities, (b) present and future economic potential for development, (c) type and nature of transportation networks, and (d) community awareness, relative strength of community institutions, and citizen participation.[96] HUD guidelines set 100 acres and 12,000 in population as minimal for new town intown federal aid, derived basically from the first approved NTIT project (Cedar—Riverside). The supply of NTIT housing must not be sacrificed to meet other objectives. New housing will probably have to be sub-

[95]U.S. Department of Housing and Urban Development, *New Communities: Problems and Potentials* (Washington, D.C., December 1976), p. 3.

[96]Harvey S. Perloff, Tom Berg, Robert Fountain, David Vetter, and John Weld, *Modernizing the Central City* (Cambridge, Mass: Ballinger, 1975), p. 388.

TABLE 11-2. Summary of New Communities Approved by HUD

Community	GUARANTEE COMMITMENT Amount ($1000s)	Projected Population	DEVELOPMENT PERIOD (Years)	Acres	Percent Residential
Maumelle, Ark.	$ 14,000	45,000	20	5,319	38
Shenandoah, Ga.	25,000	70,000	20	7,200	32
Park Forest South, Ill.	30,000	110,000	15	8,163	59
St. Charles Communities, Md.	38,000	75,000	20	7,408	59
Cedar-Riverside, Minn.[b,d]	24,000	30,000	20	101	83[f]
Jonathan, Minn.[a,d]	21,000	50,000	20	8,194	29
Gananda, N.Y.[c,d]	22,000	50,000	20	4,733	51
Radisson, N.Y.		18,000	20	2,670	34
Riverton, N.Y.[d]	16,000	25,600	16	2,437	49
Roosevelt Island, N.Y.		18,000	7	143	27
Soul City, N.C.	5,000	30,000	20	5,180	33
Newfields, Ohio[d]	18,000	40,000	20	4,032	54
Harbison, S.C.	13,000	23,000	20	1,740	42
Flower Mound, Tex.[a]	18,000	64,000	20	6,156	49
San Antonio Ranch, Tex.[e]	18,000	88,000	30	9,318	45
The Woodlands, Tex.	50,000	150,000	20	17,000	37
Total	$294,000				

Key: [a]Acquired by HUD.

[b]Future is determined by the court and the city government.

[c]HUD has determined that it lacks potential and will end its commitment.

[d]Bonds have been called.

[e]State Land Development Agency projects: Obligations not guaranteed by HUD, but project is eligible for other program benefits. Subject to final CDC review.

[f]Open space and schools in elevated buildings are counted under residential and commercial uses.

Source: U.S. Department of Housing and Urban Development, HUD News, HUD No. 76-346 (Sept. 29, 1976); HUD No. 78-19 (Jan. 18, 1978).

sidized for low- and moderate-income families. Relocation costs may be an expensive part of NTIT development.

Central city development may be subsidized for land acquisition and clearance, and improvements as well as planning. Federal loans may also reduce financing costs. Various housing subsidy programs are generally used.

The Urban Development Action Grant Program is designed for urban areas in distress and requires strong private funding before a city can be eligible.[97]

[97]1977 Housing and Community Development Act.

Minimum criteria include average unemployment (for large cities only), age of housing in the community, percentage of persons at the poverty level, lag in per person income, lag in population growth, and stagnating manufacturing and retailing employment.

Summary

This chapter has briefly described major federal housing programs. These programs have an economic, social, and environmental influence on society. As indicated, the programs were often enacted to achieve goals apart from housing. Thus, in terms of evaluation, one must consider whether the program achieves its objectives, whether benefits outweigh costs, who benefits, and if the program is efficient.

Two guides in analyzing programs are vertical and horizontal equity. Vertical equity states that the poorest persons receive the most aid; horizontal equity states that persons in the same circumstances receive equal treatment.

Federal housing programs may develop in several directions. Housing allowance experiments may lead to greater demand for consumer subsidies. Economic concerns may create more incentives for production. Cost increases and inflation may promote aid for moderate and middle-income families. Energy policy may dictate the structure and type of new housing.

Terms

conditional grant   grant that must be repaid if a property owner does not meet preset conditions.

deep subsidy   an especially large amount of financial aid.

forgivable loan   loan that does not have to be repaid if certain conditions are met.

homesteading   property claimed by a household under homestead law.

housing authority   a public body which provides and manages housing, especially for low-income groups.

statutory   created by law.

subpoena   court order for a person or documents to be presented in court.

subsidy   financial aid provided by the government.

Suggested Readings

Aaron, Henry J., *Shelter and Subsidies.* Washington, D.C.: The Brookings Institution, 1972.

Ahlbrandt, Roger S., Jr., "Delivery System for Federally-Assisted Housing Services: Constraints, Locational Decisions and Policy Implications," *Land Economics,* I (August 1974), 242–50.

Brooks, Richard O., "The Policy Issues of New Towns: One Failure of Law to Guide Planning in America," *Urban Lawyer* 8 (Winter 1976), 94–122.

Brueggeman, William B., "Federal Housing Subsidies: Conceptual Issues and Benefit Patterns," *Journal of Economics and Business* 27 (Winter 1975), 141–49.

Downs, Anthony, "Housing the Urban Poor: The Economics of Various Strategies," *The American Economic Review,* LIX, Part 1 (September 1969), 646–50.

Drewes, Chris W., "Homesteading 1974: Reclaiming Abandoned Houses on the Urban Frontier," *Columbia Journal of Law and Social Problems,* 10 (Summer 1974), 416–55.

Hartman, Chester W., *Housing and Social Policy,* Englewood Cliffs, N.J.: Prentice-Hall, 1975.

Hirshen, Al, and Vivian N. Brown, "Too Poor for Public Housing: Roger Starr's Poverty Preferences," *Social Policy* 3 (May/June 1972), 28–32.

Landreth, Duane P. "Four Elements—Planning, Citizen Participation, Housing Assistance and A-95 Review—Under Title I of the Housing and Community Development Act of 1974," *The Urban Lawyer* 9 (Winter 1977), 61–121.

Lord, Tom Forrester, *Decent Housing: A Promise to Keep.* Cambridge, Mass.: Schenkman, 1977.

Marcuse, Peter, "Homeownership for Low Income Families: Financial Implications," *Land Economics* 48 (May 1972), 134–43.

Meehan, Eugene J., "Looking the Gift Horse in the Mouth: The Conventional Public Housing Program in St. Louis," *Urban Affairs Quarterly* 10 (June 1975), 423–63.

Meeks, Carol B., "Review of the Housing Allowance Program," *The Journal of Consumer Affairs,* 10 (Winter 1976), 208–23.

Phares, Donald, ed., *A Decent Home and Environment: Housing Urban America.* Cambridge, Mass.: Ballinger, 1977.

Prescott, James R., and Bakir Abu Kishk, "Some Evaluative Aspects of Alternative Housing Subsidies," *Journal of Economics and Business,* 27 (Winter 1975), 159–71.

"Public Housing and Urban Policy: Gautreaux v. Chicago Housing Authority," *The Yale Law Journal,* 79 (March 1970), 712–29.

Shostak, Arthur B., "New Towns and Social Welfare Prospects: 1975–2000 A.D.," *Journal of Sociology and Social Welfare,* 3 (November 1975), 131–35.

Solomon, Arthur P., *Housing the Urban Poor.* Cambridge, Mass.: MIT Press, 1974.

Steiner, Gilbert Y., *The State of Welfare.* Washington. D.C.: The Brookings Institution, 1971.

Tullock, Gordon, "Subsidized Housing in a Competitive Market: Comment." *The American Economic Review,* LXI (March 1971), 218–24.

Weinstein, Jerome I., "Housing Subsidies: An Overview," *Journal of Urban Law,* 51 (May 1974), 723–50.

Welfeld, Irving, "American Housing Policy: Perverse Programs by Prudent People," *Public Interest,* 48 (Summer 1977), 128–44.

Wendt, Paul F., Housing Policy—The Search for Solutions. Berkeley, Calif.: University of California Press, 1963.

STATE AND LOCAL
GOVERNMENT POLICIES

1. IDENTIFY MAJOR ROLES OF STATE GOVERN-
   MENT WHICH EFFECT HOUSING.

2. HOW DO REGULATIONS SUCH AS BUILDING
   CODES OR ZONING EFFECT HOUSING
   PRICES?

3. DISCUSS THE RELATIONSHIP OF PROPERTY
   TAXES TO HOUSING.

4. ARE PROPERTY TAXES REGRESSIVE OR PRO-
   GRESSIVE?

5. WHAT ARE GOVERNMENTS DOING TO EN-
   COURAGE ENERGY CONSERVATION?

Many activities of state and local governments affect housing. Some governments have specific housing policies. Other policies, such as those related to land use, building codes, and highway construction, also impinge on housing. These activities help communities to choose and develop local or state policy.

State Government

In the early twentieth century, the location, character, and quantity of housing were mainly a matter of private responsibility and local control. This tradition ended with the Depression and the post World War II years as the federal government created housing programs.[1] State governments began to take a major role in the late 1960s as more statewide activities were required. Early state actions included attempts to standardize building codes and their administration, establishment of housing finance agencies, and revision and equalization of the landlord-tenant relationship.

Most states have a government agency responsible for housing policy and community development (Table 12-1). State community affairs agencies take an active role in housing. Departments of Community Affairs are organized as cabinet-

---

[1]Spencer Parratt, *Housing Code Administration and Enforcement*, PHS Publication N. 1999, (Washington, D.C.: U.S. Government Printing Office, 1970), p. viii.

Building codes regulate new construction.

level departments in thirty states and as major offices or divisions in fifteen states.[2] They generally plan activities and support local planning efforts. These agencies often provide local governments with information and technical aid. State activities related to housing include:

1. Research or policy analysis.
2. Housing finance.
3. Land use legislation and planning.
4. State housing and building codes.
5. Environmental standards.
6. Landlord-tenant relationships.

Since 1970, at least half of the states have established home ownership programs.[3] Most of the programs are for moderate-income families, and most provide aid in financing the home. The program often begins with the establishment of a state housing finance agency (HFA).

STATE HOUSING FINANCE AGENCIES

A powerful force in housing development lending, state housing finance agencies (HFAs) have been growing in number since the early 1960s. More than

[2]State Departments of Community Affairs (Washington, D.C.: Council of State Community Affairs Agencies, June 1978).

[3]"Survey of State Programs Designed to Encourage Homeownership," *Law Project Bulletin* V (January/February 1975), 3–10.

TABLE 12-1. Functions and Capabilities of State Housing and Development Agencies, by State

	FUNCTIONS OF HFAs[1]						FUNCTIONS OF DCAs			STATE LEGISLATION			
	Housing Finance or Housing Development Agency	Mortgage Loans	Construction Loans	Acquire Land	Rehab Programs: including tax incentives	Technical Assistance	DCA or Planning and Development Agency	Comm. Dev. Programs	Housing Programs	Statewide Bldg. Act[4]	Statewide Housing Code[3]	State Land Use Controls General[2]	State Environmental Review Programs[5]
Alabama							X	X	X	X		1	X
Alaska	X	X	S	S	S	X	X	X	X			2	X
Arizona							X	X	X			2	
Arkansas	X		S	S		S	X	X	X			2	
California	X	S	S		S		X	X	X	XM	XM	2	X
Colorado	X	X	X		X	X	X	X	X			X	X
Connecticut	X	X	X	S	X	X	X	X	X	XO	XM	2	X
Delaware	X	S	X	S	X	X	X	X	X			2	X
Florida							X	X	X			X	X
Georgia	X	X	S		S	S	X	X	X		XM	2	X
Hawaii	X	X	X	X	S	X						X	X
Idaho	X	X	X	X	S	S	X	X	X			X	X
Illinois	X	X	X	X	X	X	X	X	X			2	X
Indiana							X	X	X	XM	XO	2	X
Iowa	X	S			S	S	X	X	X	XO		2	X
Kansas							X		X			2	
Kentucky	X	S	S	S	S	X	X	X	X			2	X
Louisiana	X		na		S	E	X	X	X			2	
Maine	X		X	S	S	X	X	X	X			2	X
Maryland	X	X	X	S	S	X	X	X	X			X	X
Massachusetts	X	X	X		X	X	X	X	X	XM	XM	X	X
Michigan	X	X	X	S	X	X	X	X		X	XM	2	X
Minnesota	X	X	X		X	X	X	X	X	XO	XM	2	X
Mississippi							X	X	X			2	
Missouri	X	X	X		X		X	X	X			2	X
Montana	X	S	S		S	E	X	X	X	X		2	X
Nebraska							X	X	X			2	
Nevada	X	S	X		S	S	X	X	X			X	
New Hampshire	X	S	S		S	S	X	X	X	X		2	
New Jersey	X	X	X	S	X	X	X	X	X	XO	XM	2	X
New Mexico	X	na	na	na	na	na	X	X	X			2	X
New York	X	X	X	X	X	X	X	X		XO	XO	X	X
N. Carolina	X				S	S	X	X	X	XM		X	X
N. Dakota							X	X	X			2	X
Ohio	X	S	S		X	X	X	X	X	XM		2	X
Oklahoma	X	S	S		S	X	X	X				2	X
Oregon	X	X	S		3	X	X	X		X		X	X
Pennsylvania	X	X	X		X	X	X	X	X			2	X
Rhode Island	X	X	X	S	X	E	X	X	X	X	XM	2	X
S. Carolina	X	S	S		S	X	X				XO	2	X
S. Dakota	X	X	X	S	S	X	X			X		2	X
Tennessee	X	X	X	S	X	X	X		X			2	

271

TABLE 12-1. Continued

	FUNCTIONS OF HFAs[1]						FUNCTIONS OF DCAs			STATE LEGISLATION			
	Housing Finance or Housing Development Agency	Mortgage Loans	Construction Loans	Acquire Land	Rehab Programs: including tax incentives	Technical Assistance	DCA or Planning and Development Agency	Comm. Dev. Programs	Housing Programs	Statewide Bldg. Act[4]	Statewide Housing Code[3]	State Land Use Controls General[2]	State Environmental Review Programs[5]
Texas							X	X	X			2	
Utah	X		S		X	X	X	X	X	X	X	2	
Vermont	X	X	S		S	S	X			X		X	X
Virginia	X	X	X	S	X	X	X				X	2	X
Washington							X			X		2	X
W. Virginia	X	X	X	X	X	X	X	X	X	X		2	
Wisconsin	X	X	X	S	S	X	X	X	X	X	XM	2	X
Wyoming	X		S			S	X	X	X			X	X
Totals	40	23	22	5	16	25	49	42	43	20	11	11	38

Key: X = Operating or enacted
S = Statutory authority, but not implemented
E = Shared function with other agencies
XM = Mandatory
XO = Optional State Model
[1] = No activity at state level
[2] = Study or state legislative consideration in progress
na = figures not available

Sources:

aCouncil of State Governments, *The Book of the States, 1978–79*, Vol. 2 (Lexington, Ky. 1978), pp. 478–82. Based on 1977 Survey.

bNatural Resources Defense Council, Inc., *Land Use Controls in the United States* (New York: Dial Press, 1977), pp. 254–55.

cAdvisory Commission on Intergovernmental Relations (ACIR), *State Action on Local Problems 1972* (Washington, D.C., 1973), p. 22

———, *State Action 1973: Toward a Full Partnership* (Washington, D.C. 1974), p. 21.

dGeorge Sternlieb, *Building Codes: The State of the Art, Strategies for the Future*, PB-240 259, prepared for the U.S. Department of Housing and Urban Development (Rutgers, N.J.: State University of New Jersey, 1973), pp. 20–21.

eU.S. Department of Housing and Urban Development, *Housing in the Seventies*, (Washington, D.C., 1974), pp. 142, 151.

three-fourths of all the states engage in housing finance.[4] Activities of HFAs include financing of single-family and multi-family developments, providing loans to lenders, buying mortgages in the secondary market, and providing loans directly to home buyers.

[4]See Nathan S. Betnun, *Housing Finance Agencies* (New York: Praeger Publishers, 1976), and Peter R. Morris, *State Housing Finance Agencies* (Lexington, Mass.: Lexington Books, 1974).

Most HFAs are public corporations that are self-supporting and pay their own operating costs and overhead. They are generally independent of state executive departments. HFAs usually offer BMIRs and aid low- and moderate-income families. Thus, they try not to compete with private lenders for the same clientele. Many HFA activities related to housing development for low- and moderate-income families are supported by moral obligation bonds, a concept that originated with the New York HFA in 1960.[5] The agency sells bonds to investors with only their word as collateral. In addition, HFAs have used the Internal Revenue Code and federal housing subsidies to support housing production, including programs such as Section 8. "As of March 1, 1976, HFAs had provided direct mortgage and/or construction financing for approximately 289,000 housing units."[6] Most of these were multi-family rental units; a few were single-family houses. The majority of multi-family units received aid through the Section 236 program.

Stegman criticized early HFA efforts to provide moderate-income suburban housing rather than housing for low- and moderate-income inner-city persons.[7] He also thought that HFAs should be more involved in rehabilitating existing housing.

In gauging the success of HFAs, several measures are possible: volume of production, levels of rents or subsidies related to incomes of families served, location of housing, number of families served compared to number eligible, and racial mixture. Betnun concluded that HFAs were somewhat better in providing racially integrated housing than HUD.[8]

Housing was better designed, larger, and more luxurious—often, however, at a higher unit cost. Rent subsidies resulted in equally low rents, and units were more often available for very-low-income families.

Changing money market conditions have influenced the HFA's ability to raise capital. The development and use of a coinsurance program between HFAs and HUD will stabilize the market for HFA obligations and contribute to their long-term production capacity. A coinsurance program would share the risk between HUD and HFA for mortgages underwritten and financed by an HFA.[9] Such a program was authorized in the 1974 Housing and Community Development Act. HUD regulations have restricted the program to low-income housing and will only insure 90 percent mortgages for nonprofit sponsors.[10]

In addition to funding housing production, HFAs may choose and requisition sites, require design service, determine the size and number of units in a project, and require support facilities. They may also survey and evaluate state needs in housing. The future role of HFAs will depend on their ability to obtain capital and subsidy funds.

The Council of State Housing Agencies (CSHA) was formed in 1974 to promote the common interest of HFAs and organizations that work with HFAs in providing housing for low- and moderate-income families. The CSHA has established a library and collaborated with the Urban Institute on a computerized sur-

[5]Advisory Commission on Intergovernmental Relations, *State Legislative Program,* Part 6, Housing and Community Development (Washington, D.C., December 1975), p. 10.

[6]Kenneth G. Hance, Jr., and Thomas A. Duvall III, "Coinsurance: The Key to the Future for State Housing Finance Agencies?" *The Urban Lawyer* 8 (Fall 1976), 722.

[7]Michael A. Stegman, "Housing Finance Agencies: Are They Crucial Instruments of State Government?" *Journal of the American Institute of Planners* 40 (September 1974), 307–20.

[8]Betnun, *Housing Finance Agencies,* p. 104.

[9]See Hance and Duvall, "Coinsurance," for more details.

[10]*Housing and Development Reporter,* The Bureau of National Affairs: Washington, D.C., 1978. p. 50:0014.

vey of HFAs and the establishment of a data bank.[11]

ENVIRONMENTAL ACTIVITIES

Today, state agencies are actively involved in preservation, conservation, and regulation of the environment. There is little evidence yet of the impact of this legislation on housing. In the future, however, the location, cost, speed of housing production, and quality of the residential environment will all be affected.

One of the major environmental tasks of states is to dispose of land or regulate land use. Traditionally, land use has been decided by local governments. There is now a growing state interest in regaining control. State leaders feel that they have a broader vision and can create a more comprehensive program.

In 1975 a state land use planning program existed in forty states. Another four states had some kind of land use planning efforts. Both Hawaii and Vermont have state land use plans.[12] A statewide program could include developing data on existing land uses, projecting future needs, and developing a set of policies or regulations to guide private decisions on land use.[13]

In addition to general land use control, some states have limited commercial and housing development in certain regions, such as coastal areas, wetlands, or moun-tain wilderness areas.[14] Several states have environmental laws on scenic and open space easements.

One way to limit or control development is to require an *environmental impact statement* (EIS). This involves costs of preparation and processing time. The EIS does produce different residential developments than would otherwise have been built.[15] Some individuals see it as a means to limit low-income and multi-family housing.[16] However, the EIS does not necessarily insure environmental quality since many factors cannot be predicted.

Energy Conservation Regulations

Energy conservation is under state control. States have the authority to enforce conservation policies through their police powers. Many states are now enacting energy conservation regulations, most of them related to building codes (Table 12-2).

Not only the worthiness of energy conservation but also its economic costs and benefits must be weighed. How many families are priced out of the market as a result of new restrictions? Payback periods can be calculated for any given situation.

Solar energy is often viewed as

[11]Council of State Housing Agencies, *1977 Annual Report* (Washington, D.C., n.d.), pp. 11–12.

[12]U.S. Department of Housing and Urban Development, *Housing in the Seventies* (Washington, D.C., 1974), p. 147.

[13]U.S. Department of Housing and Urban Development, *Survey of State Land Use Planning Activity* (Washington, D.C.: The American Institute of Planners Research Office, Jan. 29, 1976), p. xii.

[14]U.S. Department of Housing and Urban Development, *State Intervention for Environmental Quality* (Washington, D.C., June 1973), p. 6.

[15]Stephen R. Seidel, *Housing Costs and Government Regulations* (New Brunswick, N.J.: The Center for Urban Policy Research, 1978), p. 241.

[16]Bruce L. Ackerman, "Impact Statements and Low Cost Housing," *Southern California Law Review* 46 (June 1973), 754–801.

TABLE 12-2. Summary of State Energy Conservation Regulations

			STATUS		COVERAGE	
State	Enacted	Proposed	Considering ASHRAE 90-75	No Activity	Single-Family	Multi-Family
Alabama				X		
Alaska		X				
Arizona		X				
Arkansas				X		
California	X[a]	X			X	X
Colorado						X
Connecticut		X	X			
Delaware		X				
Florida		X	X			
Georgia		X				
Hawaii		X				
Idaho		X				
Illinois		X				
Indiana		X	X			
Iowa		X				
Kansas		X	X			
Kentucky				X		
Louisiana		X				
Maine		X				
Maryland		X	X			
Massachusetts		X	X[b]			
Michigan		X	X			
Minnesota	X				X	X
Mississippi				X		
Missouri				X		
Montana			X			
Nebraska				X		
Nevada		X			X	X
New Hampshire		X				
New Jersey		X	X			
New Mexico		X				
New York		X			X	X
North Carolina	X		X		X	X
North Dakota		X				
Ohio	X					X
Oklahoma				X		
Oregon	X		X		X	X
Pennsylvania		X				
Rhode Island		X	X			
South Carolina		X	X			
South Dakota		X				
Tennessee		X				
Texas		X				
Utah		X				
Vermont		X				
Virginia	X		X		X	X
Washington		X			X[c]	X
West Virginia		X				
Wisconsin		X			X[d]	X
Wyoming		X				

(See Notes, p. 276.)

environmentally sound; state programs are now beginning to encourage its use (Table 12-3). Incentives related to property taxes, income, and sales taxes are being tried. States may also promote solar energy by sponsoring research and development projects.

Community Controls

Municipal or local controls are based on the police power of the state. This power provides for laws on the health, safety, and welfare of its citizens. The primary regulations that affect housing are building and housing codes, *zoning* ordinances, and *subdivision ordinances*. Not every locality has all three, nor is it always clear what each regulation covers.

BUILDING CODES

One of the regulations on housing construction is a *building code*. This controls new construction and is generally used by local governments to set minimum standards. Nearly half of all local governments have building codes. However, state involvement is increasing. Fifteen states now have statewide codes affecting one- and two-family dwellings, while four more have codes on multi-family units.[17] Nine of the fifteen codes are mandatory.

CODE CONTENT AND ENFORCEMENT   Building codes, as noted above, regulate new construction. They establish material and systems standards for durability, prevention of unsanitary or unhealthy conditions, and protection against fire or other safety hazards. The codes may vary in content and comprehensiveness.

The standards set by codes are usually expressed as *specifications* or *prescriptions* of what an item should be. A more progressive and flexible approach is the use of *performance* specifications, which state the requirements for a building component, such as the amount of load a wall must bear. Performance standards enable manufacturers and testing laboratories to evaluate new materials and procedures. Over 150 groups, including trade associations, government testing labs, and standards associations, develop standards.

In the 1974 Housing and Community Development Act, the National Institute of Building Sciences (NIBS) was created.[18] Its function is to develop, publicize, and maintain nationally recognized performance criteria, standards, and other technical means of maintaining life, safety, health, and public welfare. These standards must be suitable for local adoption with due regard for consumer problems. Thus, the NIBS provides a technical foundation for building codes.

The building code is used for evaluation; a building must be satisfactory be-

---

[17]Seidel, *Housing Costs and Government Regulations*, p. 76.

[18]Title VIII, Public Law 93-383, 42 U.S.C. 5301.

Notes:

aNonresidential regulation under development by the Energy Resources Conservation and Development Commission.

bAdopted ASHRAE 90-75 effective January 1, 1976, but state building code commission placed an idefinite moratorium on that action.

cThermal insulation standards in statewide code vetoed by governor; waiting for uniform building code to adopt thermal standards.

dRegulations suspended by Legislative Joint Committee for Review of Administrative Roles.

Source: Building Energy Authority and Regulation Survey: State Activity (Washington, D.C.: National Bureau of Standards, March 1976).

TABLE 12-3. State Acts Relating to Solar Energy, 1974–1976

	Real Property Tax Exemptions	Income Tax Credits or Deductions	Sales Tax Exemption or Refund	Easements and Zoning	Standards and/or Certification	Code Provisions	Provide State Promotion, Investigation or R&D	State Buildings to Use Solar Energy	Loans or Grants
Alabama									
Alaska		X							
Arizona	X	X	X				X		
Arkansas		X					X		
California		X			X	X	X		X
Colorado	X	X		X			X	X	
Connecticut	X		X	X	X				
Delaware									
Florida				X	X	X	X		
Georgia	X		X	X					
Hawaii	X	X					X		
Idaho		X		X					
Illinois	X								
Indiana	X								
Iowa	X						X	X	
Kansas	X	X		X					
Kentucky									
Louisiana									
Maine	X						X		
Maryland	X			X			X		
Massachusetts	X		X						X
Michigan	X	X					X		
Minnesota	X			X	X		X		
Mississippi									
Missouri									
Montana	X	X					X		X
Nebraska							X		
Nevada	X					X		X	
New Hampshire	X								
New Jersey	X		X						
New Mexico		X		X	X		X	X	
New York	X						X		
N. Carolina	X	X					X		
N. Dakota	X	X		X					
Ohio							X		
Oklahoma		X							
Oregon	X	X		X					X
Pennsylvania									
Rhode Island	X								
S. Carolina									
S. Dakota	X								
Tennessee	X								X
Texas			X						
Utah									
Vermont	X	X					X		
Virginia	X			X			X		

TABLE 12-3. Continued

	Real Property Tax Exemptions	Income Tax Credits or Deductions	Sales Tax Exemption or Refund	Easements and Zoning	Standards and/or Certification	Code Provisions	Provide State Promotion, Investigation or R&D	State Buildings to Use Solar Energy	Loans or Grants
Washington	X								
West Virginia									
Wisconsin		X							
Wyoming									

Sources: U.S. Department of Commerce, National Bureau of Standards, *Research and Innovation in the Building Regulatory Process* (Washington, D.C.: U.S. Government Printing Office, 1977), p. 110; National Solar Heating and Cooling Information Center, *State Solar Legislation* (Washington, D.C.: U.S. Government Printing Office, 1978).

fore it is ready for use. In addition to stating standards, the building code defines terms and licensing requirements. Also, it often spells out the administrative structure and appeals process in case the developer differs with the municipality.

The building inspector or official interprets and enforces the building code. Enforcement may be weak and inconsistent due to personnel problems. Field and Rivkin report that inspectors' salaries are low, preventing high-quality personnel, and limited budgets restrict on-the-job training ur updating of skills.[19] Many officials have a background in the construction industry and close ties with local builders. Seven out of eight are appointed, making them vulnerable to political pressure.[20]

UNIFORMITY Lack of uniformity is a major criticism of building codes. The "larger" builder who works in different communities is particularly affected by a variety of codes. A uniform building code might:

1. Eliminate restrictions that add to production costs.
2. Promote the development of new construction materials and techniques by widening the market.
3. Reduce the cost of research and testing.
4. Reduce the inventory needed by a large builder who works in several communities.

Some exceptions may need to be made for regional variations in climate or condition, such as earthquakes or snow load.

Model codes are one attempt to develop uniform standards. There are four major groups with model codes: the Building Officials Conference of America (BOCA), which uses the *Basic Building Code*; the International Conference of Building Officials (ICBO), with the *Uniform Building Code;* the Southern Building Codes Conference, with the *Southern Standard Building Code;* and the *National Building Code* of the American Insurance

[19]Charles G. Field and Steven R. Rivkin, *The Building Code Burden* (Lexington, Mass.: Lexington Books, 1975), p. 47.

[20]Ibid., p. 51.

Codes often set plumbing standards and performance requirements.

Association. The former three codes were written mainly by professional building inspectors and are updated periodically.

HUD, through the FHA, has established minimum standards that serve as guides for federally financed housing. The National Conference of States on Building Codes and Standards, which aims to promote cooperation between states, is another attempt at improving uniformity. The National Bureau of Standards has developed a set of model documents to aid state regulatory agencies in obtaining uniformity. New York has the most extensive state development program of model building codes. The state Building Construction Code has

been adopted by 462 communities out of 598 in New York State.

Model codes have not created uniformity since they differ somewhat in content; local interpretation increases the complexity and confusion. Nearby communities may adopt different model codes, may not keep them current, and may enforce them differently. In 1970, 73 percent of cities used one of the four model codes as the basis for their city code.[21] Older and more industrialized sections of the country were more likely to use locally drafted codes.[22]

---

[21]Ibid., p. 42.

[22]Ibid., p. 44.

COSTS Building regulations impose real costs on the construction industry and the housing consumer. Building codes may raise housing prices by increasing the number of items a builder must use and slowing the adoption of cost-saving materials and procedures. Building codes may limit choice in design, materials, and construction methods. Several studies suggest that the codes add about 3 percent to the cost of housing.[23] Until there is more research on the economic costs and benefits of building codes, their impact on building safety, construction costs, and efficiency will continue to be debated.

HOUSING CODES

Whereas building codes are primarily concerned with construction standards for new housing, *housing codes* deal with minimum standards for existing buildings. Housing codes cover facilities and equipment, and occupancy, maintenance, and use related to the health and safety of both occupants and neighbors. Included are standards for plumbing facilities, fire exits, heat, light, ventilation, electrical service, general sanitary conditions, potential fire hazards, internal and external structural repair, and insect and rodent infestation.

BACKGROUND Housing code standards evolved from laws passed in the mid-1800s by New York State to combat the dismal conditions of New York City tenements. The original Tenement Housing Act of 1867 required sleeping rooms to be ventilated; roofs to be in good repair; stairs to have banisters; at least one water closet or privy to be provided for every twenty occupants; and the building to be kept clean to the satisfaction of the Board of Health. Since it was practically impossible to enforce and housing conditions remained poor, the law continued to change.

Reis and Veiller were leaders in the movement to improve urban housing.[24] However, little was done in the prosperous 1920s, and the Depression of the 1930s halted all efforts. In the late 1930s, the American Public Health Association worked to define basic health conditions that housing should provide.[25] The first federal law related to housing codes was the 1954 Housing Act.

Two major elements in this act strongly affected code enforcement and related activity: (1) the "workable program" requiring communities to develop their own plan of action to stop the spread of urban decay in order to receive federal aid, and (2) a change in the program of "slum clearance and urban redevelopment" to "urban renewal," which could now be used for conservation and rehabilitation of blighted but salvagable areas as well as the clearance and redevelopment of slums.[26] Lieberman notes that the workable program requirement

[23]Sherman J. Maisel, *Housebuilding in Transition* (Berkeley, Calif.: University of California Press, 1953), p. 249; and Leland S. Burns and Frank G. Bittelbach, "Efficiency in the Housing Construction Industry," Report of the President's Committee on Urban Housing: Technical Studies Vol. II (Washington, D.C.: U.S. Government Printing Office, 1969).

[24]J. Ford, *Slums and Housing* (Cambridge, Mass.: Harvard University Press, 1936), pp. II, 9.

[25]American Public Health Association, Committee on the Hygiene of Housing, *Basic Principles of Healthful Housing*, 2nd ed. (New York: American Public Health Association, 1939).

[26]Housing Act of 1954, Public Law 83-560, 68 Stat. 622-23, 1954.

was directly responsible for the adoption of a housing code, or the updating of an existing code, in 67 percent of thirty-nine cities he surveyed.[27] An additional boost was given housing codes in Section 117, Title I, of the 1965 Housing Act, which authorized direct federal aid to cover the cost of code enforcement.[28] All federal initiatives to improve housing through code adoption and enforcement depend upon state and local action.

UNIFORMITY Many local housing codes are based on a model state code or on those available from professional code developers. Each model code contains different minimum standards that stress health and safety requirements, construction and maintenance requirements, or legal and administrative provisions, depending on the publisher of the code.[29]

Many states, stimulated by federal programs for code enforcement, have developed their own housing codes. These can be adopted or adapted by local communities. One example is the *New York State Model Housing Code*.[30]

A ready-made code has certain supposed advantages. The most recent advances in technology may be used, and innovation is encouraged. Codes are unbiased and free from local influences. Regulations are based on sound principles of safety. Above all, initial cost to local governments for drafting, editing,

and printing are kept to a minimum, with yearly updates available.[31]

Meeks and Oudekerk compared the content of the BOCA code with the housing codes of sixty-two communities in New York State.[32] They found that the communities generally agreed about minimum standards for basic facilities and equipment, water supply, and sewage disposal, as well as thermal standards and light and ventilation minimums. Occupancy minimums for habitable space were more varied. Over half the codes had been revised or updated.

ENFORCEMENT Wolman suggests that housing codes have done little to enforce minimum housing standards because programs are poorly funded and staffed.[33] Usually only the city can bring suit for a violation, enforcement remedies are weak or punitive, and the owner is often unable to afford the necessary repairs. One exception to this is in New Jersey, where the state has the right to enter, inspect, and investigate if necessary.[34] The state may also prosecute and has a variety of legal remedies available. However, strict enforcement may lead to abandonment. Economic incentives

---

[27]Parratt, *Housing Code Administration and Enforcement*, p. viii.

[28]Housing and Urban Development Act of 1965, Public Law 89-117, 79 Stat. 478, 1965.

[29]See Building Codes.

[30]New York State Division of Housing and Community Renewal, *State Model Housing Code: A Demonstration Project* (New York, 1974).

---

[31]Richard L. Sanderson, *Codes and Code Administration* (Chicago, Ill.: BOCA, 1969), pp. 48–49; Walter H. Lewis, "Solving Building Code Problems," in *Readings in Code Administration*, ed. Richard L. Sanderson (Chicago, Ill.: BOCA, 1974), p. 51.

[32]Carol B. Meeks and Eleanor Oudekerk, "Comparative Analysis of the Housing Codes of Selected New York State Municipalities and Two Model Codes," *The Building Official and Code Administrator* 11 (October 1977), 14–18.

[33]Harold L. Wolman, *Housing and Housing Policy in the U.S. and the U.K.* (Lexington, Mass.: Lexington Books, Heath, 1975), p. 88.

[34]Sol A. Metzger. "Statewide Code Enforcement—New Jersey, The Test Case," *Rutgers Law Review*, 27 (Spring 1974), 662.

would help landlords or owners to maintain housing.

Meeks and Oudekerk found that residents' complaints were most often used to trigger inspection and enforcement. Lack of resources were reported by 43 percent of the sample as a major obstacle to code administration and enforcement.[35] Enforcement budgets for the 133 New York State communities sampled ranged from zero to $20 million. Average per capita spending in communities under 100,000 ranged from $.82 to $1.87.

COSTS Regulations of any kind impose costs. Little is known about how housing codes affect the cost of housing. Papageorge reported that compliance with the code decreased substandard housing in Mobile, Alabama. This generally raised rents from $4 to $10 per month, but in all cases, "the tenants felt the improved living conditions were well worth the increased rent.[36]

Whether the renter, landlord, or owner bears the cost of housing codes is not known. Preferences and local housing market conditions will partially dictate how willing the parties are to assume the cost burden. Research is needed on their effect on the quality and cost of housing. The National Commission on Urban Problems reported these major needs in relation to housing codes: (1) to raise the minimum standards for health, safety, and welfare, (2) to increase enforcement, and (3) to extend coverage.[37]

ZONING

Zoning is a public regulatory power used to safeguard or promote public health, safety, morals, or general welfare through control of land use and the building exterior. "More than 90 percent of cities with 5,000 or more residents, and all large cities except Houston, have some form of zoning based on the concept of 'external' diseconomies."[38],[39] Zoning inhibits land uses which would lower the value of nearby properties.

State involvement in zoning is usually limited to environmental issues or to large-scale developments. Wisconsin has laws governing *floodplain* areas. Oregon and Vermont authorize state zoning when local communities do not.

In 1916 New York City passed one of the first police power zoning ordinances in the country. In 1926 the U.S. Supreme Court declared it to be constitutional.[40] Zoning was established to:

1. Prevent the spread of fire.
2. Protect health by preventing the spread of disease.
3. Protect property values by assuring compatible land use.
4. Protect public facilities from overload.
5. Improve community life.

Prior to zoning ordinances, land could be controlled through law. First, a landowner could attach a covenant to the title of the land prohibiting certain activities.

[35]Carol B. Meeks and Eleanor Oudekerk, *Housing Codes in New York State* (Ithaca, N.Y.: New York State College of Human Ecology, Cornell University, 1977), p. 9.

[36]George T. Papageorge, "Housing Code Success in Mobile," *HUD Challenge*, 5 (December 1974), 22.

[37]National Commission on Urban Problems, *Building the American City*, (Washington, D.C.: U.S. Government Printing Office, 1968), pp. 274–75.

[38]Muller, Thomas. *Economic Impacts of Land Development: Employment, Housing, and Property Values*, URI 15800. Washington, DC: The Urban Institute, September 1976.

[39]For a discussion of land development in Houston, see Bernard H. Siegan, *Land Use Without Zoning* (Lexington, Mass.: Lexington Books, 1972).

[40]*Village of Euclid* v. *Ambler Realty Co.*, 272 US 365. 47 S.Ct 114., Nov. 22, 1926.

USDA Soil Conservation Service.

Rural fringe area of Kansas City, Missouri: Open space in the foreground, industrial area in the center, and the metropolitan skyline in the background.

Second, neighbors could sue under the common law of nuisance if a landowner's activities were injuring their enjoyment of their land. Plaintiffs had to show that the use was unreasonable in that location and reduced the value of their property.

Zoning puts land to use for which it is best suited and promotes orderly community development. It regulates land use, population density, site requirements, and structure dimensions. Sometimes, zoning laws regulate parking, signs, and minimum house size. In particular, zoning often sets lot sizes, prohibits apartment houses or mobile home parks, and gives subdivision requirements.

Zoning does not force changes in existing use, and parcels of land may be exempted from the zoned use. The process of singling out one parcel of land for special usage, for the benefit of the owner rather than the community, is known as spot zoning.

Special zones now limit or prevent development, including agricultural and conservation districts, floodplains, wetlands, and wilderness areas. These zones can limit the supply of land for urban development and increase land prices. They also reduce the land's value for the landowner.

Sometimes compensation is paid to owners whose development rights have been restricted. Hagman suggests that the money come from *windfalls* other property owners receive from public improvements.[41] Another type of zoning is incentive zoning.[42] This is a plan whereby, in return for including certain features or amenities in a building, a developer is allowed to use a design not otherwise permitted.

Transferable Development Rights (TDR) is a new approach to make land use controls more acceptable. It has already been tried in some areas—Collier County, Florida; Suffolk County, New York; and Boulder, Colorado. Two types of plans are proposed. One involves a private market with prices determined by demand and supply. The other calls for government participation in all TDR purchases or sales.[43] TDR is another way of compensating the owner for the loss of value due to land use restrictions.

Zoning affects housing prices by controlling the supply of sites, influencing rents and prices when it reduces or increases the supply of multi- or single-family developments, and providing requirements that will add to the cost of the land or the unit. Hamilton suggests that as much as 50 percent of the variation in housing prices in different cities may be due to zoning restrictions on land supply.[44] Moss suggests that minimum lot size requirements may not only increase land prices but also accelerate rural-urban land conversion.[45] However, if suburban property taxes increase as fast as or faster than rural taxes, rural-urban land conversion is retarded.[46] Other concerns are that zoning reinforces racial and economic segregation, stifles innovation, does not really protect neighborhoods, and disintegrates into administrative problems.

A major criticism of zoning is its "exclusionary" effect. "Exclusionary zoning may be defined as the complex of zoning practices which results in closing suburban housing and land markets to low- and moderate-income families."[47] Large-lot zoning has been most criticized for increasing sprawl, adding to the cost of housing, and eliminating "undesirables" from an area.

As an alternative to zoning, neighborhood organizations similar to condominium associations could be formed to protect neighborhood quality.[48] This organization would control the area's collective property rights. Nelson further suggests that future neighborhood use be the result of private competition. According to Brown and Coke, people are looking for innovations in land use policy.[49] Everyone wants to protect communities

[41]Donald G. Hagman, *Windfalls and Wipeouts,* as quoted in Bergman et. al., p. 22.

[42]David J. Benson, "Bonus or Incentive Zoning—Legal Implications," *Syracuse Law Review,* 21 (Spring 1970), 895–906.

[43]For more detail, see Franklin J. James and Dennis E. Gale, *Zoning for Sale: A Critical Analysis of Transferable Development Rights Programs* (Washington, D.C.: The Urban Institute, April 1977).

[44]Bruce W. Hamilton, "Zoning and the Exercise of Monopoly Power," *Journal of Urban Economics,* 5 (January 1978), 130.

[45]William G. Moss, "Large Lot Zoning, Property Taxes, and Metropolitan Area," *Journal of Urban Economics,* 4, (October 1977), 424.

[46]Ibid., 426.

[47]Paul Davidoff and Linda Davidoff, "Opening the Suburbs: Toward Inclusionary Land Use Controls," *Syracuse Law Review,* 22 (Winter 1971), 519.

[48]Robert H. Nelson, *Zoning and Property Rights* (Cambridge, Mass.: The MIT Press, 1977).

[49]Steven R. Brown and James G. Coke, *Public Opinion on Land Use Regulation* (Columbus, Ohio: Academy for Contemporary Problems, January 1977), p. 2.

from unchecked and uncontrolled development.

SUBDIVISION REGULATIONS

Subdivision controls are a major form of control in community planning. Subdivision regulations govern the residential development of raw land. They control streets (right-of-way, grading, sidewalks, curbs), streetscape (lighting, signs, and trees), water, sewer and storm drains, utilities, and open space. Subdivision regulations often require a developer to donate to the city land for schools, parks, utility easements, and streets. The cost of these items is then passed on to the consumer in the home's purchase price. Local requirements will vary with the type of project and the area involved.

Subdivision regulations were developed in the early 1920s to deal with the problem of land speculation. On vast amounts of subdivided land, public water and sewers were supplied. Earlier, Michigan (1873) and Wisconsin (1849) had required surveying and registration of land and public approval. Usually subdivision regulations are applied uniformly throughout the city.

Subdivision controls protect buyers by assuring them of access and meeting community development needs. The city, on the other hand, does not have to provide streets and other public services. Subdivision regulations also enable communities to plan for public facilities, traffic, open space, and the funds needed to meet the service demands of new residents.

Performance bonding may be required by local governments to assure that subdivision requirements are met by the developer. A performance bond helps guarantee the buyers of lots in the development that public improvements will be made. Few court actions have resulted from performance bonding, but the courts seem to easily accept its validity. "The rationale for . . . acceptance appears to be a feeling that if the legislature can allow local governments to improve conditions for plot approval on subdividers then the legislature can surely permit the local governments to allow performance bonding to accomplish this end."[50] Performance bonding eases the financial burden on developers and protects the community.

PLANNED UNIT DEVELOPMENT REGULATIONS

Another important local tool is the planned unit development ordinance. This "combines zoning, subdivision control, and land use procedures to allow a developer more design flexibility, while replacing the traditional, rigid, limited use zoning district standards with broad general standards. . . ."[51]

Planned Unit Developments (PUDs) are usually large scale, with clustered housing units and common areas, rather than individual lots. Proponents of PUDs argue that they provide higher-quality living environments with more open space at a lower cost. PUDs allow the use of innovative, efficient, and topographically suitable site and building patterns. At least half a dozen states now authorize the adoption of the PUD approach.

Although PUDs have the advantages

---

[50]Richard M. Yearwood, *Land Subdivision Regulation* (New York: Praeger Publishers, 1971), p. 138.

[51]Advisory Commission on Intergovernmental Relations, *Environment, Land Use and Growth Policy*, Part 5 (Washington, D.C.: ACIR State Legislative Program, 1975), p. 120.

noted, the community also has more control over the development. Approval of construction, architecture, and planning concepts may be required which would not be needed if the property were already zoned for the use intended.[52] A developer pays a higher price than the local authorities if a proposed project is not built. PUDs have been used by cities to foster luxury apartments and higher rents.

GROWTH CONTROLS

Local governments are increasingly interested in growth management. The main concerns are to limit municipal costs and to preserve the physical and social environment. Growth controls may also be exclusionary.

The most popular growth control ordinance is the sewer moratorium,[53] which has been used in the Far West, South Florida, and the North Central and Middle Atlantic states.[54] A sewer moratorium may involve a freeze on new sewer authorizations or connections, building permits, subdivision requests, or zoning. Such action is legally justified as police power in public health issues. Results depend on how long the moratoriums are in effect. Large lot development with septic systems often result. They affect the home building industry, encourage sprawl, and add to housing prices.

Other techniques used include: adequate public facilities ordinances, phased development controls, population and building permit limitations, and urban services areas. A public facilities ordinance states that public facilities must be available for approval to develop. Phased development controls provide a timetable for future development decisions through a capital improvement plan. Population and building permit limitations limit the number of building permits issued or the number of dwelling units or total population in the community. An urban service area is an area where enough public services are available to support urban development. Other areas are then marked as rural or agriculture service areas and intended to be sparsely developed.

CONCLUSION

Building and housing codes protect consumers from poorly designed, constructed, and maintained dwellings. Since new buildings will be part of the housing stock for forty to sixty years, these controls will in part determine the shape of future living environments.

Zoning controls land use and the building exterior. The purpose is to maintain property values and good housing development. Subdivision regulations protect both consumers and developers.

These community controls may overlap. Areas may have all of them, some, or none. The effects of controls have not really been studied, although they are assumed to benefit consumers and communities. However, the long-term results of increased regulation have not been fully considered. Also, government regulations do increase costs.

Today there is increased concern about the environmental, social, and economic

---

[52]Siegan, *Land Use Without Zoning*, p. 155.

[53]Seidel, *Housing Costs and Government Regulations*, p. 199.

[54]Rivkin/Carson, Inc., *The Sewer Moratorium as a Technique of Growth Control and Environmental Protection* (Washington, D.C.: U.S. Department of Housing and Urban Development, June 1973), p. 1.

impact of land development. For this reason, many developers must invest a lot of time and money analyzing development alternatives and their effects.[55] Longer public review and processing times mean higher land option costs, interest, taxes, and overhead, as well as construction costs. "Changes in regulations or regulatory practices increase the risks associated with initial investments in development projects . . . and are likely to increase the profit requirements of developers."[56]

Property Taxes

The tax policies of local governments, especially on property, affect housing. *Property taxes* influence land price, use, and urban development. They also increase the cost of housing and influence the size and distribution of disposable income since they take a larger proportion of smaller income.[57] The property evaluation *assessment* rate and the tax rate are key factors in property taxes. Many states offer exemptions or tax relief to certain groups.

Real estate taxes fall on land and buildings or housing units attached to the land. The land and buildings may be assessed separately. Land accounts for a larger proportion of the assessment in rural areas, buildings in urban areas. In 1973, nineteen states based property taxes on the full *market value* or its equivalent.[58] Property tax rates vary widely from area to area. Property taxes are the chief source of local government revenue.[59]

Two major property tax issues will be discussed here: first, the problem of who bears the cost of the tax; second, programs developed to give tax relief to certain groups. In 1970 homeowners paid an average of 4.9 percent of their income in property taxes (a median of 3.4 percent).[60] The Advisory Commission on Intergovernmental Relations (ACIR) notes that 22 million households paid 5 percent or more of income and 17 million households paid 6 percent or more.[61]

REGRESSIVE OR PROGRESSIVE TAX The property tax is continually criticized by policy makers, academics, and the public. "In a poll conducted for the Advisory Commission on Intergovernmental Relations, respondents chose the property tax less often than any other tax as the fairest tax" and more often than any other as the least fair tax.[62]

Tax incidence is the effect of a tax on

---

[55]Joseph Rabianski, Neil G. Carn, and Nicholas Ordway, *Measuring the Effects of Increasing Citizen Participation and Technical Review on the Costs of Housing: An Empirical Study of Amending The Atlanta Zoning Ordinance 1971–76,* (Atlanta, Ga.: Department of Real Estate and Urban Affairs, Georgia State University, December 1977), p. 1.

[56]Ibid.

[57]Walter A. Morton, *Housing Taxation* (Madison, Wis.: University of Wisconsin Press, 1955), p. 7.

[58]U.S. Department of Commerce, Bureau of the Census, *Property Values, Subject to General Property Taxation in the United States: 1973,* Series GSS, No. 69 (Washington, D.C.: U.S. Government Printing Office, December 1974).

[59]For a history of property taxation, see Jens P. Jensen, *Property Taxation in the U.S.,* (Chicago, Ill.: University of Chicago Press, 1931).

[60]U.S. Department of Commerce, Bureau of the Census, *Census of Housing: 1970,* Vol. V (Washington, D.C.: U.S. Government Printing Office, 1973), pp. 121, 123.

[61]Advisory Commission on Intergovernmental Relations, *Financing Schools and Property Tax Relief—A State Responsibility,* A Commission Report A-40 (Washington, D.C., January 1973), p. 39.

[62]ACIR, *Financing Schools,* p. 12.

real income. This comes about in three ways: (1) through changes in the person's tax liability (the amount paid); (2) through changes in the price of things the person sells (labor and the services of any capital or land owned); (3) through changes in the prices of goods and services purchased. A typical tax will affect all three types of incidence, and these effects may be cumulative or offsetting for a given individual. For the sake of simplicity, tax incidence is usually treated in terms of its effect on average income in various income classes.[63]

Is the property tax *regressive* or *progressive?* A regressive tax is one that taxes the poor at a higher rate than the rich. A progressive tax, in contrast, increases with income. The property tax is usually considered regressive because housing—and, therefore, property taxes—take up a larger proportion of the poor person's budget.[64]

Recent economic analysis suggests that the property tax is not really regressive.[65]

The property tax reduces the after-tax rate of return on all capital goods. Since capital is distributed progressively in terms of normal income, the same is true of the property tax.

TAX RELIEF PROGRAMS State property tax relief programs are major social programs with several goals: "Reducing the regressivity of the property tax; shielding low income households from large tax liabilities; enabling the elderly to retain their homes; slowing neighborhood deterioration; and influencing voting behavior."[66] Since these programs give certain groups more money to buy or rent housing, they can be viewed as subsidies which can influence housing prices. Generally prices would rise as the demand for housing increases.

A 1974 HUD survey identified twenty-five state-mandated *circuit breaker* programs and forty state-mandated *homestead exemption* programs (Table 12-4). In addition, eighteen other tax relief programs were available.[67]

A circuit breaker is like a negative income tax on property tax liability. Tax relief increases as income decreases. Income is used to determine eligibility and the amount of relief received. Circuit-breaker programs usually separate the tax payment from the actual granting of relief. Claimants usually file for tax relief and receive either an income tax credit or a tax rebate check. "Super" circuit-

[63]ACIR, *Financing Schools*, p. 31.

[64]See Dick Netzer, *Economics of the Property Tax* (Washington, D.C.: The Brookings Institution, 1966); Richard A. Musgrave and Peggy B. Musgrave, *Public Finance in Theory and Practice* (New York: McGraw-Hill, 1973), p. 368; Joseph A. Pechman and Benjamin A. Okner, *Who Bears the Tax Burden?* (Washington, D.C.: The Brookings Institution, 1974), Table 4-8, variant 3b p. 59, as listed in *Property Tax Relief Programs for the Elderly, Final Report*, prepared for the U.S. Department of Housing and Urban Development, Office of Policy Development and Research, by Abt Associates, Inc., Cambridge, Massachusetts (HUD-PDR-153, May 1976); Charles L. Schultze, Edward R. Fried, Alice M. Rivlin, and Nancy H. Teeters, *Setting National Priorities*, The 1973 Budget (Washington, D.C.: The Brookings Institution, 1972), as listed in *Financing Schools and Property Tax Relief—A State Responsibility*, A Commission Report, (Washington, D.C.: Advisory Commission on Intergovernmental Relations, January 1973).

[65]For a complete discussion, read Henry J. Aaron, *Who Pays the Property Tax?* (Washington, D.C.: The Brookings Institution, 1975).

[66]Abt Associates, Inc., *Property Tax Relief Programs for the Elderly, Final Report*, HUD-PDR-153 (Washington, D.C.: U.S. Department of Housing and Urban Development, Office of Policy Development and Research, May 1976).

[67]For a detailed description of state property tax relief programs, see John Shannon, "The Property Tax: Reform or Relief?" in *Property Tax Reform*, ed. George E. Peterson (Washington, D.C.: The Urban Institute, 1973).

TABLE 12-4. Property Tax Relief Programs

PROGRAM DESCRIPTION	NUMBER OF PROGRAMS	NUMBER OF STATES REPRESENTEDa
State-mandated	65	44b
(circuit breakers)	(25)b	(24)b
(homestead exemptions)	(40)	(23)
Local option	6	6
Tax deferrals	5	5
Tax freeze	2	2
Renter's credits	4	4
Low-income comprehensive tax credit	1	1
Total	83	49b

aColumn does not add since there are several different programs in many states.

bIncludes the District of Columbia.

Source: Survey of State Property Tax Relief Programs; and State Statutes reported in U.S. Department of Housing and Urban Development, *Property Tax Relief Programs for the Elderly, A Compendium Report,* HUD-PDR-153-2 (Washington, D.C., April 1975), p. 16.

breaker programs benefit both elderly and nonelderly claimants, usually favoring the elderly. States vary widely in eligibility requirements and payment formulas, and are likely to remain so.[68]

The formulas used in circuit breakers may be unrelated to actual property taxes. These formulas base taxes on estimated or actual spending on housing rather than on ownership of capital and property tax deviations from the nationwide average. Since such formulas are unrelated to actual taxes, their fairness should be evaluated as income maintenance or housing allowance formulas.[69]

A homestead exemption operates like a direct grant, reducing the assessed value of homes of all eligible persons by the same amount. Although income may help determine eligibility for homestead exemption relief, it is *not* used to set the amount received. Homestead exemption relief is usually granted by reducing either the assessment or the taxes due on the property.

Since 1970, state tax relief programs have been mainly circuit breakers. In 1975 these programs served about 3 million people at a cost of more than $450 million.[70] Elderly recipients in 1974 numbered about 1.7 million with an average claim of $144 (Table 12-5). Homestead exemption programs delivered greater benefits to more elderly applicants, and the average payment was higher: 6.3 million claimants received more than $1 billion in 1973; the average claim was $173.[71] At least 1.3 million were elderly homeowners. Over 70 percent of the total relief for both types of programs, however, was delivered by three states: California, Michigan, and Minnesota.[72]

In 1974 eighteen states offered renters relief from property taxes in their

---

[68]See also S.D. Gold, "A Note on the Design of Property Tax Circuit-Breakers," *National Tax Journal,* 29 (December 1976), 477–81; and Advisory Commission on Intergovernmental Relations (ACIR), *Property Tax Circuit Breakers' Current Status and Policy Issues* (Washington, D.C., February 1975), pp. 4–5

[69]*Property Tax Relief Programs,* pp. 62–63.

[70]ACIR, *Property Tax Circuit Breakers,* pp. 4–5.

[71]HUD Compendium, p. ii.

[72]Ibid., p. ii.

TABLE 12-5. Tax Relief Programs

PROGRAM TYPE	NUMBER OF PARTICIPANTS	TOTAL BENEFITS ($000)	AVERAGE BENEFITS
Circuit-breaker programs[a]			
Elderly	761,000	108,000	$142
Elderly & selected others (disabled, etc.)	1,021,000	148,900	145
No age limitation[b]	1,470,000	207,100	141
Total	3,253,000	464,000	143
Homestead exemption programs[c]			
Elderly	1,311,000	140,000	108
Elderly and disabled	270,000	22,500	83
No age limitation	4,790,000	900,000	188
TOTAL	6,371,000	1,100,000	173

[a]Data for calendar year 1974.

[b]Does not include elderly or disabled claimants.

[c]Data are from three years—1972, calendar year 1973, or estimates for 1975.

Source: U.S. Department of Housing and Urban Development, Property Tax Relief Programs for the Elderly, A Compendium Report, HUD-PDR-153-2 (Washington, D.C., April 1975), pp. 19, 27.

circuit-breaker programs. Renters tend to receive less relief than homeowners.[73] Owners in eight states received an average of $154, while renters in the same states received $120. Fewer renters than homeowners participate in tax relief programs. However, renters may be in different income groups, or the proportion of rent estimated to be property tax could be understated.[74] In addition, some states gave special property tax abatements or reduced payments to renters living in subsidized housing and nonprofit nursing homes.[75]

How well have the tax relief programs met their objectives? The results are either mixed, scanty, or not available. HUD found no evidence that these programs slow neighborhood decay.[76] Whether property tax relief motivates the elderly to move is unknown. These programs may influence voting behavior of the general public on public finance questions, but the elderly vote seems unchanged.

Property tax relief can easily be made regressive.[77] If federal aid were used simply to absorb a bit of local school spending, or if all property tax rates for education were trimmed uniformly, upper-income suburban families would benefit most. From their vigorous lobbying for property tax cuts, many homeowners may already have reached this conclusion.

Property tax relief programs may result in economic windfalls to some investors at the expense of others and intergovernmental movements caused by property tax reduction. In some states, property tax relief is prevented by law.

Investors choose between different in-

[73]HUD Compendium, p. 23.

[74]HUD Compendium, p. 25.

[75]HUD Compendium, p. 58.

[76]HUD Final Report, pp. 3–4.

[77]Arthur P. Solomon and George E. Peterson, Property Taxes and Populist Reform, Working Paper #16 (Cambridge, Mass.: Joint Center for Urban Studies, MIT and Harvard University, October 1972), p. 20.

vestments mainly on the basis of the expected return. Thus, they must take into account different taxes or tax rates affecting the investment. A sudden change in property taxes will influence the investor's view of the market, possibly with dramatic economic effects.[78]

TAX REFORM Today, tax policy makers are considering four approaches to property tax reform. They are: actions to insure fair property assessment, reclassification of property, a uniform statewide property tax, and *site value taxation*.[79]

Property tax assessment might be improved by *full-value assessment* and *appraisal*. Today many communities tax housing on some percentage of market value. Full-value assessment has certain advantages. Sloppy, politically oriented, or corrupt assessment is reduced. Costs drop, too, since there is maximum use of market information. Taxpayers become more knowledgeable and administration is more efficient since the appraisal and the assessment are the same. However, there are disadvantages. Start-up costs are high since most communities are a long way from full-value assessment, and there are increased work loads for assessors and their staffs in keeping records current.

A statewide property tax instead of local property taxes should lower the tax rate in poor communities and raise the rate in wealthier ones. At the same time, a uniform tax rate should increase the proportion of the property tax paid by real estate owners—who, by and large, are wealthier than their tenants.[80]

Land value taxation is also being considered. This method assesses land at current market value based on its highest and best use rather than its present use. This would encourage more rapid, lower-priced land sales decreasing *"leapfrog" development*.

ASSESSMENTS In addition to property taxes, real estate may be subject to special assessments. These are benefit taxes that help finance public improvements. The improvements, such as sewers and sidewalks, are likely to increase property values. Usually the improvements are paid for over five to ten years.

CONCLUSION

Property taxes are a major source of local government revenue and affect housing quality and price. The question of who bears the tax burden is a major political issue. Tax relief programs of both a circuit-breaker and homestead exemption type are offered by a majority of states. Tax reform is always under consideration.

Summary

State and local governments adopt many policies which directly or indirectly affect housing quality and price. In recent years, the number and role of state government agencies in housing have increased rapidly. Two major areas of concern are the financing of housing and the housing environment, as well as the impact of housing development on the external environment.

Communities can control housing

---

[78]ACIR, *Financing Schools*, p. 83.

[79]ACIR, *Financing Schools*, p. 69.

[80]Solomon and Peterson, *Property Taxes*, p. 20.

characteristics in many ways, including building and housing codes, zoning, and subdivision regulations.

Property taxes have an impact on housing costs and selection. Many states and communities are enacting circuit-breaker and homestead exemption programs to provide tax relief for certain groups.

Terms

appraisal valuation of property.

assessed value estimate of current market value for tax purposes.

assessment the process of estimating current market value for tax purposes.

building code regulation of new construction.

circuit breaker tax relief based on income.

environmental impact statement report of the effect of an action on the surrounding area.

equalization process of evening out differences in assessment levels among land assessment districts

flood plains areas which flood frequently.

full-value assessment worth of property as determined by demand and supply in an area.

homestead exemption reduction in assessment or taxes on the property of eligible groups.

housing code regulation of existing housing units.

leapfrog development housing development that skips an area of vacant, higher-priced land closer to the city in favor of land farther away.

market value worth of property as determined by demand and supply in an area.

performance-based building requirement states the allowable or desirable end goal to be achieved. Unlike prescriptive building requirements, they set forth the results expected rather than the means of achievement.

prescriptive building requirement states the allowable or permitted dimension, size, engineering type, assembly method, or material that must be incorporated into the building project. These prescribe allowable design solutions.

progressive tax tax that increases with income.

property tax tax on land and buildings.

regressive tax tax that decreases as income increases.

site value taxation taxation based on the worth of a location regardless of the improvements.

specification code see *prescriptive building requirement.*

subdivision ordinances regulations on land development. These may include lot size and layout, and public facilities requirements.

tax incidence who bears the burden of the tax.

wetlands land that contains much moisture, such as marsh land.

windfall an unexpected or sudden gain.

zoning regulation of land use, including location, bulk, height, shape, and coverage of buildings on the land.

Suggested Readings

Aaron, Henry, "The Property Tax: Progressive or Regressive? A New View of Property Tax Incidence," *The American Economic Review,* 64 (May 1974), 212–21.

———, *Who Pays the Property Tax?* Washington, D.C.: The Brookings Institution, 1975.

Advisory Commission on Intergovernmental Relations, *Super Circuit-Breakers: New Advances with a Flexible Concept.* Information Bulletin 74-1. Washington, D.C., January 1974.

———, *Property Tax Relief for Farmers: New*

Use for Circuit Breakers. Information Bulletin No. 75-8. Washington, D.C., August 1974.

———, State Legislative Program Part 6, *Housing and Community Development.* Washington, D.C., December 1975.

Courant, Paul N., "On the Effect of Fiscal Zoning on Land and Housing Values," *Journal of Urban Economics,* 3 (January 1976), 88–94.

Field, Charles G., and Steven R. Rivkin, *The Building Code Burden.* Lexington, Mass.: Lexington Books, Heath, 1975.

Gaffney, Mason, "What Is Property Tax Reform?" *The American Journal of Economics and Sociology,* 31 (April 1972), 139–52.

Hance, Kenneth G., Jr., and Thomas A. Duvall III, "Coinsurance: The Key to the Future for State Housing Finance Agencies?" *The Urban Lawyer,* 8 (Fall 1976), 720–46.

McConnaughey, John S., Jr., *Economic Impacts of Building Codes.* Washington, D.C.: National Bureau of Standards, Jan. 28, 1977.

Musgrave, Richard A., "Is a Property Tax on Housing Regressive?" *The American Economic Review,* 64 (May 1974), 222–29.

Pechman, Joseph A., and Benjamin A. Okner, *Who Bears the Tax Burden?* Washington, D.C.: The Brookings Institution, 1974.

Shannon, John, "The Property Tax: Reform or Relief?" in *Property Tax Reform,* ed. George E. Peterson. Washington, D.C.: The Urban Institute, 1973.

U.S. Department of Commerce, Bureau of the Census, "Real Estate Tax Data for Homeowner Properties for the United States and Regions: 1971," *1970 Census of Housing,* HC(S1)17. Washington, D.C.: U.S. Government Printing Office, June 1973.

———, National Bureau of Standards, *Model Documents for the Evaluation Approval and Inspection of Manufactured Buildings.* Washington, D.C.: U.S. Government Printing Office, July 1976.

U.S. Department of Housing and Urban Development, *A Study of Property Taxes and Urban Blight,* HUD-PDR-29-3, vol. 1, parts 1 and 2. Washington, D.C.: U.S. Government Printing Office, January 1973.

———, *A Land Use Resources List Emphasizing Community Development,* HUD-412-A. Washington, D.C.: Library Division, September 1975.

———, Office of General Counsel, *State Laws Enacted in 1973 of Interest to the Department of HUD,* HUD-OGC-53-1. Washington, D.C.: U.S. Government Printing Office, December 1974.

———, *Property Tax Relief Programs for the Elderly, An Evaluation.* Washington, D.C.: U.S. Government Printing Office, November 1975.

———, *Property Tax Relief Programs for the Elderly, Final Report,* HUD-PDR-153. Washington, D.C.: U.S. Government Printing Office, May 1976.

Yearwood, Richard M., *Land Subdivision Regulation.* New York, Holt, Rinehart and Winston, 1971.

GOVERNMENT POLICIES AFFECTING HOUSING

Besides the direct housing policies discussed in Chapters 11 and 12, other government actions and policies have an indirect effect. Tax policies, welfare, and environmental policies, as well as actions to end discrimination, affect housing consumption and production. This chapter describes these policies and briefly analyzes their effect on housing.

Income Tax Policy

A major policy that affects housing is the personal income tax policy. Personal income taxes, both national and in many states, allow persons to deduct mortgage interest and property taxes and to defer capital gains. These deductions encour-

age home ownership and may promote increased housing consumption. They are most beneficial to wealthy homeowners.

In 1976 these deductions cost the federal government an estimated $9.0 billion.[1] "The mortgage interest deduction alone would have amounted to $5.3 billion in 1976; the real estate tax alone, to $4.4 billion."[2] The individual items summed do not equal the two combined because if either were disallowed, more taxpayers would use the standard deduction.

These tax deductions favor the wealth-

---

[1] *Ninth Annual Report on the National Housing Goal,* Message from the President of the United States, House Document No. 95-53, 95th Congress, 1st Session, Jan. 19, 1977, p. 15.

[2] Ibid.

The single-family home has been supported by federal income tax policy.

ier taxpayer since tax savings vary directly with the income tax bracket. Persons with low income pay little tax and receive less benefit (see Table 13-1). More than half the benefits go to upper-income groups—contradicting our ideas of equity and efficiency.

Homeowners who itemize deductions benefit from this policy. It lowers the cost of owned housing compared to rental housing and to other goods and services. The tax liabilities of a renter and a homeowner are compared in Table 13-2. Both earn $18,000 per year and have $21,500 in assets. All the renter's assets yield taxable income. The homeowner has $15,000 of his assets as equity in his home. Since the tax system is not neutral, the renter pays more tax than the homeowner. Thus, *horizontal equity* does not exist.

Aaron has examined the effect of tax policy on housing consumption. He reports that for every 1 percent drop in housing costs, the amount of housing demanded will increase by 1 to 1.5 percent.[3]

It has been argued that (1) homeowners maintain their dwellings in better condition and (2) home ownership makes the neighborhood more stable by increasing the person's financial interest in the area. If these arguments are valid, society benefits. This benefit repays the homeowner through reduced income tax payments. However, Ozanne and Struyk report no systematic differences in housing services received by higher-income

---

[3]Henry J. Aaron, *Shelter and Subsidies: Who Benefits from Federal Housing Policies?* (Washington, D.C.: The Brookings Institution, 1972), p. 62.

TABLE 13-1. Estimated Revenue Cost of Allowing Homeowners Deductions for Mortgage Interest and Real Estate Taxes, 1976

Adjusted Gross Income, by Class	Returns (thousands)	Percent of all returns filed in class	Average tax savings	Total revenue cost (millions)	Revenue cost as percent of total tax paid by members of class
Under $5,000	264	1	$ 72	$ 19	3.5
$5,000–$10,000	2,318	11	119	275	2.7
$10,000–$15,000	5,140	32	181	932	4.7
$15,000–$20,000	5,236	44	247	1,296	5.5
$20,000–$30,000	5,560	66	416	2,729	8.1
$30,000–$50,000	2,605	79	810	2,111	9.5
$50,000–$100,000	796	84	1,451	1,154	7.0
$100,000 and over	191	88	2,680	512	3.9
All returns	23,109	26	391	9,028	6.5

Returns with tax savings

Source: Office of Tax Analysis, the Secretary of the Treasury, *Ninth Annual Report on the Nation Housing Goal*, Message from the President of the United States, House Document No. 95-53, 95th Congress, 1st Session (Jan. 17, 1977), p. 32.

renters compared to owners.[4] They conclude that there is no basis to assume that society benefits from home ownership as income increases.

A tax expenditure or subsidy must usually serve a valid public purpose, have benefits that exceed the costs, and be the most efficient means available. Since personal income tax deductions do not meet these criteria, several reforms have been proposed. Ozanne and Struyk suggest that income tax reforms:

1. Allow some advantage to all homeowners because of neighborhood stability effects.

2. Give low-income owner-occupants larger income tax deductions relative to tenant/landlords to maintain the high level of dwelling maintenance that low-income owners do.

3. Minimize inequity.

4. Be administratively feasible.[6]

They suggest limiting the amount of personal deductions to $1,500 and ignoring imputed rent—the amount of rent an owner-occupant would receive if the home were rented. Other tax reforms include disallowing the deduction and including imputed net rent in the homeowner's taxable income. This is usually calculated as gross rent less de-

[4]Larry Ozanne and Raymond J. Struyk, *Housing From the Existing Stock, Comparative, Economic Analyses of Owner-Occupants and Landlords*, an Urban Institute Paper, 221-01 (Washington, D.C., May 1976), p. 23.

[5]George F. Break and Joseph A. Pechman, *Federal Tax Reform, The Impossible Dream* (Washington, D.C.: The Brookings Institution, 1975).

[6]Ozanne and Struyk, *Housing From the Existing Stock*, p. 129.

TABLE 13-2. Personal Tax Liabilities of a Renter and a Homeowner with Equivalent Earnings, Assets, and Expenses[a]

IN DOLLARS	RENTER	HOMEOWNER
Income		
Earnings	18,000	18,000
From assets of $21,500		
Interest (at 5 percent)	1,075	325
Imputed net rent on $15,000 equity in house	. . .	(750)
Money income	19,075	18,325
Housing cost[b]		
Money expenditure	4,500	3,750
Imputed net rent	. . .	(750)
Residual money income	14,575	13,825
Taxable income		
Money income	19,075	18,325
Less standard deductions and personal exemptions	6,200[c]	3,000[c]
Less mortgage interest and property taxes, and other deductions	. . .	4,600
Total	12,875	10,725
Tax liability	1,748	1,290

[a]Based on 1978 tax rates for a four-person household with no members age sixty-five or over. The renter claims a zero bracket amount, formerly called a standard deduction, of $3,200 and has personal exemptions of $3,000. The homeowner itemizes and claims as deductions $2,600 in mortgage interest and property taxes, and $2,000 in other deductions. Personal exemptions also amount to $3,000.

[b]Real housing costs are 25 percent of earnings for both renter and owner. Costs of home ownership include $750 in net profit or net imputed rent, $1,800 in mortgage interest (8 percent on a $22,500 mortgage), $800 in property taxes, and $1,150 for maintenance and depreciation.

[c]Personal exemptions are not deducted separately on 1978 tax forms. The $750 deduction for each exemption and dependent has already been allowed for in the tax tables. The standard deduction is also allowed for in the tax tables, not deducted separately.

Source: Adapted from Richard Goode, "Imputed Rent of Owner Occupied Dwellings Under the Income Tax," *Journal of Finance*, 15 (December 1960), 505–506, and Henry J. Aaron, *Shelter and Subsidies, Who Benefits from Federal Housing Policies?* (Washington, D.C.: The Brookings Institution, 1977), p. 54. See also Internal Revenue Service, *Your Federal Income Tax: 1979 Edition*, publication 17 (Washington, D.C., November 1978).

preciation, maintenance, and repair costs. The taxing of imputed rent, other things equal, would probably discourage middle-income groups from buying a home.[7]

TAX TREATMENT OF CAPITAL GAINS

Besides the deduction of mortgage interest and property taxes, the capital gain on housing property is taxed at 40

[7]Robert H. Litzenberger and Howard B. Sosin, "Taxation and the Incidence of Homeownership Across Income Groups," mimeo (Murray Hill, N.J.: Bell Laboratories, n.d.).

percent of the rate of earned income. Capital gain is the increase in value less improvements of the property over the time it is owned.

A homeowner who sells one home and buys another of equal or higher value within eighteen months will not be taxed immediately on any capital gain realized. The gain can be deferred until the owner's death, when it cannot be taxed. Thus, a homeowner is encouraged to remain a homeowner.

Elderly homeowners face problems when they wish to move to smaller, less expensive housing. Thus, Congress has provided, in the 1978 Tax Revenue Act, that any gain up to $100,000 of profit from the sale of a home realized by a taxpayer fifty-five years or older can be excluded from tax.[8] This provision may be used only once in a lifetime and only if the home was a principal residence for three of the five years preceding the sale.

TAX BENEFITS ON RENTAL PROPERTY

Tax benefits on rental property influence the decision to rent or buy. The major benefit on rental property is deduction of depreciation. According to Aaron, "Owners may depreciate rental property for tax purposes at a rate appreciably above the true decline in market value."[9] Owners are not taxed on the excess until the time of sale. If the rental market is competitive, rents will drop. As with the subsidy for homeowners, the impact on rents from the depreciation deduction will depend on the owner's tax bracket and the size of the deduction in relation to rents. Brueggeman concludes that changes in tax treatment of rental property would raise rents in the long run.[10]

Other benefits on rental property are deduction of construction period interest and taxes and a five year write-off of rehabilitation spending on low- and moderate-income rental property.

In the 1976 Tax Reform Act, Congress limited real estate tax shelters but exempted low- and moderate-income government-subsidized rental housing until

1982.[11] Studies are now underway to develop other subsidies for this type of housing.[12]

CONCLUSION

Income tax subsidies affect the use of resources, income distribution, and housing tenure; they also increase housing consumption. If these tax shelters are eliminated, costs would increase for both owners and renters, and consumption would decrease. If, on the other hand, income tax rates decrease as a result of increased revenues, poor and elderly renters would benefit more than homeowners.

Environmental Policies

Environmental laws affect the quality of the housing environment and the cost of housing (Table 13-3).[13] Specific regulations govern the quality of air, water, solid waste, and noise. They aim to improve air and water quality and reduce noise levels. All these regulations involve costs to housing consumers.

One of the most important and controversial parts of the 1969 National Environmental Policy Act (NEPA) is Section 102 (2) (C). This requires each agency to prepare for every major action "signifi-

[8]The Revenue Act of 1978, Public Law 95-600, Sec. 404, at 2869.

[9]Aaron, *Shelter and Subsidies*, p. 66.

[10]William B. Brueggeman, "Tax Reform, Tax Incentives and Investment Returns on Rental Housing," HUD Mimeo (March 1977), p. 86.

[11]Public Law 94-455 (Oct. 4, 1976), Title II and III.

[12]U.S. Congress, Congressional Budget Office, *Real Estate Tax Shelter Subsidies and Direct Subsidy Alternatives* (Washington, D.C., May 1977).

[13]*U.S. Code Congressional and Administrative News,* National Environmental Policy Act of 1969, Public Law 91-190; 83 Stat 852, Laws of 91st Congress, 1st sess, Vol. 1, 1969.

Multifamily residential structures are treated differently under the tax systems from single-family dwellings. Wollaston Manor apartment complex, Quincy, Massachusetts.

cantly affecting the quality of the human environment" an environmental impact statement. This document must be available to other interested federal, state, and local agencies as well as the public, and must "accompany the proposal through the existing agency review processes."[14]

This requirement has been criticized on the ground that the costs outweigh the benefits. There are costs for preparation

---

[14]42 U.S.C. SS 4332(2) (c).

TABLE 13-3. Review of National Environmental Legislation

TITLE	DATE	CONTENT
National Environmental Policy Act 42 U.S.C. §§4321 et. seq.	1969 1970	Environmental protection in areas of air, water, noise, solid waste, and marine life. Council of Environmental Quality (CEQ) has authority to issue guidelines, review and appraise programs, and resolve environmental issues. Environmental Protection Agency (EPA) given authority by three enabling acts: the Clean Air Act of 1967, the Water Pollution Control Act of 1972, and the Noise Control Act of 1972.
Clean Air Act P.L. 90-148, 81 Stat. 485 Amendments P.L. 91-604, 84 Stat. 1676.	1967 1970	Authorizes regulation of mobile and stationary sources of pollution; sets primary and secondary air quality standards. Also, Clean Air Act Amendments of 1974 (P.L. 93-319, 88 Stat. 246).
Water Pollution Control Act P.L. 92-500, 86 Stat. 816; §402(h), 86 Stat. 883; §208, 86 Stat. 839.	1972	Regulates pollution emission and sets effluent guidelines. Section 402(h) empowers EPA or the state to ban or restrict sewer connections. Section 208 requires integrated area wide waste treatment management programs for a twenty-year period.
Noise Control Act P.L. 92-574, 86 Stat. 1234.	1972	Regulates noise emissions from aircraft, airports, motor carriers, railroads, etc. HUD Handbook 1390.2 calls for standards for external and interior noise exposures and insulation between units in housing developments.
NEPA's Environmental Impact Statement (EIS) 42 U.S.C. § 4332(2) (C) 1970; amendment 42 U.S.C. §4332(2) (D) (Supp. v. 1975).		Special environmental clearance required for certain federal housing developments and federal funding.

and review, as well as others to meet the requirements. Throughout the process there are still other costs for delays, not to mention outlays for the bureaucracy involved.

Enforcement of NEPA has resulted in legal battles. Different court rulings are related to NEPA requirements on HUD's housing programs.[15] In *Silva* v. *Romney* the district court prevented HUD from approving a mortgage guarantee to a housing developer until a proper impact statement was submitted, on the basis that HUD and the developer had a binding contract.[16] Another case in which the courts ruled that NEPA applied was *Goose Hollow Foothills* v. *Romney*. This concerned a HUD construction loan on a sixteen-story high rise in Portland, Oregon.[17]

[15]Frederick R. Anderson, *NEPA in the Courts*, Resources for the Future, Inc. (Baltimore, Md.: Johns Hopkins University Press, 1973), p. 87.

[16]342 F. Supp. 783, 2 E.L.R. 20385 (D. Mass. 1972), remanded 473 F. 2d. 287, 3 E.L.R. 20082 (1st Cir. 1973), reversed and remanded, 482 F. 2d. 1282 (1st Cir. 1973).

[17]334 F. Supp. 877, 1 E.L.R. 20492 (D. Ore. 1971).

Wildlife habitat. Environmental policies impact on housing development.

NEPA was held not to apply on HUD issuance assistance for a proposed apartment building in Los Angeles[18] or to HUD's intention to insure a loan on an apartment complex in Houston, Texas.[19] Until clear precedents are established by both the courts and the agency, HUD projects will be judged individually.

---

[18]*Echo Park Residents' Committee* v. *Romney* 323F. Supp. 487, 3 E.L.R. 20175 (N.D. Cal. 1972).

[19]*Hiram Clark Civic Club* v. *Romney* 330 F. Supp. 918, 2 E.L.R. 20362 (S.D. Tx. 1971).

Brooks suggests that environmental protection programs have these effects on housing costs:

1. There are higher standards for all federally assisted housing. These include improving drainage, sewage, landscaping, and open space; avoiding poor locations; and bringing subsidized housing standards closer to FHA standards.

2. Land available for housing development is more expensive.

301

3. Certain construction standards are imposed.

4. Costs for servicing and maintenance of housing developments are affected.

5. Site selection and preparation for housing development is made more difficult.

6. Federal review and funding will escalate the cost of land. The time lag between development and completion further increases the demand for these lands.

7. Enviromental controls on certain resources (e.g., timber) will make them more difficult to get and more expensive to transport.

8. The energy crisis has its own impact. Builders are pressured to raise the initial cost of construction to provide savings in energy use and maintenance later.

9. Maintenance standards are higher —heating, drainage, sewage, air and water quality monitoring.

10. Preparation costs of environmental impact statements are passed on to the developer—not allowable in mortgage applications.[20]

One growing concern is the possibility of layered and inconsistent environmental controls as states and other agencies pass laws or regulations. Also, there is as yet no way to verify or disprove the impact of environmental protection laws on the cost or quality of housing.[21] Since

some lands are unavailable for housing development, the supply goes down; thus, the price of land will rise. But protection of wetlands, coastal zones, open spaces, and water resources may enhance the environment and so outweigh the costs.

The U.S. coastal zone, including the Great Lakes, has received careful attention. Coastal areas can be destroyed by poor development, although more than half the population lives in counties bordering the oceans and Great Lakes and seven of the largest metropolitan areas are on the coastal zone. Besides housing development, coastal zones are attractive to industries and developers of natural resources such as oil.

In 1972, Congress passed the Coastal Zone Management Act, which preserves, protects, develops, restores, or enhances coastal zone resources. As incentives, grants were given to states for program development, administration, and acquisition of coastal areas. In addition, federal agencies must cooperate with state programs once they are approved.

Welfare Policies

Welfare policies have a considerable impact on housing. HEW estimates suggest that in 1972 about $4.6 billion in state and federal welfare funds were spent on housing.[22]

State welfare programs vary greatly in the amount allocated to housing within a household's budget. Some states have specific allocations; others pay any

[20]Mary E. Brooks, *Housing Equity and Environmental Protection: The Needless Conflict* (Washington, D.C.: American Institute of Planners, Now American Planning Association, 1976).

[21]Arthur P. Solomon, "The Effect of Land Use and Environmental Controls on Housing," *Resources for Housing* (San Francisco: Federal Home Loan Bank, December 1975), pp. 177–92.

[22]U.S. Department of Housing and Urban Development, *Housing in the Seventies* (Washington, D.C., 1974), p. 46.

their determination on prevailing rents in the area.

In 1972 Connecticut granted the highest rental allotment—$162 (Table 13-4); only fifteen states paid more than $100. In 1977, twenty-nine states reported that the amount of money included in Aid to Families with Dependent Children (AFDC) programs for rent was no longer identifiable since consolidated standards were now used to determine need.[23] Without welfare support, these families would generally be worse off. But the support given is often not enough to buy standard housing.

One important issue is the relationship between public assistance and housing assistance. The use of "flat grants" makes it difficult to identify funds used for housing needs. In addition, Congress specified that although families living in public housing were to pay no more than 25 percent of their income for rent, this requirement was not to apply if this reduced welfare assistance, nor could a public welfare agency reduce a tenant's assistance if the housing authority reduced its rent. In 1974 Congress required that where rent and utilities were calculated separately in any state, rent paid in public housing should equal this amount. Because of these requirements, more federal aid through operating subsidies is supporting public housing.

President Carter has directed HEW to develop a welfare reform plan that includes a reduction of expenditures on housing programs with the funds to be used to provide cash transfers to poor families. Khodduri et al. argue that such a plan will not significantly improve housing conditions of the poor.[24] They suggest there is still a need for supplyside aid, the level of support will not allow the poor to live in a standard quality unit or to improve the level of housing services provided.

Discrimination

Today discrimination related to many aspects of housing is illegal. There are laws on the rental, sale, or financing of housing. However, data suggest that discrimination still exists. This is a problem for all because it affects the economic, social, and political climate of society.

When slavery existed, minorities could be denied the right to buy or rent property because of their racial or ethnic origin. The first steps taken to change this were the passage of the Thirteenth Amendment and the abolition of slavery.

CIVIL RIGHTS ACT OF 1866

The Civil Rights Act of 1866 guaranteed to all U.S. citizens the right to inherit, buy, lease, sell, hold, and convey real and personal property. In *Jones* v. *Alfred H. Mayer Co.,* the Supreme Court held that this act "bars all racial discrimination, private as well as public, in the sale or rental of property."[25] In so ruling, the Court, unlike Title VIII, allowed no exceptions. Every housing unit in the United States was covered. Although the 1866 act is declaratory only, the Court held that its broad equity power made injunctive relief appropriate.

---

[23]Juanita Henderson, "Rents, Subsidies for AFDC Recipients," *Journal of Housing,* 35 (October 1978), p. 469.

[24]Jill Khodduri, Katharine Lyall and Raymond Struyk, "Welfare Reform and Housing Assistance: A National Policy Debate," *AIP Journal* 44 (January 1978), p. 10.

[25]*Jones* v. *Alfred H. Mayer Co.,* 392 U.S. at 413.

TABLE 13-4. Estimated Spending for Housing Through Public Assistance Programs in 1972

State	AFDC Monthly Rent Allowance	AFDC Caseload	AFDC Monthly Housing Cost for Caseload	OAA Monthly Rent Allowance	OAA Caseload	OAA Housing Cost for Caseload
Alabama	$19	42,927	$815,613	$40	113,403	$4,563,120
Alaska	140[a]	4,021	562,940	145	1,997	289,565
Arizona	81	18,829	1,525,149	49	13,719	672,231
Arkansas	35	21,911	766,885	35	58,245	2,038,575
California	140	444,865	62,281,100	63	307,748	19,388,124
Colorado	69	30,580	2,110,020	45	31,137	1,401,165
Connecticut	162	31,853	5,160,186	103	8,288	853,664
Delaware	63	9,282	589,766	66	2,987	197,142
District of Columbia	94	26,668	2,506,792	68	4,055	275,740
Florida	81	89,562	7,254,522	50	68,535	3,426,750
Georgia	46	96,252	4,427,592	40	91,578	3,663,120
Guam	20[b]	610	12,200	20[b]	479	9,580
Hawaii	157	11,553	1,813,821	59	2,975	175,525
Idaho	68	6,824	464,032	76	3,405	258,780
Illinois	97	186,019	18,043,643	97	34,202	3,313,594
Indiana	100	47,680	4,760,800	100	16,005	1,600,500
Iowa	70	24,258	1,698,060	33	21,581	712,173
Kansas	125	21,068	2,633,500	125	10,251	1,281,375
Kentucky	52	41,451	2,155,452	23	57,167	1,314,841
Louisiana	22	63,171	1,389,762	35	114,050	3,991,750
Maine	115	18,408	2,116,920	43	11,017	473,731
Maryland	41	57,444	2,355,204	41	9,934	407,294
Massachusetts	78	81,130	6,328,140	50	58,027	2,901,350
Michigan	145	160,305	23,244,255	145	42,675	6,185,265
Minnesota	130	38,510	5,006,300	105	18,116	1,902,180
Mississippi	50	44,445	2,222,230	50	82,867	4,143,350
Missouri	40	64,646	2,585,840	40	93,188	3,727,520
Montana	58	6,552	380,036	29	3,029	87,841
Nebraska	100	12,024	1,202,400	100	7,255	725,500
Nevada	58	4,773	276,834	52	3,063	109,270
New Hampshire	85	5,861	498,185	70	4,604	322,280
New Jersey	100	109,919	10,991,900	75	20,497	1,537,275
New Mexico	47	16,187	760,789	37	8,422	311,614
New York	105	355,491	37,326,555	75	115,428	8,657,100
North Carolina	62	47,215	2,927,330	72	35,139	2,530,008
North Dakota	72	4,364	314,208	62	4,234	262,508
Ohio	96	130,512	12,529,152	58	50,275	2,915,950
Oklahoma	40	30,237	1,209,480	30	66,125	1,983,750
Oregon	54	25,218	1,361,772	42	7,450	312,900
Pennsylvania	86	173,592	14,928,912	65	50,018	3,251,170
Puerto Rico	20	53,693	1,073,860	20	20,302	406,040
Rhode Island	80	14,051	1,124,080	80	3,997	319,760
South Carolina	40	26,304	1,157,376	35	17,343	607,005
South Dakota	95	6,246	593,370	100	3,723	372,300
Tennessee	33	54,666	1,803,978	33	48,852	1,612,116

TABLE 13-4. Continued

State	AFDC Monthly Rent Allowance	AFDC Caseload	AFDC Monthly Housing Cost for Caseload	OAA Monthly Rent Allowance	OAA Caseload	OAA Housing Cost for Caseload
Texas	33	117,971	3,893,043	33	207,000	6,831,000
Utah	75	12,619	946,425	36	2,823	101,628
Vermont	104	5,259	546,936	104	4,097	426,088
Virgin Islands	16	755	12,080	12	317	3,804
Virginia	95	44,055	4,185,225	95	14,665	1,392,225
Washington	91	45,097	4,103,827	61	19,251	1,174,311
West Virginia	38	20,319	772,122	33	13,013	429,429
Wisconsin	130	40,097	5,212,610	130	20,257	2,633,410
Wyoming	100	2,052	205,200	65	1,348	87,620
Total (monthly)			275,163,579			108,621,906
Total (annual)			3,301,962,948			1,303,462,872
Total (both programs)						4,605,425,820

[a]Figure not reported; estimate based on California figure since California need standard is most comparable.

[b]Figure not reported; estimate based on Puerto Rico figure, since Puerto Rico need standard is most comparable.

Source: Department of Health, Education, and Welfare, National Center for Social Statistics.

The 1866 Civil Rights Act provides a quick, direct way of fighting racial discrimination in housing; the complainant takes the case directly to a federal court. The court can stop the rental of the housing to someone else. It can enable the complainant to rent the housing desired. Finally, it can award damages and court costs or take other action to benefit the complainant.

The courts have held that the 1866 act does not apply to denial of housing alone. Illegal discrimination exists if minority home buyers are given less favorable terms or charged higher prices.[26] In a 1974 case, black homeowners in south Chicago argued that the 1866 Civil Rights Act prohibits the charging of higher prices for houses in black neighborhoods than for comparable houses sold to whites in white neighborhoods. The court of appeals ruled against the defendants, who had argued that pricing disparities were justified by the demand in the black housing market. This argument was rejected.[27]

TITLE VIII, CIVIL RIGHTS ACT OF 1968

Discrimination based on race, color, religion, or national origin in the rental or

[26]*Contract Buyers League* v. *F&F Investment*, 300 F. Supp. 210 (N.D. Ill. 1969), *aff'd with respect to other issues sub nom. Baker* v. *F&F Investment*, 420 F.2d 1191 (7th Cir. 1970), *cert. denied*, 400 U.S. 821 (1970).

[27]*Clark* v. *Universal Builders, Inc.*, 501 F.2d 324 (7th Cir. 1974); *cert. denied*, 419 U.S. 1070 (1974). The plaintiffs showed that appraisers had pegged the sale prices of south Chicago houses built by Universal Builders, Inc., at $3,729 to $6,508 above the going prices for comparable houses located in Chicago's suburbs.

U.S. Department of HUD.

Quality of housing is affected by welfare policy.

sale of housing is illegal under Title VIII of the Civil Rights Act of 1968.[28] The following acts are prohibited by the Fair Housing Law (Title VIII):

1. Discrimination in the sale and rental of most housing because of race, color, religion, or national origin.
2. Discrimination in advertising, sale, or rental of housing; financing of housing; or real estate brokerage services.

Title VIII provides three ways of fighting discrimination:

1. Discriminatory acts covered by the Fair Housing Law can be reported to HUD, which will investigate the complaint. If it is covered by the law and the Secretary of HUD decides to resolve it, HUD must use informal methods to end the practice or inform the complainant of his or her right to immediate court action. In appropriate cases, HUD may refer the complaint to the U.S. Attorney General. Or the complaint may be referred to a state or local agency that administers a law that is comparable to the federal law. If the state or local agency does not begin to act

---

[28]42 U.S.C. 3601 *et seq.* 1970.

within thirty days and continue with reasonable speed, HUD may require the case to be returned. Either way, the complainant will be notified of the type of action to be taken. On receiving a complaint, HUD will give a copy to the person charged. This person may then file an answer in writing.

2. A person may take a complaint directly to the U.S. District Court, or to a state or local court, within 180 days of the alleged discriminatory act, whether or not a complaint has been filed with HUD. In appropriate cases, an attorney may be appointed for the complainant, and the payment of fees, costs, or security can be waived. If HUD or the state or local agency cannot obtain voluntary compliance, the complainant may file suit in the appropriate U.S. District Court. The court can grant permanent or temporary injunctions, temporary restraining orders, or other relief. It may award actual damages and a maximum of $1,000 in punitive damages. The courts are also directed to expedite cases and to hear them as soon as possible.

3. Alleged discrimination in housing may also be reported to the U.S. Attorney General. If his investigation indicates that there is a pattern or practice of resistance to full enjoyment of rights granted under Title VIII, or that a group of persons has been denied such rights and the denial raises an important public issue, the Attorney General may bring court action.

In 1973 HUD averaged about 230 complaints per month under Title

VIII,[29] about 25 percent more than 1972 and about 200 percent that of 1971. By 1976 HUD was averaging 278 complaints per month.[30] Title VIII also has a short statute of limitations—180 days after the alleged discriminatory act occurred. HUD must further the purposes of the act through research and conferences.

Discrimination based on sex was prohibited in the 1974 Housing and Community Development Act. On January 20, 1975, the Department of Justice made its first charge of sex discrimination, based on this amendment to title VIII.[31] The charge concerns the refusal of an apartment management firm in Richmond, Virginia, to include a wife's income in determining the financial qualifications of apartment applicants. In addition, the Department has filed its first suit alleging that the refusal to rent to citizens of certain foreign countries in effect discriminates on the basis of race, color, and national origin in violation of Title VIII.

More than 7,300 complaints have been filed under Title VIII. The Department of Justice filed 135 suits between January 1969 and June 1973. During the same period, HUD referred 110 Title VIII complaints to the Justice Department with recommendation for legal action.[32] Of these, the Justice Department has instituted at least 20 suits. During the same period, HUD conciliated 1,218 com-

[29]42 U.S.C. 3601 et seq. 1970, p. 31.

[30]U.S. Department of Housing and Urban Development, *1976 Statistical Yearbook* (Washington, D.C.: U.S. Government Printing Office, December 1977), p. 24.

[31]*Housing in the Seventies*, p. 50.

[32]*Twenty Years After Brown: Equal Opportunity in Housing*, a report of the United States Commission on Civil Rights (Washington, D.C., December 1975), p. 90.

plaints. It is expected that the number of cases involving multi-family units of twenty-five or less will be investigated and conciliated quickly, as the HUD staff increases and gains greater expertise and improves management practices.

A study of fifty randomly selected fair housing cases resulted in Ward concluding that fair housing cases have been more successful since Title VIII.[33] The average award of monetary damages was $3200. Compensatory damages for injury resulting from the loss of civil rights, humiliation and mental anguish have also been awarded. However punitive damages were seldom awarded and awards of attorneys' fees was also limited. Ward listed the primary causes of ineffectiveness with judicial enforcement of fair housing laws as:

1. The high costs of litigation,
2. The inordinate length of time involved before final resolution of these cases, and
3. The relatively short statutues of limitations.[34]

RELATED ACTS

Title VI of the 1964 Civil Rights Act prohibits discrimination on the grounds of race, color, and national origin by recipients of federal aid. HUD can withhold or withdraw funds from offenders.[35] More than 1,330 complaints were filed under Title VI by 1972.[36]

Executive Order 11063, issued in 1962, prohibits discrimination in the sale and rental of federally subsidized and insured housing.[37] HUD may defer or retract funds or cancel contracts with offenders.

Neither Title VI or Executive Order 11063 prohibits discrimination based on sex or marital status.[38]

Executive Order 11246, as amended by Executive Order 11375, prohibits discrimination in employment by federal or federally assisted construction contractors.[39]

The National Housing Act section 207(b) prohibits discrimination against families with children in the rental of FHA insured units.[40]

DISCRIMINATION IN LENDING

Discrimination based on race, color, religion, sex, or national origin in making housing loans is prohibited. The agencies listed on page 309 have issued statements and guidelines that must be followed by the supervised lending institutions:

The statements and guidelines of these agencies represent affirmative action consistent with Title VIII of the 1968 Civil Rights Act as amended to include sex. All complaints dealing with discrimination in lending should be forwarded to HUD.

In 1972–1973, the Commission on Civil Rights investigated mortgage lending policies and practices in Hartford, Connecticut—a city they considered typically American and representative of

---

[33]Clark Gable Ward, "An Analysis of Remedies Obtained through Litigation of Fair Housing Cases: Title VIII and the Civil Rights Act of 1866." Washington, D.C.: U.S. Department of Housing and Urban Development, September 1978, pp. 48–49.

[34]Ibid., p. 49.

[35]42 U.S.C. 2000 d. 1970.

[36]*Housing in the Seventies*, p. 50.

[37]3 C.F.R. 652 1962.

[38]42 U.S.C. 2000 d. 1970; 3 C.F.R. 652 1962.

[39]Exec. Order No. 11, 246, 30 Fed. Reg. 12, 319 (1965), amended by Exec. Order No. 11, 375, 31 Fed. Reg. 14,303 (1967).

[40]National Housing Act, 12 U.S.C. §1713 (1976).

FEDERAL FINANCIAL REGULATORY AGENCY	TYPE OF LENDING INSTITUTION SUPERVISED
1. Comptroller of the Currency	National banks: any bank with "National" in its name
2. Federal Deposit Insurance Corp.	Banks, other than national banks and state member banks of the Federal Reserve System
3. Federal Reserve System	State member banks of the Federal Reserve System, etc.
4. Federal Home Loan Bank Board	Savings and loan associations insured by the Federal Savings and Loan Insurance Corporation
5. Farm Credit Administration	Federal land banks and federal land bank associations; federal intermediate credit banks; production credit associations
6. National Credit Union Admin.	Federal credit unions

other U.S. cities.[41] It reported that using traditional banking processes and standards, the mortgage finance system does not provide fair treatment for minorities and women. Discrimination against minorities was subtle; against women, blatant. At that time, an employed wife's income was discounted. Today every lender making a federally related mortgage loan must consider the combined income of husband and wife. The single woman, especially if she was young and unmarried, had the most trouble getting a mortgage. A widow was in a better position. The separated woman had problems because of her uncertain legal status. A divorced woman had trouble because she was allegedly unstable economically and because of the social stigma attached to divorce. A lending institution today may not refuse to lend to members of one sex, or require higher standards of credit worthiness, or different criteria for one sex.

A 1974 pilot study of eighteen SMSAs revealed significant differences in acceptance and rejection rates on mortgage loans for minority and majority applicants.[42] Even if economic factors such as income, assets, and credit worthiness were held constant, more minority applicants were rejected.

A study of six rural housing markets examined race or sex discrimination in housing.[43] Four Southern sites (blacks) and one South Dakota site (American Indians) showed clear evidence of racial discrimination. No evidence of discrimination against the Spanish-surnamed was found in the New Mexico site. Sex inequality was observed on all sites.

RURAL-URBAN COMPARISONS Discrimination may differ not only by race or sex but also by location. A U.S. Department of Agriculture study reported that credit terms on single-family homes were higher and credit was used less often in nonurban

---

[41]U.S. Commission on Civil Rights, *Mortgage Money: Who Gets It?* Clearinghouse Publication 48 (Washington, D.C.: U.S. Government Printing Office, June 1974).

[42]U.S. Senate, Committee on Banking, Housing and Urban Affairs, *Report on Fair Lending Enforcement by the Four Federal Financial Regulatory Agencies,* 94th Congress, 2d Session, June 3, 1976.

[43]*Discrimination in Rural Housing, Vol. 1: Analysis and Findings* (Cambridge, Mass.: Urban Systems Research and Engineering, Inc., August 1975), p. 1.

than in urban areas in 1970.[44] In nonurban areas, the median interest rate was higher, terms of loans were shorter, and fewer properties were mortgaged. However, the situation had improved since 1960. More savings and loan associations and federal agencies became active in rural areas, and the need for home mortgages dropped sharply from 1960 to 1970. However, in 1975, there was still much less home mortgage credit available in rural areas.[45] A 1973 survey by the Office of Economic Opportunity and another by the Congressional Research Service also revealed that rural lenders require a higher down payment and shorter term than urban institutions.[46]

REDLINING Redlining, as noted earlier, occurs when an area or neighborhood is marked as a poor risk. In such an area few, if any, mortgages will be made—or, if they are, the terms will be less favorable than in other areas. Redlining results from and promotes neighborhood decay.[47] Lenders have generally used age and *economic obsolescence* of a neighborhood as loan criteria.[48] Thus, it is often difficult to separate redlining from sound financial judgment.

A practice related to redlining is disinvestment. Here, the lending institution receives funds from the community, usually as deposits, and then invests them in another area. This often involves transfering money from an inner-city neighborhood to more attractive investment in the suburbs. Thus, the funds from one community build up another, and the original community becomes "disinvested" of its economic power.

The 1976 Home Mortgage Disclosure Act attempts to combat redlining by requiring depository institutions to provide information showing whether they are meeting the housing needs of their community and to aid consumers in deciding where to place their deposits.[49] One reason for a *federal* law regulating disclosure is to equalize any competitive imbalance among states that regulate disclosure and those that do not.

Regulation C, adopted in June 1976 by the Board of Governors of the Federal Reserve, spells out the information to be provided and defines terms used in the act.[50] Each federally chartered depository institution with assets of $10 million or more in a Standard Metropolitan Statistical Area (SMSA) must compile and make available to the public, for inspection and copying, the number and total dollar amount of mortgage loans which were

---

[44]Hughes H. Spurlock, *Differences in Housing Credit Terms and Usage Between Metro and Nonmetro Areas in the United States,* Agricultural Economic Report #305, ERS (Washington, D.C.: U.S. Department of Agriculture, August 1975).

[45]Hughes H. Spurlock and Ronald Bird, *Housing Credit: A Rural–Urban Comparison* (Washington, D.C.: U.S. Department of Agriculture, November 1978), p. iv.

[46]Office of Economic Opportunity, *The Place I Belong, A Report on Southern Rural Housing,* Vol. II (Washington, D.C.: U.S. Government Printing Office, 1973), Chapters II and IV; Congressional Research Service, *Rural Housing: Credit Availability and Federal Programs,* Committee on Agriculture and Forestry, U.S. Senate (Mar. 4, 1975).

[47]For background on redlining, see Center for Urban Studies, Urban-Suburban Investment Study Group of the University of Illinois, *Redlining and Disinvestment as a Discriminatory Practice in Residential Mortgage Loans* (Washington, D.C.: U.S. Department of Housing and Urban Development, U.S. Government Printing Office, 1977).

[48]"Redlining Solution Requires Unified Approach," *Mortgage Banker* 37 (April 1977), 47.

[49]Public Law 94-200, 12 U.S.C.A. Sec. 2801 et seq. Some states have also enacted disclosure statutes. 10 Cal Admin. Code, Ch. 2 2453 (1975) and Ill. Ann Stat. Ch. 95, Sec. 201, NY Super of State Banking Dept. issued disclosure regulations.

[50]41 *Federal Register,* p. 23, 939, 1976.

originated or bought by that institution during each fiscal year. The information must be itemized by location of the loan inside or outside SMSAs and within SMSAs by census tract or zip code.

Consumers must take the initiative to check the information. The act assumes that consumers armed with information are more effective than administrative regulations.

The act resulted from pressure by community groups and housing activists. The number of applications and rejections for an area is also important but not required by law. Another flaw is the failure of the act to require disclosure of terms, rates, down payments, and other mortgage costs.

Lenders object to the Home Mortgage Disclosure Act because:

1. It is not sound financial policy to invest in declining neighborhoods and they are required by statute to invest wisely.[51]
2. They are against government interference in the private market.
3. Areas become deteriorated long before financial support is withdrawn.
4. They fear misinterpretation of the data.

There may also be federal redlining.[52]

Along with redlining is the concept of *greenlining*. This is the demand by citizen groups that lending institutions invest in their area under threat of depositor withdrawals. The demand also usually includes full disclosure of mortgage lending performance, advertising when funds are available, and equal mortgage terms in different service areas.

On the municipal level, two regulations prevail: the depository ordinance and the civil rights-based ordinance.[53] The most typical is the depository ordinance. This states that for a lending institution to become a depository of municipal funds, information on mortgage lending practices must be disclosed. Usually the total number and dollar amount of home mortgage loans must be given for each home and branch office within the municipality. The flaw here is that the ordinance applies only to lending institutions that wish to receive municipal funds. Many may prefer not to hold these funds rather than disclose their lending activity.

The second municipal model is the civil rights-based model. Here the preexisting municipal civil rights ordinance is amended to prohibit discrimination in home mortgage and home rehabilitation loans because of the "social or economic or environmental conditions" in the local area.[54]

The 1977 Community Reinvestment Act encourages institutions to meet the credit needs of their communities, including low- and moderate-income neighborhoods, consistent with safe and sound operations. It requires the institutional regulators—Comptroller of the Cur-

[51]USC 1421-49, 1970.

[52]Marcia Duncan, Edwin T. Hood, and James L. Nect, "Redlining Practices, Racial Resegregation, and Urban Decay," *Urban Lawyer* 7 (Summer 1975), 518–19.

[53]Robert E. Wisniewski, "Housing Mortgage Redlining: An Introduction to the Parameters of Federal, State and Municipal Regulation," *Municipal Attorney*, 18 (February 1977), 49. For a description of city disclosure ordinances, see Robert E. Wisniewski, "Mortgage Redlining (Disinvestment): The Parameter of Federal, State, and Municipal Regulation," *University of Detroit Journal of Urban Law*, 54 (Winter 1977), 367–429.

[54]Wisniewski, "Housing Mortgage Redlining," p. 49.

rency, Federal Deposit Insurance Corporation, Federal Home Loan Bank Board, and Federal Reserve Board—to assess the records of the institutions in meeting community credit needs and to take these assessments into account when considering applications by institutions for branches, mergers, charters, insurance, and other approvals.

CONCLUSION

Although these civil rights laws and actions suggest that discrimination is part of history, segregated housing continues to be a problem.[55] Regulation itself does not bring about change; enforcement is needed as well as attitude change. Education of all parties as to their rights and responsibilities is also important.

Summary

Many government actions affect housing. This chapter has discussed tax policy, environmental and welfare policies, and laws related to discrimination. The personal income tax policy of the federal government and in many states is designed to encourage home ownership by allowing deductions for mortgage interest and property taxes. Environmental policies improve the quality of the housing environment but increase costs. Welfare agencies provide many funds for housing costs. Governments at all levels have policies and laws to combat discrimination in housing.

Terms

disinvestment investment of deposits from one area in a different area.

greenlining demand by a group that lending institutions invest in their area under threat of depositor withdrawal.

horizontal equity equal treatment of like individuals.

imputed rent value which could be attributed to the home if it were rented by the owner.

redlining designation by a lending institution of an area or neighborhood as a poor risk in which few or more stringent mortgages will be made.

Suggested Readings

Aaron, Henry, "Income and Taxes," *The American Economic Review*, 60 (December 1970), 789–806.

Abrams, Stanley D., and Elizabeth B. Baldwin, "Local Fair Housing Legislation: Adoption, Enforcement and Related Problems," *The Urban Lawyer*, 2 (Summer 1970), 277–413.

Break, George F., and Joseph A. Pechman, *Federal Tax Reform, The Impossible Dream.* Washington, D.C.: The Brookings Institution, 1975.

Brooks, Mary E., *Housing Equity and Environmental Protection: The Needless Conflict.* Washington, D.C.: American Institute of Planners, 1976.

---

[55]See A. Sorensen, K.E. Taeuber, and L.J. Hollingsworth, Jr., *Indexes of Racial Residential Segregation for 109 Cities in the United States 1940 to 1970* University of Wisconsin: Institute for Research on Poverty (1974); E. Grier and G. Grier, "Equality and Beyond, Housing Segregation in the Great Society," in Norman R. Yetman and C. Hoy Steele, eds., *Majority and Minority: The Dynamics of Racial and Ethnic Relations* (Boston: Allyn & Bacon, 1971), p. 453; Thomas L. VanValey, Wade Clark Roof, and Jerome E. Wilcox, "Trends in Residential Segregation: 1960–1970," *American Journal of Sociology,* 82 (January 1977), 826–44.

"Chicago Housing Group Erasing 'Redlines,'" *Street*, 15 (Winter 1976), 18–19.

Goode, Richard, "Imputed Rent of Owner Occupied Dwellings Under the Income Tax," *Journal of Finance,* 15 (December 1960), 504–30.

Landler, David, "Income Tax Incentives for Owner-Occupied Housing," in *The Taxation of Income from Capital,* ed. Arnold C. Harberger and Martin J. Baily. Washington, D.C.: The Brookings Institution, 1969.

Polikoff, Alexander, *Housing the Poor: The Case for Heroism.* Cambridge, Mass.: Ballinger, 1978.

Reidy, Daniel F., "Urban Housing Finance and the Redlining Controversy," *Cleveland State Law Review,* 25 (1976), 110–37.

Schlafly, Joseph, "A Proposal for Eliminating Redlining: The Missouri Financial Institutions Disclosure Act of 1976," *St. Louis University Law Journal,* 20 (1976), 722–51.

Tolley, George S., and Douglas B. Dramind, "Homeownership, Rental Housing and Tax Incentives," mimeo. Washington, D.C.: U.S. Department of Housing and Urban Development, February 1977.

U.S. Commission on Civil Rights, *Mortgage Money: Who Gets It?* Clearinghouse Publication 48. Washington, D.C.: U.S. Government Printing Office, June 1974.

U.S. Department of Housing and Urban Development, *Equal Opportunity in Housing: A Bibliography of Research.* Washington, D.C.: September 1974.

Werner, Frances E., William J. Frej, and David M. Madway, "Redlining and Disinvestment: Causes, Consequences, and Proposed Remedies," supplement, *Clearinghouse Review,* 10 (October 1976), 501–42.

White, Melvin, and Anne White, "Horizontal Inequality in the Federal Tax Treatment of Homeowners and Tenants," *National Tax Journal,* 18 (September 1965), 225–59.

Wisniewski, Robert E., "Housing Mortgage Redlining: An Introduction to the Parameters of Federal, State and Municipal Regulations," *Municipal Attorney,* 18 (February 1977), 47–50.

Author Index

Subject Index